A graded
SPANISH REVIEW GRAMMAR
with composition

A graded SPANISH REVIEW GRAMMAR with composition

by

F. COURTNEY TARR

and

AUGUSTO CENTENO

SECOND EDITION

revised by

PAUL M. LLOYD

University of Pennsylvania

Prentice-Hall, Inc., Englewood Cliffs, New Jersey

Printed in the United States of America

ISBN: 0-13-362160-X

Library of Congress Catalog Card Number: 72-85926

10 9 8 7 6

PRENTICE-HALL INTERNATIONAL, INC., *London*
PRENTICE-HALL OF AUSTRALIA, PTY. LTD., *Sydney*
PRENTICE-HALL OF CANADA, LTD., *Toronto*
PRENTICE-HALL OF INDIA PRIVATE LIMITED, *New Delhi*
PRENTICE-HALL OF JAPAN, INC., *Tokyo*

To the Memory of

F. COURTNEY TARR
and
AUGUSTO CENTENO

preface

A Graded Spanish Review Grammar with Composition has occupied a special place in Spanish language teaching in the United States since it first appeared forty years ago. Many other texts have had a brief popularity and have disappeared, but Tarr and Centeno seems to go on forever. The book continues to enjoy a reputation as one of the most useful Spanish review grammars available. Although it was planned by the authors for both elementary and advanced classes of grammar review, it has probably been used more often in advanced classes, for students who have already completed at least two years of college Spanish. Its usefulness derives both from the organization of the material in each lesson, with basic points being stressed in the first half and more advanced or subtle matters being dealt with in the second half, and from the use of colloquial Spanish to illustrate grammatical points. The systematic review of verbs and the emphasis on idiomatic uses of verbs has proved equally valuable. The authors stated in their original preface that they hoped "the arrangement of material will have the advantage of being not only orderly and logical, but progressive and practical as well." Their hopes have been amply fulfilled, and their material has stood the test of time.

Why then is a revision needed? To make extensive alterations might well destroy the book's distinctive character. Nevertheless, in view of the changes in approach to language learning that have taken place since 1933, some additional material could well prove useful for many classes. When *A Graded Spanish Review Grammar* was written, language teaching in the United States tended to be dominated by what was later called the "grammar-translation" approach. Many, if not most, language teachers believed that the most effective way to teach a foreign language was to describe the grammatical structure of the language to the student (in English, of course), giving a few examples of each construction and then to test whether the student had understood the point by having him translate English phrases and sentences into the foreign language. Conversational use of the language was postponed for special "conversation" courses. Tarr and Centeno followed this practice, and at the end of each half of each chapter they provided a series of what they called "exercises" that were simply isolated English sentences whose Spanish equivalents illustrated various aspects of Spanish grammar. Today, language classes tend to place far greater emphasis on practice of the language through the use of drills intended to enable the student to speak the language he is learning. Many teachers hold that the learning of grammatical structure can best be achieved by practice in Spanish of each usage and construction studied, rather than through passive absorption from grammatical descriptions plus some translation.

It is with these considerations in mind that I have undertaken to revise *A Graded Spanish Review Grammar.* I have not attempted to make the book a completely audio-lingual one, since to do so would have necessitated a radical recasting of almost everything; the result would have been a new book. Therefore I have kept the original text intact for the most part, although I have not hesitated to reword some of the grammatical descriptions when I thought they could be made clearer to the average English-speaking student, for example, in the case of §30 on the preterit and imperfect tenses, §72 on the possessive pronouns, §111 on the theory of the subjunctive. The organization of the original text has been maintained also, with only two minor changes: §116 has been put in chapter eight, after §105, and renumbered §106, and §67 has been retitled. I have also added to the examples in cases where it seemed appropriate.

Arrangement of Material. The authors' original description needs no emendation: "The first thirteen chapters deal with the syntax of the verb and of the pronoun, arranged in the order of fundamental importance and increasing complexity. For example, the infinitive and the subjunctive are taken up in chapters eight to ten (thus occupying the center of the book) and the study of the verb culminates in the discussion of the passive voice and related constructions—in many ways the most difficult chapter of Spanish syntax. The remainder of the material is presented in the traditional order of the parts of speech (article, noun, adjective, etc.). But in order that the student may have at his disposal before writing the exercises the indispensable minimum concerning the forms and uses of the articles, nouns, and adjectives, the entire treatment is preceded by two preliminary lessons in which these points are covered."

Exercises. The chief difference between the first edition of this text and the revision is to be found in the exercises. In keeping with the modern emphasis on active practice, I have added a number of learning drills in Spanish wherever they seemed appropriate.* These drills are in many cases substitution drills that involve manipulating a sentence and varying it in a number of ways, as, for instance, by changing vocabulary, altering a verb, adding or omitting material, etc. These drills may be done orally in class or written out if the teacher wishes to stress writing. In the preliminary lessons I have indicated how these drills may be used as a basis for oral practice in class by adding a series of *preguntas* whose answers require the use of the sentences found in the drills. I have not added these questions to the rest

*In some places the material did not lend itself to these drills and nothing has been added, as in Part II of chapter nineteen.

of the text, since it seemed to me that a teacher could easily make up any questions desired, basing himself on the material of the drills.

Translations. Those teachers who wish to use translation as a method of testing, if not for learning, will find the original "exercises" intact, except that they are now more accurately labelled "translations." In a few cases, I have added a few words. The verb and idiom review sections have also been retained in their original order. As the authors said in their original preface, "The teacher may take up this material in connection with either Part I or Part II of each chapter, or as a whole, after the Preliminary Lessons and Part I have been covered. These exercises provide a review, in the order named, of regular, radical-changing, orthographic-changing, and irregular verbs. In addition a number of common verbs that offer no irregularities in form but are the basis of many current idioms are included. One of the purposes of these exercises is to impart a feeling for some of the most widely used verbs in Spanish by showing not only the variety of their uses, but the underlying connection between them." I have added a few idioms to some sections.

Themes for Composition. The sections on composition, like the "exercises" of the original edition, are translations from English to Spanish. They differ from the translations in the grammatical chapters of the text only in being a connected narrative, and in being based on the themes, vocabulary and idioms found in the Spanish text. As in the grammatical review, I have endeavored to retain as much of the original text as possible. Some changes, of course, had to be made, since the first edition reflected the Spain of the 1920s, a country in many ways quite different from the Spain of the 1970s. The social and political upheavals of the Civil War and its aftermath have made many changes in the surface of Spanish life. The economic boom of the 1960s and the rapid industrialization of the country have made Spain a much more modern and typically European country than it was fifty years ago. Therefore I have had to make some changes in the content and order of the composition texts to make them fit the Spain of today. *Tema 18*, which consisted mostly of a list of modern Spanish authors from different regions, seemed to be unnecessary for most classes in view of the large number of anthologies of Spanish literature now available for all levels of classes, and I have therefore omitted most of it. *Tema 19*, with its picture of Spaniards unused to tourists and the more obvious aspects of modern life, seemed especially out of place at a time when many millions of tourists visit Spain every year.

In order to continue the emphasis on the use of Spanish in its own terms without reference to English, I have added four new sections that do not involve translation but rather direct composition in Spanish within certain limits. *Tema cuarto* rather strictly controls what the student writes by giving him only vocabulary and a limited choice of things to do with it. *Tema noveno* offers somewhat greater freedom to the student within the limits of the questions that must be answered. *Tema quince* follows the same format, and *Tema veintiuno* allows the student to write more or less as he pleases on the topics suggested. It is not my intention to confine the teacher or the student in these new sections, but rather to provide a guide for further composition. Teachers who find that their students need more practice of fundamentals can compose further exercises like those found in *Tema cuarto*, while more advanced classes may deal with themes like those suggested in the other sections. For additional practice of the idioms found in the translation sections, the teacher may require that in a specific dialog or paragraph the student use the idioms found in a particular theme. Many other variations are possible.

Typographical conventions. Parentheses have been used in all translations and themes to present explanatory or additional material to be included in the Spanish translation. Brackets have been consistently used for material that is to be omitted in the Spanish translation. The abbreviation **Ud.** is used in examples and translations, chiefly for the sake of convenience.

Appendix. In addition to the forms of the regular, radical changing, orthographic-changing, and irregular verbs, the Appendix retains the complementary material, such as lists of verbs used directly before infinitives, verbs requiring a preposition before a dependent infinitive, adjectives and participles that vary in meaning according to their position and to their use with **ser** and **estar**, interjections, numerals, etc. Usefulness, rather than completeness, was the criterion in compiling these lists. A condensed treatment of the rules for the formation of diminutives, augmentatives, and depreciatives is found in §§275, 276 and 277.

Augusto Centeno was one of my Spanish teachers when I was a student at Oberlin College, and I still have pleasant memories of his classes in Spanish literature. Therefore, it has been especially gratifying for me to have had a hand in this second edition of Tarr and Centeno.

I wish to thank Mrs. Sophia Serrano and Mrs. Elizabeth D. Centeno, heirs of the authors, for authorizing this revision of *A Graded Spanish Review Grammar with Composition*. Many thanks are due also to Luis Javier Casanova, cultural attaché to the Spanish embassy, for useful information incorporated in the revised sections of the compositions.

P. M. L.

contents

Preface vii

preliminary lesson one 1

The definite article. Nouns. Personal accusative. Interrogation and negation.
Review of regular conjugations. **Echar, tirar, saltar**

preliminary lesson two 8

The indefinite and neuter articles. Adjectives. **Que.** Adverbs in **-mente.**
Review of radical-changing verbs, class I. **Sentar, contar, perder, volver, soler**

chapter one 15

Ser and **estar.** Expressions signifying *to become.*
Review of radical-changing verbs, classes II and III. **Pedir, servir, entender**

chapter two 25

Tenses of the indicative. *Will* and *would.*
Verbs with orthographic changes. **Tocar, pegar, jugar, coger**

chapter three 37

Personal pronouns. The imperative.
Verbs ending in **-aer, -eer, -oír, -uir, -üir** and those whose stem ends in **-ll** or **-ñ. Caer**

chapter four 48

Personal, reflexive, and neuter pronouns.
Verbs ending in **-ecer** and **-ocer. Saber, conocer**

chapter five 58

Demonstratives and possessives.
Verbs ending in **-ucir** and **-ducir. Parecer, quitar**

chapter six 69

Relative pronouns.
Dar

chapter seven 80

Interrogatives and negatives.
Poner, meter

chapter eight 90

The infinitive. **Por** and **para.**
Sacar, tomar

chapter nine 102

The subjunctive mood in noun clauses.
Hacer

chapter ten 112

The subjunctive mood in adjective and adverb clauses.
Decir, dejar

chapter eleven 124

The gerund, participles, and auxiliaries.
Querer, poder, convenir

chapter twelve 135

Impersonal and reflexive verbs.
Haber, tener

chapter thirteen 144

The passive voice and related constructions.
Ser, estar, andar

chapter fourteen 154

The article.
Quedar, seguir

chapter fifteen 163

Nouns.
Ir, tardar

chapter sixteen 175
Adjectives.
Venir, traer, constar

chapter seventeen 185
Adverbs and expressions of comparison.
Llevar, subir, bajar

chapter eighteen 197
Indefinites and numerals.
Salir, entrar, ocurrir

chapter nineteen 209
Prepositions and conjunctions.
Pasar, tratar, valer, caber, cumplir, faltar, bastar, sobrar, acabar

composition 223

temas
1. *La travesía* 225
2. *En Madrid* 226
3. *Impresiones de Madrid* 228
4. *Temas para escribir* 230
5. *Un paseo por la Castellana* 231
6. *Una tertulia de café* 234
7. *En el museo del Prado* 235
8. *En Toledo* 237
9. *Temas para escribir* 239
10. *Diversiones españolas* 240
11. *Teatros y corridas* 242
12. *Planeando una excursión* 243
13. *Ávila y Segovia* 245
14. *Por tierras de Castilla* 247
15. *Temas para escribir* 249
16. *De Madrid a Murcia* 250
17. *En Sevilla* 251
18. *En Granada* 253
19. *De compras* 255
20. *Carta de Madrid* 257
21. *Temas para escribir* 259

Appendix

Regular verbs §§222–225 263
Radical-changing verbs §226–228 266
Orthographic-changing verbs §229–231 268
Irregular verbs §§232–266 270
§267 *Common verbs of differing regimen* 280
§268 *Verbs governing direct infinitive* 280
§269 *Verbs governing prepositions* 281
§270 *Adjectives that vary in meaning when used with* **ser** *and* **estar** 284
§271 *Adjectives that vary in meaning according to position* 285
§272 *Irregular absolute superlatives* 285
§273 *Definite article with place names* 286
§274 *Gender of nouns* 286
§275 *Augmentative suffixes* 286
§276 *Diminutive suffixes* 286
§277 *Depreciative suffixes* 287
§278 *Interjections* 287
§279 *Numerals* 289
§280 *Days of the week and months of the year* 290

VOCABULARY (Spanish–English) 293

VOCABULARY (English–Spanish) 317

INDEX 345

A graded
SPANISH REVIEW GRAMMAR
with composition

preliminary lesson one

NOTE. Neither the rules nor the exceptions in the two preliminary lessons are complete. Reference is made in parentheses after each paragraph heading to the more extended treatment of the same topic.

1. Forms of the definite article (§155)

	SINGULAR	PLURAL
MASC.	**el** } *the*	**los** } *the*
FEM.	**la** } *the*	**las** } *the*

2. Gender of nouns (§165)

1. Nouns in Spanish are either masculine or feminine.
2. Nouns ending in **o** are usually masculine; nouns ending in **a** are usually feminine.

el edificio	*building*	**la casa**	*house*
el retrato	*portrait*	**la alcoba**	*bedroom*
el aeropuerto	*airport*	**la pierna**	*leg*

EXCEPTIONS: **la mano** *hand*, **el día** *day*, and many masculine nouns ending in **a** (§165).

3. Nouns denoting male beings are masculine, those denoting female beings are feminine—regardless of ending.

el guía	*guide*	**la actriz**	*actress*
el marinero	*sailor*	**la prima**	*cousin*
el conferenciante	*lecturer*	**la madre**	*mother*
el actor	*actor*	**la modelo**	*the (artist's) model*

4. The names of the days and months are masculine.

3. Contraction of the definite article (§156)

The article **el** contracts with the prepositions **a** *to* and **de** *of* to form **al** and **del** respectively.

Los árboles del jardín.	*The trees of the garden.*
Vamos al teatro.	*We are going to the theatre.*

4. Plural of nouns and adjectives (§166)

The plural of Spanish nouns and adjectives is formed *(a)* by adding **s** to words ending in an unaccented vowel or diphthong, *(b)* by adding **es** to those ending in a consonant (including **y**). *(c)* Nouns with final unaccented syllable in **-s** do not change their form in the plural.

a. **el caballo**	*the horse*	**los caballos**
la torre	*the tower*	**las torres**
blanco	*white*	**blancos**
b. **la virtud**	*virtue*	**las virtudes**
el papel	*the paper*	**los papeles**
la ley	*the law*	**las leyes**
fácil	*easy*	**fáciles**
c. **el lunes**	*Monday*	**los lunes**
la tesis	*the thesis*	**las tesis**

5. Orthographic changes

In spelling the plural of nouns and adjectives, *(a)* final **z** changes to **c**, *(b)* words having a final stressed syllable ending in **n** or **s** lose the written accent, *(c)* words having a final unstressed syllable ending in **n** acquire a written accent.

a. **el lápiz**	*the pencil*	**los lápices**
la luz	*the light*	**las luces**
b. **la reunión**	*the gathering*	**las reuniones**
cortés	*courteous*	**corteses**
c. **el joven**	*the youth*	**los jóvenes**

EJERCICIOS

Escríbase el plural de las palabras siguientes:

1. juez 2. margen 3. tradición 4. solidez 5. ramplón 6. vez 7. fácil 8. alemán 9. crisis 10. holgazán 11. fugaz 12. burlón.

6. Personal accusative (**§§99, 118, 168, 173**)

When the noun object of a verb is a definite person or personified thing (including animals), it is preceded by the preposition **a.** This construction ("personal accusative") is one of the peculiar characteristics of the Spanish language.

He visto a mi amigo.	*I have seen my friend.*
Amo a España.	*I love Spain.*
Tuvieron que matar al perro.	*They had to kill the dog.*

EJERCICIOS

Póngase en los espacios de las frases siguientes cada una de las palabras entre paréntesis con la preposición **a** donde sea necesario:

1. Vamos a visitar ______. (mis abuelos, la catedral, don Juan, el profesor, el barrio viejo)
2. Echaron a la calle ______. (el muchacho, la basura, el gato, el viejo, la amiga de María)
3. Mañana van a recoger ______. (Diego, los papeles, el aparato, nuestros compañeros, mi tío)
4. Quiero mucho ______. (Margarita, Sevilla, la tertulia, un curso nuevo, el jefe).

PREGUNTAS

1. ¿Qué vamos a visitar? ¿A quién (quiénes) vamos a visitar?
2. ¿Qué echaron a la calle? ¿A quién echaron a la calle?
3. ¿Qué van a recoger mañana? ¿A quién van a recoger mañana?
4. ¿Qué quiere Ud. mucho? ¿A quién quiere Ud. mucho?

7. Uses of the definite article (**§§ 157, 159**)

1. The definite article is used more frequently in Spanish than in English. It is used *(a)* with abstract nouns, *(b)* with nouns used in a generic sense, both singular and plural, *(c)* with days of the week and other expressions of time, *(d)* with parts of the body and articles of personal wear (instead of the possessive adjectives, as in English, see §73).

a. **La religión, la ciencia y el arte son las grandes creaciones de la humanidad.**	*Religion, science, and art are the great creations of humanity.*

b. **El petróleo y la electricidad son muy necesarios en la vida moderna.** *Oil and electricity are very necessary in modern life.*
Las abejas poseen una organización social. *Bees possess a social organization.*

c. **Saldremos el lunes.** *We will leave Monday.*
Llegaremos a las cinco y media. *We will arrive at half past five.*
El verano pasado estuvimos en Europa. *Last summer we were in Europe.*
Eran las tres menos cuarto. *It was quarter to three.*

EXCEPTION: **Ayer fue jueves, hoy es viernes, mañana será sábado.** *Yesterday was Thursday, today is Friday, tomorrow will be Saturday.*

d. **Sacó el reloj.** *He took out his watch.*
Tiene los ojos negros. *He has black eyes* (his eyes are black).

EJERCICIOS

Sustitúyanse las palabras entre paréntesis por las palabras subrayadas:

1. La civilización es un producto de los esfuerzos de hombres extraordinarios. (arte, ciencia, literatura, gobierno, técnica, transportación moderna)
2. Los hombres[a] suelen preocuparse más por los asuntos personales[b].
   a. (las mujeres, los jóvenes, los estudiantes, los americanos)
   b. (las enfermedades, la sociedad, la patria, la salud).

Sustitúyanse los nombres de los días de la semana por las palabras subrayadas:

3. Estarán aquí para el viernes.
4. Mañana es jueves, ¿no?
5. Me gusta ir al parque todos los días.

Sustitúyase cada palabra entre paréntesis por las palabras subrayadas:

6. El viejo se puso los zapatos. (el abrigo, la camisa, la corbata, los pantalones)
7. Elena tiene los ojos azules. (el pelo rubio, las pestañas largas, la boca chica, las piernas delgadas, las manos grandes)
8. Vamos a quitarnos el sombrero. (la corbata, el jersey, la chaqueta, los anteojos).

PREGUNTAS

1. ¿Qué es la civilización?
2. ¿Quiénes se preocupan más por los asuntos personales?
3. ¿Cuándo estarán aquí?
4. ¿Qué día es mañana?
5. ¿Le gusta a Ud. ir al parque todos los días?
6. ¿Qué se puso el viejo?
7. ¿Cómo es Elena?
8. ¿Qué vamos a quitarnos?

2. The definite article is also used—but with specific exceptions—*(a)* before **señor** (but *not* **don**) and other titles, *except* in direct address, *(b)* with adjectives of nationality denoting language, *except* after the preposition **en** and the verbs **hablar** *to speak*, **escribir** *to write*, **estudiar** *to study*, and **aprender** *to learn.*

	a. **El señor Martínez ha llegado hoy.**	*Mr. Martínez has arrived today.*
	El general Marina y el cardenal Casares paraban en el mismo hotel.	*General Marina and Cardinal Casares stopped at the same hotel.*
But:	**—Por aquí, señor Rodríguez.**	*(Come) this way, Mr Rodríguez.*
	Don Miguel Gómez es amigo mío.	*Mr. Miguel Gómez is a friend of mine.*
	b. **El español no es difícil.**	*Spanish is not difficult.*
But:	**Me gusta hablar español.**	*I like to speak Spanish.*
	La señorita Sierra estudia alemán.	*Miss Sierra is studying German.*

NOTE. The definite article is also omitted after **de** *of* before adjectives of nationality denoting language, in cases such as **la clase (lección) de español** *the Spanish class (lesson)*, **el profesor (libro) de inglés** *the English teacher (book).*

8. Interrogation and negation

In an interrogative sentence *(a)* the subject follows the verb; in a negative sentence *(b)* the adverb **no** *not* precedes the verb.

a. **¿Está Juan en Madrid?** *Is John in Madrid?*
¿Está cerrada la puerta? *Is the door locked?*
b. **Juan no está en Madrid.** *John is not in Madrid.*

NOTE. The English adjective *no (=not any)* is usually rendered by the adverb **no** in Spanish: **No tengo libros** *I have no books.*

EJERCICIOS

Póngase la forma correcta de los nombres y títulos siguientes en los espacios: (el general Marina, el señor Alvar, doña Antonia, la señorita Alonso, el capitán Moreno, el profesor Carvajal, don Miguel)

1. Hoy llega ______.
2. —Pase Ud., ______.
3. En el nuevo parador se encontraban ______ y ______.
4. ¿Quiere Ud. algo, ______?

PREGUNTAS

1. ¿Quién llega hoy?
2. ¿Quién va a pasar?
3. ¿Quiénes se encontraban en el nuevo parador?
4. ¿Quién quiere algo?

TRANSLATION

1. I have five pencils. 2. The gardens are very large. 3. The nations of the world should seek peace. 4. The cities of Cuba are not very modern. 5. Mr. Vilches and Mr. Borrás are actors. 6. We visited the President. 7. We fear death. 8. Dogs are domestic animals. 9. Miss Vela is very pretty. 10. Senator Díaz will arrive tonight. 11. Modern science has conquered time and space. 12. Today is Sunday. We do not work [on] Sundays. 13. Write this exercise in Spanish. 14. Yesterday I saw Mr. López. 15. He picked up his cane and his hat. 16. I will go to New York next week. 17. Italian, French, and Spanish come from Latin. 18. Has Mr. Domínguez sent the package? 19. The house has four bedrooms. 20. Classes begin at eight thirty. 21. I cannot mail this letter; I haven't any stamps. 22. Cotton has many uses. 23. Your parents are very young. 24. We go every morning to the Spanish class. 25. I am going to speak to (greet) a friend. 26. Mr. Alvarez is our Spanish teacher. 27. We are sailing next Monday. 28. I like coffee, but I don't like wine.

VERBS AND IDIOMS

Review the conjugation of the regular verbs (§222).

Echar(se) *to throw, cast, take to, start to, etc.*[1]
1. Don't put (throw) the blame on him. 2. They threw him out of the theatre. 3. Will you [please] mail this letter? 4. I am going to lie down (*refl.)* a while. 5. Do you want more coffee?—Yes, pour me a little more. 6. She gave me an angry look. 7. You are very fond of paying compliments. 8. Let's take **(por)** the short cut. 9. We started to run down the street. 10. They all burst out **(echarse a)** laughing. 11. This has spoiled all my plans. 12. He thinks he is a **(se las echa de)** Don Juan.

Tirar(se) *to draw, pull, throw* (violently), *throw away, etc.*
1. A cart drawn by oxen. 2. Military life attracts him. 3. It's about **(habrá)** five kilometers at most. 4. She has blonde hair approximating reddish. 5. He threw a book at my head. 6. The poor woman threw herself off the bridge. 7. Throw away that cigar; it smells bad. 8. Let's take **(por)** the short cut. 9. The soldiers were firing at the target.

Saltarse *to jump over, come out* or *off* (suddenly).
1. He jumps over all obstacles. 2. I skipped all the descriptions in the book. 3. Tears came to his eyes **(se le saltaron las lágrimas).** 4. A button has come off my **(del)** vest.

[1]*Etc.* is not used vaguely, but to indicate that there are other meanings used in the translations which are related to or derived from those given in the definitions at the head. These meanings and idioms are either given in parentheses or recorded in the Vocabulary. Onc of the purposes of these translations is to impart a feeling for some of the most widely used verbs in Spanish by showing not only the variety of their uses but also the underlying connection between them. It must be constantly kept in mind that frequently the "idiom" is in English rather than in the Spanish expression, which is often more literal, direct, and concrete. In order to facilitate the acquisition of a real feeling for the literal meaning of the Spanish expression, this is given in parentheses whenever necessary or possible.

preliminary lesson two

9. The indefinite article, forms and uses (§§158, 161–163)

1.

	SINGULAR		PLURAL	
MASC.	**un**	*a, an (one)*	**unos**	*some*
FEM.	**una**		**unas**	

2. The indefinite article is used less frequently in Spanish than in English. The most frequent omission of this article in Spanish is before an *unmodified* predicate noun denoting a social class or an occupational, political, or religious group.

Mi cuñado es arquitecto.	*My brother-in-law is an architect.*
El primer ministro es socialista.	*The prime minister is a socialist.*
La mujer de Miguel es católica.	*Miguel's wife is a Catholic.*

3. Spanish, like English, expresses the partitive by omitting the article. Spanish possesses no unstressed partitive corresponding to the English unstressed *any, no.*

En esta tienda se venden plantas y flores.	*In this shop plants and flowers are sold.*
¿Tiene Ud. fósforos?	*Have you any matches?*
No tengo fósforos.	*I have no matches.*

EJERCICIOS

Sustitúyanse las palabras entre paréntesis por las palabras subrayadas:

1. Mi padre[a] es abogado[b].
   a. (tu hermano, el presidente, el comandante, nuestro tío)
   b. (aristócrata, médico, estudiante, republicano, izquierdista, protestante)
2. En España se cultivan naranjas. (aceitunas, manzanas, uvas, toronjas)

3. Pedro tiene libros[a] interesantes[b].
   a. (parientes, profesores, hermanas, pinturas)
   b. (importantes, excelentes, tradicionales, extraordinarios).

PREGUNTAS

1. ¿Qué es su padre?
2. ¿Qué se cultiva en España?
3. ¿Qué tiene Pedro?
4. ¿Qué es Ud.?
5. ¿Qué tiene Ud.?

10. The neuter article (§§78, 126, 164)

The neuter article **lo** *the* is not used with nouns. It is used with adjectives (and participles) to form concepts equivalent to abstract nouns. (This construction is often equivalent to the English *thing*, *part*, or the suffix *-ness*.)

Lo mejor del libro.	*The best part in the book.*
Lo raro de la situación.	*The queerness of the situation.*
Lo nuevo del caso.	*The newness of the matter.*

EJERCICIOS

Sustitúyanse las palabras entre paréntesis por las palabras subrayadas:

Me gusta[a] lo bueno[b] del libro[c].
   a. (extraña, molesta, intriga, encanta)
   b. (raro, extraordinario, interesante, nuevo, original)
   c. (caso, situación, cosa, asunto).

PREGUNTAS

1. ¿Qué le gusta a Ud.?
2. ¿Qué le extraña a Ud.?
3. ¿Qué le molesta a Ud.?
4. ¿Qué le intriga a Ud.?
5. ¿Qué le encanta a Ud.?

11. Feminine of adjectives (§176)

The masculine and feminine forms of adjectives are *(a)* identical, ***except:*** *(b)* when the masculine ends in **o**, the feminine ends in **a**, *(c)* adjectives of nationality ending in a consonant add **a** to form the feminine, and lose the written accent if the final syllable of the masculine form is stressed and ends in **-n** or **-s**.

a. **difícil** *difficult*, **gris** *gray*, **audaz** *audacious.*
b. **blanco, -a** *white*, **bonito, -a** *pretty*, **maravilloso, -a** *marvellous.*
c. **español, -a** *Spanish*, **francés, -a** *French*, **alemán, -a** *German.*

NOTE. Adjectives of nationality are not capitalized in Spanish, even when used as nouns.

12. Agreement of adjectives (§§179, 184)

An adjective agrees in gender and number with the noun it modifies.

La casa amarilla estaba rodeada de árboles frutales.	*The yellow house was surrounded by fruit trees.*

EJERCICIOS

Combínense los sustantivos y adjetivos siguientes:

1. nación, juventud, cuñado, paisaje, fenómeno, sombrero, lápiz
2. triste, alemán, hermoso, andaluz, pintoresco, malo.

13. Apocope of adjectives (§185)

Certain adjectives have shortened or apocopated forms when used in unstressed position before the noun. They fall into the following groups: *(a)* those which lose the final **o** before a masculine singular noun, *(b)* those which lose the final syllable. In *(a)* belong: **uno,** *one ;* **alguno,** *some, any ;* **ninguno,** *none, no ;* **bueno,** *good ;* **malo,** *bad ;* **primero,** *first* and **tercero,** *third.* In *(b)* belong: **ciento** *(a, one) hundred*, which becomes **cien** before all nouns and colloquially when used alone; **grande** which becomes **gran** before a noun in the singular; and **Santo** *Saint* which becomes **San** before any masculine singular name unless it begins with **To-** or **Do-**. *(c)* **Cualquiera** *any* is in a class by itself since it drops the final -a before all nouns.

a. **Estas naranjas tienen muy buen sabor.**	*These oranges have a very good flavor.*
Algún día se lo contaré a Ud.	*I will tell you some day.*

NOTE. The apocopated forms **algún** and **ningún** bear the written accent.

b. **Hemos recorrido hoy cien kilómetros.**	*We have covered one hundred kilometers today.*
Aquí hay casi cien.	*Here there are almost a hundred.*
San Jerónimo y Santo Tomás fueron doctores de la Iglesia.	*Saint Jerome and Saint Thomas were doctors of the Church.*
c. **Podemos hacerlo cualquier día.**	*We can do it any day.*

EJERCICIOS

Combínense los adjetivos de **§13** con los sustantivos siguientes:

médico, princesa, estudio, manzana, libro, esfuerzo.

14. Position of adjectives (**§§180, 187**)

1. Determinative adjectives (articles, demonstratives, possessives, numerals, and indefinites) precede the noun modified.

mis libros	*my books*	**unos sellos**	*a few stamps*
esta corbata	*this necktie*	**doce habitaciones**	*twelve rooms*

2. Descriptive adjectives normally follow the noun when they differentiate the noun modified from others of the same class. A few common adjectives **(bueno, malo, grande)** usually precede because in most cases they have lost their differentiating force.

la torre blanca	*the white tower*	**un viaje marítimo**	*a sea trip*
un gato persa	*a Persian cat*	**la literatura medieval**	*medieval literature*

3. In interrogative sentences, the predicate adjective precedes the subject, if the latter is a noun.

¿Es muy caro el libro? — *Is the book very expensive?*

EJERCICIOS

Combínense los adjetivos y sustantivos siguientes:

1. este, cinco, nuestro, malo, grande, bueno
2. adjetivo, fotografías, traje, perro, novelas, sillas.

15. *Que*

Que may be *(a)* a conjunction (English *that*), *(b)* a relative pronoun *(that, who)*, and *(c)* the comparative adverb *than.*

a. **Dice que llega esta tarde.**	*He says that he will arrive this afternoon.*
b. **El niño que abrió la puerta es su sobrino.**	*The boy who opened the door is her nephew.*
c. **Dolores estudia más que su hermano.**	*Dolores studies harder* (more) *than her brother.*

NOTE. *Than* is **de** before numerals: **tengo más de mil fotografías en mi álbum** *I have more than a thousand photographs in my album.*

EJERCICIOS

Combínense las frases siguientes en una sola frase con el relativo **que**, por ejemplo, **Pedro dice algo. Le gusta hablar.→ Pedro dice que le gusta hablar:**

1. Juan dice algo. Su madre viene.
2. El hombre indica algo. Hay que dar una vuelta.
3. El niño es su sobrino. El niño abrió la puerta.
4. Mi hermano es un abogado famoso. Mi hermano vive en Madrid.
5. El viaje fue interesante. Hicimos un viaje.
6. El libro es caro. Compramos el libro.

PREGUNTAS

1. ¿Qué dice Juan?
2. ¿Qué indica el hombre?
3. ¿Qué es el niño? ¿Quién abrió la puerta?
4. ¿Qué es su hermano? ¿Dónde vive su hermano?
5. ¿Qué hicieron Uds.?
6. ¿Qué compraron Uds.?

Si Enrique trabaja mucho, su hermano Pedro trabaja poco, y su primo Jacinto no trabaja nunca,

7. ¿Quién trabaja menos que Pedro?
8. ¿Quién trabaja más que Jacinto?
9. ¿Quién trabaja más que Enrique?
10. ¿Quién trabaja menos que Enrique?

16. Adverbs in *-mente* (§191)

Adverbs of manner are freely formed by adding **-mente** to the feminine singular of adjectives. If the adjective has a written accent the latter is retained in the derived adverb.

lento	*slow*	**lentamente**	*slowly*
frío	*cold*	**fríamente**	*coldly*
rígido	*rigid*	**rígidamente**	*rigidly*

TRANSLATION

1. That gentleman is an Englishman; his wife is a very tall blonde. 2. Mr. Rivas is an employee of the company. 3. Charles is a doctor; he is a famous oculist. 4. I am going to buy some bread. 5. We haven't any money. 6. The most interesting [part] of the trip was the visit to the Roman ruins. 7. This is the absurd [side] of the project. 8. These armchairs are very uncomfortable. 9. The first lessons are not very difficult. 10. We could see the English coast. 11. He played several Portuguese airs. 12. Those mountains are not very high. 13. I like this blue overcoat. 14. My study is very small. 15. He won the third prize. 16. He is going to write an essay on the Spanish novel. 17. We are taking (following) a course in (of) contemporary art. 18. We had very bad weather. 19. Are these girls Irish? 20. This author writes very confusedly. 21. This map costs more than two dollars. 22. It is evident that he hasn't read the book. 23. He talks very rapidly. 24. The gardens (which) we are going to visit belong to the Governor. 25. John earns more than Louis.

VERBS AND IDIOMS

Review radical- (stem-) changing verbs of Class I (§226).

Sentar *to seat, lay down, agree with, be becoming to*; **sentarse** *to sit down, be seated.*
1. This climate does not agree with me. 2. The new suit was very **(muy bien)** becoming to her. 3. Let's sit down here. 4. In the picture (photograph) some persons were seated and others (were) standing. 5. Before discussing the matter we should **(conviene)** lay down a few principles. 6. Mix **(mézclense)** the ingredients and let **(déjese)** set for (during) an hour.

Contar *to count, recount, tell*; **contar con** *to count on* or *with, have.*
1. He couldn't get to sleep, so **(y)** he began to count (up) to a thousand. 2. The president of the University was (counted) at that time some fifty years [old]. 3. The

shoemaker's wife would tell us stories every night. 4. Don't tell it to me, tell it to him. 5. He manages (directs) everything; the director is of no importance (does not count for anything). 6. You (may) count on my help. 7. This province has great [natural] resources.

Perder *to lose, miss.*
1. We missed the train by a few minutes. 2. Don't miss (for yourself) the trip to the mountains.

Volver (§266)[1] *to go back, return* (intrans.), *turn* (trans.); **volver a** *to* (do) *again;* **volverse** *to turn (over, back), become (turn, go).*
1. Let's go back (to) home. 2. Don't do it again. 3. Please recopy this letter. 4. Turn the page. 5. That noise is driving me crazy. 6. I don't know why he turns his back [on] me. 7. I have a pain in this shoulder which will (does) not let me turn over on **(de)** that (this) side. 8. The deal is closed; don't go back on it **(atrás).** 9. That fellow must have gone crazy. 10. These people have become (turned) very suspicious. 11. There are nothing but (everything becomes) difficulties.

Soler *to be accustomed (used) to, to* (do) *usually.*
1. I usually stay at home at night. 2. We used to go together to the café. 3. What do you (does one) usually give as a **(de)** tip?

[1]This reference is always to call attention to irregularities in the conjugation.

chapter one

Ser and **estar**
Expressions signifying *to become*

I

17. *Ser* (§259) and *estar* (§245)

1. **Ser** and **estar** both mean *to be.* **Ser** means *to be* in essence, while **estar** means *to be* in location, state, or condition.[1]

2. **Ser** is used when the predicate is *(a)* a noun or an adjective used as a noun, *(b)* an adjective denoting an essential quality or characteristic, *(c)* a prepositional phrase denoting origin, material, or ownership, *(d)* an expression of time, *(e)* part of an impersonal expression.

a. **Pedro es arquitecto.**	*Pedro is an architect.*
Carmen es madrileña.	*Carmen is a Madrilian.*
El sol es un planeta.	*The sun is a planet.*
Soy casado.	*I'm married (i.e., a married man).*
b. **La torre es muy alta.**	*The tower is very high.*
El señor Martínez es viejo.	*Mr. Martínez is old.*
c. **La mesa es de madera.**	*The table is (made) of wood.*
Este abrigo es de mi hermano.	*This overcoat is my brother's.*
Soy de Málaga.	*I am from Malaga.*
d. **Son las tres y media.**	*It is half past three.*
Es de día.	*It is daytime.*
Hoy es el quince de marzo.	*Today is the 15th of March.*

[1]This distinction is also reflected in the nouns **ser** *being* and **estado** *state, condition.*

e. **Es probable.**	*It is probable.*
Es evidente.	*It is evident.*
Es tarde.	*It is late.*

NOTE. Adjectives such as **interesante, caro, popular,** and **cómodo,** which denote the product of essential characteristics, are construed with **ser: el libro era muy interesante** *the book was very interesting,* **la silla es cómoda** *the chair is comfortable.* But **yo estoy cómodo** *I am comfortable* (condition).

EJERCICIOS

1. Combínense los nombres en la sección *(a)* con los adjetivos y sustantivos en la sección *(b)* usando el verbo **ser:**

   a. Carlos, Miguel, Antonio, el médico, mi tío, María
   b. profesor, famoso, estudiante, escritor, muy popular, soltero, rico, guapo, alto

   Preguntas: ¿Qué es *Carlos* (Miguel, etc.)? ¿Quién es *el profesor* (famoso, etc.)?

2. Combínense los sustantivos de la sección *(a)* con los de *(b)* para indicar que los de *(b)* son el material de que están hechos, por ejemplo, **cuaderno, papel→el cuaderno es de papel:**

   a. cuaderno, casa, máquina de escribir, vestido, reloj
   b. papel, piedra, aluminio, seda, plata

   Preguntas: ¿De qué es *el cuaderno* (la casa, etc.)?

3. Combínense los sustantivos de la sección *(a)* con los hombres de *(b)* para indicar que pertenecen a los de *(b)*, por ejemplo, **libro, tío → el libro es de mi tío:**

   a. artículo, automóvil, edificio, barco, pistola
   b. hermano, Jorge, gobierno, Jacinto, guardia

   Preguntas: ¿De quién es *el artículo* (el automóvil, etc.)?

3. The more frequent uses of **estar** are: *(f)* to express location, *(g)* with present participles to form the so-called progressive tenses, *(h)* with past participles to denote the condition resulting from the action of a verb, and *(i)* with adjectives signifying state or condition.

f. **Estamos en los Estados Unidos.**	*We are in the United states.*
La Giralda está en Sevilla.	*The Giralda is in Seville.*
El sol está lejos de la tierra.	*The sun is distant from the earth.*
g. **Estamos estudiando.**	*We are* (in the act of) *studying.*

h. **La ventana está cerrada.**	*The window is closed.*
El artículo está bien escrito.	*The article is well written.*
El cielo está nublado.	*The sky is cloudy.*

NOTE. **Ser** is never used with past participles except to form the passive voice (**§148**).

i. **Juan está contento.**	*Juan is happy.*
Mi primo está enfermo.	*My cousin is ill.*

EJERCICIOS

1. Contéstense las preguntas siguientes, usando los sujetos entre paréntesis: ¿Dónde está ______? (su padre, la Giralda, el Prado, los astronautas, nosotros, yo)
   Cámbiense las frases siguientes según el modelo: **el vaso se rompió → el vaso está roto.**
2. La novela se escribió en inglés.
3. Se cerraron las iglesias.
4. Se murió mi tío.
5. Se suprimió el periódico.
6. Se prohibió toda manifestación pública.

4. From the above summary it is evident that the distinction between **ser** and **estar** should offer no difficulty except when the predicate is an adjective *(b* and *i)*. When this occurs choice is made between the two verbs according to whether the predicate adjective denotes *(b)* an essential quality or characteristic, or *(i)* a state or condition.

Isabel es muy morena.	*Isabel is very dark* (of complexion—essential characteristic).
Isabel está muy morena.	*Isabel is very dark* (from the air and sun—condition).

5. If the subject of **ser** is a person the predicate adjective usually approximates the force of a noun denoting a general class or type.

Mi sobrina es rubia.	*My niece is (a) blonde.*
Mi cuñada es joven.	*My sister-in-law is (a) young (woman)*
Mi amigo Carlos es rico.	*My friend Carlos is rich.*

NOTE. **Ciego** *blind*, **sordo** *deaf*, and the like, belong to this category, as does **feliz: soy feliz** (but **estoy contento**) *I am happy.*

6. **Estar** may be regarded as the graphic verb *to be* and, in contrast to the more abstract **ser,** often has the force of *look, feel, taste, act*, etc. **Estar** emphasizes the effect that a quality has on the person perceiving it. (See **§270** for a list of adjectives whose meaning is different after **ser** and **estar**.)

Antonio es malo.	*Antonio is bad* (wicked).
Antonio está malo.	*Antonio is ill* (feels bad).
Rosario es pálida.	*Rosario is pale* (by nature).
Rosario está pálida.	*Rosario is* (looks) *pale.*
Luis es muy raro.	*Luis is very queer.*
Luis está muy raro hoy.	*Luis acts very queer today.*
El caldo es muy bueno para los enfermos.	*Broth is very good for sick people.*
Este caldo está muy bueno.	*This broth tastes very good.*

EJERCICIOS

Combínense las palabras en la sección *(a)* con las de *(b)* primero con el verbo **ser** y después con el verbo **estar:**

a. Luis, el jefe, yo, Jacinto y su amigo, las muchachas, nuestros padres
b. malo, aburrido, cansado, extraño, listo, divertido

Preguntas: ¿Cómo está *Luis* (el jefe, etc.)? ¿Cómo es *Luis*?

7. The graphic quality of **estar** is well illustrated in the progressive tenses, which in Spanish always refer to action in progress.

Estoy leyendo una novela.	*I am* (in the act of) *reading a novel.*
But: **Leo muchas novelas.**	*I read many novels* (general statement).
Ahora vivo en Nueva York.	*I am living* (live) *in New York now.*

EJERCICIOS

Cámbiense los verbos en las frases siguientes del presente al progresivo con **estar,** con adición de la frase **en este momento,** por ejemplo, **estudio mis apuntes → en este momento estoy estudiando mis apuntes.**

1. Mi profesor nos ayuda.
2. Los obreros construyen un edificio nuevo.
3. Los estudiantes protestan las injusticias.
4. El autor escribe una novela.
5. El tren llega a la estación.

18. Expressions signifying *to become*

To become, like *to be*, is rendered in Spanish in a more varied and more graphic fashion than in English.[2] If the predicate is *(a)* a noun or an adjective used as a noun, **hacerse** is used to denote the result of conscious effort; if the predicate is *(b)* an adjective or participle, **ponerse** is used to indicate changes in physical, mental, or emotional states.

a. **Miguel se hizo periodista.**	*Miguel became a newspaper man.*
Un pobre puede hacerse rico.	*A poor man can become rich.*
b. **Fernando se puso pálido (furioso, gordo).**	*Fernando became pale (furious, fat).*
El cielo se puso muy oscuro.	*The sky became very dark.*

EXCEPTIONS: **se hace tarde** *it is getting (becoming) late;* **se hace (de) noche** *it is getting dark* (night time).

EJERCICIOS

Combínense las palabras en la sección *(a)* con los de *(b)* con los verbos **hacerse** o **ponerse:**

a. yo, mi compañero de cuarto, el profesor, los ciudadanos, la princesa
b. rico, enojado, abogado, ingeniero, enfermo

TRANSLATION A

1. Who is that gentleman? He is a friend of my father's. 2. What are those papers?—They are letters. 3. How is your brother?—He is sick. 4. My nephew wants to be an engineer. 5. We would like to be in Seville during (the) Holy Week. 6. That building is high. It is [made] of steel and concrete. 7. These apples are not ripe. 8. I am from Zaragoza; my parents are still there. They are old. 9. The door is closed and the lights are out. 10. This house belongs to my brother-in-law. 11. My office is not far from your hotel. 12. These shoes are comfortable, but too expensive. 13. I don't like these cigarettes. They are dry. 14. Today is the first of June. Next month we will be in Europe. 15. Be generous. 16. Be ready at five o'clock. 17. The book I am reading now is interesting and is very well written. 18. You are very busy this morning.—I have been busy the whole week. 19. The proprietor of the store was lame. 20. How beautiful the sea looks this evening!

[2] NOTE, in this connection, the many graphic Spanish equivalents of the English *do, make, have, get, give, take,* etc., registered in the Verbs and Idioms.

21. I am not [a] nervous [person], but I feel restless today. 22. Do you like this ice cream?—Yes, it is (tastes) good. 23. You have become pale. Are you ill? 24. It became late and we had to return. 25. My roommate has become [a] lawyer. 26. We were eating when he came in.

II

19. Additional remarks on *ser*

1. **Ser,** not **estar,** is used in the following cases, where occurrence and definition, not actual location, are expressed.

La escena es en Madrid.	*The scene is* (takes place) *in Madrid.*
Aquí es donde vive.	*This* (here) *is* (the place) *where he lives.*
La guerra fue en Babilonia.	*The war was (occurred) in Babylonia.*
La conferencia es a las tres.	*The lecture is at three.*

EJERCICIOS

Sustitúyase la forma debida del verbo **ser** por los verbos en las frases siguientes:

1. La ceremonia tuvo lugar en el ministerio.
2. Se armó una batalla en el campo.
3. La conferencia empieza a las ocho.
4. La función se verificó anoche.
5. Darán la fiesta en casa de mi tío.

2. In Spanish the subject frequently follows the verb. Consequently, **ser** sometimes agrees in number with the predicate, not the subject, especially if the predicate is felt to be the logical subject.

Lo más interesante de la obra son las escenas cómicas.	*The most interesting part of the work is the comic scenes.*

3. **Ser de** gives to a following infinitive an impersonal passive meaning.

Es de esperar . . .	*It is to be hoped . . .*
Era de oír . . .	*You should have heard* (it was worth hearing)

20. Additional remarks on *estar*

1. **Estar** also indicates location in time in the following idiomatic expressions:

¿A cuántos (del mes) estamos hoy?	*What date is today?*
Estamos a quince de marzo.	*It is the fifteenth of March.*

NOTE. These sentences may also be rendered: **¿qué fecha es hoy?** and **hoy es el quince de marzo.**

2. As a result of the difference between **ser** and **estar,** certain adjectives and participles vary distinctly in meaning according to whether they are used with one or the other. (For a longer list of these adjectives and participles see Appendix, §**270.**)

Este producto es muy rico en vitaminas.	*This product is very rich in vitamins.*
Este plato está muy rico.	*This dish is (tastes) delicious.*
Joaquín está muy cansado.	*Joaquín is very tired.*
Joaquín es muy cansado.	*Joaquín is very tiresome* (a bore).
Es un hombre muy distraído.	*He is a very absent-minded man.*
Estaba distraído.	*I wasn't paying attention* (was distracted).

3. The graphic character of the progressive tenses and especially of resultant conditions may be increased by replacing **estar** with auxiliaries of more concrete meaning:

Voy cansándome de esto.	*I am getting tired of this business.*
Anda distraído.	*He is* (going around) *absent-minded.*
Vengo indignado.	*I am* (coming from somewhere) *indignant.*

EJERCICIOS

Cámbiense los verbos en las frases siguientes a las construcciones con **-ndo** y los verbos **estar, ir, andar,** y **venir**: por ejemplo, **escucho los chismes → estoy (vengo, etc.) escuchando los chismes.**

1. Cantamos las canciones populares.
2. Mi amigo mejor escucha todo lo que dicen.
3. Ese tonto molesta a todos.
4. Aquella muchacha hermosa atrae a todos los jóvenes.
5. Nuestros compañeros se cansan de los estudios.

4. The use of **estar** to stress the impact that something makes on the speaker is revealed with special force when it appears with adjectives which usually are found with **ser** or even, in a few rare cases, with nouns. In such sentences the emphasis is not on the identification of the subject with the predicate as with **ser** but on how the subject *appears* to the speaker, independent of what or how it is in reality. The best English equivalent of this use is *seem* or *look.*

El pobre de don Alejandro está tan viejo estos días.	*Poor Alexander looks so old these days.*
¡Estaba tan niña, tan muñeca!	*She seemed so child-like, so doll-like!*
¡Qué idiota estás!	*How idiotic you're acting!*

NOTE. After **ser** and **estar** the distinction between nouns and adjectives is largely neutralized. See §**17**, 5. Compare also **él es muy caballero** *he is very gentlemanly;* **es muy verdad** *it is very true;* **esos chicos son muy amigos** *those boys are great friends.*

21. Expressions signifying *to become* (§139, note)

Spanish possesses no general equivalent to the abstract English verb *to become.* The Spanish equivalent will vary according to the specific meaning in each case. In addition to **hacerse** and **ponerse** the following are also used: *(a)* **llegar a ser** (with nouns) to indicate the final result or culmination of a process, *(b)* **volverse** (with adjectives) to denote a violent or radical change, *(c)* **convertirse en** (with nouns) to denote any change, natural or unexpected, *(d)* **meterse a** (with nouns) to denote an unexpected change of occupation, and *(e)* certain reflexive verbs like **calentarse** *grow warm* and **enfriarse** *grow cold* and a number of verbs ending in **-ecer,** like **endurecer** *harden,* **empobrecer** *become poor,* **enriquecer** *grow rich,* **entristecer** *become sad,* **esclarecer** *grow light,* **oscurecer** *grow dark,* etc. In some cases, however, *(f)* a complete change in construction is required.

a. **Napoleón llegó a ser emperador.**	*Napoleon became emperor.*
Llegaron a ser amigos inseparables.	*They became (came to be) inseparable friends.*
b. **Se volvió loco.**	*He became (went) crazy.*
Se volvió republicano.	*He became (turned) republican.*
c. **El agua se convierte en vapor.**	*Water becomes (turns into) steam.*
El mitin se convirtió en un motín.	*The (political) meeting became (turned into) a riot.*
d. **Se metió a novelista.**	*He became (turned his hand to being) a novelist.*

NOTE. With **monja** *nun* and **fraile** *monk, friar,* **meterse** is used: **se metió monja** *she became a nun.*

e. **La comida se ha enfriado.** *The meal has become cold.*
Anochece. *It is getting dark.*
Se ha enriquecido. *He has become rich.*
f. **Vivió diez años en el destierro.** *He became an exile for ten years.*

NOTE. The English idiom *what has become of?* is translated **¿Qué ha sido de?** or **¿Qué se ha hecho de?**

EJERCICIOS

Contéstense, utilizando en las respuestas las palabras entre paréntesis y las expresiones de la sección 21:

1. ¿Qué ha sido de su primo? (ingeniero, rico, dramaturgo, loco, general, sacerdote)
2. ¿Qué le pasó al amigo de usted? (socialista, reaccionario, amigo del presidente)

Cámbiense las frases siguientes, utilizando los verbos inceptivos, según el modelo:
La comida está fría → la comida se ha enfriado.

3. Mi madre está triste.
4. El cielo está claro (oscuro).
5. El agua está caliente.
6. La tierra está dura.
7. La muchacha tiene la cara roja.

TRANSLATION B

1. What date is today?—It is the 18th of February. *(two ways)* 2. I was talking with Miss Pardo. She is a very nice girl. 3. Her parents are spending the winter in Majorca. They are both painters. 4. The plays of Zorrilla were very popular. 5. The hill is very steep. 6. This coffee is very hot. 7. I have been awake the whole night and now I am tired. 8. Your father-in-law is always in a (of) good humor. 9. The resemblance of the portrait was astonishing. 10. Charles is a writer. He is never satisfied with **(de)** his work. 11. What (how) is your fiancée [like]?—She is tall and blonde. 12. I want to buy this hat. How much is it?—It is very cheap. 13. Mr. Sánchez is [a] very silent [individual], but tonight he has been talking all the time. 14. I have never been so happy. 15. You act very strange. —Yes, I am worried. 16. You are [a] very absent-minded [person].—Oh, no, you are mistaken. 17. We were very bored. 18. The film was very boring. 19. The waiter became so furious that I thought he had gone crazy. 20. I am getting fat.

It is very disagreeable. 21. What has become of your cousin George?—He is married now. 22. He has become president of the firm. 23. You are becoming very intolerant. 24. The word "speed" has become the symbol of this age. 25. Is it here that you bought the suit? 26. All this is to be regretted. 27. The best [part] of the program is the works of Falla.

III

VERBS AND IDIOMS

Review radical-changing verbs of Classes II and III **(§§227, 228).**
1. I regret I did not do (not having done) it before. 2. He heard (felt) a tremendous noise. 3. I don't think we will sleep at all **(nada)** tonight. 4. Where is John?—Upstairs, sleeping soundly. 5. His father died **(morírsele)** yesterday.

Pedir *to beg, ask for, request.*
1. He asked me to go with him. 2. Ask him for it. 3. You (one) can't ask for anything better (more). 4. Ask for (it) in all good drug stores. 5. I have borrowed his tuxedo. 6. I am going to ask you a favor. 7. We saw some beggars asking for alms.

Servir (de) *to serve (as)*, **(para)** *be of use, good for;* **servirse de** *make use of;* **sírvase** *please.*
1. His daughter was employed (serving) in the home of a doctor. 2. In this hotel they serve very good meals **(muy bien de comer)**. 3. Help (serve) yourself [to] bread. 4. At night the patio served as a dining room. 5. The boy acted as a chauffeur, a waiter, and even a secretary for him. 6. This key is no good. 7. What is this used for?—It is no good at all (for nothing). 8. He is no good as an (for) aviator. 9. What is the use of denying it? 10. Please close the door.

Entender *to make out (hear, understand*[3]*;* **entenderse** *to come to an understanding* or *agreement, to get along together;* **entender de** *to know about* (through practice).
1. Speak louder; I can't (do not) hear (understand) you well. 2. I can't read (do not make out) his handwriting. 3. [It is by] talking [that] people come to understand each other. 4. Those two do not get along well together. 5. That was not what [was] agreed on. 6. Is it clear?—Yes, sir. 7. He knows a lot about machinery. 8. Apparently you know [something] about everything.

[3]In contrast to **oír (§251)** *to hear* (physically) and **comprender** *to comprehend* (rationally).

chapter two

Tenses of the indicative
will and *would*

I

(For tense forms of the indicative, see §**222**)

22. The present tense

The simple present tense is employed more frequently in Spanish than in English, being used *(a)* to render the ordinary English present progressive tense and *(b)* to render the English present perfect when the act or state lasts down to the present. This latter construction is particularly identified with impersonal **hace (§137)** with temporal **desde (que)**, and with the verb **llevar** used with temporal meaning.

a. **¿Adónde va Ud.?**	*Where are you going?*
Ahora vivo en el campo.	*I am living in the country now.*

NOTE. The progressive tenses in Spanish have much more graphic force than their English equivalents (see §§**17,** 7; **20,** 3).

b. **Hace una semana que estamos aquí.**	*We have been here a week.*
Estamos aquí desde el lunes.	*We have been here since Monday.*
No la he visto desde que estoy aquí.	*I haven't seen her since I have been here.*
Llevamos aquí una semana.	*We have been here a week.*

NOTE. Similar to *(b)* is the idiomatic use of **acabar de** to represent action just previously completed: **acaba de llegar el tren** *the train has just pulled in.*

EJERCICIOS

Contéstense:

1. ¿Desde cuándo estudia usted el español?
2. ¿Cuánto tiempo hace que usted vive aquí?
3. ¿Lleva usted mucho tiempo estudiando en esta universidad?
4. ¿Cuántos días hace que usted no ve a sus padres?

23. The preterit

1. English has but one simple past tense. Spanish possesses two, the preterit and the imperfect. Of these, the preterit is the one that more closely corresponds to the English simple past. It is essentially a narrative tense, presenting bald facts viewed as a completed and undivided whole, regardless of duration. Consequently it is used *(a)* to record a single completed fact or phenomenon, and *(b)* to sum up a series of acts or states which, viewed as a whole, constitute a single completed fact or phenomenon.

a. **Cerró la puerta con violencia.**	*He slammed the door.*
Ayer llovió.	*Yesterday it rained.*
Estuvimos en España en el verano de 1972.	*We were in Spain in the summer of 1972.*
El viaje duró seis días.	*The trip lasted six days.*
b. **La semana pasada escribí dos cartas a mi hermana.**	*Last week I wrote two letters to my sister.*
Mataron ocho toros en la corrida.	*Eight bulls were killed in the bullfight.*
En el siglo XVI los españoles hicieron muchos viajes de exploración.	*In the sixteenth century the Spaniards made many voyages of exploration.*

2. The English *ago* is rendered by **hace . . . que** with the preterit. **Hace** may follow the verb, in which case **que** is omitted.

Hace una semana que llegué. **Llegué hace una semana.**	*I arrived a week ago* (*lit.* It makes a week since I arrived).

EJERCICIOS

Cámbiense las frases siguientes al pretérito:

1. Me levanto y me lavo la cara.
2. Luego me visto y me pongo el mejor traje que tengo.

3. Suena el teléfono.
4. Descuelgo el receptor y digo: —Diga.
5. Después me desayuno y voy a ver a mi amiga.

24. The imperfect

1. The imperfect tense corresponds roughly to the English past progressive. Consequently, the imperfect is essentially a descriptive tense and indicates that an act or state is viewed *(a)* as being in progress. It is also used *(b)* to indicate habitual, recurrent, or continuous action in the past, corresponding to the English *used to*, *would*, *(c)* to represent indirect discourse, and *(d)* to give the time of day.

a. **Estaba en Sevilla cuando le vi por primera vez.**	*I was in Seville when I first saw him.*
Llovía sin parar.	*It was raining continuously.*
La comitiva fúnebre pasaba lentamente.	*The funeral procession was passing slowly.*
Las olas se estrellaban contra las rocas.	*The waves were breaking on the rocks.*
b. **Iba al café todas las tardes.**	*He would (used to) go to the cafe every afternoon.*
c. **Dijo que lo sabía.**	*He said he knew it.*
d. **Eran las seis en punto cuando terminé.**	*It was six o'clock on the dot when I finished.*

2. Since the imperfect is the past form of the present, it is used in the **hace . . . que, desde, llevar,** and **acabar de** constructions **(§22)** to render the English pluperfect.

Hacía una semana que estábamos allí. / **Llevábamos una semana allí.**	*We had been there (for) a week.*
Estábamos allí desde principios de mes.	*We had been there since the first of the month.*
El tren acababa de llegar.	*The train had just pulled in.*

EJERCICIOS

Cámbiense las preguntas en los ejercicios de la sección 22 al imperfecto.

Cámbiense las frases siguientes al imperfecto:

1. Hace un día espléndido.
2. Los pájaros cantan en los árboles.

3. El cielo está azul.
4. Oigo los ruidos de la calle.
5. Son las siete y cuarto.
6. Me siento listo para todo.

25. The future

The Spanish future tense corresponds in general to the English. The following differences are to be noted: *(a)* the future is used in Spanish to indicate a probability or conjecture which the speaker is reasonably certain will prove to be true ("future of probability"); *(b)* the future is not used in Spanish to render the English *will* when the latter means *be willing.*

a. **¿Quién llama?—Será el cartero.** — *Who is knocking?—It must be the postman.*

NOTE. This use of *must* in English must be differentiated from the *must* denoting obligation.

b. **No quiere venir con nosotros.** — *He will not ("won't") come with us.*

NOTE. The future is used after **si** *whether*, but not after **si** *if*: **no sé si vendrá** *I don't know whether he will come (or not)*, but **si le veo se lo daré** *if I see him I shall give it to him.*

26. The conditional

Just as the imperfect represents the present in the past, so the conditional tense represents the future in the past. The Spanish tense corresponds in general to the English, but with the same differences as noted in §**25** for the future.

¿Quién llamaba?—Sería el cartero. — *Who was knocking?—It must have been the postman.*

No quería venir con nosotros. — *He would not (did not want to) come with us.*

EJERCICIOS

Cámbiense las frases siguientes al futuro:

1. Mañana voy a Nueva York.
2. Dentro de poco estamos allí.
3. Muy pronto lo sabes todo.
4. Jorge puede hacerlo.
5. No quieren hacer el trabajo necesario.

En las frases siguientes cámbiense las expresiones con **deber (de)** e infinitivo al futuro y luego al condicional, por ejemplo, **debe de verlo → lo verá.**

1. Deben de ser las cuatro.
2. Debe de ser mi hermano.
3. Mi libro debe de estar perdido.
4. Aquella vieja debe tener más de ochenta años.
5. Deben de haber ido al teatro.

27. The perfect tenses

The perfect tenses are formed with **haber** and the invariable past participle. The present perfect and pluperfect are *(a)* normally used as in English—except in constructions denoting lapse of time (§§**22** and **24**). The future perfect and conditional perfect express *(b)* in past time the same functions as the future and the conditional.

a. **Le he dado mi opinión sobre el asunto.**	*I have given him my opinion on the subject.*
Le había dado mi opinión sobre el asunto.	*I had given him my opinion on the subject.*
b. **¿Quién ha mandado el paquete?—Habrá sido mi primo.**	*Who has sent the package?—It must have been my cousin.*

NOTE. The conditional perfect of probability is quite rare.

EJERCICIOS

Cámbiense los verbos en las frases siguientes del presente al perfecto:

1. Vamos muchas veces al teatro.
2. Allí se presentan muchas obras dramáticas.
3. Hasta ahora no vuelvo a mi patria.
4. ¿Tienes una cosa semejante?
5. No lo hace nunca.

28. Will *and* would

The student should bear in mind that the English auxiliaries *will* and *would* represent not only the future and conditional tenses but also the present and past tenses of **querer** *to be willing*, *to want* and that *would* often represents the imperfect tense in the meaning *used to*.

Dijo que vendría.	*He said he would come.*
No quiere (quería) venir con nosotros.	*He won't (wouldn't) come with us.*
Iba al café todos los días.	*He would go to the cafe every day.*

TRANSLATION A

1. We are going to the theatre. Are you coming too? 2. Somebody is calling you on the (by) telephone. 3. I have been here for three months. Tomorrow I am leaving for Spain. 4. Goytisolo's latest novel has just come out. 5. I haven't been to (in) the movies since I have been here. 6. You have been studying for two hours. 7. I saw your grandfather in Philadelphia, but I didn't talk to him. 8. The Secretary of [the] Treasury arrived this morning. 9. The conductor asked us for the tickets. 10. The apartment has five rooms. 11. The sea was very rough. 12. Last year I used to take my meals in a restaurant. 13. I didn't hear what he was saying. 14. The steamer was entering the bay when the collision occurred. 15. It was half past one when the game started. 16. When we lived in the country we would get up at six o'clock every morning. 17. Charles V was King of Spain and Emperor of Germany. 18. In the Middle Ages Medina del Campo was famous for its fairs. 19. He had been sick for a long time. 20. I had been two years in America when we became friends. 21. [I wonder] where my dictionary is?—It must be on the shelf. 22. The child must have been four years old. 23. He told me he would see me tomorrow. 24. I wouldn't like to live in this town. 25. The owner of the dog said that he would not sell him. 26. I must have lost the key of my trunk. 27. We had forgotten that it was Sunday and the stores were closed.

II

29. Uses of the graphic present

The present tense is used, especially in the spoken language, as a graphic substitute for other tenses in the following constructions: *(a)* as an emphatic future, when certainty is implied, *(b)* in interrogations, when immediate future time is involved, *(c)* for the conditional perfect, in contrary to fact conditions, *(d)* for the simple past, in historical narrative, in rapid sequences, or with **por poco**, *(e)* for the imperative, by stating the command not as a wish but as a fact.

a. **Mañana le despido.**	*I* (surely) *will discharge him tomorrow.*
Nos reunimos esta tarde.	*We will get together* (of course) *this afternoon.*
Eso lo hago yo cualquier día.	*I'll do that any day.*
b. **¿Vamos ahora?**	*Shall we go now?*
¿Pongo el desayuno en la mesa?	*Shall I put the breakfast on the table?*

NOTE. In negative sentences the Spanish graphic present often has the force of *can* or *will* in English: **no entiendo su letra** *I can't make out his handwriting*; **el ruido no me deja dormir** *the noise will not let me sleep.*

c. **Si hubiera entrado** (or **entra**) **en aquel momento, le tiro algo a la cabeza.**	*If he had entered at that moment I would have thrown something at his head.*
d. **Salgo de casa, me encuentro con Enrique, me convida a café y luego nos fuimos al teatro.**	*I left the house, met Enrique, he "treated" me to coffee, and then we went to the theatre.*
Por poco me caigo.	*I almost fell down.*
e. **Deja Ud. el paquete en el correo y vuelve aquí.**	*Leave the package at the post office and return here.*

30. Preterit and imperfect *(cont.)*

1. The difference between the preterit and the imperfect is a modal rather than a temporal one. The preterit stresses final result, the imperfect stresses process. It follows, therefore, that the same statement may have a different meaning according to which past tense is used. When the imperfect is used, the speaker regards the meaning of the verb as being in progress and forming the background of other acts that may be taking place. The difficulty encountered by speakers of English lies in the fact that while in English one may often use a past progressive in the same sense as a Spanish imperfect, the English simple past may also be used in sentences which in Spanish would require an imperfect. Also, there are some verbs in English which rarely appear in the progressive construction, e.g., *to be*, *to have*, *to seem*, etc.

A las once de la mañana el barco entró en el puerto.	*At eleven o'clock in the morning the ship entered the port.*
A las once de la mañana el barco entraba en el puerto.	*At eleven o'clock in the morning the ship was entering the port.*

In the preceding examples, we can see that the first sentence simply reports a past fact as finished and done with, while the second sentence implies that while the action was taking place, i.e., while the ship was entering the port, some other events were taking place and the entering of the ship was simply a background for them. For example, while the ship was entering the port, it struck a sand bar, or the captain had a heart attack, etc. In isolated sentences where there is no visible context, it is the speaker's mental attitude, i.e. the unexpressed context, that determines the tense of the verb used.

En el siglo XVI España fue una gran potencia europea. — *In the sixteenth century Spain was a great European power* (viewed in résumé and implying contrast with some subsequent situation, e.g., **para 1800 España había perdido mucha de su importancia anterior.**)

En el siglo XVI España era una gran potencia europea. — *In the sixteenth century Spain was a great European power* (viewed as the background for further statements about what was happening during the time that Spain was a great power, e.g., **en esa época se llevó a cabo la conquista de mucho del Nuevo Mundo**).

En el verano de 1972 estuvimos en España. — *In the summer of 1972 we were in Spain* (summed up as a single experience).

En el verano de 1972 estábamos en España. — *In the summer of 1972 we were in Spain* (the speaker may go on to relate what happened during the period spent in Spain. In English it would be impossible to say, *we were being in Spain*).

EJERCICIOS

Cámbiense las frases siguientes al pasado:

1. Mi amigo Peña me acompaña todos los días al parque.
2. Cada mañana llega a mi casa a las diez.
3. Por lo general tomamos una taza de café y luego salimos.
4. Un día Peña toca el timbre mientras todavía duermo.
5. De repente me despierto y veo que son las siete.
6. —¿Qué diablos será eso?—me pregunto.
7. Abro la puerta y Peña me saluda cordialmente.

8. Entra y me explica que unos compañeros suyos que viajan por el país quieren hacer una excursión a El Escorial.
9. Por eso nos invitan a ir con ellos.
10. Acepto la invitación, nos desayunamos, y vamos. Nos divertimos mucho.

2. As a result of the difference between the preterit and imperfect, certain verbs such as **conocer, saber, poder, tener,** and **querer** have different meanings in these two tenses.

No lo sabía.	*I did not know it.*
Lo supe ayer.	*I found it out (learned it) yesterday.*
No conocía a ese señor.	*I did not know that gentleman.*
Le conocí ayer.	*I met him yesterday.*
No quería salir.	*He would not (did not want to) go out.*
No quiso salir.	*He refused to go out.*
No podía levantarse.	*He could not* (was not able to) *get up.*
No pudo levantarse.	*He could not* (tried but failed to) *get up.*
Ayer tuvo carta de su madre.	*He received a letter from his mother yesterday.*

NOTE. With **poder** and **querer** the difference in meaning between the preterit and imperfect is much more evident when the sentence is negative.

3. The imperfect is the past equivalent of the graphic present and as such is used as a graphic substitute for the conditional, especially in colloquial speech.

Si no hablaba se moría.	*If he couldn't have talked he would have died.*
Si hubiera entrado en aquel momento, le tiraba algo a la cabeza.	*If he had entered at that moment I would have thrown something at his head.*

4. The preterit (usually with **ya**) stresses the completion of action in immediate past time.

Ya terminamos.	*We have finished.*
Se acabó.	*It's all over.*

5. The imperfect is frequently used instead of the present tense *(a)* in polite interrogations with **desear** or its equivalent, and *(b)* with **merecer.**

a. **¿Qué deseaba el señor?**	*What does the gentleman wish?* (Used by waiters and shopkeepers.)
b. **Merecía que le ahorcaran.**	*He deserves to be hanged.*

EJERCICIOS

Cámbiense los infinitivos entre paréntesis a la forma debida del pasado:

1. Ayer yo (conocer) al nuevo decano cuando fui a la reunión.
2. Enrique tenía el brazo roto y no (poder) levantar el peso.
3. Manuel esperaba un regalo de su madre pero sólo (tener) una carta.
4. Las dos camareras (conocer) a muchos de los parroquianos de la cafetería.
5. Un día nosotros (saber) una noticia importante.
6. Pedro me dijo que no (querer) salir porque estaba muy ocupado.
7. Las tropas insurgentes fracasaron porque no (poder) apoderarse de la capital.

31. The future as imperative

The future is occasionally used as a categorical imperative.

Hará Ud. lo que le digo.	*You will do what I say.*

32. Special uses of the present perfect

The present perfect may be used *(a)* in clauses introduced by **hace . . . que,** especially if negative, *(b)* in colloquial speech in Spain as equivalent to the simple past when referring to recent events, or even *(c)* with the force of an imperative, stating the command as an already accomplished fact.

a. **Hace mucho que no le he visto.**	*I haven't seen him for a long time.*
b. **Han llegado esta mañana.**	*They arrived this morning.*
¿Lo han entendido?	*Did they understand?*
c. **¡Ya se ha callado Ud.!**	*You shut up!*

EJERCICIOS

Póngase el presente del perfecto o el presente de los verbos entre paréntesis:

1. Hace muchos días que no (trabajar) Pepe.
2. Hace mucho que nosotros (estar) en esta ciudad.
3. Hace sólo una semana que yo te (conocer).
4. Hace un rato que él no (venir) por aquí.
5. Hace tiempo que ellos no (salir) de casa.

33. The archaic pluperfect

In literary Spanish one may still find a sporadic case of the archaic pluperfect, identical in form with the imperfect subjunctive in **-ra.**

La criada se guardó el dinero que le diera su señora.	*The servant kept the money her mistress gave (had given) her.*

34. Further constructions with *desde* (temporal)

1. In expressing an act or state that lasts down to a point in the present (or the past) **desde hace** (or **desde hacía**) may be used to indicate the time elapsed.

Estoy aquí desde hace una semana.	*I have been here a week.*
Estaba allí desde hacía una semana.	*I had been there a week.*

2. In past time the preterit (not the imperfect) is used with **desde que,** which expresses the moment *from* which (not the time *during* which).

No la he visto desde que llegué.	*I have not seen her since I arrived.*
No la había visto desde que salí de España.	*I had not seen her since I left Spain.*

TRANSLATION B

1. I [will] stay (at) home tomorrow. 2. If it had not been for the policeman he would have killed me. 3. The vender of lottery tickets was crying: "It comes out tomorrow." 4. What [do you say], shall we dance? 5. You go to the store, pay the bill, and come back at once. 6. We want to get our passports, but the office was closed. 7. That very day the troops entered the city. 8. Eight o'clock had just struck. When we arrived at the station the train was pulling out. 9. It was a cool and pleasant morning; the walk didn't tire us at all. 10. There were many people there whom I did not know, but later on I made friends with some of them. 11. The taxi driver refused (did not want) to accept the tip the lady gave (had given) him. 12. I tried to call him on the telephone, but I couldn't. 13. We went to see you last night. You were not [in]. 14. I had not been to (at) a horserace for several years. 15. I have not gone out to the street since I fell sick. 16. He said that if he did not arrive on (a) time he would lose the position. 17. It is useless. He will not

listen. 18. We will come back right away. 19. I would not take it seriously. 20. He and I were then very good friends, but later on we quarrelled. 21. I took out my wallet and noticed that I did not have any money. 22. In 1840 my great-grandfather made a trip from Madrid to Malaga; it lasted twenty days. Journeys were very long in those times. 23. I thought you were away. When did you return? 24. I learned the news this afternoon. 25. If I don't [get an opportunity to] talk, I [shall] die. 26. Shall we leave now? 27. The danger is over (passed) now.

III

VERBS AND IDIOMS

Review verbs with orthographic changes **(§229).**
1. Don't begin yet. 2. I began the work. 3. Nobody can **(no hay quien)** convince him. 4. Don't I convince you? 5. Send (address) the mail to this address **(señas).** 6. Go (direct yourself) to the manager. 7. Find out what is going on.

Tocar *to touch, play* (an instrument or music), *ring* (a bell); impers. *to be one's turn, get* (as one's share or lot).
1. Do not (it is prohibited) touch the objects. 2. You (one) must not mention (touch on) this topic to him, because he gets angry. 3. His oldest daughter plays the piano very well. 4. The orchestra played several modern Spanish works. 5. Don't ring the doorbell, it is out of order. Knock (with your hand). 6. I have just had my examination in **(examinarme de)** chemistry; it's your turn tomorrow. 7. How much does each one (of) us get?

Pegar *to stick, beat, give* (blow, shot, kick, shout, jump, etc.).
1. I am putting (sticking) these pictures in my album. 2. Don't beat the child! 3. I shot (*or* stabbed) one of the robbers. 4. You can't fool me **(pegármela).**

Jugar (§250) *to play, gamble.*
1. Did you play (at) tennis yesterday?—Yes, I played three sets **(partidos).** 2. If you do not wish to play, don't play.

Coger *to gather, catch, take (pick, select).*[1]
1. Anna was gathering flowers in the garden. 2. Don't catch your finger! 3. His coming took (caught) me unawares. 4. I must catch the seven o'clock train. 5. He has caught a cold. 6. He took me by **(de)** the hand and led me to his study. 7. Here is (you have) the box of cigars; take a few.

[1]**Coger** is often a graphic alternative for **tomar** (p. 101) in this sense.

chapter three

Personal pronouns. The imperative

I

35. Table of personal pronouns

(For neuters and reflexives, cf. §§**52, 55**).

		SINGULAR		
PERSON	SUBJECT	INDIRECT OBJECT	DIRECT OBJECT	PREPOSITIONAL FORM
1.	**yo** *I*	**me** *to me*	**me** *me*	**mí** *me*
2.	**tú** *you (thou)*	**te** *to you (thee)*	**te** *you (thee)*	**ti** *you (thee)*
3.	**él** *he*	**le** *to him, it* (m).	**le** *him*, **lo** *it* (m.)	**él** *him*
	ella *she*	**le** *to her, it* (f.)	**la** *her, it* (f.)	**ella** *her*
	usted *you*	**le** *to you* (m. and f.)	**le** *you* (m.), **la** *you* (f.)	**usted** *you*
		PLURAL		
1.	**nosotros (-as)** *we*	**nos** *to us* (m. and f.)	**nos** *us* (m. and f.)	**nosotros (-as)** *us*
2.	**vosotros (-as)** *you*	**os** *to you* (m. and f.)	**os** *you* (m. and f.)	**vosotros (-as)** *you*
3.	**ellos** *they* (m.)	**les** *to them* (m.)	**los, les** *them* (m.)	**ellos** *them*
	ellas *they* (f.)	**les** *to them* (f.)	**las** *them* (f.)	**ellas** *them*
	ustedes *you* (m. and f.)	**les** *to you* (m. and f.)	**les** *you* (m.), **las** *you* (f.)	**ustedes** *you*

36. Pronouns of address

1. **Usted** (often abbreviated **Ud., Vd., V.**) and **ustedes** (abbreviated **Uds., Vds.,** or **VV.**) are the pronouns that ordinarily correspond to the English *you.* Being contractions of **vuestra merced** and **vuestras mercedes,** they are third person pronouns, as are the object forms **le, la, les, las.**
2. The second person forms **tú** and **vosotros (-as)** are used only in intimate or familiar address. (The same holds true for **te** and **os.**) These second person forms are chiefly used between relatives, young people (including university students even when they do not know each other), and close friends of any age. In Andalusia and in Spanish America **vosotros** and the corresponding verb forms have been replaced by **ustedes.**

37. Titles of address

1. **Señor** *Mr.*, **Señora** *Mrs.* and **Señorita** *Miss* (abbreviated **Sr., Sra., Srta.**), **don** and **doña** (abbreviated **D.** and **Dª**) are used according to the following scheme:
   Señor (etc.): **Sr. Gómez, Sr. D. Miguel Gómez** (used especially in addressing letters).
   Don (etc.): **D. Miguel, D. Miguel Gómez, Sr. D. Miguel Gómez.**

   NOTE. **Don** was formerly used in Spain only by nobles. Today anyone having the *bachillerato* is entitled to put **don (doña)** before his first name.
2. For the use and omission of the definite article with **Señor,** see §7, 2*a*. **Señor, señora,** and **señorita** may be used as nouns meaning *gentleman*, *lady*, and *young lady*.

38. Conventional and intimate imperative (§§29, e; 31; 32, c; 58; 108, 3; 115; 132, 4, n.)

1. The third person forms of the present subjunctive are used with **usted** to form *(a)* the ordinary or conventional imperative. The forms of *(b)* the imperative mood are second person forms and are used only when **tú** and **vosotros** would apply.

a.	**compre Ud.**	*buy*	**aprenda Ud.**	*learn*	**viva Ud.**	*live*
	compren Uds.	*buy*	**aprendan Uds.**	*learn*	**vivan Uds.**	*live*
b.	**compra**	*buy*	**aprende**	*learn*	**vive**	*live*
	comprad	*buy*	**aprended**	*learn*	**vivid**	*live*

NOTE. In colloquial speech the second person plural imperatives have become identical with the infinitive: **¡ hijos, venir aquí !** *Children, come here !*

EJERCICIOS

Cámbiense los verbos en las frases siguientes al imperativo según el modelo: **La señora Alas habla → hable Ud., señora Alas.**

1. El señor Gómez viene mañana.
2. Pepe tiene cuidado.
3. Los señores traen los papeles al juez.
4. Isabel me dice la verdad.
5. El capitán obedece las órdenes del general.
6. La señorita Ramírez pedirá ayuda a su padre.
7. Tomás se pone el jersey.
8. Antonia nos compra unos recuerdos en España.

2. The first person plural of the present subjunctive is used for the first person plural imperative, the only exception being **vamos** *let's go.*

Estemos contentos por ahora.	*Let us be satisfied for the present.*
Defendamos nuestros derechos.	*Let us defend our rights.*

NOTE. **Vamos a** + infinitive of a verb is used instead of the imperative form whenever the action is to be performed immediately: **vamos a comer** *let's eat* (now), in contrast to the more general **no comamos demasiado** *let us not eat too much* (at any time).

EJERCICIOS

Contéstense las preguntas utilizando primero la construcción con **vamos a** y luego el subjuntivo según el modelo: **¿Entramos? → Sí, vamos a entrar; entremos.**

1. ¿Salimos?
2. ¿Comemos?
3. ¿Trabajamos?
4. ¿Escribimos?
5. ¿Bailamos?
6. ¿Bebemos?

39. Subject pronouns

Usted is the only subject pronoun normally expressed with the verb, the others being adequately indicated by the inflectional ending. Any subject pronoun may be used, however, when needed for clearness, contrast, or emphasis. The subject pronouns **él, ella, ellas, ellos,** when so used always refer to persons, never to things. Subject pronouns referring to things are not expressed.

Él pintaba y ella escribía.	*He was painting and she was writing.*
Él lo dijo, yo no.	*He said it, not I.*
Son grandes y cómodos. (los autobuses)	*They are large and comfortable.* (the buses)
Ella es muy buena.	*She is very kind.*

NOTE. To render the English impersonal *It is I, it was they,* etc., the Spanish uses the inflected forms of **ser: soy yo (somos nosotros), eran ellos,** etc.

EJERCICIOS

Quítense los sujetos de los verbos en las frases siguientes, sustituyendo el pronombre donde es necesario:

1. Carlos iba mucho al teatro pero María prefería ir al cine.
2. Mis padres suelen viajar mucho.
3. Los chicos juegan en la calle después que terminan las clases.
4. Ese señor lleva mucho tiempo aquí y su mujer también.
5. La cocinera no quiso preparar lo que le mandó su patrón.

40. Object pronouns of the third person

The following peculiarities of object pronouns of the third person must be noted: *(a)* **lo** as direct object ordinarily refers to things, **le** to persons; *(b)* **los** and **las** as direct objects refer to both persons and things; *(c)* **le** and **les** as indirect objects are both masculine and feminine; *(d)* masculine **usted (ustedes)** has the direct object form **le (les)** and feminine **usted (ustedes), la (las).** In Spanish America **lo** is usually used for all masculine direct objects, both persons and things.

41. Position of object pronouns

1. Object pronouns, both direct and indirect, are placed immediately before the verb. These are called *conjunctive* pronouns, in contrast to the *disjunctive* or *prepositional* forms. The former are consequently unstressed and the latter stressed forms.

Le hablé ayer.	*I spoke to him (her) yesterday.*
Hablé con él ayer.	*I talked with him yesterday.*

2. When, however, the conjunctive pronoun is object of *(a)* an infinitive, *(b)* a present participle, or *(c)* an affirmative *(not negative)* imperative, the pronoun follows the verb and is annexed to it.

a. **Tenemos que copiarlas.** (cartas)	*We have to copy them.* (letters)
b. **Estaba leyéndola.** (novela)	*He was reading it.* (novel)
c. **Démelo Ud.** (lápiz)	*Give it to me.* (pencil)
But: **No me lo dé Ud.**	*Do not give it to me.*

NOTE. When the pronoun is annexed, the stressed syllable of the verb remains the same, and requires a written accent in all cases except when only one pronoun is appended to an infinitive.

EJERCICIOS

Sustitúyanse los pronombres por los sustantivos objetos de los verbos en las frases siguientes:

1. Los estudiantes van a ver al señor rector. (decano, secretaria, muchachas)
2. Mi primo verá la exposición pronto. (las pinturas, los monumentos, el museo)
3. Señalamos el peligro a nuestros compañeros. (los colores, el palacio, la casa)
4. El obrero invitó a los forasteros a tomar una copa. (la gente, los hombres, las chicas)
5. Tienen que comunicar la noticia a los demás. (los informes, las ideas, la decisión)
6. ¿Por qué no nos muestran los ejemplos? (las pinturas, los periódicos, el programa)

En las frases del ejercicio de §38, 1, sustitúyanse los pronombres por los sustantivos objetos de los verbos. Luego háganse todas las frases negativas, e.g., **La señora Alas toma café → Señora Alas, tómelo Ud.; no lo tome Ud.**

42. The redundant construction

1. When the context does not clearly indicate the antecedent of **le, la, los, las,** or **les,** ambiguity is avoided by adding after the verb the proper prepositional form.

Le di el libro { **a él.** / **a ella.** / **a Ud.** } *I gave the book to him (her, you).*

2. This construction is also used *(a)* for purposes of emphasis, contrast, or clearness and *(b)* when the indirect object is a noun denoting a person (or personified thing).

a. **No me lo diga Ud. a mí.**	*Don't tell it to me.*

NOTE. For further emphasis, the prepositional form may precede: **a mí no me importa** *I don't care.*

b. **Le expliqué el caso a mi hermano.**	*I explained the matter to my brother.*

NOTE. When **todo(s)** is the direct object, **lo(s)** must also be used: **lo tengo todo aquí** *I have everything here;* **los he visto todos** *I have seen them all.*

EJERCICIOS

Sustitúyanse los pronombres por los objetos de los verbos en las frases siguientes, utilizando siempre la construcción enfática **a él, a ella,** etc.

1. Le ofrecí el dinero al conserje, no a la portera. (mujer—hombre, empleados—jefe)
2. Les escribimos la tarjeta postal a nuestros padres, y también a nuestras hermanas. (los amigos—el profesor, mi madre—mi sobrino)
3. ¿Podemos enseñar la lección a los alumnos? (el profesor, nuestros compañeros)
4. Les entregaron los paquetes al cartero. (la bibliotecaria, el artista)
5. José le pidió un duro a su padre. (su madre, sus compañeros).

43. The construction of *gustar*, etc.

With certain verbs and verb phrases the English direct object becomes the subject (and follows the verb). The English subject becomes the indirect object.

Me gustan los perros.	*I like dogs. (Lit.* Dogs are pleasing to me)
Me hace falta un sombrero.	*I need a hat.*
Me falta dinero.	*I lack money.*
Me encanta la literatura.	*Literature delights me.*
Me agradan mis compañeros.	*I like my companions.*
¿Te sienta bien ese traje?	*Does that suit suit you?*
Nos parece aburrido.	*We think it's boring.*

EJERCICIOS

Sustitúyanse las palabras en las secciones *a)* y *b)* por las palabras subrayadas:

1. Me gusta[a] la pintura moderna[b].
   a. atraer, agradar, aburrir
   b. los viajes, el Quijote, el vino francés, los periódicos extranjeros
2. ¿Le falta[a] a Ud. dinero?[b]
   a. hacer falta, parecer interesante, contentar, espantar
   b. un perro, un gato, sellos nuevos, joyas raras, la información

TRANSLATION A

1. Please show me that hat. 2. Buy me that typewriter, dad. I need one. 3. Let us go to my study. We will talk there. 4. Let us go for a walk. 5. Let us forget the incident. 6. Son, open the window. 7. He was reading and she was sewing. 8. You suggested it, he didn't. 9. They have a country house. It is small, but very pretty. 10. Who is downstairs?—It is they. *(masc.)* 11. We sent you *(sing.)* a present. Did you *(sing.)* receive it? 12. We used to visit him every evening. 13. I met Miss García in the post office and accompanied her home. 14. We saw them *(masc.)* and greeted them. 15. Where are your glasses?—I have left them home. 16. How many sentences are there in this section?—I haven't counted them. 17. We are going to propose a plan to you *(sing.)* 18. I intend to give them a copy. 19. Here are the suitcases. I am going to check them. 20. All right, do it now, don't leave it for tomorrow. 21. Did you write down the addresss of the boardinghouse?—I am doing it at this moment. 22. It would be better to talk to him, not to her. 23. Well, don't accuse *me!* 24. Tell them *(masc.)* what happens. 25. Last night I sent **(poner)** a telegram to the cashier of the bank. 26. Address the letter to Mr. Pedro Fernández Carvajal, calle de San Bernardo, [number] 32. 27. Sell it all.

II

44. Pronouns of address *(cont.)*

Following are some special uses of pronouns of address: *(a)* **tú** (and **te**) are used in prayers and apostrophes, *(b)* **vosotros** and corresponding forms are frequently used in addressing an audience, in advertisements, and in general notices.

a. **Padre nuestro que estás en los cielos . . .**	*Our Father who art in Heaven . . .*
b. **Quisiera presentaros esta noche . . .**	*I should like to present to you tonight . . .*
c. **Comprad la hoja de afeitar "Toledo".**	*Buy Toledo razor blades.*

NOTE. **Vos** (second personal plural, with singular or plural meaning) is used in archaic or poetic style. **Nos,** the paternal *we,* is still used by high ecclesiastical authorities.[1]

45. Titles of address and family names *(apellidos)*

1. **Señor** is used in addressing or referring to titled persons and officials.[2]

¿Está el señor rector?	*Is the President* (of a university) *in?*

2. Officially a Spaniard has two family names **(apellidos)**, his father's and his mother's: **D. Manuel Carrillo (y) Gayangos.** (In modern usage the **y** is usually omitted.)

3. A married woman retains her own family name as her legal name, adding to it her husband's, preceded by **de.** Thus **Mercedes Linares Castellanos** becomes, on marrying the above-mentioned gentleman, **Dª Mercedes Linares de Carrillo,** and their son **Rafael** is called **Rafael Carrillo Linares.**

EJERCICIOS

La señorita Nieves Muñoz Castro se casa con Francisco Salinas e Ibáñez.

1. ¿Cómo la llaman después del casamiento?
2. ¿Cuál será el nombre completo de su hija Pilar?
3. Si Pilar se casa con Diego Aguilar Pastor, ¿cómo la llamarán?

[1]In many parts of Spanish America **vos** is colloquially used instead of **tú,** with special verb endings, e.g., **amás, comés, escribís.** Only in Argentina, however, has it become accepted as standard.

[2]Certain offices and ranks have a special form of address **(tratamiento),** such as **Usía** (contraction of **Vuestra Señoría)** and **Vuecencia** (contraction of **Vuestra Excelencia).**

46. Compound subject

In the case of compound subjects of different persons the verb is first person plural if one of the subjects is first person, and second person plural if they are second and third person.

Usted y yo vamos.	*You and I go.*
Tú y él vais.	*You and he go.*

47. Forms of the conjunctive pronouns *(cont.)*

The following deviations from normal usage are frequently met with, chiefly in colloquial style: (1) **lo** instead of **le** as direct object referring to masculine persons *(loísmo)*; (2) **les** instead of **los** as direct object referring to masculine persons *(leísmo)*; (3) **la** as the indirect object referring to feminine persons *(laísmo)*.

NOTE. The use of **le** as masculine direct object referring to things *(leísmo)* is provincial and archaic.

48. Special uses of conjunctive pronouns

1. Following are some important idiomatic uses of the conjunctive pronouns: *(a)* when the direct or indirect noun object precedes the verb, it is usually recapitulated by the corresponding conjunctive pronoun; *(b)* the feminine pronoun **la** (also **las** and rarely **ella**) is used elliptically in many idiomatic and colloquial expressions, as equivalent to an indefinite *it* (see §**77**, 2 for **la(s)** used in set expressions); *(c)* in literary style (and in archaic and provincial speech) the conjunctive pronouns are occasionally annexed to finite forms of the verb, especially at the beginning of a sentence or clause.

a. **El dinero lo perdió en la calle.**	*(As for) the money, he lost it in the street.*
b. **¡Buena la hiciste!**	*You made a fine mess of it!*
Las caza al vuelo.	*He is quick at catching on.*
Se las echa de Don Juan,	*He puts on airs of being a Don Juan.*
Se las da de intelectual.	*He pretends to be an intellectual.*
Voy a habérmelas con él.	*I'm going to have it out with him.*
Esa materia se las trae.	*That subject is a problem.*
¡Me las pagará!	*He'll pay for that!*

Quiero arreglármelas. *I want to settle things.*
No las tenía todas conmigo. *I didn't have my wits about me.*
c. **Hallóse sin protección de nadie.** *He found himself without any backing.*

49. Special uses of the prepositional forms

In addition to the uses set forth in §**42**, the prepositional forms of the pronoun are employed *(a)* after verbs of motion, *(b)* to replace the disjunctive forms when the verb is omitted.

a. **Me dirigí a ella.** *I went up to her.*
Vino a mí y me dijo . . . *He came to me and said . . .*
b. **¿Le gusta a Ud.? A mí no.** *Do you like it? I don't.*

NOTE. After **entre** *between* the subject pronouns are used: **entre tú y yo** *between you and me.*

TRANSLATION B

1. Buy national products. 2. Advertise in this magazine. 3. Ladies and gentlemen: I would like to indicate to you. . . . 4. He and I were classmates. 5. [As for] the house, he has it mortgaged. 6. [As for] his son, he has him in a military academy. 7. We approached them to hear what they were saying. 8. The man was running towards us. 9. We moved away from them. 10. The Ambassador will see you later. 11. Consult the secretary. 12. Those girls are talking about us. 13. They have invited you, not me. 14. Does the project interest you?—It doesn't [interest] me. 15. I haven't answered them *(masc.)* yet. I am going to dictate the letter to you. 16. Don't type it. Write it in (with) pencil. 17. I can't go to see them *(fem.)*. Give them *(fem.)* [my best] regards. 18. I gave the stamps to you. Where have you put them? 19. We would like to hear her sing. Have you heard her? 20. Men do not like to shop. Women do. 21. This soil needs water. 22. Is it you, Frank?—Yes, it is I. 23. He wouldn't tell them, but I did. 24. Are you going to the theatre with them?—No, I am not [in the mood] for it. 25. He'll pay me [for] this *(fem. pl.)*!

III

VERBS AND IDIOMS

Verbs ending in **-aer, -eer, -eír, -oír, -uir, -üir,** *and those whose stem ends in* **-ll** *or* **-ñ (§§ 229, 230, 231).** 1. I found (saw) myself in a very difficult situation.

2. The night was so dark that nothing could be (was) seen. 3. I can't stand (see) that fellow. 4. Thinking that you were not coming, we (have) started to eat. 5. They believed that we had heard the conversation. 6. I have always thought so (the same). 7. She is always laughing. 8. He laughed *(refl.)* loudly (much) when I told him (it). 9. I do not hear well. 10. He said it in [a] loud voice so that we [could] hear it. 11. Look here! Porter! 12. Let us wait until he finishes talking. 13. They finished the job and left (went away). 14. He dyed his hair and moustache.

Caer (§236) *to fall, get (fall to one's lot), fit (become);* **caer en (la cuenta de)** *to remember (see the point);* **caerse** *to fall (of persons).*
1. A tree has fallen *(invert)*. 2. Look out! **(¡Cuidado!)** Don't fall! 3. I almost **(por poco)** fell (fall). 4. (To) my friend Manuel has won (fallen) a prize in the lottery. 5. The dress fitted her very well. 6. Don't drop it (let fall). 7. I know that man in **(de)** the derby, but I can't (do not) remember who he is (may be). 8. You know to whom I refer.—Yes, now I remember. 9. In what direction is **(¿hacia dónde cae?)** the museum? 10. He hasn't got a penny to his name **(No tiene donde caerse muerto).** 11. The children have taken a liking to their father's friend **(les ha caído en gracia).**

chapter four

Personal, reflexive, and neuter pronouns

I

50. Two conjunctive pronoun objects

When both the direct and the indirect object pronouns are used, the indirect object precedes the direct. The two pronouns either precede or follow the verb according to the rules for the position of a single pronoun object.

Me lo dio esta mañana.	*He gave it to me this morning.*
Démelo Ud.	*Give it to me.*
No quiso dármelo.	*He refused to give it to me.*

51. The conjunctive pronoun *se*

If both pronoun objects are of the third person, the indirect object invariably has the form **se** (instead of **le** or **les**). The redundant construction is used with **se** in accord with the principles of §**42**.

Juan se lo vendió { **a él.** / **a ella.** / **a usted.** / **a ellos.** / **a ellas.** / **a ustedes.** } — *John sold it to him (her, you, them).*

Se lo dio a mi hermano.	*He gave it to my brother.*

NOTE. This conjunctive pronoun **se** must not be confused with the reflexive **se**.

EJERCICIOS

Primero cámbiense las palabras subrayadas por las palabras entre paréntesis, y luego sustitúyanse los pronombres por los objetos de los verbos:

1. Le mostraron las casas nuevas[a] al señor ministro[b].
2. Le dio el aparato[a] a tu hermano[b].
3. Le da los fondos[a] al banquero[b].
4. Les ofreció la oportunidad a los extranjeros.

a. (los libros, la flor, las armas, el barco)
b. (el rector, los oficiales, la señora, el profesor)

52. Reflexive pronouns

Reflexive pronouns are object pronouns which are identical with (*i.e.*, "reflect") the subject of the verb. The reflexive pronouns of the first and second persons have the same forms as the corresponding personal pronouns. *(a)* The conjunctive form for the third person, both singular and plural, direct and indirect, is **se**; *(b)* the corresponding prepositional form is **sí**; *(c)* with the preposition **con** the special forms **conmigo, contigo,** and **consigo** are used; *(d)* reflexive **se** whether direct or indirect object, always precedes any other conjunctive pronoun.

a. **Ellas se están vistiendo.**	*They are getting dressed* (dressing themselves).
b. **Hablaba para sí.**	*He was talking to himself.*
c. **Lo trajo consigo.**	*He brought it with him(self).*
d. **Se me acercó.**	*He came up to me.*

EJERCICIOS

Pónganse los pronombres reflejos en los espacios, cambiando los sujetos a **yo, tú, nosotros,** y **ellos**:

1. Juan ______ hizo un favor.
2. María ______ compró unos bombones.
3. Pedro ______ llevó el libro.
4. Miguel nunca ______ niega nada.
5. Ricardo lo trajo con ______.

53. Dative of interest

The Spanish indirect object expresses more varied relations than its English counterpart *(person to whom)*. It denotes, in general, the person to whose benefit or disadvantage the action redounds. This relation is traditionally called the "dative of interest." (Contrast **me dió el libro** *he gave me the book* with **me cambió el neumático** *he changed the tire for me.*) The more usual types of relation expressed by this dative of interest are *(a)* possession and *(b)* separation. This object when reflexive, *(c)* often serves to give an intensifying force to the action by doubling the reference to the subject.

a. **Me duele la cabeza.**	*My head aches.*
Le rompí el bastón.	*I broke his cane* (for him).
Me hizo una fotografía.	*He took my picture* (for me).
Se puso el sombrero.	*He put on his hat.*
b. **Le compramos la quinta.**	*We bought the country house from him.*
El ruido me quitó el sueño.	*The noise prevented me from sleeping* (*i.e.*, took sleep away from me).
c. **Se fue (se marchó) a Francia.**	*He went (off, away) to France.*
Se estaba días enteros sin hablar.	*He would remain entire days without speaking.*
Se bebió una botella de vino.	*He drank (up) a bottle of wine.*

NOTE. The more usual verbs in this category are: **irse, marcharse** *to go away*, **quedarse, estarse** *to remain, stay*, **llevarse** *carry off, away*, **caerse** *fall down*, and **pararse** *to stop* (intrans.).

EJERCICIOS

Pónganse los pronombres debidos en los espacios según los objetos entre paréntesis:

1. ______ robaron el reloj de plata.
2. ______ perdió una gran oportunidad.
3. ______ pueden hacer la ropa para mañana.
4. ______ dejó el recado.
5. ______ han explicado el caso.
6. ¿______ puede planchar la camisa?

(a él, a ella, a nosotros, a Miguel y Jacinto, a mí, a ti, a ustedes)

54. Verbs having material and personal objects

When a Spanish verb has two objects, one personal and the other material, the person affected usually becomes the indirect object and the thing affected the direct object. In English the reverse is often the case; note the English equivalents of the Spanish construction with the verbs **pagar, pedir, agradecer, avisar, impedir,** and the like.

Se lo agradezco mucho. (el regalo)	*I am grateful to you for it.* (the gift)
Me la pagó en seguida. (la cuenta)	*He paid me right away.* (the bill)
Se lo impedimos. (el acto)	*We prevented him from doing it.* (the act)
Me lo pidió. (un libro)	*He asked me for it.* (a book)

EJERCICIOS

Sustitúyanse los pronombres por los objetos de los verbos en las frases siguientes:

1. Le agradezco mucho a Ud. la carta de recomendación.
2. Te pidió el regalo.
3. Nos avisó que había peligro.
4. Les pagaron la cuenta.
5. Nos impidieron que saliéramos.

55. Neuter pronouns

Neuter personal pronouns, like neuter demonstratives (**§69**), have as their antecedents a phrase, a clause, a general idea, or a specific object of indeterminate gender, either expressed or understood. They have the following forms: *(a)* the subject pronoun **ello,** which in modern usage is rarely employed, *(b)* the conjunctive pronoun **lo,** and *(c)* the prepositional form **ello.**

a. **Ello es que nunca volvió.**	*The fact is he never came back.*
b. **Tiene Ud. que contármelo.**	*You must tell me (it).*
c. **Cuente Ud. con ello.**	*Count on it* (what I have said).

56. Predicate *lo*

The Spanish language, in contrast to the English, possesses a strong feeling for grammatical completeness. As a consequence, the neuter pronoun **lo** is used *(a)* after the verbs **ser** and **estar,** to recapitulate the idea expressed in a previous adjective or even noun, and *(b)* after **creer, decir, preguntar,** and similar verbs of discourse where in English the object idea is either unexpressed or rendered by the particle *so.*

a. **¿Es Ud. español (española)? —Lo soy.**	*Are you Spanish?—I am.*

	¿Está Ud. enfermo?—Lo estoy.	*Are you ill?—I am.*
But:	**¿Quién es? ¿Juan?—No, soy yo.**	*Who is it? John?—No, it is I.*
b.	**Dígaselo Ud.**	*Tell him.*
	¿Cree Ud. que perderemos el tren?—No, no lo creo.	*Do you think we will miss the train?—No, I don't think so.*
	Voy a preguntárselo.	*I am going to ask him.*

EJERCICIOS

Contéstense con el pronombre debido, sustituyendo las palabras entre paréntesis por las palabras subrayadas:

1. ¿Es Ud. americano? (español, francés, chino)
2. ¿Es abogado su padre? (arquitecto, médico, periodista)
3. ¿Están Uds. contentos? (tristes, alegres)
4. ¿Son interesantes los estudios? (aburridos, técnicos)
5. ¿Cree Ud. que todo va bien? (que la vida es mala, que el mundo se acaba)
6. ¿Les dijeron Uds. a sus padres qué van a hacer durante las vacaciones? (por qué no van a casa, cómo están)

57. *Mismo (-a, -os, -as)*

Mismo *self* may be used to intensify both subject and object pronouns.

Él mismo tuvo que reconocerlo.	*He himself had to admit it.*
Me lo repetía muchas veces a mí mismo.	*I would repeat it to myself many times.*

TRANSLATION A

1. I am going to return it *(masc. sing.)* to you. 2. They want to sell it *(fem. sing.)* to her. 3. Don't send them *(fem. pl.)* to Charles. He has them already. 4. Where is the umbrella?—George took it away (with him). 5. He got up from the chair and came toward us. 6. Put your coat on. Don't take it off. 7. I am going away tomorrow. Why don't you come with me? 8. When I went to your house, you had gone. 9. Stay here while I shave *(refl.)*. 10. Who was talking with him?—Nobody, he was talking to himself. 11. The injured [man] came to. 12. Did you fall down?—No, but I thought I was going to (fall down). 13. Don't be grateful to me; be grateful to her. 14. Let him know about it. 15. Did I pay the shoemaker for the shoes?—I don't think so, but ask him. 16. They disarranged my

papers and broke my ash tray. 17. You have ruined my suit. 18. Well, the fact is that we never saw him again. 19. The janitor told us all [about] it. 20. It was very unpleasant; I don't want to think of it. 21. I don't want to mix in it. 22. That man is an Englishman, isn't he?—Yes, he is. 23. You don't look old.—No, I don't but I am. 24. I am going to borrow these books from him. 25. Don't lose heart. Cheer up! 26. Are you ready?—Yes, I am. 27. If you want his permission ask for it. 28. Please copy this page for me. 29. He ate it all up. 30. She told me herself.

II

58. Imperative of reflexive verbs

In the first person plural imperative reflexive verbs lose the final **s** of the termination when the pronoun **nos** is annexed; in the second person plural (intimate) imperative the final **d** is similarly dropped when **os** is annexed.

Sentémonos aquí.	*Let's sit down here.*
Sentaos, muchachos.	*Sit down, boys.*

NOTE. The only exception is **idos** *go away.*

EJERCICIOS

Cámbiense las expresiones siguientes al subjuntivo, primero en frases positivas, y luego en frases negativas, sustituyendo las palabras entre paréntesis por las palabras subrayadas:

Vamos a <u>ponernos el sombrero</u> (quitarnos los zapatos, acordarnos del asunto, divertirnos, atrevernos, casarnos, apresurarnos, despedirnos, quedarnos, irnos)

59. Further uses of the prepositional forms

As a result of the rules for position of pronoun objects, when the direct object of a verb is a pronoun of the first or second person and the indirect object is a pronoun of the third person, the latter takes the prepositional form.

Me presentó a ella.	*He introduced me to her.*
Nos acercamos a él.	*We approached him* (See §**49**.)
Te recomendamos a ella.	*We recommended you to her.*

NOTE. **Me la presentó** can only mean *he introduced her to me.* But **se le acercó** meaning *he approached her* is possible because **se**, whether direct or indirect object, always precedes other pronouns.

EJERCICIOS

Constrúyanse frases completas con las palabras dadas, e.g., **Manuel/presentar/a mí/a ella → Manuel me presentó a ella; Manuel me la presentó.**

1. Eduardo/presentar/a nosotros/a él.
2. Mi amigo/recomendar/a ellos/a ella.
3. Nuestros padres/presentar/a él/a ellos.

60. Position of pronoun objects *(cont.)*

There is a growing tendency in modern Spanish to place the pronoun objects of the infinitive or gerund immediately before the auxiliary instead of annexing them to the dependent verb.

No me lo quiso dar or **No quiso dármelo.**	*He wouldn't give it to me.*
Se lo voy a dar or **Voy a dárselo.**	*I am going to give it to him.*
Le estoy escribiendo or **Estoy escribiéndole.**	*I am writing to him.*

EJERCICIOS

Sustitúyanse los pronombres por los objetos de los verbos en las frases siguientes:

1. El gerente va a ofrecerme un puesto.
2. Ramón quería escribir la solicitud al jefe.
3. Manuel puede encontrar los periódicos.
4. Vamos a decir el cuento de hadas a las niñas.

61. Dative of interest *(cont.)*

The dative of interest often expresses many subtle shades of advantage or disadvantage, rendered *(a)* often by the English *on*, *at* or *(b)* occasionally impossible of direct translation.

a. **Me hizo una jugada.**	*He played a mean trick on me.*
La niña le ponía una carita muy graciosa.	*The little girl would make a cute little face at him.*

b. **Me temo que no resulte.**	*I am afraid that it will not turn out.*
Sé lo que me hago.	*I know what I am doing.*

NOTE. Sometimes two dative values may be combined: **se le murió el caballo** *his horse died ("on" him)*. **Morir** states a bald fact **(murió el rey** *the king died,* **murieron muchos en el combate** *many died in the battle)* while **morirse** indicates a personal concern on the part of the speaker.

62. Reflexive verbs with material complement

In contrast to the situation in §54, a number of reflexive verbs require a preposition to introduce the material complement, *e.g.*, **alegrarse de, enterarse de, oponerse a, contentarse con.** See §269 for a list of frequently used verbs that require a prepositional complement.

Me alegro de su éxito.	*I am glad of your success.*
Se enteraron del asunto.	*They learned about the affair.*
Me opuse al arreglo.	*I opposed the arrangement.*

63. Reciprocal pronouns

The plural reflexive pronouns may be used with reciprocal meaning. The redundant construction **uno a otro, el uno al otro,** etc., is employed when needed for clearness or emphasis.

Se ayudaban en sus estudios.	*They helped each other in their studies*
No podían soportarse el uno al otro.	*They couldn't stand each other.*
Nos llevábamos muy bien, él y yo.	*We got along very well (together), he and I.*

64. Predicate *lo (cont.)*

1. Predicate **lo** is used to recapitulate, not only adjectives, but also nouns regardless of gender.

Parece mentira, pero no lo es.	*It seems incredible but it is not.*
Creen que para mí es una satisfacción. Y lo es, lo es.	*They think it is a pleasure for me. And it is, it is.*

65. Personal pronouns with partitive value

If the antecedent of a conjunctive pronoun is partitive, the pronoun likewise has partitive value. In such cases the English either omits the pronoun or uses the indefinites *any*, *some*, *none*, etc.

¿No tiene vergüenza?—Sí, la tiene. *Hasn't he any shame?—Yes, he has.*
¿No hay árboles en este pueblo?—No, no los hay. *Are there no trees in this town?—No, there aren't any.*

NOTE. The omission of the pronoun is gaining ground in modern colloquial Spanish: **¿Tiene Ud. fósforos?—Sí tengo** *Have you any matches?—Yes, I have.*

TRANSLATION B

1. Let us get up very early. 2. Let us get together later on. 3. Rejoice, friends! 4. He recommended me to you. 5. He recommended you to me. 6. We are going to organize it *(masc.)*. 7. Be careful with the radio; you are going to get it out of order. 8. Buy a dozen from me, said the flower vender to us. 9. Translate this poem for me. I don't understand it very well. 10. He ate up all the grapes. 11. He would come late to the office (on me), he would carry off my writing paper and even sell my books. 12. His mother died a year ago. 13. She died from grief. 14. His illness grew worse. 15. Fatigue took away my appetite. 16. The dog got away from him. 17. We shall oppose it. 18. Let us be contented with this solution. 19. They used to see each other in the café. 20. When I entered the room they were insulting each other. 21. I myself opened the door for them. 22. We ourselves had warned (it to) him. 23. We were afraid of finding difficulties, but there were none. 24. Is there running water in this room?—Yes, there is. 25. Were there any visitors this afternoon?—Yes, there were. 26. She seized the letter and prevented me from reading it. 27. Are you the landlady?—Yes, sir, I am.

III

VERBS AND IDIOMS

Review verbs ending in **-ecer** *and* **-ocer (§239).**

Saber (§257) *to know (have information concerning:* **sabe mucho español** he knows a great deal of Spanish), *know how to, find out; taste of* (a); **conocer** *to know (be acquainted with persons or things:* **conoce muy bien el español** he knows Spanish very well), *recognize, be evident.*

1. He does not know how to read or **(ni)** write. 2. I did not know that you were here. 3. I know that the road is in very bad condition *(pl)*. 4. He knows a great deal of medicine. 5. Do you know [any] French? 6. Do you know [the way] to the post office? 7. I know **(me sé)** that book by heart. 8. He never knows his **(la)** lesson. 9. What is he going to say when he finds it out? 10. It is not known where he is. 11. This water tastes of iron. 12. Do you know General Domínguez? 13. He is well acquainted with Spanish customs. 14. He also knows Spanish music. 15. He met (got acquainted with) her at the seashore. 16. I had changed so much that he did not know me. 17. At the station I spoke **(saludar)** to several acquaintances. 18. It is evident that you do not live here. 19. His scar does not show **(conocérsele)** at all. 20. I did not know that this gentleman was a foreigner; he does not show it at all. 21. We know a great deal about this fellow. 22. We know this fellow very well. 23. You will find out tomorrow. 24. [I want you to] know that that is not true.

chapter five

Demonstratives and possessives

I

66. Demonstrative adjectives

Spanish possesses three demonstrative adjectives corresponding to the demonstrative adverbs **aquí** *here* (near to the speaker), **ahí** *there* (near the person addressed), and **allí** *there* (removed from both, yonder).

SINGULAR			PLURAL		
MASC.	FEM.		MASC.	FEM.	
este	**esta**	*this* (here)	**estos**	**estas**	*there* (here)
ese	**esa**	*that* (there)	**esos**	**esas**	*those* (there)
aquel	**aquella**	*that* (yonder)	**aquellos**	**aquellas**	*those* (yonder)

From the above it follows *(a)* that the demonstrative adjective agrees in gender and number with the accompanying noun and is repeated before nouns of different gender, *(b)* that **este** indicates an object near to, associated with, or possessed by the speaker, *(c)* that **ese** indicates an object near to, associated with, or possessed by the person spoken to, and *(d)* that **aquel** indicates an object distant from both or unrelated to either.

a. **Este hombre y esta mujer.**	*This man and woman.*
b. **Esta silla es muy cómoda.**	*This chair* (I am sitting in) *is very comfortable.*
No veo bien con estos lentes.	*I don't see well with these glasses* (I have on).
c. **Déme Ud. esa pluma.**	*Give me that pen* (you have).
Me gusta ese sombrero.	*I like that hat* (you are wearing).
d. **Mire Ud. aquella casa.**	*Look at that house* (yonder).
Aquellos árboles son robles.	*Those trees* (yonder) *are oaks.*

EJERCICIOS

Sustitúyanse los adjetivos demostrativos por los artículos definidos en las frases siguientes, cambiando las palabras subrayadas por las palabras entre paréntesis:

1. El libro que tengo aquí es más interesante que el libro que Ud. tiene. (la revista, las fotos)
2. Vemos los árboles en las montañas distantes. (la nieve, las rocas, los esquiadores)
3. El monumento que tú has visto es muy famoso. (la iglesia, el museo, las casas antiguas)
4. La pluma aquí es más cara que la pluma allí en la mesa. (el aparato, los platos, la radio)

67. Pronouns resulting from deletion of a noun

One of the most common processes of Spanish grammar is the formation of a pronoun by deleting the noun found in a noun phrase. (See §§**68, 72, 84, 181, 186** for examples.) Thus one may form the demonstrative pronoun by removing the noun modified by a demonstrative adjective. In writing, the demonstrative pronoun must have an accent written over the stressed vowel. For example, from **aquellas corbatas** one may get **aquéllas,** from **este coche** → **éste,** etc.

No me gustan estas corbatas, aquéllas sí.	*I don't like these neckties (but) I do (like) those.*
Esta silla es más cómoda que ésa.	*This chair is more comfortable than that one.*

EJERCICIOS

Quítense los sustantivos modificados por los demostrativos, sustituyendo las palabras entre paréntesis por las palabras subrayadas:

1. Quiero ver estas cosas, no aquellas cosas. (libros, camisas, caja, traje)
2. Se me acercaron esos muchachos, pero aquellos muchachos se marcharon. (hombres, guardias, señoritas)
3. Déme Ud. esa pluma porque esta pluma está rota. (plato, lápiz)
4. ¿Prefiere Ud. esta manzana o esa manzana? (melón, galletas, vasos)
5. Este sombrero me sienta mejor que ese sombrero. (traje, camisa, corbatas)

68. Demonstrative *el*

Another example of the formation of a pronoun by deleting a noun is seen in the use of the definite article plus the relative pronoun **que** or the preposition **de** by removing the noun between them. Thus from **el hombre que vino** → **el que vino, la mujer que sirve** → **la que sirve, la plata del Perú** → **la del Perú,** etc. (See §84 for further examples.)

Los recursos de Chile y los del Perú.	*The resources of Chile and those of Peru.*
Esta tienda y la de la esquina.	*This store and the one on the corner.*
Este diccionario y el que Ud. tiene.	*This dictionary and the one (which) you have.*
La del vestido azul marino.	*The (woman) in the navy blue dress.*

EJERCICIOS

Quítense los sustantivos después de los artículos definidos de las frases siguientes según el modelo, cambiando las palabras subrayadas por las palabras entre paréntesis, e.g., **este helado es el helado que más me gusta** → **este helado es el que más me gusta.**

1. Estas flores son las flores que prefiero. (calcetines, corbatas, zapatos)
2. Mi prima es la muchacha del vestido verde. (pelo negro, ojos azules, sonrisa alegre)
3. Estos libros son los libros que Ud. quería ver. (pinturas, objetos, fotos, vasos)

69. Neuter demonstratives

Since there are no neuter adjectives, the neuter demonstrative pronouns **esto, eso, aquello,** and **lo** bear no written accent. They are used to refer to a general idea, a phrase, a clause, or an object of indeterminate gender. **Lo** is chiefly used in the combination **lo que** *what (that which).*

Esto me preocupa.	*This* (situation) *worries me.*
Eso no es verdad.	*That* (what you have said) *is not true.*
Lo que ocurrió ayer.	*What* (that which) *happened yesterday.*

70. Possessive adjectives

1. There are two forms of possessive adjectives in Spanish, the stressed and the unstressed. The former follow the noun and are used only under special circumstances, the latter precede the noun and are the ones normally used.

POSSESSIVE ADJ. NORMAL FORM			POSSESSIVE ADJ. STRESSED FORM	
SINGULAR	PLURAL		SINGULAR	PLURAL
1. **mi**	**mis**	*my*	**mío, mía**	**míos, mías**
2. **tu**	**tus**	*thy*	**tuyo, tuya**	**tuyos, tuyas**
3. **su**	**sus**	*his, her, its, your*	**suyo, suya**	**suyos, suyas**
1. **nuestro, -a**	**nuestros, -as**	*our*	**nuestro, -a**	**nuestros, -as**
2. **vuestro, -a**	**vuestros, -as**	*your*	**vuestro, -a**	**vuestros, -as**
3. **su**	**sus**	*their, your*	**suyo, -a**	**suyos, -as**

2. The possessive adjective agrees in gender and number not with the possessor (as in English) but with the thing possessed. **Mi, tu,** and **su,** however, have the same form for masculine and feminine. They are repeated before nouns of different gender or number.

Éstas son mis habitaciones.	*These are my rooms.*
¿Han traído Uds. su baúl?	*Have you* (pl.) *brought your trunk?*
Este autor me regala todos sus libros.	*This author gives me all his books.*
Mi tío y mis primos.	*My uncle and cousins.*

3. The stressed forms are chiefly used only *(a)* in direct address, *(b)* exclamations, and *(c)* as equivalents of the English *of mine, of yours,* etc.

a. **No tardes, hijo mío.**	*Don't be long, my son.*
b. **¡Dios mío!**	*My Lord!*
c. **Consuelo es muy amiga suya, ¿verdad?**	*Consuelo is a good friend of yours, isn't she?*

4. The English possessive case *('s)* is rendered by **de** with the possessor noun or pronoun.

La casa de mi amigo.	*My friend's house.*
Esto no es de nadie.	*This is nobody's* (*i.e.*, does not belong to anybody).

EJERCICIOS

Sustitúyanse los sustantivos entre paréntesis por las palabras subrayadas, y sustitúyanse los adjetivos posesivos por otros adjetivos posesivos:

1. ¿Dónde está su madre? (sobrino, tío, abuela, padres)
2. Mi coche es nuevo. (barco, calcetines, tocadiscos)
3. El violinista es un amigo mío. (compañero, primo, pariente)

71. Substitutes for *su*

Since **su** (and **suyo**) may mean either *yours* (sing, and plural), *his*, *hers*, *theirs*, or *its*, it is very frequently replaced, to avoid ambiguity, by the phrases **de él, de ella, de usted,** etc., following the noun.

Es una idea de ella.	*It's (one of) her idea(s).*
He leído el artículo de Ud.	*I have read your article.*

NOTE. In conversation **su** (and **suyo**) normally mean *yours* (referring to the person addressed). In more formal style the **su** may be retained in addition to the explanatory **de usted: he leído su artículo de Ud.** *I have read your article.*

EJERCICIOS

Sustitúyanse los pronombres con **de** que corresponden a los nombres entre paréntesis por el adjetivo **su(s)** en las frases siguientes: e.g. **su clase → la clase de ella, la clase de ellos,** etc.

1. Vamos a ver su casa.
2. Sus ideas son siempre interesantes.
3. Sus carteles están en la mesa.
4. Josefa es una amiga suya.

(María, Ana y Jorge, Jacinto, los hermanos de Pablo, las señoras, usted, ustedes)

72. Possessive pronouns

(a) Possessive pronouns, being stressed words, are formed by deleting the noun in noun phrases composed of the article, the noun, and the stressed possessive adjective or the possessive expressed by **de** plus a noun or pronoun, **la casa tuya → la tuya, el libro mío → el mío, los perros de él → los de él, las flores de usted → las de usted,** etc. *(b)* **El suyo** normally

means *yours;* in other meanings it is replaced, to avoid ambiguity, by **el de él, el de ella,** etc. *(c)* The demonstrative **el** may be omitted only after the verb **ser** (§17, 2*c*).

a. **Este comedor es más grande que el nuestro.**	*This dining room is larger than ours.*
Sus maletas están aquí, las mías no.	*Your suitcases are here, mine are not.*
b. **Aquí está mi abrigo. ¿Dónde están el suyo y el de Pepe?—Aquí está el de él, pero no veo el mío.**	*Here is my overcoat. Where are yours and Joe's?—Here is his but I don't see mine.*
c. **Esta corbata es mía.**	*This necktie is mine.*
Esta cochera es del vecino; la de la esquina es la nuestra.	*This garage is our neighbor's; the one on the corner is ours.*

NOTE that demonstrative **el** may be retained after **ser** to indicate contrast or emphasis.

EJERCICIOS

Sustitúyanse los pronombres posesivos por los sustantivos subrayados, cambiando las palabras entre paréntesis por las palabras subrayadas:

1. Ud. tiene mi paraguas. (guantes, billete, libro)
2. Nuestro coche está en la calle. (bicicletas, amigo)
3. Sus maletas están en el hall. (compañero, baúl, amiga)
4. ¿No tienes tus billetes? (libro, corbata, pantalones)
5. Éste es mi número. (libro, permiso, cartas)
6. ¿Ése es su libro? (guante, coches, impermeable)

73. Substitutes for the possessive adjective

The possessive adjective is used less frequently in Spanish than in English. Its place can be taken by the definite article (§7, 1*d*) or by the dative of interest or possession (§53).

Saqué el reloj.	*I took out my watch.*
Me duele la cabeza.	*My head aches.*
Nunca se sabe la lección.	*He never knows his lesson.*
Estoy perdiendo el tiempo.	*I am wasting my time.*

NOTE that this construction is not confined to parts of the body or objects of personal wear but may be extended to any object directly associated with the subject of the sentence.

TRANSLATION A

1. These shoes are [too] big for me. 2. Who is that girl seated at the window? 3. What are you doing with that gun? 4. Which of those gentlemen is your uncle?—The one with the moustache. 5. Please show me that overcoat. No, not that one, the one with the belt. 6. This writing desk is too (very) low. I like better (more) the one you have in your study. 7. Have you seen this?—No, what is it? 8. Why do you say that? 9. What you ask for is impossible. 10. I have met Mrs. Torrijos; her daughter Teresa is studying in the university. 11. Are all those prints yours?—No, these are my brother's. 12. Our house is near theirs. 13. My son, don't neglect your studies. 14. That impatience of yours will be your ruin. 15. The editor of that newspaper is a classmate of mine. 16. I don't share your opinion. 17. That was a remark of his. 18. Is this your briefcase?—No, mine is on the table. 19. Are those dresses hers?—No, hers are in the trunk. 20. This car is his; ours is in the garage. 21. Those mountains are higher than the ones we saw on our trip. 22. I am very glad to meet you.—The pleasure is mine. 23. I don't remember what he said. 24. These handkerchiefs are not ours; they must be somebody else's. 25. I have told you many times that that is your drawer and that this one is mine. 26. I have lost my hat. 27. Don't put your head out of (through) the window.

II

74. *Acá* and *allá*

The adverbs **aquí** and **allí** have the more indefinite forms **acá** *(over) here* and **allá** *(over) there.*

Allá en las montañas hace frío.	*Over there in the mountains it is cold.*
Venga Ud. acá.	*Come over here.*

NOTE. These adverbs when used with **por** have many special meanings: **por aquí** *around here, this way*; **por ahí** *somewhere around, around town*; **por allí** *around there, that way*; **por acá** *in this region, neighborhood*: **Venga Ud. por acá** *Call on us some time.*

75. Agreement

A demonstrative adjective modifying two nouns of different gender need not be repeated if the nouns are plural and form a single concept.

estas ideas y proyectos	*these ideas and plans*

76. Special uses of the demonstratives

Following are some special uses of **este, ese,** and **aquel:** *(a)* with temporal, as well as locative, meaning; this use is particularly characteristic of **aquel:** *(b)* in a series of two, **éste** (the last mentioned) means the *latter* and **aquél** (the first mentioned) *the former; (c)* in correspondence **en (a, por) ésta** and **en (a, por) ésa** mean *here* and *there*, respectively, a noun such as **ciudad** being understood; *(d)* the pronoun **ése (ésa,** etc.) when applied to persons conveys an idea of contempt; *(e)* the adjective **ese** imparts a graphic flavor, especially in certain set phrases with **por.**

a. **En estos días.**	*In these days.*
En esa época.	*At that time.*
En aquel entonces.	*At that time* (definitely past).
Aquel asunto me salió mal.	*That* (past) *affair turned out badly for me.*
b. **Bolívar y Wáshington son los dos grandes libertadores americanos; éste murió en 1799, aquél en 1830.**	*Bolivar and Washington are the two great American liberators; the former died in 1830, the latter in 1799.*
c. **Llegaré a ésa el lunes próximo.**	*I shall arrive there next Monday.*
d. **¿Quién es ése?**	*Who is that fellow?*

NOTE. **Éste (ésta,** etc.) are used familiarly[1] with the meaning *he (she,* etc.*)* when pointing to a person present: **eso es lo que éste dice** *that's what he says.*

e. **por esas calles**	*through the streets* (graphic)
por esos mundos de Dios	*throughout the wide world*

77. Special uses of *el* and *la*

1. **De los (las) que** and **de lo que** may be used as equivalent to the English *of the kind (sort) which.*

Ése es de los que tiran la piedra y esconden la mano.	*That fellow is the kind who throws stones without showing his hand.*
Es de lo que no hay.	*There's nothing better than this (i.e.,* its like does not exist).

2. The feminine **la** and **las** are used with **de** *(a)* to refer familiarly to the female members of a family, *(b)* in a number of set idiomatic phrases, exactly

[1]In literary style, **éste** (etc.) when beginning a sentence, is equivalent to the English emphatic *he* (*she, it,* etc.) or *the latter.*

parallel to the use of **la(s)** as an object pronoun (**§48, b**), *(c)* with adjectives in certain idiomatic expressions.

a. **La de Bringas.**	*Mrs. Bringas* (or *the Bringas woman).*
Las de Fernández.	*The Fernández girls.*
b. **Pasó las de Caín.**	*He went through great suffering.*
Hubo la de San Quintín.	*There was a big fight.*
Se armó la de Dios es Cristo.	*A big fight started.*
Tomó las de Villadiego.	*He took to his heels.*
¡La de gente que había!	*What a big crowd there was!*
¡La de preocupaciones que tenemos!	*What a lot of worries we have!*
c. **Ésta es la nuestra.**	*This is our opportunity.*
Se armó la gorda.	*They started a good one (fight).*
Pasamos las negras.	*We had a tough time.*
Me llevas la contraria.	*You oppose me.*
Miguel ha hecho una de las suyas.	*Michael has pulled one of his tricks.*
Se salió con la suya.	*He got his own way.*

NOTE. A similar construction is found in the idioms **fue ella, será ella: Cuando llegamos a casa, fue ella.** *When we got home, the trouble started.*

78. Special uses of the neuter demonstratives

The neuter demonstratives **lo, esto, eso, aquello** are used frequently *(a)* to form adverbial phrases, *(b)* with **de** to form appositional phrases and clauses. **Lo** in these phrases is the same as the neuter article. (See **§§10, 164.**)

a. **por eso**	*for that reason, therefor, that's why*
en esto	*at this juncture*
con esto	*thereupon*
b. **Lo de ayer.**	*The (incident) of yesterday.*
Eso es lo de menos.	*That is the least important (part).*
Esto de escribir a máquina me molesta.	*This (business) of typewriting annoys me.*
Eso de que lo niegue Ud. ahora . . .	*(The idea) that you should deny this now . . .*
Aquello del "Titanic".	*The Titanic disaster.*

NOTE. **¡Eso es!** or simply **¡Eso!** means *That's it! Exactly!*

EJERCICIOS

Sustitúyanse **eso, esto, aquello** o **lo (de)** por las palabras subrayadas:

1. La idea de que no hay que trabajar es absurda.
2. El incidente de don Juan y la criada debe olvidarse.
3. ¡Qué rara la manía de Enrique, no querer volver a casa!
4. El accidente que tanto daño hizo a Susana nos pesó a todos.
5. La cosa de tu abuelo sí que fue interesante.

79. Additional remarks on possessives

1. The stressed form of the possessive adjective is used in a number of prepositional phrases.

de parte mía	*on my behalf, from me*
a pesar suyo	*to his (her,* etc.*) regret*
por cuenta mía	*on my account*
a costa nuestra	*at our expense*
en busca suya	*in search of him*
en contra tuya	*in opposition to you*

NOTE. The unstressed form may also be used in the above phrases: **de mi parte,** etc.

2. The neuter possessives **lo mío, lo tuyo**, etc., are used with various shades of meaning: indefinite, abstract, or collective.

Siempre has confundido lo mío y lo tuyo.	*You have always confused my property and yours.*
Ellos van a lo suyo.	*They are going after what they want.*
Se llevó lo suyo.	*He got what was coming to him.*

NOTE. But **los míos,** etc., may mean *my people,* etc. (family, partisans, etc.).

TRANSLATION B

1. Galdós and Pereda are two Spanish novelists; the latter was born in Spain, the former in the Canary Islands. 2. He *(pointing)* says he has nothing to do with that. 3. When shall we see you in this [city]? 4. That [fellow] is the one who wanted to sell me those shares. 5. He is always wasting time in the (those) cafés. 6. He is the kind that never says anything. 7. They took to their heels. 8. The [countess] of Cantarranas and her friends were still there. 9. Come this way. The children must be over there in the garden. 10. Do you remember those wonderful mornings in Granada? 11. He has gone in search of you. 12. I will do it on (for) my own

account. 13. I haven't been able to attend to that [affair] of your son. 14. That [affair] of the strike was a very serious thing. 15. Do you mean to tell me that those documents were false?—Yes, that's it. 16. That was a blessing from God. 17. In those moments of affliction the inhabitants showed their great courage and heroism. 18. I don't like this [idea] of eating so late. 19. We were all talking there and at this moment we heard a great noise. 20. They laughed at his expense. 21. All I have is at your disposal. 22. Where is the servant?—She must be somewhere around. 23. The liberal leader and his [followers] were arrested. 24. They gave him his [deserts].

III

VERBS AND IDIOMS

Review verbs in **-ucir** *and* **-ducir (§238)**

1. Translate five pages. 2. I should like you to translate this page for me. 3. I want you to conduct the negotiations. 4. He took (conducted) us to his study.

Parecer *to have the appearance of (seem, look like), put in an appearance (turn up, show up)*[1]*;* **parecerse a** *to resemble.* (**Parecer** is very frequently used impersonally: **me parece** *it seems to (strikes, impresses) me, I believe;* **¿qué le parece?** *how do you like? (what do you think of?);* **¿le parece que . . .?** *what do you say to . . .? shall we . . .?)*

1. They are so sunburned that they look like Indians. 2. He seems to be very happy **(contento)**. 3. She looks like a different person (doesn't look like the same). 4. Those jokes are unseemly (do not look well) in a person like you. 5. The child was not to be seen anywhere. 6. [They] have **(ya)** turned up the papers I **(que se me)** lost. 7. Emilia looks a great deal like (resembles) her grandmother. 8. It is a very original work; it is not like (resembles) anything which I am acquainted with. 9. The picture is **(tiene)** a very good likeness **(parecido)**. 10. Apparently (it seems to be that) he has given up the plan. 11. His conduct is to all appearances **(al parecer)** quite innocent. 12. It seems unbelievable **(mentira)** that you should say that. 13. I believe it is going to rain. 14. That does not strike me favorably **(bien)**. 15. How did you like the bullfight? 16. Shall we leave now? 17. He does all that for appearances' sake **(por el buen parecer)**.

Quitar *to remove, take away (off, from), etc.*

1. Take the books off the table. 2. He took off his coat. 3. I took the collar off the dog. 4. Don't take away his illusions. 5. Get (yourself) out of here. 6. He must be gotten out of the way **(de en medio)**. 7. Love keeps me from sleeping (takes sleep away from me). 8. The one [thing] does not exclude the other. 9. Cut it out! **(¡Quita!)**

[1]**Aparecer** means *to put in an appearance.* Hence it may also be used in 5 and 6.

chapter six

Relative pronouns

I

80. Simple and compound relatives

There are two fundamental distinctions which must be clearly understood before the use of relative pronouns in Spanish can be mastered. These distinctions concern the *use*, not the *form* of relative pronouns. The first is between simple and compound relatives: *(a)* a simple relative pronoun has an antecedent in the main clause; *(b)* a compound relative pronoun contains its own antecedent.

a. **La carretera que Ud. ve es la de Madrid.**	*The road that you see is the one to Madrid.*
b. **Quien calla otorga.**	*He who keeps silent gives consent.*

81. Complementary and supplementary relative clauses

The second fundamental distinction concerns complementary and supplementary relative clauses: *(a)* a complementary (or restrictive) relative clause is one which is necessary to complete the meaning of the antecedent, the two forming a single concept; *(b)* a supplementary (or non-restrictive) relative clause is one which adds an accessory or parenthetical fact, not an essential part of the antecedent. This latter type of relative clause is usually indicated by a comma in writing or by a pause in speaking.

a. **El señor que acaba de llegar ha subido a su habitación.**	*The gentleman who has just arrived* (*i.e.*, the newcomer) *has gone up to his room.*

b. **El señor Herrera, que acaba de llegar, ha subido a su habitación.** *Mr. Herrera, who has just arrived, has gone up to his room.*

82. *Que*

Que (uninflected) *which, that, who, whom* is by far the most frequent relative pronoun. It is the ordinary simple relative and is used *(a)* in complementary relative clauses both as subject and object and referring to both persons and things; *(b)* similarly in supplementary relative clauses; *(c)* after the common prepositions **de, a, en, con,** especially when referring to things.

a. **El oficial que vino a verme es un primo mío.** *The officer who came to see me is a cousin of mine.*

Éste es el libro que me dieron. *This is the book (that) they gave me.*

NOTE 1. The object relative pronoun is never omitted in Spanish as in English: **el asunto a que Ud. se refiere** *the matter you refer to.*

NOTE 2. The personal accusative is normally not used in complementary relative clauses: **el hombre que acabo de saludar** *the man I just spoke to.*

b. **Mi tío, que es un hombre de buen humor, nos divirtió mucho.** *My uncle, who is a humorous man, amused us very much.*

c. **El avión en que fuimos a Cuba.** *The plane on which we went to Cuba.*

La reunión a que asistimos. *The meeting which we attended.*

EJERCICIOS

Combínense los pares de frases siguientes en frases completas, e.g., **Éste es el libro. Me dieron el libro. → Éste es el libro que me dieron.**

1. Los amigos nos saludaron. Los amigos llegaron ayer.
2. Mi plan es de viajar por México. Mi plan no está completo.
3. El estilo de arquitectura de los edificios es muy moderno. Vimos los edificios.
4. La residencia es vieja. Vivo en la residencia.
5. El hombre es un amigo mío. Usted vio al hombre ayer.
6. La conferencia fue interesante. Fuimos a la conferencia.
7. El auto es de mis padres. Viajamos en el auto.
8. El profesor es de España. Te hablé del profesor.

83. *Quien* (pl. *quienes*) *who, whom*

Quien refers only to persons, never to things. It is used with growing infrequency *(a)* after prepositions, *(b)* as a compound relative, especially in set phrases.

a. **La persona de quien Ud. me habló.**	*The person of whom you spoke to me.*
El amigo por quien me enteré.	*The friend through whom I found out.*
b. **Quien calla, otorga.**	*He who keeps silent gives consent.*

NOTE. **Quien** (and **el cual**) may still be found in supplementary relative clauses: **lo consulté con mi padre, quien (el cual) me dio buenos consejos** *I talked it over with my father, who gave me good advice.* This use of **quien** and **el cual,** which purists insist on, is more characteristic of the written than the spoken language.

EJERCICIOS

Combínense los pares de frases siguientes en frases completas; e.g. **El chico es chileno. Hablo con el chico.**→**El chico con quien hablo es chileno.**

1. Los muchachos son de Chile. Viajamos con los muchachos.
2. La mujer es mi novia. Compré el regalo para la mujer.
3. Los pasajeros eran ciudadanos americanos. Dejaron desembarcar a los pasajeros.
4. No conozco al hombre. Usted habló con el hombre.
5. El hombre es banquero. Tomé el dinero del hombre.

Sustitúyase **quien** por **el que** en las frases siguientes:

6. El que no se atreve no pasa la mar.
7. El que da luego, da dos veces.
8. El que lo dijo, lo afirma.

84. *El que (la que, los que, las que, lo que)*

El que composed of the articles **el, la, los, las** and the relative **que** (see **§68**) refers to both persons and things. It is used *(a)* as the compound relative pronoun equivalent to the English *he who*, etc., *the one which*, etc., and *(b)* as a simple relative in competition with **el cual** and **quien**, especially after prepositions. *(c)* The neuter form **lo que** is the equivalent of the English *what (=that which)*.

a. **El que tiene dinero lo gasta.**	*He who has money spends it.*
Las que vinieron ayer son unas estudiantas cubanas.	*Those (girls) who came yesterday are (a group of) Cuban students.*
Este helado es el que más me gusta.	*This ice cream is the (kind) I like best.*
Mi prima, la que está casada con el ingeniero.	*My cousin* (the one) *who is married to the engineer.*

b. **Los pueblos por los que pasamos eran muy pintorescos.** *The towns through which we passed were very picturesque.*
El amigo por el que me enteré. *The friend through whom I found out.*

c. **Lo que me cuenta Ud. me asombra.** *What you tell me astonishes me.*
Lo que llevaba en la cabeza era un cántaro. *What she was carrying on her head was a water jar.*

EJERCICIOS

Quítense las palabras subrayadas en las frases siguientes, sustituyendo las palabras entre paréntesis; luego quítense los sustantivos:

1. El hombre que lo dice, miente. (la mujer, los muchachos, las personas)
2. Las muchachas que no saludaron son mis compañeras de clase. (los chicos, el estudiante, la señorita)
3. La persona que trabaja más, debe recibir más. (el estudiante, los hombres, las mujeres)

Combínense los pares de frases siguientes en frases completas:

4. Las montañas estaban cubiertas de nieve. Pasamos por las montañas.
5. El pueblo está lejos de aquí. Partí desde el pueblo.
6. La iglesia grande es la catedral. Hay una cruz encima de la iglesia.

Combínense los pares de frases siguientes en frases completas, sustituyendo **lo que** por **algo**, e.g., **Ud. me cuenta algo. Me asombra.**→**Lo que Ud. me cuenta me asombra.**

7. Algo ocurrió. Fue increíble.
8. Vimos algo. No es nada raro.
9. Ese individuo decía algo. No me llamó la atención.
10. Le regalaron algo. Era un libro recién publicado.

85. *El cual (la cual, los cuales, las cuales, lo cual) which, who, whom*

El cual also refers to both persons and things. It is never used as a compound relative. It is steadily being driven out by **el que,** especially in the spoken language. **El cual** is used *(a)* to indicate the more distant of two possible antecedents, thus preventing ambiguity, and alternates with **el que** *(b)* after prepositions other than **de, a, en, con.** *(c)* The neuter **lo cual** is used in supplementary clauses when the antecedent is a clause or a phrase.

a. **Comí con el hijo de la casera, el cual fue compañero mío.** *I dined with my landlady's son, who was a classmate of mine.*

b. **Había una torre muy alta desde la cual (la que) se veía toda la ciudad.** *There was a very high tower from which the entire city could be seen.*

c. **Se negó a verme, lo cual (lo que) me extrañó mucho.** *He refused to see me, which* (fact) *astonished me greatly.*

NOTE. **Lo cual** can never be used as equivalent to the compound relative **lo que** *what.*

EJERCICIOS

Combínense los pares de frases siguientes en frases completas, utilizando **el cual, la cual, lo cual,** etc.

1. La hija del presidente hizo una visita a los Estados Unidos. La hija había estudiado inglés.
2. Los pastores eran enemigos del gobierno. El fugitivo vivía entre los pastores.
3. El edificio es el ayuntamiento. Hay un museo detrás del edificio.
4. Recibió una gran cantidad por sus esfuerzos. Le agradó mucho.

86. Summary

The chief uses of the relative pronouns are summarized in the following table, the forms in parenthesis being alternative but less frequent.

ANTECEDENT	COMPLEMENTARY (SUBJ. OR OBJ.)	SUPPLEMENTARY	COMPOUND	AFTER PREPOSITIONS
Person	**que**	**que** (**el cual, quien**)	**el que** (**quien**)	**quien** (**el que, que**)
Thing	**que**	**que** (**el cual**)	**el que**	**que** (after **de, a, en, con**) **el que, el cual** (after other prepositions)

NOTE 1. **Donde** *where (=in which)* is frequently used in relative clauses: **el pueblo donde viven mis padres** *the town where my parents live.*

NOTE 2. If the subject of the relative clause is a noun it usually follows the verb (see preceding example).

87. *Cuyo* and *cuanto*

1. **Cuyo (-a, -os, -as)** *whose, of which* is the possessive relative adjective referring to both persons and things and agreeing in gender and number with the thing possessed.

El terremoto cuyos efectos fueron tan desastrosos. *The earthquake, the effects of which were so disastrous.*

2. **Cuanto (-a, -os, -as)** is a compound relative (both pronoun and adjective) equivalent to **todo el que,** etc. The neuter **cuanto** is the form most frequently used.

Le debo a Ud. cuanto soy y tengo. *To you I owe all I am and all I have.*

NOTE. **Todo** and **cuanto** may be used in combination: **estoy conforme con todo cuanto Ud. dice** *I agree with everything you say.*

EJERCICIOS

Combínense los pares de frases siguientes en frases completas, e.g. **Ese hombre es guapo. Vemos su casa.→ Ese hombre cuya casa vemos es guapo.**

1. Aquella casa es bonita. Su puerta está abierta.
2. Aquel estudiante no se preocupa. Sus padres pagan todos los gastos.
3. Los alumnos tienen que gastar mucho. Sus libros son caros.
4. Los chicos van a México. Sus padres van de vacaciones.

TRANSLATION A

1. Who are the gentlemen who were here this morning? 2. Mr. La Barrera, who is on his way to France, will stop here tomorrow. 3. I like immensely the photograph you sent me. 4. We couldn't find the porter to whom we had given our check. 5. The man through whom I got the job has just telephoned me. 6. He who perseveres goes very far. 7. My partner's secretary *(f.)*, who left last week, is a Puerto Rican. 8. The maid said they weren't at home, which surprised me a good deal. 9. We read many essays, among which was yours. 10. What he said was untrue, but very amusing. 11. Of all the museums we have visited this is the one we like best (most). 12. Now we are studying Goya, whose influence on contemporary art has been so great. 13. Don't pay any attention to what they say. 14. I will give you all the envelopes I have. 15. There are three trains every day; the one which has just left is the express. 16. Why don't you publish that story you read us? 17. The girl you were talking to is the same one I was telling you about. 18. I will have to borrow some money from my cousin Albert, (the one) who is in Belgium. 19. The driver, who was not what we would call a gentleman, answered him very rudely. 20. Their gardener, who is an Italian, speaks no English. 21. The writer, whose works you admire so much, died yesterday. 22. My friends, who were Americans, landed before I [did]. 23. The passengers who were American citizens could land before those who were not. 24. All I have is at your disposal. 25. We lived in a large house on top of which there was a roof-garden. 26. The

square has high arcades under which the people walk. 27. The town we stopped in was very small. 28. We saw for the first time the Spanish flag, the colors of which are red and yellow. 29. I have finished the job your friend gave **(encargar)** me. 30. This is the café where we get together.

II

88. Agreement

The verb in the relative clause usually agrees with the antecedent in person and number.

Tú, que la conoces bien, habla primero.	*You, who know her well, speak first.*
Yo soy el que (quien) lo digo.	*It is I who say it.*

NOTE. In sentences such as the latter, the third person is more frequent: **yo soy el que (quien) lo hizo** *I am the one who did it.*

89. Special constructions with *que*

Que may be used *(a)* referring to persons after the prepositions **de** and **con,** *(b)* as a relative adverb equivalent to **en que** *on which, when, (c)* as a compound relative when followed by an infinitive.

a. **El empleado de que le hablé a Ud.**	*The employee about whom I spoke to you.*
La gente con que suele reunirse.	*The people with whom he usually associates* (in gatherings).

NOTE. The use of **que** instead of **quien** imports a more indefinite or general meaning of the antecedent.

b. **El día que nací.**	*The day* (when) *I was born.*
c. **Esto me da que pensar.**	*This gives me something to think about* (cause for reflection).

NOTE. **Donde** may be used similarly: **no había donde sentarse** *there wasn't any place to sit down.*

EJERCICIOS

Combínense los pares de frases siguientes en frases completas:

1. El oficial nos ayudó. Te hablé del oficial.
2. Los muchachos son simpáticos. Vivo con los muchachos.
3. El día fue mi cumpleaños. Fui a ver a mi madre ese día.

90. Indefinite *quien*

Quien is used with indefinite value, in certain set constructions.

Hay quien asegura . . .	*Some people assert . . .*
Como quien dice.	*As one might say.*

91. Special constructions with *el que*

1. **El que** (or **quien**) may be used as the simple relative as predicate of **ser**.

Es el pequeño el que se ha caído.	*It is the youngest child who has fallen down.*
Fue el miedo lo que nos hizo retroceder	*It was fear that* (*i.e.*, Fear was what) *caused us to go back.*

2. **El que** is sometimes found as a stressed alternative for simple **que** after prepositions:[1]

Con un desdén al que no fué insensible.	*With a scorn to which he was not insensible.*

3. When the compound relative is object of a preposition the following peculiarities are to be noted: *(a)* the preposition always comes before **el que (lo que)**, which cannot be split, unless *(b)* the demonstrative **el** may be replaced by the more emphatic **aquél** or **ése.**

a. **¿Sabe Ud. al que me refiero?**	*Do you know the one I am referring to?*
Sé de lo que eres capaz.	*I know what you are capable of.*

NOTE. By attraction, a similar construction is occasionally used with nouns: **al único que hace caso es a Ud.** *the only person he minds is you.* Furthermore, the preposition may be repeated: **es por él por quien me preocupo** *he is the one I am worried about*; **¡a ése es al que (a quien) se lo di!** *that's the fellow I gave it to!*

b. **Aquello a que me referí . . .**	*What I referred to . . .*
Pocos eran aquellos a quienes no invitaron.	*There were (very) few who were not invited.*

4. **Lo que es** in initial position has the special meaning *as for.*

Lo que es simpatía, sí que la tiene.	*As for charm, she certainly has it.*
Lo que es yo no voy.	*As for me, I won't go.*

[1]The history of **el que** is one of steady encroachment on the territory of the other relatives.

92. Special construction with *cuyo*

Cuyo *(a)* is replaced by **a quien** in constructions corresponding to the dative of interest or possession, and *(b)* is occasionally used as a relative adjective replacing adjectival **el cual**, which is still more infrequent.

a. **El señor a quien le robaron la cartera.**	*The gentleman whose wallet was stolen.*
b. **Por cuya razón** (or **por la cual razón** or **por lo cual)**	*For which reason.*
Salieron para Coín, a cuyo pueblo llegaron al mediodía.	*They left for Coin, at which town they arrived at noon.*

NOTE. The appositional form **pueblo a que** is more usual in such constructions.

93. Correlatives

Both **quien** and **cual** are used *(a)* in literary style as correlatives—with the written accent to distinguish them as such—either in the singular or plural. *(b)* **Tal** and **cual** (sometimes **como**) also form a correlative pair, as do **el que más** and **el que menos** *the best* and *the worst (of them)*.

a. **Quiénes (cuáles) a pie, quiénes (cuáles) a caballo, los campesinos acudían al mercado.**	*Some on foot, others on horseback, the peasants were hastening to the market.*
b. **Tal para cual.**	*Two of a kind.*
Pinta las costumbres del pueblo tales cuales (como) son.	*It depicts the customs of the people just as they really are.*

94. The relative conjunction *que*

In colloquial speech especially, a personal pronoun may be used to recapitulate the antecedent, the relative then becoming a mere connective.

Tiene una letra que no la entiende nadie.	*He has (so bad) a handwriting that nobody understands it.*
Tendrá sus defectos, que no los veo yo.	*He may have his faults, but I don't see them.*

EJERCICIOS

Combínense los pares de frases en frases completas:

1. Tiene un geniazo. Nadie lo aguanta.
2. Es un tipo. No sé por qué no le meten en la cárcel.
3. La pobre lloraba. Daba lástima.

TRANSLATION B

1. The afternoon I saw you I had an accident. 2. We will go to the beach where we used to bathe last summer. 3. It was the bad condition of the road that made us give up our trip. 4. As for courage, he certainly has it. 5. You who are a good friend of his ought to tell him. 6. I am the one who proposes it. 7. We visited Jerez, which [city] pleased us greatly. 8. Most of the tourists who come here are Americans. 9. You are the one who has to decide. 10.As for her, she said nothing. 11. From (by) what I have just seen we cannot come to an agreement. 12. The prisoner, whose hands and feet they tied, could not escape. 13. He is one of those for whom idleness doesn't exist. 14. That's the one I want to talk to. 15. He maintains that he speaks seven languages, which I know isn't true. 16. The villagers, who are very shrewd people, wanted to cheat us. 17. Tell (talk to) us about what you did. 18. That's what I wanted to ask you about. 19. It's the translation that is difficult. 20. Many were those whose eyes would fill with tears. 21. We had an interview with those against whom the accusation had been made. 22. It's a critical situation (the one) we are in. 23. We who love him well will try to dissuade him. 24. The actors he can rely on are all amateurs. 25. There wasn't any place to put the car. 26. Children give a great deal of trouble (to do). 27. It is a difficulty which I had not realized. 28. He has [such] a temper that nobody can stand him.

III

VERBS AND IDIOMS

Dar (§241) *to give, etc.; to strike, hit, etc.;* **darse** *to occur;* **darse por** *to consider oneself*. (**Dar** is frequently used to form verb phrases out of nouns.)
1. What is on (are they giving) at the theatre tonight? 2. This soil produces splendid melons. 3. Various cases of typhus have occurred *(invert)*. 4. It makes no difference to me. 5. The windows faced on the garden. 6. He thanked me for the favor. 7. Jump! 8. You have to hurry. 9. I did not realize it. 10. He

caused a scandal. 11. They gave us very good meals. 12. Let's take a stroll through the streets. 13. The two aviators intend to go around the world. 14. You can't get around it **(no hay que darle vueltas)**. 15. I have forgotten to wind my watch. 16. He gave me to understand that the article was his. 17. He did not consider himself beaten. 18. I will not let on. 19. It struck twelve. 20. You have hit **(en)** the mark. 21. I have just got **(me ha dado)** a pain in my arm. 22. It makes me feel sorry **(da pena)** to see him like that **(así)**. 23. It made him feel ashamed to have to borrow money. 24. I feel afraid to go in. 25. I [suddenly] felt like **(ganas de)** hitting him with my umbrella. 26. The clerk answered insolently: I won't **(no me da la gana)** 27. He came upon his friend. 28. I have taken to **(me ha dado por)** collecting stamps. 29. They slapped each other. 30. At it again **(¡ dale !)** 31. That fellow is always boring **(dar la lata)**. 32. He put the bite on me for some money **(Me dio un sablazo)**. 33. My girlfriend jilted me **(dar calabazas)**. 34. They put on airs **(darse bombo)**. 35. He misrepresented the matter to me **(me dio gato por liebre)**. 36. She deceived me **(dársele con queso)**. 37. He never does things right **(dar pie con bola)**.

chapter seven

Interrogatives and negatives

I

95. Interrogatives

1. All interrogative adjectives and pronouns bear the written accent to differentiate them from relatives and conjunctions of identical form. This accent is retained in indirect questions.

¿Quién ha dicho eso?	*Who has said that?*
¿Adónde va Ud.?	*Where are you going?*
No sé cuándo llegará.	*I do not know when he will arrive.*

2. **¿Quién?** (pl. **¿quienes?**) *who?* refers only to persons. *Whom?* is **¿a quién?** and *whose?* is **¿de quién?** (always followed immediately by **ser**).

¿Quiénes eran esos señores?	*Who were those gentlemen?*
¿A quién saluda Ud.?	*Whom are you greeting?*
¿De quién es este lápiz?	*Whose pencil is this?*

NOTE. **Cuyo** is not used as an interrogative.

3. **¿Qué?** (uninflected) *what? which?* is both (*a*) pronoun and *(b)* adjective.

a. **¿Qué dijo él?**	*What did he say?*
b. **¿Qué montañas son éstas?**	*What mountains are these?*
¿En qué barco vino Ud.?	*In what* (which) *boat did you come?*

4. **¿Cuál?** (pl. **¿cuáles?**) *which (one)?* is used only as a pronoun.

¿Cuál es su habitación?	*Which* (one) *is your room?*
¿Cuál es su tío?	*Which one is your uncle?*

NOTE. In Spanish America **cuál** is also used as an adjective. **¿Cuál libro quiere Ud.?** *Which book do you want?*

5. The English *what is?* is rendered in Spanish *(a)* by **¿qué?** (=**¿qué cosa?**) when definition or identification rather than selection is called for *(b)* by **¿cuál?** when selection is stressed (English *which*). The latter is, of course, more frequent.

a. **¿Qué es esto?** — *What is this?*
¿Qué es la justicia? — *What is justice?*
¿Qué es ese señor?—Es médico. — *What is* (*i.e.*, does he do) *that gentleman?—He is a doctor.*

NOTE. Contrast **¿Quién es ese señor?—Es el señor Ruíz.**

b. **¿Cuál es la capital de Chile?** — *What* (*i.e.*, which city) *is the capital of Chile?*
¿Cuál es el número de su teléfono? — *What* (which one) *is your telephone number?*

6. **¿Cómo?** *how?* always implies manner *(in what way?)*

¿Cómo está Ud.? — *How are you?*
¿Como le gustan los huevos?—Me gustan fritos. — *How do you like your eggs* (prepared)*?—I like them fried.*

NOTE. The English *how do you like?* in the sense of *What do you think of?* is rendered by **¿Qué le parece (parecen) a Ud.?**: **¿Qué le parece a Ud. Montevideo?—Me gusta muchísimo.** *How do you like Montevideo?—I like it very much.*

7. **¿Cuánto?** *how much? how many?* is fully inflected and is used as both adjective and pronoun.

¿Cuánto es? — *How much is it?*
¿Cuántas semanas dura el viaje? — *How many weeks does the trip last?*

8. *What kind of ?* is normally **¿qué clase de?**

¿Qué clase de madera es ésta? — *What kind of wood is this?*

EJERCICIOS

Háganse preguntas de las frases siguientes:

1. Ese señor será el nuevo juez.
2. Aquellos edificios son del Ministerio de Gobernación.
3. Los árboles en este jardín fueron plantados hace muchos años.
4. Los turistas pueden ir en avión de Nueva York a Madrid en seis horas.
5. Cuzco es una de las ciudades más pintorescas de la América del Sur.
6. Le encantan a Ud. los cuadros de Diego Rivera.
7. Hablé con mi confesor.
8. Prefieres el café con leche
9. Ese libro me costó un ojo de la cara.
10. El número de mi cuarto es 212.

96. Interrogatives used as exclamations

1. **¡Qué!** corresponds *(a)* to English *how!* before adjectives and adverbs and *(b)* to English *what! what a!* before nouns; if the noun *(c)* is modified by a following adjective, **tan** or **más** is placed before the adjective.

a. **¡Qué bonito!**	*How pretty!*
¡Qué lejos vive Ud.!	*How far (away) you live!*
b. **¡Qué paciencia tiene Ud.!**	*What patience you have!*
c. **¡Qué edificio tan (más) alto!**	*What a tall building!*

2. **¡Cuánto!** *how much! how many!* is fully inflected and is used both as pronoun and as adjective.

¡Cuántos árboles hay en esta finca!	*How many trees there are on this estate!*
¡Cuánto me alegro!	*How happy I am!*

NOTE. The shortened adverb **¡cuán!** *how!* (used only before adjectives and adverbs) is exclusively literary.

EJERCICIOS

Háganse frases exclamativas de las frases siguientes:

1. Estoy muy contento.
2. Tenemos que leer muchos libros en este curso.
3. Aquel parque es muy pintoresco.
4. Me fastidia la conducta de los estudiantes.
5. La conferencia fue muy interesante.

97. Simple negation

1. Simple negation is expressed in Spanish by the adverb **no,** which precedes the verb and its conjunctive pronoun objects. Spanish **no** renders both *(a)* the English *do not*, *is not*, etc., *(b)* the English adjective *no.*

a. **No lo hice.**	*I did not do it.*
¿No viene esta tarde?	*Is he not coming this afternoon?*
Viene esta tarde ¿no es verdad?	*He is coming this afternoon, isn't he?*

NOTE. **¿no es verdad?** is frequently shortened to **¿no?** or **¿verdad?**

b. **No tengo suerte.**	*I have no luck.*

2. If no verb is present, **no** usually follows pronouns and adverbs, as does **sí** when similarly used.

Todavía no. *Not yet.* **Ahora no.** *Not now.*
No me gusta a mí, pero a él sí. *I don't like it but he does.*

98. Strong negation

1. Negative *(a)* adverbs, *(b)* pronouns, and *(c)* adjectives may be used to reinforce the negation or define it more specifically. Of these the more usual are *(a)* **nunca, jamás** *never*, *(b)* **nada** *nothing*, *(c)* **ninguno** *no*. If these negatives follow the verb **no** must also be used; if they precede the verb **no** is not required. Consequently, Spanish, unlike English, may have more than one negative in the same sentence. In fact, in the Spanish negative sentence all forms are negative.

a. **No lo he visto jamás.** — *I have never seen it.*
Ni yo tampoco. — *Nor I (n)either.*
Nunca dice nada a nadie. — *He never says anything to anybody.*

NOTE. **Tampoco** is the negative corresponding to **también** and is used after a preceding negative statement.

b. **Aquí nadie sabe nada.** — *Here nobody knows anything.*
No he visto a ninguno de esos hombres. — *I have seen none of those men.*
c. **No voy a ninguna parte.** — *I am going nowhere (I am not going anywhere).*

2. The negative forms are used even when the negative is merely implied.

Comió más que nunca. — *He ate more than ever.*
¿Ha estado Ud. jamás en Venezuela? — *Have you ever been in Venezuela?*
Baila mejor que nadie. — *She dances better than anyone.*
Una llanura sin agua ni árboles. — *A plain without water or trees.*

EJERCICIOS

Háganse negativas las frases siguientes:

1. Tengo mucho.
2. Fuimos algunas veces a la capital.
3. Algunos de esos papeles pertenecen al profesor.
4. Él va y yo también.
5. Un día recibimos una carta.
6. Alguien puede ayudarme.
7. Visité muchos lugares.

99. *Alguien, algo, alguno*

1. Corresponding to the negatives **nadie, nada, ninguno** are the affirmative indefinites **alguien** *somebody, anybody,* **algo** *something, anything,* **alguno** *some, any.*

Alguien llama a la puerta.	*Somebody is knocking at the door.*
Que conteste alguien.	*(Let) anybody answer.*
¿Hay algo de particular?	*Is there anything special?*
Sí, algo que me extraña.	*Yes, something which surprises me.*
Algún día lo sabrá Ud.	*Some day you will find (it) out.*
Conozco a algunos pero no a todos.	*I know some but not all.*

NOTE. The personal accusative is used with **alguien, nadie, alguno,** and **ninguno.**

EJERCICIOS

Háganse positivas las frases siguientes:

1. Nadie vendrá con nosotros.
2. Nunca dirá nada de lo que le pasó.
3. Aquí no hay nada de interés.
4. Ninguno de esos chicos me saludó.
5. Ella no estudió ni él tampoco.

2. **Algo** and **nada** may be used as adverbs.

El libro es algo pesado.	*The book is somewhat (rather) dull.*
No son nada orgullosos.	*They aren't a bit (at all) proud.*

EJERCICIOS

Sustitúyanse **algo** o **nada** por **muy** en las frases siguientes:

1. Aquel señor es muy pesado.
2. Los estudios no son muy estimulantes.
3. Mi viaje a España no fue muy caro.
4. Los que no aprecian el arte son muy tontos.

TRANSLATION A

1. What are you doing?—I am reading.—Reading what? 2. To whom did you give the package? 3. Whose razor is this?—Which one?—The one (which is) on the dresser. 4. Which is your wife?—The one (who is) dressed in **(de)** white.

5. What is your brother?—He is a travelling salesman. 6. What is this [made] of? 7. Which is your desk? 8. The bank is closed. What is today? 9. What date is today? 10. What is the date of the capture of Granada? 11. Which color do you like best? 12. What is the result of the test? 13. What is your opinion? 14. What is your second family name? 15. What shouts are those? 16. How many acts has the play? 17. How much have you lost?—I have lost all I had. 18. How did your speech turn out?—It turned out very well. 19. How did you like the show? 20. What kind of engine is this? 21. What a cool morning! 22. What a delicious dessert! 23. How generous he is! 24. How nice these people are! 25. I haven't any appetite. 26. Aren't you coming with us?—No, I can't now. 27. The orchestra played better than ever. 28. Don't let anyone come in! 29. We don't have anything to do with them. 30. I can't hear anything. 31. With whom did you go to the movies?—With no one. 32. Do you want something?—No, I don't want anything. 33. Has anyone been here?—No, sir, no one. 34. His reply wasn't a bit courteous. 35. This lesson is rather (somewhat) difficult, isn't it?—No, not at all. 36. Have you ever been to (at) a bull fight?

II

100. Interrogatives *(cont.)*

1. It must be noted *(a)* that the adjective **¿qué?** often has the same value as the pronoun **¿cuál?**, *(b)* that the pronoun **¿qué?** may be replaced in colloquial and emphatic style by **¿qué cosa?**

   a. **¿En qué barco vino Ud.?** — *In what* (which) *boat did you come?*
   ¿Cuál es el barco en que vino Ud.? — *Which is the boat you came in?*
   b. **¿Qué cosa es la propiedad?** — *What is property?*

2. **¿Cómo?** is also used as the polite equivalent of the English *what (did you say)?* and is equivalent to the English emphatic query *what (do you mean)?*

   Esa señorita es su hermana.—¿Cómo su hermana? — *That young lady is his sister.—What do you mean his sister?*
   No lo sé.—¿Cómo que no lo sabe Ud.? — *I don't know.—What, (do you mean) you don't know?*

3. **¿A cómo?** and **¿a cuánto?** are used in asking the price of articles sold by the pound, the dozen, etc.

   ¿A cómo (cuánto) se vende el ciento de naranjas? — *What is the price of oranges by the hundred?*
   ¿A cuánto (cómo) está la merluza? — *What is the price of hake* (today)?

4. **¿ Qué tal ?** *how? (what kind of?)* is used when function **(ser)** or condition, result **(estar)** is involved.

¿Qué tal es el coche?	*How is the car working?*
¿Qué tal abogado es Vallejo?	*What kind of a lawyer is Vallejo?*
¿Qué tal está el camino?	*In what shape is the road?*
¿Qué tal estuvo el concierto?	*How was the concert?*

EJERCICIOS

Háganse preguntas de las frases siguientes:

1. La tecnología es un peligro para la humanidad.
2. La mantequilla se vende a cien pesetas el kilo.
3. Los camarones están a ciento cincuenta pesetas el kilo hoy.
4. El señor Gómez es un músico muy dotado.
5. El estreno del drama estuvo magnífico.

101. Exclamations *(cont.)*

1. The following special constructions should be noted: *(a)* **¿ a qué ?** in the sense of *why, for what purpose?; (b)* **¡ qué de !** meaning *what a !, how many !, (c)* **¡ lo que !** for **¡ cómo !** and **¡ cuánto !** in exclamations and *(d)* in direct questions; in this latter type an inflected adjective may intervene between **lo** and **que.**

a. **¿A qué viene todo esto?**	*Why all this* (discussion)?
b. **¡Qué de gente!**	*What a crowd!*
c. **¡Cómo / ¡Cuánto / ¡Lo que** } **nos divertimos con eso!**	*How we enjoyed that!*

NOTE. The construction **¡ La de gente que había !** (§77, 2*b*) is an outgrowth of the exclamatory and quantitative **¡ Lo que !**

d. **No sabe Ud. lo que le aprecia.**	*You don't know how much he esteems you.*
No tiene Ud. idea de lo bonitas que son.	*You haven't an idea how pretty they are.*

EJERCICIOS

Cámbiense las frases siguientes según el modelo: **Las playas de la Costa Brava son muy hermosas. → ¡ Ud. no sabe lo hermosas que son! Jorge sabe mucho. → ¡ Ud. no se imagina lo que sabe!**

1. El paisaje de México nos encantó.

2. Las muchachas de ese lugar son muy monas.
3. La vida hoy es muy cara.
4. Los precios han subido mucho.
5. Estas cartas son muy importantes.

102. Interjections

Interjections are used much more frequently in Spanish than in English. (For a list of the more common interjections, see Appendix, §278.) Some of the most frequent are:

¡Hombre!	*Man (alive)!*	**¡Oiga!**	*See here! Listen!*
¡Cuidado!	*Look out!*	**¡Ay!**	*Alas! Ouch!*

NOTE. Note the following uses of **¡ay!** and **¡cuidado!**: **¡Ay de mí!** *Woe is me!* **¡Cuidado con los rateros!** *Look out for pickpockets!*

103. Negatives *(cont.)*

1. Except for the cases cited in §97, the position of **no** when the verb is not expressed is usually the same as in English.

He escrito la mayor parte pero no todo.	*I have written most but not all.*

2. Some expressions, affirmative in origin, have acquired negative force: *(a)* **alguno** following the noun at the end of a negative sentence is equivalent to an emphatic affirmation of the negation; *(b)* **en mi vida, en absoluto,** and similar expressions, by analogy to **nunca** and the like, have acquired a strong negative value even when used before the verb or as independent expressions; *(c)* **dejar de** means *to leave off, stop* and, by extension, *to fail to, refrain from.*

a. **No tengo inconveniente alguno.**	*I have no objection (at all).*
b. **En mi vida he oído tal cosa.**	*I have never heard such a thing in all my life.*
En absoluto.	*Not at all.*
Me importa un bledo.	*I don't care a bit.*
c. **No deje Ud. de escribirme.**	*Don't fail to write me.*

3. The adverb **nada** is frequently used *(a)* as an exclamation and *(b)* in the form **nada de.**

a. **¡Nada, hombre, nada! Descuide Ud.**	*Of course, of course! Don't worry.*

b. **Hacía un tiempo magnífico; nada de calor, nada de humedad.** *The weather was splendid; no heat, no humidity.*

4. **Ni** is used *(a)* in the correlative **ni . . . ni** *neither . . . nor* (usually with plural verb) and *(b)* in the combinations **ni siquiera, ni aún** *not even,* **ni un(o)** *not a single.*

a. **Ni Juan ni Jorge dijeron nada.** *Neither John nor George said anything.*

NOTE. When **no** is used the first **ni** is often omitted: **no tiene padre ni madre** *he has neither father nor mother.*

b. **Ni siquiera me escribe.** *He doesn't even write to me.*
No tengo ni un céntimo. *I haven't a single* ("a red") *cent.*

NOTE 1. **Ni** often has the value of *not even*: **ni su mismo padre le hubiera reconocido** *not even his own father would have recognized him;* **quedó que ni pintado** *it was just right* (*i.e.*, not even if specially painted could it have been better).
NOTE 2. **Ni** is used in certain colloquial expressions as an emphatic negative: **¡ni hablar!** *By no means!* e.g., **¿Vienes con nosotros?—¡Ni hablar!** It is also used to emphasize a statement: **Ellos son tan tontos, de estudios ¡ni hablar!** *They're so dumb, there's no question of studying!* Other emphatic negative expressions are: **ni pensarlo, ni por pienso, ni en sueños, ni soñarlo, ni de milagro,** etc.

EJERCICIOS

Cámbiense las frases siguientes según el modelo: **No tengo libros → No tengo ni un libro; no tengo libro alguno. Pedro no escribe a sus padres. → Pedro ni (siquiera) escribe a sus padres.**

1. Aquí no tenemos las comodidades de la vida moderna.
2. Desde aquí el humo es tan espeso que no se ve el fin de la calle.
3. No hay esperanzas para la paz mundial.
4. Los de esa familia no trabajan un día de la semana.
5. Esos revolucionarios no han aprendido las lecciones de la historia.

Cámbiense las frases según el modelo: **Escríbame → No deje de escribirme.**

6. Llámame por teléfono el lunes.
7. Tráigame Ud. unos churros.
8. Saluden Uds. de mi parte a su padre.

5. A redundant **no** is occasionally used in Spanish, when the sense of the subordinate element is negative.

Prefiero morir a no vivir así. *I prefer to die than to live this way.*

TRANSLATION B

1. In which house do you live? 2. To which club does he belong? 3. What is all this noise for? 4. How they shouted! 5. How many soldiers on the streets! 6. I couldn't tell you how angry they *(f.)* were! 7. How was the game?—Fair. 8. How does she drive?—Pretty well. 9. What kind of a student is he?—One of the best. 10. I am in no hurry [at all]. 11. Don't fail to give him the message. 12. Neither you nor he has any reason to complain. 13. When are you going to stop typing? I can't sleep. 14. Thank you very much.—Don't mention it, [old] man. 15. [Be] careful! The sidewalk is very slippery. 16. He had neither work nor money. 17. I haven't had a single moment's rest. 18. I [never] laughed more in my life. 19. Don't [answer back], don't [answer back]! Do what I tell you. 20. Not even you will be able to convince him. 21. I didn't sign the check.—What [do you mean] you didn't? 22. You cannot imagine how animated the dance was. 23. How (much) we danced last night! 24. Would you like an ice cream?—No, no ice cream *(pl.)* for me.

III

VERBS AND IDIOMS

Poner (§254) *to place, put, etc.;* **ponerse** *to put on, start to, become, set* (sun).
1. He put the bread on the table. 2. What are they putting [on] tonight at the Opera? 3. You have got (put) me in a predicament. 4. Let's send him a telegram. 5. This always puts him in a **(de)** bad humor. 6. Such things make me nervous. 7. They have made him **(de)** overseer of the estate. 8. They are to start housekeeping **(casa)** in Madrid. 9. What name have they given the child? 10. Keep me informed **(al corriente)** of what goes on. 11. This hen does not lay. 12. Put on your overcoat. 13. He took it **(ponérsele)** into his head to do it. 14. We all stood up **(de pie)**. 15. I am **(voy)** getting old. 16. The sky became very dark. 17. It was impossible to come to an agreement. 18. The girl started to sing. 19. The train started off **(en marcha)**. 20. In summer the sun sets very late.

Meter *to put into, etc.;* **meterse** *to get (put) oneself into, etc.*
1. I have to put all this into the trunk. 2. He put his hand in his pocket. 3. We went into the woods. 4. Now he has gone in for painting **(a pintor)**. 5. I don't like to get [involved] in other people's affairs. 6. I don't want to get [mixed up] in that. 7. They have gotten into a mess. 8. Don't get [into a conflict] with him. 9. We have put our foot **(la pata)** [in it]. 10. Don't make so much noise. 11. He is always butting in **(meter la cuchara)**.

chapter eight

The infinitive
Por and **para**

I

104. The infinitive

1. The infinitive is the verbal noun. As such its construction is always that of a noun, being either *(a)* subject or *(b)* object of a verb or *(c)* introduced by a preposition. But being also a verb in meaning, the infinitive may have its own subject, object, or other verbal modifiers (see example *a*).

a. **Me gusta acostarme tarde.**	*I like to go to bed late.*
b. **Quería ir al teatro.**	*I wanted to go to the theatre.*
c. **No tengo ganas de comer.**	*I don't feel like eating.*

2. The Spanish infinitive corresponds not only to the English infinitive with *to* but also to the verbal noun in *-ing*. Hence, after prepositions it is the infinitive (not the gerund) which is used in Spanish.

Ver es creer.	*Seeing is believing.*
No tardará en llegar.	*He will not be long in arriving.*
Hable Ud. con él antes de marcharse.	*Speak with him before leaving.*

3. The dependent infinitive is used regularly in Spanish—more so than in English—when there is no change in subject. A change in subject usually causes the infinitive to be replaced by a finite verb introduced by **que** (*i.e.*, a noun or an adverb clause—see §§**111, 112**).

Siento no poder ir.	*I am sorry I can't go.*
Afirma haberlo visto.	*He asserts he saw it.*

Sigamos hasta concluir. — *Let's keep on until we finish.*

But **Afirma que ella se lo dijo.** — *He asserts she told him (so).*

Sigamos hasta que él llegue. — *Let's keep on until he arrives.*

EJERCICIOS

Cámbiense las frases según el modelo. **No lo ha visto (afirma) → Afirma no haberlo visto.**

1. Volamos por el aire. (creemos, queremos, esperamos)
2. Han jugado a los naipes. (confiesan, sienten, olvidan)
3. Tomás toca el piano. (piensa, prefiere, necesita)
4. Hiciste todas tus tareas. (lograste, esperaste, intentaste)
5. Vuelvo a casa. (espero, me gusta, temo)

4. In Spanish certain verbs, verb phrases, adjectives, and nouns require a preposition as a link to their noun complements. This preposition is retained when the noun is replaced *(a)* by an infinitive or *(b)* by a noun clause.[1] See **§269** for a list of verbs requiring a prepositional complement.

a. **Me alegro de saberlo.** — *I am glad to know it.*
Insiste en hacerlo. — *He insists on doing it.*
Estoy seguro de convencerle. / Tengo la seguridad de convencerle. — *I am sure of convincing him.*

b. **Me enteré de que no había venido.** — *I found out that he had not come.*
Insistí en que no lo había dicho. — *I insisted that he had not said it.*
Tengo la seguridad de que no lo dijo. — *I am certain that he did not say it.*

NOTE. The preposition **a** is regularly used with verbs signifying motion, expressed or implied: **voy a hablarle** *I am going to speak to him,* **me obligan a hacerlo** *they oblige me to do it.*

EJERCICIOS

Cámbiense las frases siguientes según el modelo: **No puedo verte. (me avergüenzo de) → Me avergüenzo de no poder verte.**

1. Oí la noticia. (me contento con, me asusto de, consiento en)
2. No vamos al teatro. (nos disculpamos de, nos resignamos a, nos extrañamos de)

[1]This uniformity of construction between the noun, the infinitive, and the noun clause is one of the distinctive features of Spanish syntax.

3. Juan hace un viaje a Europa. (insiste en, se compromete a, no se atreve a)
4. Mis padres me ayudarán. (se alegran de, se desviven por, se cansan de)
5. Sacaste buenas notas. (te alegras de, te niegas a, te ocupas en)

5. Conversely, when the noun complement is not introduced by a preposition, there is no preposition corresponding to the English *to* used with the infinitive.

Me gusta el teatro—ir al teatro.	*I like the theatre—to go to the theatre.*
Le prometí el dinero—dárselo.	*I promised him the money—to give it to him.*

105. Infinitive after verbs of causation and perception

1. The dependent infinitive with its immediate modifiers usually comes directly after the main verb. This is especially to be noted—in contrast to the English usage—after verbs of perception and causation.

Oyeron cantar a Fleta.	*They heard Fleta sing.*
Hizo venir al médico.	*He had the doctor come.*
Vimos caer al suelo al oficial herido.	*We saw the wounded officer fall to the ground.*

2. When a verb of causation or perception and its dependent infinitive both have noun objects, *(a)* the object of the main verb is the indirect object of the verb and the subject of the infinitive and usually comes last. *(b)* If the object of the main verb is a pronoun it naturally precedes the verb. *(c)* If both objects are third person pronouns the indirect object becomes **se** and both precede the main verb. *(d)* If the object of both verbs is a reflexive pronoun, the pronoun appears only once, before the main verb.

a. **Mandó traer el desayuno al criado.**	*He ordered the servant to bring breakfast.*
Oyeron hablar español al camarero.	*They heard the waiter speaking Spanish.*
Oímos cantar "La Paloma" a una chica guapa.	*We heard a pretty girl sing "La Paloma".*
b. **Le veo dejar caer el periódico.**	*I see him drop the newspaper.*
Nos miraron firmar nuestros nombres.	*They watched us sign our names.*
c. **Se lo veo dejar caer.**	*I see him drop it.*
Se la oí cantar.	*I heard her sing it.*
Se lo mando hacer.	*I order him to do it.*

d. **Me permito sonreír.** — *I allow myself to smile.*
No se dejaba convencer. — *He did not let himself be convinced.*

3. If the dependent infinitive has no object, the object of the main verb is the direct object.

La vimos entrar. — *We saw her enter.*
Oigo sonar las campanas. — *I hear the bells ring.*
Las oigo sonar. — *I hear them ring.*

EJERCICIOS

Cámbiense las frases siguientes según el modelo: **El médico vino. (vieron) → Vieron venir al médico.**

1. El pianista tocó una pieza de Falla. (escuchamos)
2. Los muchachos corrieron por la calle. (vi)
3. Las azafatas ayudaron al pasajero enfermo. (hicieron)
4. La mujer gritaba desesperadamente. (oyó)
5. Los bomberos se acercaron al incendio. (miramos)

Sustitúyanse las formas debidas de los pronombres por los objetos subrayadas:

6. Vi acercarse a nosotros a un viejo extraño.
7. Escuchamos gritar al marido furioso.
8. Yo oía silbar a los pájaros.
9. El chófer mira reparar el auto al mecánico.
10. Vieron al hombre pegar a su compañero.

106. Special constructions

(a) **al**+infinitive is equivalent to the English *on, when, (b)* **que** introduces the infinitive depending on an indefinite pronoun or on a noun modified by an indefinite or numerical adjective, *(c)* certain verbs (*e.g.*, **dejar, consentir, pensar**) vary in constructions with the dependent infinitive, according to their variations in meaning, *(d)* **aprender, empezar,** and **enseñar,** although transitives, take a complementary infinitive in **a,** probably by analogy to verbs of motion.

a. **Al entrar en la casa.** — *On entering (when he entered) the house.*

b. **Tengo algunas cartas que contestar.** — *I have some letters to answer.*
Deja mucho que desear. — *It leaves much to be desired.*
No hay nada que decir. — *There is nothing to say.*

c. **Déjeme Ud. hacerlo.** *Let me do it.*
Deje Ud. de hacerlo. *Stop doing it.*
Piense Ud. en su deber. *Think of your duty.*
Piensa salir mañana. *He intends to leave tomorrow.*

d. **Estamos aprendiendo a conducir.** *We are learning to drive.*
Empezó a llover. *It started to rain.*

NOTE. **Seguir** and **continuar** *to keep on, continue* are followed by the gerund, not the infinitive: **siga Ud. leyendo** *keep on reading.*

EJERCICIOS

Cámbiense las frases siguientes según el modelo: **Cuando entré en la casa, me fijé en el espejo roto. → Al entrar en la casa, me fijé en el espejo roto.**

1. Cuando nos enteramos de la verdad, fuimos a verle.
2. Cuando hizo el trabajo, olvidó sus problemas.
3. Cuando terminé la carta, dejé de llorar.
4. Cuando la vi por primera vez, me enamoré en seguida.

Pónganse las formas de **tener, dejar** y **haber (hay, había, habrá, hubo)** en el espacio y sustitúyanse las palabras entre paréntesis por las palabras subrayadas:

5. ______ poco[a] que decir[b].
   a. (mucho, algo, nada, varias cosas, algunos asuntos)
   b. (hacer, sugerir, proponer, acabar)

107. *Por* and *para*

The preposition **por** must be clearly differentiated from its derivative **para**, especially in translating the English *for*. **Para** is more restricted in meaning and consequently it is more helpful to learn its uses first.

1. **Para** corresponds to the English *for* in the sense of *(a)* destination and purpose, *(b)* comparison, and *(c)* limit of time (usually *by* in English). It is frequently used *(d)* to introduce infinitives indicating purpose *(to, in order to)*.

a. **Estas cartas son para Ud.** *These letters are for you.*
Mi sobrino estudia para arquitecto. *My nephew is studying (to be) an architect.*
Salimos para la Habana. *We left for Havana.*

b. **Tiene muy buena pronunciación para un extranjero.**	*He has a very good pronunciation for a foreigner.*
c. **Dejémoslo para mañana.**	*Let's leave it for tomorrow.*
Se concluirá para el sábado.	*It will be over by Saturday.*
d. **Estoy esperándole para hablarle.**	*I am waiting for him to talk to him.*

EJERCICIOS

Sustitúyanse las palabras entre paréntesis por las palabras subrayadas:

1. El libro[a] es para Ud.[b]
   a (este papel, los billetes, las cartas)
   b. (mí, tí, mi amigo, Carlos)
2. Ud. es muy discreto[a] para un joven[b].
   a. (listo, cínico, inocente, inteligente)
   b. (americano, estudiante, muchacha)
3. Lo tendremos[a] para mañana[b].
   a. (sabrá, comprarán, venderás, obtendrán)
   b. (jueves, la semana que viene, pasado mañana, esta noche)
4. Trabajo[a] mucho para ganar[b] mucho.
   a. (estudiamos, gastan, Ud. habla)
   b. (aprender, gozar de la vida, estar a gusto, no aburrirse)

2. **Por** corresponds to the English *(a) through (along, around)*, *(b) by* expressing agency, means, manner, unit of measure, *(c) for* in the sense of *because of, on account of, in behalf of, in exchange for, during, as, (d) by* and *for* in oaths and exclamations.

a. **Vamos a dar una vuelta por las calles.**	*Let's take a walk through the streets.*
Pase Ud. por aquí.	*Come this way.*
b. **Estaba muy tostado por el sol.**	*He was very sunburned.*
Consiguió el cargo por su propio mérito.	*He obtained the position by his own merit.*
Íbamos a cien kilómetros por hora.	*We were going at 100 kilometers an* (by the) *hour.*
c. **Le suspendieron en los exámenes no por su mala suerte sino por falta de preparación.**	*He failed in the examinations not because of his bad luck but for lack of preparation.*
Hágalo Ud. por mí.	*Do it for me (my sake).*
Recibió muy poco por su trabajo.	*He received very little for his work.*
¿Por cuánto tiempo va Ud. a España?	*For how long are you going to Spain?*
Por ejemplo.	*For example.*

d. **Juro por mi honor.** — *I swear by (on) my honor.*
¡Por Dios! — *For Heaven's sake!*

NOTE. *Because* (conjunction) is **porque,** but *because of, on account of* is **por** or **a causa de.**

EJERCICIOS

Sustitúyanse las palabras entre paréntesis por las palabras subrayadas:

1. Dimos un paseo[a] por el parque[b].
   a. (caminé, andaban, paseamos)
   b. (el barrio viejo, la plaza, las calles)
2. Pedro me gusta[a] por su buen humor[b].
   a. (nos ayudó, te encanta, estudia mucho)
   b. (generosidad innata, buenas cualidades, deseo de ser ingeniero)
3. Pagamos[a] poco (mucho) por esos libros[b].
   a. (hacemos, trabajan, gané)
   b. (nuestra patria, sus ideales, mis esfuerzos)
4. Culparon[a] a Pepe por su inatención[b].
   a. (multaron, condenaron, pagaron)
   b. (infracción de la ley, traición a la causa, trabajo)
5. Estuve[a] allí por varias semanas[b].
   a. (va, se quedó, estará)
   b. (tres días, el resto de su vida, un mes)

TRANSLATION A

1. I don't feel like going out. I prefer to stay here reading. 2. We were very tired from playing (at the) tennis. 3. I am convinced that you are right. 4. They refused to sign the petition. 5. They insisted that they had signed it. 6. He hastened to close the deal. 7. Be careful not to burn your fingers. 8. Don't bother to copy it. 9. We heard the night watchman move away. 10. He had the road repaired. 11. Let's keep on walking until we get to the bridge. 12. I don't think I have seen it before. 13. He makes many gestures when he talks. 14. Leave the door open when you go out. 15. He broke a leg jumping through the window. 16. Will you let him talk? 17. We are going to stop working. 18. I intend to answer his letter this morning. 19. He was thinking of resigning. 20. I wouldn't put up with that. 21. He consented to lower the price. 22. There is nothing to see here. 23. He has much to learn. 24. He is teaching us to ride horseback. 25. We are leaving for London tonight and we will be back by September. 26. Let us go for a walk along the bank of the river. 27. The pier was destroyed by the storm. 28. It is very warm for April. 29. What is this?—It is a machine for cutting

papers. 30. How much do you want for the painting? 31. There was room at the table for six people. 32. This company pays a dividend of seven per cent. 33. He remained silent out of prudence. 34. I hold your project (for) impossible. 35. I'll see you tomorrow morning. 36. Answer by telegram.

II

108. The infinitive *(cont.)*

1. The generic definite article **el** may be used with an infinitive or a noun clause to heighten its noun force,[2] especially if the infinitive or noun clause precedes the main verb or is separated from it.

El callar a tiempo es una virtud.	*Opportune silence is a virtue.*
El que diga Ud. eso tiene mucha gracia.	*Your saying that is very amusing.*

NOTE. The subjunctive is used in this type of clause. See **§116, 3.**

2. The use of the infinitive as a noun is *(a)* especially characteristic of poetic style, and *(b)* in some cases such infinitives have come to be felt as pure nouns.

a. **El susurrar de las hojas.**	*The rustling of the leaves.*
b. **Sus gestos y andares.**	*Her gestures and manner of walking.*
Mis pesares.	*My troubles.*

3. Infinitives, like nouns, are sometimes used in exclamations equivalent to elliptical commands or entreaties, either *(a)* with **a**[3] or *(b)* absolutely. A similar use occurs *(c)* in interrogations.

a. **¡A la cama y a descansar!**	*(Go) to bed and rest!*
¡A trabajar, compañeros!	*(Let's get) to work, fellows!*
¡A ver!	*(Let's* or *let me) see (it)!*
b. **¡Serenidad, muchachos y apuntar bien!**	*(Let's have) calm, men, and take good aim!*
Callarse. No hacer ruido.	*Be quiet. Let's have no noise.*

NOTE. Compare the frequent use of the general **hay que** with much the same meaning: **hay que tener cuidado** *one (we) must be careful.* Compare also a similar use of the perfect infinitive: **¡Pues no haberlo hecho!** *Well then I (you, he, etc.)*

[2]See footnote, page 91.

[3]This construction is essentially the same as the so-called "historical" (really exclamatory and emotional) infinitive: **¡Nosotras a coser, nosotras en la cocina, nosotras a planchar!** *We women always sewing, always in the kitchen, always ironing.*

shouldn't have done it! In all these cases the infinitive refers to a specific person or persons made clear by the context. Consequently, in Spanish the negative infinitive is not used for general prohibitions as in English. *No smoking (admittance, etc.)* is rendered by the Spanish formula **Se prohibe fumar (la entrada,** etc.).[4]

c. **¿Qué hacer?**	*What (is there) to be done?*
¿Cómo volver a casa?	*How (are we) to get home?*

NOTE. The infinitive is used absolutely in the following type: **entender, lo han entendido** *as far as understanding goes they understood it.*

EJERCICIOS

Cámbiense las frases siguientes según el modelo: **Descánsense Uds.** → **¡A descansarse!**

1. Cállese.
2. Vuelvan Uds.
3. Estudien Uds.
4. Llamen Uds.

Contéstense según el modelo: **Ud. se ríe.** → **¿Yo? ¿Reírme?**

5. Uds. se burlan.
6. Ud. canta bien.
7. Uds. no estudian.
8. Ud. olvida.
9. Uds. faltan a clase.

4. Even when there is no change in subject, the more concrete and graphic **que** clause is frequently used in the spoken language, instead of the infinitive, especially after verbs of saying and thinking.

Dice que no lo ha visto.	*He says he didn't see it.*
Fingí que dormía.	*I pretended I was asleep.*

5. **De, a,** and **con** are occasionally used with infinitive in place of *(a)* any conditional clause **(de)**, *(b)* contrary to fact conditions **(a)**, and *(c)* concessive clauses **(con)**.

a. **De no poder hacerlo, avíseme Ud.**	*If you aren't able to do it, let me know.*
b. **A no tener a mano el diccionario no podría trabajar.**	*If I didn't have the dictionary at hand I couldn't work.*
c. **Con tener tantos amigos ninguno le socorrió.**	*Although he had so many friends no one helped him.*

[4]But the absolute infinitive is gaining ground in general directions and in advertisements as an alternative for the imperative in **-d (§44*c*)**.

6. For Spanish equivalents of the English passive infinitive, see §**154.**

EJERCICIOS

Cámbiense las frases según el modelo: **De no querer ir, llámeme. → Si Ud. no quiere ir, llámeme.**

1. De estarde acuerdo, no tendremos inconveniente.
2. De decir la verdad, no podrán errar.
3. De haber suficiente para todos, nadie se quejará.

Cámbiense las frases según el modelo: **A no tener ayuda, no aprenderíamos nada. → Si no tuviera ayuda, no aprenderíamos nada.**

4. A estar listos, podríamos salir.
5. A considerar bien el problema, tendrías la solución.

Cámbiense las frases según el modelo: **Con tener dinero, no eres popular. → Aunque tienes dinero, no eres popular.**

6. Con trabajar tanto, nunca gano bastante.
7. Con cumplir con sus deberes, no están muy contentos.
8. Con tratar de parecer muy intelectual, todos saben que es tonto.

109. *Por* and *para (cont.)*

1. After **ir, mandar, preguntar,** and similar verbs the English *for* is rendered by **por,** the Spanish viewing the relationship as one of desire or motive rather than destination or purpose.

Tengo que ir a la ventanilla por los billetes.	*I have to go to the window for the tickets.*
Envía por su baúl.	*He sends for his trunk.*

NOTE. In conversational usage in Spain one may hear **voy a por (agua).**

2. After **estar, para** denotes *(a)* disposition (physical and mental) *to be about to, ready for,* while **por** denotes *(b)* desire, inclination, *to stand for, be in favor of.* Consequently, **estar por** in this sense is used only with personal subjects.

a. **Está para nevar.**	*It's about to snow.*
No estoy para bromas.	*I'm in no mood* (disposition) *for jokes.*
b. **Está por las cosas prácticas.**	*He is in favor of (stands for) practical things.*
Estoy por quedarme en casa.	*I am in favor of (want to) staying at home.*

3. In general, the infinitive with **para** indicates *(a)* purpose or intention; with **por** it indicates *(b)* cause, desire, or motive, and *(c)* unfinished or future action (English passive infinitive).

a. **Es un día muy hermoso para ir a la playa.** — *It is a very fine day to go to the seashore.*

NOTE. After verbs of motion **para** may be used instead of **a** if the idea of purpose is to be stressed: **fue a Filadelfia a (para) ver a un amigo** *he went to Philadelphia to (in order to) see a friend.*

b. **No le dije a Ud. nada por no disgustarle.** — *I didn't say anything to you (because I didn't want) to trouble you.*

c. **El puente está por construir.** — *The bridge is (yet) to be constructed.*

NOTE. The infinitive with **por** often corresponds to a causal clause in English: **no asistió a la reunión por estar enferma su madre** *he didn't come to the meeting because his mother was ill.*

4. In a number of cases English *in order to* may be rendered by either **por** or **para,** depending on the shade of meaning desired.

Estudio derecho por complacer a mi padre. — *I am studying law in order to* (with the desire to) *please my father.*
Estudio derecho para complacer a mi padre. — *I am studying law in order to* (with the purpose of) *please my father.*

EJERCICIOS

Sustitúyanse las palabras entre paréntesis por las palabras subrayadas:

1. Estamos para terminar. (salir, rendirnos, dormir)
2. Es buen día[a] para estudiar[b].
   a. (lugar, oportunidad, hace buen tiempo)
   b. (divertirse, cantar, trabajar)
3. Ernesto está por quedarse. (dejarlo todo, probarlo, divertirse)
4. El puente[a] está por construir[b].
   a. (la tarea, las palabras, el problema)
   b. (concluir, aprender, resolver)

TRANSLATION B

1. Smoking like that is not good for your health. 2. That you don't want to admit it is one thing and that it isn't true is another. 3. The neighing of the horses woke me. 4. We stopped at a country house called "Quitapesares." 5. I count on

being back tomorrow. 6. If you can't take the seven o'clock train wait until tomorrow. 7. Children, [go] to sleep. 8. Come, [you must] cheer up. 9. But, how [are we going to] tell him? 10. [As for] writing I haven't written.—Well, [you should] have told me before. 11. I did not find it out until I arrived at Gibraltar. 12. He is going for the mail. 13. I have come from New York to have the pleasure of meeting you. 14. She said that to tease him. 15. I will do my best to find work for you. 16. The show is about to start. 17. I am [in favor of] telling him no. 18. The party is [yet] to be organized. 19. We aren't here to waste time. 20. That's arguing for the sake of arguing. 21. Go on playing the piano. Don't stop on my account. 22. I don't know what I would do if I didn't have you here. 23. Although he is such a good lawyer he couldn't win the case. 24. This happens to you for being so stubborn. 25. They didn't have any friends because they couldn't speak the language. 26. She is living here now in order to be near her son. 27. We will accept the invitation in order not to slight them. 28. [My] not having written does not mean that I have forgotten you.

III

VERBS AND IDIOMS

Sacar (§229.1) *to take out, pull out, bring out, get out, get, obtain, infer, etc.*
1. He took a letter from his pocket. 2. Get me out of this predicament! 3. The dentist will have to pull this tooth (for me). 4. Don't stick your arm out. 5. It is impossible to get him away from his books. 6. Sugar is obtained from beets *(sing.)* 7. He has won the first prize. 8. He has gotten a great deal **(gran partido)** out of his travels. 9. You do not gain anything by **(con)** getting angry. 10. Have you bought (got) seats for the bull fight? 11. I have got a headache from this argument. 12. Make out two copies of this letter. 13. What is [to be] inferred from that? 14. He has not got anything clear **(en limpio)** out of his readng. 15. He has taken care of **(sacar adelante)** the entire family. 16. I asked her to **(sacar a)** dance.

Tomar *to take, have* (usually in the sense of *choose* or *receive*, used chiefly with food, drink, etc., and in various special meanings).
1. What are you going to have (take), tea or coffee? 2. Have you had breakfast? 3. Finish drinking your coffee. 4. I am going to have an ice cream. 5. The doctor took his pulse. 6. We have taken an apartment in Madrid. 7. He used to take many sun baths. 8. Let's take a taxi. 9. Have you any cigarettes?—Yes, have [one]. 10. Everywhere they took him for a Spaniard. 11. We shall have to take a hand **(cartas)** in the matter. 12. He got ahead **(la delantera)** of us. 13. You are teasing me. 14. Why, of course! **(¡Toma!)** That's true.

chapter nine

The subjunctive mood in noun clauses

I

110. Tenses of the subjunctive (§222)

1. In English the subjunctive mood has almost died out, its place being taken by the modal auxiliaries *may*, *might*, *should*, *would*, *could*, but in Spanish the subjunctive is still very much alive.
2. The present subjunctive is formed on the stem of the first person singular present indicative (the only exceptions are **sea, sepa, vaya** and **haya**). The two forms of the past subjunctive are formed on the preterit stem. Of these two forms the one in **-ra** is the more common, especially in spoken speech. *(a)* The future subjunctive has been replaced in ordinary usage by the present subjunctive. *(b)* There are no subjunctive forms for the conditional, for the future perfect, and for the preterit perfect tenses, the past, present perfect, and pluperfect being the only past tenses. With these exceptions, *(c)* the use and sequence of tenses is normally as in English.

a. **No creo que llegue esta noche.**	*I do not think he will arrive tonight.*
b. **Temía que no llegara a tiempo.**	*I feared he would not arrive on time.*
Es posible que haya llegado.	*It is possible that he has arrived.*
Sentí que lo hubiera hecho.	*I regretted that he had done it.*
c. **Dudo que fuera él.**	*I doubt it was he.*

111. Theory of the subjunctive

The subjunctive ("subjoined") *mood* possesses two essential characteristics: (1) it is used primarily in subordinate clauses, and (2) the assertion contained in the subordinate clause is dependent upon the meaning of the main verb, and is not related as an independent fact. Thus a statement of fact will appear in the indicative in an independent sentence.

Juan está aquí.
Los hombres no viven en paz.

If these statements are not related as facts, but are somehow dependent upon other statements, especially those denoting emotion (doubt, uncertainty, joy, etc.), volition (ordering, advising, requesting, asking, etc.), or causation, they will appear in a dependent clause in the subjunctive.

Me alegro de
Siento
Le molesta } **que Juan esté aquí.**
Temen
Es dudoso

Queremos
Es imposible } **que los hombres vivan en paz.**
Es difícil
Ruego

A convenient method for learning the uses of the Spanish subjunctive is to classify them according to the type of clause in which they occur.

112. Types of clauses

Clauses are either principal or subordinate. A subordinate clause is dependent for its full meaning on the nature of its relation to the principal clause. This relation may be that of *(a)* a noun, *(b)* an adjective, *(c)* an adverb. Noun clauses are introduced *(a)* by the conjunction **que** *that*, *(b)* adjective (or relative) clauses by relative pronouns (chiefly by **que** *that*, *which*), and *(c)* adverb clauses by adverbial conjunctions of time, cause, purpose, result, manner, concession, etc. (the majority of which are formed by adding **que** to adverbs and prepositions). Noun clauses *(a)*, like nouns and infinitives, function either as subject, object, or prepositional complement of the governing expression in the principal clause.

a. **Creo que se ha ido.** — *I think he has gone.*
Es verdad que se ha ido. — *It is true he has gone.*
Estoy seguro de que se ha ido. — *I am sure he has gone.*

NOTE. **Que,** unlike English *that,* is rarely omitted in Spanish.

b. **Me gusta la casa que ha comprado Ud.** — *I like the house you have bought.*

c. **Se lo digo a Ud. para que se lo repita a él.** *I am telling it to you so that you repeat it to him.*
Comeré aunque no tengo ganas. *I shall eat although I don't feel like it.*
Él salía cuando yo llegué. *He was leaving when I arrived.*

113. The subjunctive in noun clauses

1. Noun clauses are more frequent in Spanish than in English, which often uses the infinitive, especially in cases where the subjunctive is required in Spanish.

Quiero ir—que Ud. vaya. *I want to go—you to go.*
Me opongo a ir—a que Ud. vaya. *I am opposed to going—to your going.*

2. The subjunctive is used in noun clauses when the governing verb or expression denotes or even implies a subjective attitude of *(a)* volition, causation, necessity, or advisability, *(b)* emotion, *(c)* doubt, uncertainty, or denial.

a. **Conviene que Ud. le hable.** *It is advisable that you talk to him.*
Le dije que esperara. *I told him to wait.*

NOTE. Some of the more frequent verbs and expressions of this type are: **querer** *to will, wish, want,* **desear** *to desire,* **preferir** *to prefer,* **oponerse a** *to oppose,* **permitir** *to permit,* **dejar** *to let, allow,* **aconsejar** *to advise,* **aprobar** *to approve,* **mandar** *to order, command,* **hacer** *to cause, have,* **conseguir, lograr** *to attain, succeed in,* **impedir** *to prevent,* **pedir** *to ask for, request,* **rogar** *to beg,* **decir** *to tell* (and other verbs of saying used in the sense of command), **conviene** *it is advisable,* **importa** *it matters,* **basta** *it is sufficient,* **es necesario** *it is necessary.*

b. **Siento que no se quede Ud. aquí unos días.** *I am sorry you are not staying here a few days.*
Se alegró de que fuéramos a visitarle. *He was glad that we came* (went) *to visit him.*
Es lástima que no podamos vernos a menudo. *It is a pity that we can't see each other often.*

NOTE. Some of the more frequent verbs and expressions of this type are: **alegrarse** *to be glad,* **extrañar(se)** *to be surprised,* **asombrarse** *to be astonished,* **sentir** *to be sorry, regret,* **temer,** *to fear,* **esperer** *to hope,* **celebrar** *to be glad,* **es lástima** *it is a pity.*

c. **No creo que vayamos al baile.** *I don't believe we will go to the dance.*
Es probable que le veamos a Ud. pronto. *It is probable that we will see you soon.*

Es difícil que me encuentre Ud. en casa.	*It is unlikely that you will find me at home.*

NOTE. The most frequent verbs and expressions of this type are **creer** *to believe,* **pensar** *to think,* **decir** *to say,* and the like, *when used negatively* (*i.e.*, when doubt or mental reservation is implied). Others are **dudar** *to doubt,* **negar** *to deny,* **es posible** *it is possible,* **es probable** *it is probable,* **es fácil (difícil)** *it is likely (unlikely)* and similar expressions.

EJERCICIOS

Sustitúyanse los verbos de las notas de 2. *(a) (b) (c)* por el verbo principal de las frases siguientes y los verbos entre paréntesis por los verbos subrayadas:

1. Quieren que Ud. trabaje.
2. Prefería que nos quedáramos.
3. Se alegraban de que llegara Pedro.
4. Siento que vayas.
5. No creemos que Jacinto haya venido.
6. Es probable que María venga.

(estudiar, pagar, escuchar, fijarse, entrar, ponerse el sombrero, comer, tener paciencia, aprender, despedirse, decidir, huir)

114. The infinitive instead of the noun clause

In certain cases the infinitive may be used instead of the noun clause, even when the subject of the subordinate clause is different from that of the principal clause. This usually occurs when the subordinate subject is a pronoun which may be regarded as the indirect object of the principal verb, *e.g.*, after *(a)* **mandar, hacer, dejar, permitir,** and **impedir,** *(b)* after certain impersonal expressions such as **me conviene, me importa, me es preciso (necesario, imposible),** *(c)* after certain verbs of perception (see §**105**, 1).

a. **No le dejaron entrar en el local.**	*They did not let him enter the place.*
Me mandaron volver.	*They ordered me to return.*
Me impidió trabajar.	*He prevented me from working* (see §**105**, 2).

NOTE. The construction with the infinitive is not used after **querer, pedir, rogar,** or **decir** (in the sense of *command*).

b. **Me conviene hacerlo.**	*It is advisable for me to do it.*
Le fue imposible acudir a la cita.	*It was impossible for him to keep the engagement.*
c. **Le oímos alejarse.**	*We heard him go away.*

EJERCICIOS

Cámbiense las frases siguientes según el modelo, sustituyéndose los verbos en bastardillas por los verbos del ejercicio de §113: **No dejan que entremos. → No nos dejan entrar; Es posible que Juan vaya. → A Juan le es posible ir.**

1. Dejó que yo pagara.
2. Es preciso que ayudemos.
3. Mandan que vuelvas.
4. Es imposible que Tomás se quede.
5. Pedro permitió que fuéramos.

115. Subjunctive in pseudo-principal clauses

Even when used in what seems to be a principal clause, the subjunctive must be considered as depending upon a subjective attitude (one of wishing, commanding, surprise, incredulity, etc.) on the part of the speaker. The English equivalent of these expressions is the construction with *let*, *may*, *have*, *I wish* (understood), *to think (imagine) that!* etc.

Que entre.	*Let (have) him enter.*
¡Que lo hagan en seguida!	*Have them (I wish them) to do it at once.*
¡Que se diviertan Uds.!	*(I hope you) have a good time.*
¡Que diga una cosa así!	*(To think) that he should say such a thing!*
¡Que te frían un huevo!	*The devil with you!*

NOTE. The use of **que** clearly shows the subordinate character of the above type of clause. It is omitted only in set phrases or formulae: **descanse en paz** *may he rest in peace*; **¡Viva la República!** *Long live (hurrah for) the Republic!*

EJERCICIOS

Utilícense los verbos del ejercicio de §113 en frases con el subjuntivo: e.g., **¡que trabaje Ud.! ¡que se queden Uds.! ¡que llegue Pedro!**

TRANSLATION A

1. I am very glad that you are feeling better. 2. Tell him not to wait for us. 3. It is useless for you to insist. 4. I don't think I'll be able to go with you *(pl.)*. 5. It

is a pity you can't accompany them. 6. I am not sure this package is for us. 7. He begged me to keep the secret. 8. I fear they will not be able to finish it on time. 9. It is sufficient that you promise it. 10. It surprises me that he hasn't said anything to me. 11. We hope he isn't offended. 12. I am sorry you weren't here last night. 13. He denied that the signature was his. 14. I asked him to bring me an envelope. 15. We would like you to stay for dinner (to dine). 16. I don't mean to say you are wrong. 17. We would regret very much your misinterpreting the situation. 18. He had us carry the armchair upstairs. 19. It is necessary that we change our clothes. 20. He had the doctor come. 21. I forbade them to bring books to the examination room. 22. I advised all the students to take notes. 23. Long live the President! 24. Have the janitor come up. 25. Good night! [I hope] you sleep well! 26. [To think] that they have deceived us so!

II

116. Subjunctive in noun clauses

1. As a corollary of the principle laid down in §**113,** 2, many verbs of the **decir** and **creer** types take the indicative when straight assertion or belief is involved, and the subjunctive whenever volition, emotion, uncertainty, supposition, etc. is implied.

Telefoneó que vendría por la noche.	*He telephoned he would come in the evening.*
Le telefoneé que viniera por la noche.	*I telephoned him to come in the evening.*

In the first example the main verb simply conveys information and is therefore followed by the indicative. In the second example the same verb is used as an equivalent of verbs like **mandar, pedir, querer, aconsejar,** etc. and is followed by the subjunctive.

Se empeñaron en que no tenía razón.	*They insisted I was wrong.*
Se empeñaron en que tomáramos un taxi.	*They insisted we take a taxi.*
Sospecho que está aquí ya.	*I suspect* (*i.e.*, believe) *he is already here.*
Sospecho que haya hecho un disparate.	*I suspect* (*i.e.*, fear) *he has done something foolish.*
¿Está Ud. seguro de que ha sido él?	*Are you sure it was he?*
¿Está Ud. seguro de que haya sido él?	*Are you really sure it was he?* (implying doubt)

Esto significa que tiene esas intenciones.	*This means* (proves) *that those are his intentions.*
Esto no significa que tenga esas intenciones.	*This does not mean* (prove beyond doubt) *that those are his intentions.*
Niego que sea verdad.	*I deny that it is true.*
No niego que es verdad.	*I do not deny* (I believe) *it is true.*
No niego que sea verdad.	*I do not deny that it may possibly be true.*

NOTE 1. Some of the more common verbs and expressions in this category are, in addition to those cited above, **escribir, insistir, quejarse, suponer, confesar, recordar, es verdad, (no) hay duda.**

NOTE 2. The subjunctive is less frequent than the indicative after negative **saber: No sabía que estaba (estuviera) Ud. aquí** *I did not know you were here.* **Esperar,** and occasionally **temer(se),** may be followed by the indicative when no emotional reaction is implied: **espero que tendrá Ud. éxito** *I hope* (I am sure) *you will be successful.*

NOTE 3. **Suponer** may be followed by the future of probability: **supongo que será él** *I suppose it must be he.* For **si** (=*whether*) clauses with the future of probability, see §**123**, 7.

2. In Spanish, the tendency is to interpret the noun clause as a reflexion of the emotional attitude of the speaker rather than as a material fact. This type of subjunctive is especially common in subject clauses, e.g., after impersonal expressions that imply that what is being affirmed is dependent on the speaker's mental attitude.

Basta que Ud. lo afirme.	*It is sufficient that you affirm it.*
Es natural que sea así.	*It is natural that it should be so.*
Comprendo (me explico) que no se lleven bien.	*I understand (it is explicable to me) how (that) they do not get along together.*
But **Es innegable que el triunfo ha sido completo.**	*It is undeniable that the victory was complete* (a material fact).

NOTE. Similarly, **consta** *it is a fact,* **resulta** *it turns out,* **se conoce** (se **ve, es evidente)** *it is evident* are followed by the indicative.

3. In subordinate clauses which precede the main verb, there is an even stronger tendency to use the subjunctive, since the speaker is often undecided as to what is to follow.

Que lo haya hecho es innegable.	*That he did it is undeniable.*

4. When the subjunctive is used instead of the infinitive after verbs and expressions of the **mandar, me conviene** type (§**114**) a less general and more emphatic turn is given to the statement.

Le mandé salir del cuarto.	*I ordered him to leave the room.*
Le mandé que saliera del cuarto.	*I told him to get out of the room.*

Le conviene hacerlo.	*It would be a good thing for you to do it.*
Conviene que Ud. lo haga.	*You ought to do it.*

EJERCICIOS

Cámbiense las frases siguientes según el modelo, sustituyéndose los verbos entre paréntesis por las palabras subrayadas: **Le mandé hacerlo. → Le mandé que lo hiciera; Permiten que lo hagamos. → Nos permiten hacerlo.**

1. Conviene[a] que quedemos[b] aquí.
2. Le mandaron[a] salir[b].
   a. (nos importa, nos es preciso, dejan)
   b. (estar tranquilo, dar un paseo, ir al teatro)

5. In Spanish the noun clause is retained in cases where the English varies the construction.

Les agradecería que me enviaran . . .	*I should appreciate (it) if you would send me . . .*

117. The subjunctive in pseudo-principal clauses *(cont.)*

1. The subjunctive is used *(a)* in elliptical contrary to fact conditions, *(b)* after the adverbs **ojalá** and **así** *I wish that, may*, and *(c)* usually with adverbs signifying uncertainty, such as **tal vez, quizá** (or **quizás**), and **acaso,** *perhaps*.

a. **¡Si me vieras ahora!**	*If you could only see me now!*
¡Nunca lo hubiera hecho!	*I wish I had never done it!*
b. **¡Ojalá estuviera aquí!**	*I wish he were here!*
¡Así me cayera muerto!	*May God strike me dead!*

NOTE. The exclamatory **¡quién!** may be used elliptically in this sense but always referring to the speaker: **¡Quién estuviera allí** *(I wish I) were there!*

c. **Quizá sea verdad.**	*Perhaps it is true.*

2. Similar to the hortatory use treated in §**115** is the concessive use of the subjunctive in alternative clauses, with or without the correlatives **ora . . . ora . . ., (ya) que . . . (ya) que** *whether . . . whether.*

Pase lo que pase no pienso desistir.	*Come what may (come) I do not intend to stop.*
Que lo crea Ud. o que no lo crea, es la verdad.	*Whether you believe it or not it is the truth.*

EJERCICIOS

Añádanse **ojalá** y **quien** a las frases siguientes según el modelo: **No puedo ir ¡Ojalá pudiera ir! ¡Quien pudiera ir!**

1. No soy actor de cine.
2. No entiendo esas cosas.
3. No te veo ahora.
4. No sé la verdad.

Añádase **quizá** a las frases siguientes:

5. Vienen a vernos mañana.
6. Volvemos a casa después del concierto.
7. Me olvidarás.

Sustitúyanse los verbos entre paréntesis por los verbos subrayados:

8. Pase lo que pase, no volveremos atrás. (hacerse, venir)
9. Que lo haga o que no la haga, me es igual. (querer, ver, traer)

TRANSLATION B

1. It is unquestionable that they did their duty. 2. It is understandable that he should be so bored. 3. Is it natural that he should take that point of view? 4. It is sufficient that you recommend him to me. 5. He wrote me that he would arrive at three o'clock and to wait for him in the office. 6. I suppose you are going away this summer. 7. Let us suppose he said that. 8. Don't you think he is a man of ability? 9. Do you suspect he is deceiving you? 10. I admit that he is impatient, but not that he is indiscreet. 11. I [can] well understand that you should oppose it. 12. Can't you understand what you ask (for) is impossible? 13. I can't conceive your taking that job. 14. We can't explain to ourselves that he should be so careless. 15. He can't understand that we should live modestly. 16. He complains that you don't write to him. 17. We don't doubt that you are sincere. 18. It is evident that he is not to blame for what has happened. 19. That they were here last night is evident. 20. Would that you were here! 21. Let him what he will, don't pay any attention to him. 22. Perhaps I am mistaken. 23. Let him come and tell me himself. 24. It would be a good thing for them to rent that house. 25. They ought to rent that house. 26. He had the boy bring up the baggage. 27. We heard them discuss it. 28. Don't let yourself be carried away by your enthusiasm.

III

VERBS AND IDIOMS

Hacer (§247) *to do, make, have (cause), be* (of weather conditions and duration of time); **hacerse** *to become;* **hacer por** *to strive to;* **hacer (el papel) de** *to take the part of, act as;* **hacerse el . . .** *pretend to be.* (**Hacer** is frequently used to make verb phrases out of nouns.)
1. Don't make me miss the train. 2. They had the doctor summoned. 3. It is a splendid day. 4. This room is very cold (it is very cold in this room). 5. Have you been waiting for me long? 6. He had arrived two weeks previously. 7. What has become of your friend? 8. He became a lawyer in three years. 9. The two became friends immediately. 10. Let's go before it becomes dark **(de noche).** 11. He has become a real **(está hecho un)** personage. 12. We are accustomed **(hechos)** to all kinds of inconveniences. 13. We were soaked to the skin **(hechos una sopa).** 14. I shall try to see him. 15. He took a very important part in the uprising. 16. I have been acting as a carpenter all day. 17. I pretended not to hear (to be deaf). 18. They make up **(las paces).** 19. Do you need the pencil? 20. Have you hurt yourself? 21. Nobody paid any attention to him. 22. It doesn't please me a bit **(no me hace maldita la gracia).** 23. They have played him a dirty trick. 24. He was afraid he would make himself ridiculous **(hacer el ridículo).** 25. We have made a fine mess of it **(¡Buena la. . . .)** 26. I thought **(haciá)** you [were] in Madrid. 27. He makes [out] he does not hear. 28. It seems to me **(a mí se me hace)** that that is not the way it is said. 29. He pretends not to see what is going on **(hace la vista gorda).** 30. They took advantage of their opportunities **(hacer su agosto).**

chapter ten

The subjunctive in adjective and adverb clauses

I

118. The subjunctive in adjective (*i.e.*, relative) clauses

The subjunctive is used only in complementary relative clauses. It is used to indicate that the antecedent is *(a)* indefinite, *(b)* hypothetical, or *(c)* non-existent. It imparts to the antecedent a value corresponding in general, to the English *any*, *whatever*, *whoever*. The idea of futurity is frequently involved, especially in types *(a)* and *(b)*.

a. **Haré lo que Ud. me dice.**	*I shall do what* (the specific thing) *you tell me.*
Haré lo que Ud. me diga.	*I shall do whatever you tell me.*
b. **Se lo pregunté a un hombre que pasaba.**	*I asked a* (definite) *man who was passing.*
Se lo preguntaré al primero que pase.	*I shall ask the first person* (whoever he may be) *who passes.*
c. **¿Hay alguien aquí que lo sepa?**	*Is there anybody here who knows it?*
No conozco aquí a nadie que juegue al golf.	*I don't know anybody here who plays golf.*

NOTE. The personal accusative is always retained with the indefinite pronouns and adjectives (**§99**), but not necessarily with nouns used indefinitely: **envíenos (a) un hombre en quien tenga confianza** *send us a man in whom you have confidence.*

EJERCICIOS

Sustitúyanse los verbos entre paréntesis por los verbos subrayados.

1. Busco a un muchacho que me ayude.
2. Necesito al mozo que me ayudaba ayer. (servir, acompañar, hacer el trabajo)
3. Vamos a coger las frutas que estén maduras.
4. Compramos sólo las frutas que están maduras. (saber bien, costar poco, contener vitaminas)

Háganse negativas las frases siguientes:

5. Hay un alumno que sabe hacerlo.
6. Conocemos a alguien que habla ruso.
7. Aquí hay un avión que va a Madrid.

119. The subjunctive in adverb clauses

1. The subjunctive is *always* used in the following types of adverb clauses: *(a)* purpose, *(b)* unaccomplished result, *(c)* proviso, supposition, and exception. This latter category does *not* include conditional sentences (with **si** *if*) or concessive clauses (with **aunque** etc. *although, even if*).

a. **Lo dijo en voz alta para que nosotros lo oyéramos.** — *He said it in a loud voice so that (in order that) we could hear it.*

NOTE. The more frequent conjunctions of this type are: **para que, a fin de que, de modo (manera) que** *in order that, so that,* **no sea que, no vaya a ser que** *lest.*

b. **Salimos sin que nadie nos viera.** — *We left without anyone seeing us.*

c. **Haré mi parte con tal que Ud. haga la suya.** — *I shall do my part provided you do yours.*

Como no esté en su cuarto, no sé dónde encontrarle. — *Unless he is in his room, I don't know where to find him.*

NOTE. The more common conjunctions of this type are: **con tal (de) que** *provided (that)*, **(en) caso (de) que** *in case that,* **supuesto que** *supposing that,* **a menos que, a no ser que** *unless,* **como** *provided,* **como no** *unless.*

EJERCICIOS

Sustitúyanse los verbos entre paréntesis por las palabras subrayadas:

1. Me dio ayuda para que (de modo que, a fin de que) fuera su amigo. (no dejarle, prestarle dinero, presentarle a mi hermana)

2. Lo hice sin que los otros lo supieran. (darse cuenta, no hacer nada, ayudarme)
3. No comprenderán nada a menos que (a no ser que) alguien se lo explique. (decir la verdad, darles la solución)
4. Con tal que todo vaya bien, tendremos buenos resultados. (salir, andar)

2. The subjunctive is used *under certain conditions* in the following types of adverb clauses: *(a)* in temporal clauses when the time is future to that of the principal clause, and *(b)* in concessive clauses, unless the statement is clearly conceded as a material fact.

a. **Se lo daré cuando le vea.**	*I shall give it to him when I see him.*
Esperaré aquí hasta que Ud. vuelva.	*I shall wait here until you return.*
Tan pronto como Ud. llegue mándeme un telegrama.	*As soon as you arrive, send me a telegram.*

NOTE. The more frequent conjunctions of this type are: **cuando** *when,* **antes (de) que** *before,* **después (de) que** *after,* **tan pronto como, así que, en cuanto** *as soon as,* **hasta que** *until,* **mientras que** *during.*

b. **No lo hará aunque se lo pida Ud. mil veces.**	*He will not do it even if you ask him a thousand times.*
Salió sin paraguas, aunque estaba lloviendo.	*He left without an umbrella although it was raining* (a material fact).

NOTE. The more frequent conjunctions of this type are: **aunque** *although, even if,* **a pesar de que** *in spite of the fact that,* **aun cuando** *even though.*

EJERCICIOS

Cámbiense las frases siguientes del pasado al futuro:

1. Entramos en la casa cuando empezó a llover.
2. Se lo dio a su amigo tan pronto como llegó.
3. Te lo repetí en cuanto me lo pediste.
4. Jugaron hasta que se cansaron.
5. Pudimos discutirlo mientras que estuvimos juntos.

Contéstense según el modelo: **¿Cuándo nos veremos? (ser posible) → Nos veremos cuando sea posible.**

6. ¿Cuándo llegará su hermano? (terminar su trabajo)
7. ¿Cuándo podemos hacerlo? (estar listo)
8. ¿Cuándo me pagará Ud.? (tener el dinero)
9. ¿Cuándo se marchan Uds.? (venir nuestro padre)
10. ¿Cuándo me escribe Ud.? (llegar a España)

Sustitúyanse **después que** y **tan pronto como (en cuanto)** por **cuando** en las frases 6–10.

120. Conditional sentences

1. Although conditional sentences with **si** *if* are in reality adverb clauses of type 2 (§**119**), they show certain peculiarities which necessitate a separate treatment. The imperfect or pluperfect subjunctive is used in the *if*-clause of conditional sentences *(a)* stressing uncertainty or *(b)* containing a condition contrary to fact. The subjunctive is not used *(c)* in neutral conditions.

a. **Si lloviera no iría.** — *If it should rain I would not go* (stressing uncertainty).

b. **Si hubiera llovido no habría ido.** — *If it had rained I would not have gone* (contrary to fact).

c. **Si llueve no iré.** — *If it rains* (does rain) *I shall not go* (neutral).

NOTE. The present subjunctive is never used after **si** *if*. Contrast with **en caso de que** (and other conjunctions of §**119**, 1, *c*): **en caso de que llueva no iré** *in case it rains* (should rain) *I will not go.*

2. **Hubiera** etc. is frequently used instead of **habría** etc. in the conclusion of a contrary to fact condition.

Si hubiera llovido no hubiera ido. — *If it had rained I would not have gone.*

NOTE. **Como si** *as if* is especially identified with contrary to fact clauses: **lo dijo como si no le importara nada** *he said it (just) as if it were a matter of no importance to him.*

3. **Si** meaning *whether* introduces an indirect question and is followed either by the infinitive or the future (or conditional) of probability.

No sabía si ir o no. — *I did not know whether to go or not.*

Me pregunto si será cierto. / **¿Si será cierto?** — *I wonder if it is (can be) true.*

EJERCICIOS

Cámbiense los verbos en las frases siguientes según el modelo: **Si Luis viene, le veremos. → Si Luis viniera, le veríamos.**

1. Si estamos de acuerdo, podemos irnos.
2. Si te lo dicen, lo crees.
3. Si es necesario, lo pagaré.
4. Si tienen bastante dinero, harán un viaje a Chile.
5. Si me lo pides, te lo daré.

Cámbiense las frases siguientes según el modelo: **Ramón no vino y no le vi. → Si Ramón hubiera venido, le habría (hubiera) visto.**

6. Mis amigos no estudiaron y no aprendieron la lección.
7. Fernando no se cuidaba, y se enfermó.
8. Llovió ayer y no fuimos al campo.
9. No trabajé mucho y no gané mucho.
10. No me mandaron la carta y no supe la verdad.

TRANSLATION A

1. Let him do whatever he wishes. 2. Let us stop at (in) a hotel where they have [an] orchestra. 3. This apartment has only four rooms. I want one that has seven. 4. Isn't there anyone here who knows you? 5. I can't find the bellboy who has my baggage. 6. I couldn't find a porter to carry my baggage. 7. The tailor has brought some samples for us to choose. 8. What are you going to do when you finish your work? 9. You can start your lecture when [ever] you want. 10. Don't do anything until we see each other tomorrow. 11. It would be better for you not to tell them unless they ask you. 12. Unless you hurry, we will never get there (arrive). 13. In case he is not in his office call him at his house. 14. I will take charge of the matter provided you give me liberty of action. 15. Before the student could answer, the bell rang. 16. The child crossed the street without anyone seeing him. 17. I couldn't finish the translation although I worked all night. 18. I will not be able to finish the translation even though I study all night. 19. The ambassador spoke so slowly that we could understand him very well. 20. I will speak very slowly so that everybody can understand me. 21. The dentist pulled my tooth out without my realizing it. 22. You shout at me as if I were deaf. 23. If we had walked faster we wouldn't have missed the trolley. 24. If you wait a moment we will go out together. 25. If you don't like it, don't buy it. 26. If you should need me tomorrow, call me on the telephone. 27. He did not say whether he would accept or not. 28. Write it down now, lest you forget it. 29. I will give it to him as soon as I see him. 30. (There is) nobody (who) can convince him of the contrary.

II

121. The subjunctive in relative clauses *(cont.)*

1. The subjunctive is used whenever the antecedent carries merely an implication of uncertainty or negation.

Hay pocos que lo sepan.	*There are few (persons) who know it.*
Apenas había quien hablara de otra cosa.	*There was scarcely a person who could talk of anything else.*

2. The subjunctive is also used *(a)* in relative clauses of concession introduced by **por (más) . . . que** *however (much)*, and *(b)* occasionally after a superlative, in order to emphasize the statement by including all possibilities.

a. **Por más esfuerzos que haga, no lo conseguirá.** — *No matter what efforts he may make, he will not succeed.*
Por mucho (más) que corra Ud., no le alcanzará. — *No matter how hard you run, you will not overtake him.*

NOTE. The indicative may be used when an actual fact is stressed: **Por mucho que trabajo . . .** *No matter how hard I (do) work. . . .*

b. **Es el poeta más grande que España haya producido.** — *He is the greatest poet that Spain has ever produced.*

3. The following types of relative clauses, corresponding to *(a)* parenthetical and *(b)* hypothetical or concessive clauses in English, are extensions of the hortatory subjunctive treated in §**115.** This construction is especially characteristic of colloquial speech and set phrases.

a. **Su padre, que en paz descanse (q.e.p.d.) . . .** — *Your father, may he rest in peace . . .*
El finado, que santa gloria haya . . . — *The deceased, may he have glory . . .*
Mi abuelo, que de Dios goce (q.d.D.g.) . . . — *My grandfather, may he be with God . . .*
Tu mujer, que en gloria esté (q.e.g.e.) . . . — *Your wife, may she be in glory . . .*

b. **La vida que le pidieran, la daría.** — *He would give his life if they asked him.*
Con dos letras que le pongas, se arregla el asunto. — *If you will only drop him a few lines the matter will be settled.*

NOTE 1. The set phrases **que yo sepa (recuerde, vea)** *that (as far as) I know (can remember, see)* have lost in most cases their original relative value: **no es hombre rico, que yo sepa** *he is not a rich man, that I know of.*
NOTE 2. The parenthetical **que digamos** *to say the least* is used to intensify a preceding negative: **no es muy justo que digamos** *it is not very fair, to say the least.*

EJERCICIOS

Sustitúyanse las palabras entre paréntesis por las palabras subrayadas:

1. Por mucho que haga, no tendrá éxito. (gritar, trabajar, saber)
2. Por más cartas[a] que escriba,[b] nadie le hará caso.
   a. (esfuerzos, oficiales)
   b. (hacer, ver)
3. Por muy hermosa que sea, no puede engañar a todos. (inteligente, trabajadora, rica, astuta)

122. The subjunctive in adverb clauses *(cont.)*

1. The subjunctive is used *(a)* in causal clauses of doubtful or rejected reason and, in antiquated style, after **como** causal, *(b)* in result clauses, when a desired, not an accomplished, result is stated, or when a result is denied, *(c)* after **aunque**, when an acknowledged fact is emotionally stressed.

a. **No lo hago porque sea conveniente, sino porque es justo.**	*I do not do it because it is convenient but because it is right.*
No es que sea fea; es que es antipática.	*It isn't that she is homely; (it is that) she is disagreeable.*
Como no pudiera ir contra la opinión pública tuvo que dimitir.	*As he could not go contrary to public opinion he had to resign.*
b. **Arregle Ud. el programa en tal forma que todos queden satisfechos.**	*Arrange the program so that everybody will be pleased.*
No soy tan tonto que me lo crea.	*I am not so foolish as to believe that.*
c. **Aunque sea Ud. mi jefe, no le puedo obedecer en esto.**	*Even though you* are *my chief, I cannot obey you in this.*

NOTE. Compare **por muy alcalde que sea, a mí no me da órdenes** *no matter how much of a mayor he may be, he can't give me orders.* **Y eso que,** on the other hand, carries no emotional value and always takes the indicative: **me pasé el día trabajando, y eso que era domingo** *I spent the day working, although it was Sunday.*

EJERCICIOS

Sustitúyanse las palabras entre paréntesis por las palabras subrayadas:

1. No trabajo porque <u>sea agradable</u>, sino porque es necesario. (gustarme, obligarme tú)
2. No es que <u>no me guste</u>; es que no tengo tiempo. (ser desagradable, irritarme, no poder hacerlo)
3. Aunque <u>vengan</u> muchos, no lo voy a tolerar. (no creerlo, esforzarse)

2. The following are developments of clauses originally temporal in value: *(a)* **ya que** *now that, since, granted that* and *(b)* **siempre que** *whenever, provided that* take the subjunctive when futurity, possibility, or an emotional attitude is stressed; *(c)* **mientras que** *as long as, until* and **hasta que** *until* when

referring to future time (and hence to action not yet accomplished) often have a redundant **no.**

a. **Ya que a Ud. no le hace falta . . .**	*Since (now that) you do not need it . . .*
Ya que no trabaje éste, que nos deje en paz.	*Since (granted that) this fellow won't work himself, let him not disturb us.*

NOTE. **Ya que** with the subjunctive is found especially in negative clauses.

b. **Siempre que viene nos trae un regalo.**	*Whenever he comes he brings us a present.*
Siempre que a Ud. no le haga falta . . .	*Provided, of course, you will not need it . . .*
c. **Mientras que no lleguen las órdenes no podemos hacer nada.**	*As long as the orders do not come* (*i.e.*, until they do come) *we can do nothing.*
No haga Ud. nada hasta que no le llame.	*Don't do anything until I call you.*

EJERCICIOS

Sustitúyanse las palabras entre paréntesis por las palabras subrayadas:

1. Ya que todo va bien ahora, podemos terminar a tiempo. (todos trabajar, no haber dificultades)
2. Ya que no haya remedio, me encomendaré a Dios. (nadie ayudarme, haber perdido todo, no tener éxito)
3. Siempre que van allí, se divierten mucho. (ver a sus padres, aprender algo, beber vino)
4. Siempre que no haya dificultades, todo irá a las mil maravillas. (hacer buen tiempo, alguien ayudarnos, conservar mi salud)
5. Mientras no hagamos nada, no le veremos. (quedarnos aquí, estar viajando, no llamarle)

3. **Como** (causal) when used with the subjunctive and referring to future time, takes on a concessive or conditional value equivalent to *in case*, *provided*, or *if*. **Como no** in this use is equivalent to *unless*. These constructions are frequent in colloquial speech.

Como tenga suerte con este negocio, doblo mi fortuna.	*If (provided) I am lucky in this undertaking, I'll double my fortune.*
Como no llegue en este tren ya no llega hoy.	*Unless he arrived on this train he won't be here today.*

123. Conditional sentences *(cont.)*

1. Distinction must be made between *(a)* neutral conditions in past time (indicative) and *(b)* conditions stressing uncertainty or contrary to fact (subjunctive).

a. **Si Arturo no estaba enfermo, lo parecía.**	*If Arthur wasn't sick, he looked it.*
b. **Si Arturo no estuviera enfermo vendría a verte.**	*If Arthur weren't sick he would come to see you.*

2. **Por si** *in case* is construed like **si,** either with the present indicative or the past subjunctive.

Deje Ud. el almuerzo en la mesa por si viene (viniera).	*Leave the lunch on the table in case he comes (should come).*

NOTE. **Por si** always follows the main clause. **Por si acaso** (colloquially **por si las moscas**) means *just in case.*

3. **Si** is frequently used in colloquial speech to introduce an emphatic assertion equivalent to the English *why.*[1]

¡Si me lo dijo él mismo!	*Why, he told me himself!*

4. **Ni que** is occasionally used colloquially in elliptical clauses with either concessive or contrary to fact value.

¡Ni que estuviera loco!	*Not even if I were mad* (would I do such a thing)*!*

5. The forms in **-ara** are occasionally found in principal clauses as equivalents of the conditional.

Más te valiera callar.	*It would be better for you to keep silent.*
Dijérase que nunca había hablado con mujer.	*One would have said that he had never talked with a woman.*
Debieras dedicarte al trabajo.	*You ought to dedicate yourself to work.*

6. The condition is occasionally stated as an alternative clause (§**117,** 2). In this case **si** is omitted and the conclusion is introduced by **y.**

[1]This construction is in origin an elliptical conditional sentence **(Si me lo dijo él, ¿por qué no lo he de creer?),** but the ellipsis is no longer felt.

EJERCICIOS

Sustitúyanse las palabras entre paréntesis por las palabras subrayadas:

1. Quedémonos aquí, por si viene Víctor. (vernos Patricio, pasar algo, haber un motín)
2. ¡Ni que me hicieran rey! (ser presidente, tener un dineral)
3. ¡Si lo trajeron ellos! (hacer, decir, comprar)
4. ¿Si vendrá Jacinto mañana? (llegar, salir, estár aquí)

Fuera el discurso menos violento de forma y nos hubiera satisfecho por completo.	*Were the speech less violent in form, it would have satisfied us completely.*

7. **Si** *whether*, followed by the future or conditional of probability, may be used *(a)* after **dudar, suponer, sospechar, pensar**, etc. (§**116**, n. 3) and *(b)* in elliptical indirect questions.

a. **Dudaba si aceptaría.**	*He was in doubt whether to accept or not.*
b. **¿Si será ella?**	*I wonder if it can be she?*

8. For the use of the graphic present and imperfect in conditional sentences, see §§**29***c*, **30**, 3.

124. The future subjunctive

(See §**110**, 2a) The future subjunctive is used only *(a)* in legal phraseology and *(b)* in a few antiquated set phrases, especially proverbs.

a. **Si la Asamblea determinare . . .**	*If the Assembly should determine . . .*
b. **Adonde fueres haz lo que vieres.**	*When in Rome do as the Romans.*
Sea lo que fuere.	*Be that as it may* (be).

NOTE. Even in these cases the present subjunctive is the usual form: **sea lo que sea, pase lo que pase** *come what may.*

TRANSLATION B

1. Is there anything he does not know? 2. No matter how much you shout he will not hear you. 3. However difficult the situation may appear we will not lose hope. 4. Lope de Vega is the most fertile author the world has ever known. 5. Is the

drug store very far?—No, in two strides (that you take) you [will] be there. 6. If you would only study one hour longer (more) you could finish the work. 7. Has anyone been here to see me?—Not that I know. 8. Even if the book is very amusing I don't think it has any literary value. 9. It isn't that I don't approve [of] your plans, (it is that) the moment to put them in practice hasn't yet come. 10. In case they aren't at home leave them a note (message). 11. We will be very glad to do it provided that we can count on the necessary authorization. 12. Since I will not be able to (go to) meet you personally I will send a friend of mine. 13. Even though you say it I prefer not to believe it. 14. Why, he told me he didn't know [any] German! 15. Who sent you this gift?—Unless it is my wife I don't know who it can be. 16. If I catch him in a **(de)** good humor, I ['ll] convince him. 17. Let's walk slowly, so that we do not tire ourselves too much. 18. Not even if I had seen it with my own eyes [could I be more certain]! 19. Don't forget to take an umbrella with you, in case it rains. 20. What a way of spending money! Not even if he were a millionaire [could he spend more]! 21. Should the party refuse . . . 22. If they invited him to dinner (dine), he would always accept. 23. If they did not invite him to dinner, he would not eat. 24. The longer I live in this town, the less I like it. 25. Since I cannot tell him, I'll tell you. 26. No matter how often I read it, I do not understand it. 27. He is afraid of firearms, although he is a soldier. 28. He is not so far away that he cannot hear us. 29. I wondered whether I could be wrong.

III

VERBS AND IDIOMS

Decir (§242) *to say, tell, speak.*
1. They say you are leaving. 2. It apparently (one would say that) is of no consequence to you at all. 3. Who would have thought (would say) it! 4. All right, I am listening **(¡ Bien, Ud. dirá !)**. 5. Time (God) will tell. 6. I have finished (spoken). 7. The fear of gossip **(el qué dirán)** does not hold him back. 8. This music means (says) nothing to me. 9. What do you mean (wish to say)? 10. His brother, I mean (say) his cousin, keeps a grocery store. 11. This law, or rather **(mejor dicho)** this bill, will be discussed tomorrow. 12. He didn't say a word **(No decir esta boca es mía)**. 13. As we said before **(lo dicho)**, we'll meet at ten o'clock. 14. There is no need to say **(excuso decir)** what happened next. 15. Your grandfather is not a boy, to say the least **(que digamos)**.

Dejar *to leave (behind, unmolested, untouched, etc.)*[2]*; let, allow;* **dejar de** (with inf.) *to stop, fail to;* **dejarse de** (with noun) *quit, stop.*
1. I have left the money at home. 2. You get out **(bajarse)** here; I'll look for a place to park (leave the car). 3. I don't want you to leave it for tomorrow. 4. Let him

[2]Intransitive *leave (=go out)* is **salir (de)**.

[alone]. 5. Let me [have] the book when you finish it. 6. The illness has left him very weak. 7. We will have to (*impers.*) give him up as **(por)** impossible. 8. You astonish me *(express as resultant condition)*. 9. He has (left) forgotten his overcoat. 10. With all this **(tanta)** conversation you keep me from (do not let me) working. 11. Don't let yourself be convinced. 12. I am going to stop smoking. 13. Don't fail to write me. 14. Quit your joking **(bromas)**. 15. Quit (it)! 16. She stood me up **(dejar plantado)**.

chapter eleven

Gerund, participles, and auxiliaries

I

125. The gerund as present participle

1. The so-called present participle in Spanish is in reality a gerund and consequently is used—without prepositions—to indicate various adverbial relations: *(a)* instrument (or means) and its derivatives: manner, cause, etc.; and *(b)* time during which. This type of clause occurs more frequently in Spanish than in English, which in many cases employs a preposition with the participle or a complete adverbial clause.

a. **Arrojándose al agua, salvó la vida de su amigo.**	*(By) throwing himself into the water, he saved his friend's life.*
Vino corriendo.	*He came running.*
Estando Juan enfermo no pudo ir.	*Since John was ill, he could not go.*
Andando despacio no se cansará Ud.	*Going slowly you won't be tired.*
b. **Viviendo en Nueva York solía asistir a los conciertos.**	*When I lived in New York I used to go to the concerts.*

NOTE. The subject, if expressed, follows the gerund.

2. The gerund (present participle) is used with **estar** to form the graphic or progressive tenses. (See §§**17**, 7; **20**, 3.)

EJERCICIOS

Sustitúyanse las palabras entre paréntesis por las palabras subrayadas:

1. Va cantando una melodía popular. (andar, venir, seguir)
2. Nadie gana nada quejándose. (hablar, dormir, estudiar)
3. Siendo estudiante, iba mucho a Nueva York. (vivir en Filadelfia, estar cerca, tener la oportunidad)

126. Uses of the past participle

(For a list of the irregular past participles, see §**266**.)

1. The past participle functions as an adjective and as a verb. Its chief function as a verb is to form the compound past tenses. (See §**27**.)
2. Participles are frequently used as adjectives with the neuter article **lo** to form an abstract concept. (§**10**.) The English equivalent of this construction is usually either an abstract **noun** or a relative clause.

Lo arriesgado de la situación.	*The riskiness of the situation.*
Entre lo dicho y lo hecho hay un gran trecho.	*Actions speak louder than words.* (There is a great difference between what is said and what is done.)
Pues, lo dicho. Hasta mañana.	*As we agreed then. Until tomorrow.*

3. The English present participle ("being in progress") is often rendered by the Spanish past participle ("final result").

Había dos sombreros colgados en la percha.	*There were two hats hanging on the rack.*
El recién llegado era un señor muy divertido.	*The newcomer was a very amusing gentleman.*

4. The past participle denoting resultant condition is frequently used with **tener**. This construction must be differentiated from the perfect tenses, for which it may serve as a graphic substitute.

Tengo escrita la carta.	*I have the letter written.*
El dinero que tenía guardado.	*The money I had put aside.*
Como te tengo dicho.	*As I have* (repeatedly) *told you.*

EJERCICIOS

Sustitúyanse las palabras entre paréntesis por las palabras subrayadas:

1. Estaba dormido cuando llegamos. (acostado, ocupado, preocupado, entretenido)

2. Lo conocido siempre sirve para algo. (amado, aprendido, ahorrado)
3. Tenían compradas algunas cosas útiles. (vendidas, preparadas, encerradas, hechas)

127. Modal auxiliaries

Modal auxiliaries may be classified according as they express *(a)* desire and willingness: **querer,** *(b)* ability and possibility: **poder, saber,** *(c)* obligation and necessity: **haber de, deber, tener que,** and the impersonal **hay que,** *(d)* inference and assumption: **deber de, haber de.** Note carefully the different meanings of **poder, deber (de),**[1] and **haber de.**

a. **Quiero hacerlo.**	*I want to do it.*
¿Quiere Ud. venir mañana?	*Would you like to come tomorrow?*
b. **No puedo hacerlo.**	*I can't do it.*
Puede ser.	*It may be.*
¿Se puede (entrar)?	*May I come in?*
Puede Ud. pasar ahora.	*You may go in now.*
No sé decirle.	*I can't tell you.*

NOTE. **Poder** is equivalent to the English *may* (permission, possibility) as well as *can, be able*; **saber** denotes mental in contrast to physical ability.

c. **Ha de venir mañana.**	*He is to come tomorrow* (certainty with a shade of obligation).
Debió venir ayer.	*He should have come yesterday* (moral obligation).
Tiene que venir mañana.	*He must come tomorrow* (necessity).
Hay que hacerlo ahora.	*It has to be done now* (necessity).

NOTE. The English *we must (have to)* is often rendered **hay que: hay que trasbordar ahora** *we have to change trains now.*

d. **Debe de ser así.**	*It must be so.*
La enfermedad debió de ser grave.	*The illness must have been very serious.*
Las consecuencias han de ser éstas.	*The consequences are sure to be these.*
¿Qué ha de hacer uno?	*What can one do?*

NOTE 1. **Haber de** and **deber de** may be regarded as strong forms of the future and conditional of probability. **Será, sería,** and **serán** could be used in the first three of the above examples.

NOTE 2. **Haber de,** being a graphic form of the future, is used only of reasonably certain inferences and assumptions. From this use is derived the faint shade of obligation recorded in *(c).*

[1]The distinction between *(c)* **deber** and *(d)* **deber de** is useful to the foreigner, although not strictly observed in actual usage.

EJERCICIOS

Añádanse verbos modales a las frases siguientes según el modelo: **Hago el trabajo.** → **Puedo hacer el trabajo; debo hacer el trabajo, tengo que hacer el trabajo,** etc.

1. Ricardo vendió su coche.
2. Mi madre preparará la comida.
3. Los estudiantes estudian más de lo común.
4. Nos vemos pronto.
5. Regresaron antes de lo pensado.

128. Correspondence of tenses

Many of the English modal auxiliaries are defective verbs, but their Spanish equivalents are used with full tense distinctions.

Podrá venir mañana.	*He will be able to come tomorrow.*
Querrá hacerlo ahora.	*He will want to do it now.*
Debí hacerlo.	*I ought to have done it.*

129. Polite or softened statement

The imperfect subjunctive forms *(a)* **quisiera** and *(b)* **debiera** are used in polite or softened statements as equivalents of the English *(a) should like* and *(b) should, ought.*

a. **Quisiera que me recomendara Ud.**	*I should like you to recommend me.*
b. **Debiera Ud. tener un poco de paciencia.**	*You ought to (should) have a little patience.*
Debiera haberlo hecho.	*I should have done it.*

NOTE. **Pudiera** is sometimes used as a substitute for **podría.**

EJERCICIOS

Cámbiense las formas de **deber** y **poder** y **querer** al subjuntivo en **-ra:**

1. Debes llamar a tu padre.
2. Podemos arreglarlo ahora.
3. Quieren mantener la paz.
4. Deben esforzarse, si van a salir adelante.
5. Josefa no debe preocuparse tanto.

130. Spanish equivalents of **may** and **might**, etc.

1. The English *may* and *might* denoting possibility are often rendered in Spanish by **puede que** or **es posible que.**

   Puede que sea verdad. *It may be true.*

2. The English-speaking student of Spanish should keep in mind that the chief difficulties in the use of modal auxiliaries arise from the peculiarities of the English rather than the Spanish usage.

TRANSLATION A

1. Taking off his cap he showed us the wound. 2. Suddenly getting up he rushed towards the door. 3. If (since) you read so fast I can't understand you. 4. The driver, putting the brakes on quickly, avoided an accident. 5. I received your letter when I was in the hospital. 6. That happened a long time ago when I was a student. 7. He fulfilled his promise (what had been promised). 8. He is a very daring man. 9. What a boring speech! 10. Give me everything concerning (referring to) this fellow. 11. The actors have the play very well rehearsed. 12. I have to finish my work before going out. 13. I don't know [how] to translate this passage. Can you help me? 14. We are to sign the contract tomorrow morning. 15. The doctor said that you ought to stay in bed, and you should follow his advice. 16. All students should learn [how] to use (handle) the dictionary. 17. I should like to see you as soon as possible. 18. Could you come to my office right away? 19. We must hurry if we want to arrive on time. 20. The [sum] collected so far amounts to several million(s of) pesetas. 21. He had to rewrite the lesson. 22. It must be very late. We have to go. 23. There were many people looking out of the window. 24. I might see him this afternoon. 25. I want to play tennis today, because it may rain tomorrow. 26. You may come when(ever) you wish. 27. Will you [please] be quiet? 28. He should have sent it sooner. 29. That is not what [we] agreed [to do]. 30. We must go out now.

II

131. Present participle

1. The Latin present participle survives in the Spanish verbal adjective in **-ante** and **-iente** (or **-ente**).[2] Some of these forms are used as adjectives, nouns, or even as prepositions.

[2]The gerunds **hirviendo** *boiling* and **ardiendo** *burning* are used as adjectives: **agua hirviendo** *boiling water.*

corriente *running, current, ordinary;* **(el) amante** *loving, lover;* **el estudiante** *student;* **presente** *present;* **durante** *during.*

2. The adjectival present participle in English is rendered in various ways in Spanish: *(a)* by the verbal adjective or by adjectives in **-oso**, **-or.** etc., *(b)* by a relative clause, *(c)* after verbs of perception by the gerund or the infinitive, *(d)* by the past participle signifying resultant condition (**§126,** 3).

a. **Un palacio flotante**	*A floating palace*
El caballo ganador	*The winning horse*
El equipo victorioso	*The winning team*
La sociedad bancaria	*The banking firm*
b. **Encontré los papeles que faltaban.**	*I found the missing papers.*
c. **Oímos ladrar a un perro.**	*We heard a dog barking.*
Veíamos a los niños jugando en la plaza.	*We could see the children playing in the square.*

EJERCICIOS

Fórmense palabras en **-nte** de los verbos siguientes. Los verbos en **-ar** toman el sufijo **-ante**, y los verbos en **-er** y **-ir** casi siempre toman el sufijo **-iente**:

1. andar, bastar, brillar, cambiar, cantar, emocionar, hablar, impresionar, insultar, participar, penetrar, representar, terminar, tirar, viajar.
2. sorprender, existir (-ente), maldecir (-diciente), salir, sonreir, contender.

132. The gerund *(cont.)*

1. Even when used adjectivally *(a)* in the so-called "pictorial" gerund or *(b)* when modifying the object of a verb, the Spanish gerund retains its verb force. This latter construction *(b)* is equivalent to a supplementary relative clause.

a. **Wáshington cruzando el Delaware.**	*Washington crossing the Delaware.*
b. **Acabo de recibir un prospecto anunciando una nueva edición del "Quijote".**	*I have just received a prospectus announcing a new edition of the "Quijote".*

NOTE. Thus *we saw them move away* may be **los vimos alejarse (alejándose, que se alejaban).** But when the English present participle is equivalent to a complementary relative clause *(the missing papers)* the gerund cannot be used **(los papeles que faltaban).**

2. The only preposition used with the gerund is **en.** This infrequent construction has a temporal or conditional meaning, *as soon as, (immediately) after, when, if.*

En terminando de comer venga Ud. a mi casa.	*As soon as you finish dinner, come to my house.*
En teniendo salud no hay que apurarse.	*As long as (if) one has his health, there is no need to worry.*

3. (**§20,** 3) In the progressive or graphic tenses **estar** is often replaced by verbs of motion **(ir, andar, venir, llevar)** which give an added graphic force to the expression in keeping with their literal meaning (often rendered in English by an adverbial modifier). **Seguir** and **continuar** 'to continue' are always followed by the gerund.

Venía andando por la carretera.	*He came walking along the highway.*
Me voy cansando de esto.	*I am getting* (gradually, beginning to get) *tired of this.*
Andaba escribiendo para los periódicos.	*He was writing for the newspapers* (sporadically).
Seguí viéndola todos los días.	*I kept (on) seeing her every day.*
Llevo dos horas estudiando.	*I have been* (spending) *two hours studying.*
Vengo diciéndoselo hace tiempo.	*I have been telling him so for some time.*

EJERCICIOS

Sustitúyanse verbos de moción por **estar** en las frases siguientes:

1. Estoy aburriéndome de esto.
2. Todos estaban diciendo lo mismo.
3. Los radicales están molestando a mucha gente.
4. Estamos aguantando lo malo de este mundo.

Cámbiense las construcciones siguientes según el modelo: **Hace unos días que estudio la materia.** → **Llevo unos días estudiando la materia.**

5. Hace poco tiempo que el médico visita a los enfermos.
6. Hace un año que mi cuñado trabaja aquí.
7. Hace varias semanas que nos vemos diariamente.

4. The gerund is frequently used in familiar epistolary and journalistic style to represent an attendant circumstance or result which, in English, would take the form of a coordinate clause or even a separate sentence.

Se ha declarado la huelga general, cerrándose todas las tiendas.	*General strike declared. All shops closed.*
El automóvil chocó contra un árbol, resultando heridos de gravedad todos sus ocupantes.	*The car crashed into a tree, and all the passengers were seriously injured.*

NOTE. The adverbial gerund is sometimes used colloquially as an exclamatory imperative: **¡Andando!** *Come along!* **¡Callandito!** *Hush!*

133. Past participles *(cont.)*

1. Past participles (and adjectives with verbal meaning) may be used in the absolute construction to express *(a)* time and *(b)* manner. In this construction the participle always agrees in gender and number with the noun it modifies and always precedes it.

a. **Firmado el pagaré me entregaron el dinero.**	*After the note was signed, they delivered the money to me.*
b. **Cogidos del brazo se paseaban por el salón.**	*They walked up and down the salon arm in arm.*

NOTE. Compound prepositions such as **antes de** *before*, **después de** *after*, and **luego de** *immediately after* may be used to specify the exact temporal relation: **luego de firmado el pagaré,** etc. The participial construction with the preterit perfect of the auxiliary in apposition **(firmado que hube el pageré)** is a survival found only (and rarely) in literary style.

EJERCICIOS

Sustitúyanse las formas debidas de las palabras entre paréntesis por las palabras subrayadas:

1. Después de (luego de) pagadas las deudas, pudimos respirar un poco. (terminar la guerra, cumplir los ejercicios, hacer los trabajos)
2. (Antes de) contado el dinero, tuvieron que llegar a un acuerdo. (escribir el contrato, salir para México, empezar la tarea)

2. With the past participle (as well as with the gerund) **estar** may be replaced by related verbs of more specific meaning: **quedarse, hallarse, encontrarse, verse.** Verbs of motion **(ir, andar, venir, seguir** etc.) may also be used to impart a graphic quality in keeping with the literal meaning of the auxiliary.[3]

[3]Spanish uses many more graphic and objective auxiliaries with the gerund and past participle than does English, which, on the other hand, uses many subjective (or modal) auxiliaries. Compare in this connection the Spanish use of the past participle stressing final result where English uses the present participle stressing "being in progress."

Se hallaba muy desanimado.	*He was very discouraged.*
Andaba preocupado.	*He was (went about) worried.*
Se vieron obligados a retirarse.	*They were forced to retire.*
Me encuentro desganado.	*I'm not very hungry.*

NOTE. Past participles may lose most or all of their verb force, becoming pure adjectives (or even nouns) in value, and being construed as a consequence with **ser** (§17, 5). A true participle always takes **estar,** etc., except to form the passive voice.

EJERCICIOS

Cámbiense las frases siguientes según el modelo: **La nieve cubrió el techo. → El techo está (se halla, se encuentra, queda) cubierto de nieve.**

1. Destruyeron la casa.
2. Ocuparon la ciudad.
3. Excluyeron a los reaccionarios.
4. Suprimieron los periódicos liberales.
5. Cerraron los teatros.

134. Substitute verbs

1. The English substitute verbs *do, have, be* are rendered in Spanish in one of several ways: *(a)* by repeating the original verb, *(b)* by omitting the verb and using the personal pronoun followed by an adverb **(sí, no,** etc.**)** or *(c)* by the proper form of **ser** with personal pronoun subject.

a. **¿Ha visto Ud. a D. Benito?—Sí, le he visto.**	*Have you seen D. Benito?—Yes, I have.*
b. **¿Va Ud. a esperar a Jorge? Yo no.**	*Are you going to wait for George? I am not.*
c. **¿Quién se ha llevado mi despertador?—Yo no he sido.**	*Who has taken away my alarm clock?—I haven't.*

NOTE. The English query *Do you?* indicating surprise or interest is rendered in Spanish by **¿De veras?** or **¿Ah, si?**

EJERCICIOS

Contéstense las preguntas según el modelo: **¿Quién ha recibido una carta?—Yo no. (Yo no he sido; Yo sí.)**

1. ¿Quién ha traído un periódico?
2. ¿Quién ha ido a ver el museo?
3. ¿Quién ha gritado?
4. ¿Quién ha estado aquí antes?

135. Modal auxiliaries *(cont.)*

1. With **poder** and **deber** either the present or the perfect infinitive may be used, the latter as in English.

He debido hacerlo.	*I should have done it.*
Debe de haberlo hecho.	*He must have done it.*
Hubiera podido hacerlo. **Podría (pudiera) haberlo hecho.**	*I could have done it.*

NOTE. In sentences such as the preceding **podía** and **debía** may be used instead of the conditional.

2. **Convenir** is frequently used to render the English *should* or *ought* in the sense of "*to be to one's advantage.*"

Conviene hacerlo ahora.	*It ought to be done now.*
Convendría que Ud. le hablara.	*You ought to talk to him.*

EJERCICIOS

Cámbiense las frases siguientes según el modelo: **Han podido ganarlo.→ Pueden haberlo ganado. Podría haberlo hecho. → Habría podido hacerlo.**

1. Debemos haber estudiado más.
2. Puede haberlo visto.
3. Debieron de pagar la cuenta.
4. Has podido encontrarlo.

TRANSLATION B

1. I am reading a very interesting book. 2. This letter is very impertinent. 3. Rice is very nourishing. 4. She has a good singing voice. 5. There is running water in all the rooms. 6. We saw the boat sinking and disappearing under the waves. 7. A man riding on horseback. 8. The box containing fifty pills costs ninety-eight cents. 9. This is a passing fashion. 10. [A] barking dog never bites. 11. We met many women carrying baskets on their heads. 12. The print represents Hernán Cortés burning his ships. 13. As soon as the game is over we will go home. 14. I see you are still very busy. 15. I will go on writing until you are ready. 16. The patient is still confined to bed. 17. We had been waiting for two hours. 18. He has been engaged in politics for ten years. 19. After the necessary preparations had been made, they started the work. 20. I don't feel well. 21. You ought to

take (do) some exercise. 22. I should have moved to another house. 23. I could have gone abroad, but I didn't want to. 24. Who (has) said that?—I don't know, I didn't. 25. Didn't you like the concert? I did. 26. He ought to know what he is doing, but I don't think he does. 27. We must do (fulfil) our duty. 28. When will you find (it) out? 29. Yesterday I wanted to talk to you, but I couldn't find you.

III

VERBS AND IDIOMS

Querer (§255) *to will, wish, want, love.*
1. Will you come in? 2. He would not (did not want to) admit it. 3. I tried to save him, but it was too **(ya era)** late. 4. He will surely **(sin duda)** want the performance to continue. 5. Do you really love her? 6. The torments of love are the subject of many poems. 7. This means that I shall not see him again **(más)**. 8. He did it without meaning to (unwillingly). 9. Just as you wish **(Como Ud. quiera)**; it makes no difference to me.

Poder (§253) *to be able, can, may.*
1. The power of illusion can blind a man. 2. I cannot *(fut.)* do it until tomorrow. 3. How can such a thing have occurred? 4. The sick man could not (was unable to) speak. 5. I was looking (*gerund*) for you yesterday, but I could not find you. 6. The situation may change from one moment to another. 7. It may be true as far as **(por lo que)** I know. 8. May I come in? **(¿Se puede?)** 9. This is my opinion, but [it] might very well turn out **(ocurrir)** quite the contrary. 10. His ambition was stronger **(pudo más)** than his love. 11. Let's rest a while, I am all "in" (I can do no more). 12. I must **(no puedo menos de)** accept his decision. 13. I like it immensely **(a más no poder)**. 14. I can't stand **(poder con)** that fellow; he is very boring.

Convenir (§263) *to agree to* **(en)**, *etc.;* impers. *to suit, befit, be a good thing for one, ought, etc.*
1. I admit (agree) that he meant well (his intention was good). 2. It's a deal! **(¡Convenido!)** 3. If the time does not suit you, set **(señalar)** another. 4. I don't think it would be (is) a good thing for me to accept the position. 5. You had better **(conviene)** go slowly. 6. It would be better if **(convendría más que)** I went with him.

chapter twelve

Impersonals and reflexives

I

136. The impersonal construction

The term *impersonal* applied to a verb or verb phrase signifies that it is used without a personal subject and, consequently, only in the third person. In English the impersonal construction is formed by using the neuter pronoun *it* to represent a subject which is *(a)* non-existent, *(b)* unexpressed, or *(c)* postponed. In Spanish no such pronoun is required, since any verb may be used with the subject either unexpressed or postponed. As a result the impersonal construction is much more widely used in Spanish.

a. **Llueve.**	*It is raining.*
Amanece.	*It is dawn(ing).*
Truena.	*It is thundering.*
Escampa.	*It is clearing off.*
Hiela.	*It is freezing.*
b. **No me importa** (eso que Ud. dice).	*It is immaterial to me* (what you say).
Es lástima.	*It's a pity.*
c. **Me conviene hacerlo.**	*It's to my advantage to do it.*
Es preciso que vaya Ud.	*It's necessary that you go.*

137. *Hacer* and *haber* used impersonally

1. Impersonals with non-existent subjects are used only in the singular. In Spanish the chief members of this group are (1) verbs describing natural phenomena (see *a.* above) and (2) **hacer** and **haber** used impersonally.

2. **Hacer** is used impersonally in *(a)* expressions of weather and *(b)* in temporal clauses to record the lapse of time during or since an act or state (§§**22***b*; **23**, 2; **24**, 2; **32***a*; **34**).

a. **Hace calor (frío, fresco).**	*It is warm (cold, cool).*
Hace buen (mal) tiempo.	*It is nice (bad) weather.*

EJERCICIOS

Pónganse las formas debidas de los verbos siguientes en el presente, el presente progresivo, imperfecto y pretérito:

nevar, tronar, helar, lloviznar, granizar, amanecer, anochecer, atardecer, oscurecer, esclarecer.

3. **Haber,** when not used as an auxiliary to form the compound tenses, is an impersonal verb equivalent to the English *there is*, *there are*, etc. It has the special form **hay** only in the present tense.

¿Hay algo de particular?	*Is there anything new?*
Hubo una gritería formidable.	*There was a huge hubbub.*
Ha habido dificultades.	*There have been difficulties.*
Había seis libros en la mesa.	*There were six books on the table.*
¿Hay sandías? Las hay.	*Are there any watermelons? There are.*

4. The demonstrative *there is* **(allí está)** must be differentiated from the impersonal *there is* **(hay). Hay** etc. stresses mere existence and is always used when the predicate is indefinite. **Estar** stresses actual presence and is always used when the English *there is* is equivalent to *there stands.*

Hay barcos en la bahía.	*There are* (some) *ships in the bay.*
But: **Allí** (en la bahía) **están los barcos.**	*There* (in the bay) *are the ships.*
Abajo hay (or **está**) **un señor que pregunta por Ud.**	*Below there is a gentleman asking for you.*
Estaban dos hombres en el muelle.	*There were two men* (standing) *on the dock.*

NOTE 1. **He aquí (ahí)** corresponds to the English *here (there) is here (there) you have, behold:* **he aquí el resultado** *here you have the result.* The personal pronouns, when used, are annexed to **he.**

NOTE 2. The preterit **hubo** is used when *there was (were)* is the equivalent of **tuvo lugar, ocurrió**, etc.

EJERCICIOS

Cámbiense las frases siguientes al pasado:

1. Hay un mitin estrepitoso en la plaza.

2. Hay muchos espectadores.
3. Hay varias razones para su conducta.
4. No hay clase hoy.
5. Hay una gran explosión en el barco.

Háganse preguntas de las frases precedentes y contéstense con los pronombres según el modelo: **¿Hay muchos estudiantes?—Sí, los hay. ¿Había muchos estudiantes?—Sí, los había.**

138. Verbs with non-personal subject

Some verbs are used *(a)* exclusively as impersonals, but *(b)* many transitive verbs, especially those denoting thought, feeling, or obligation, are used in the impersonal construction with the indirect object of the person affected (dative of interest) in cases where the English would use a personal subject. (Compare the archaic English *methinks.*)

a. **Sucedió algo extraordinario.** — *An extraordinary thing happened.*
Basta que sea Ud. amigo mío. — *It suffices that you are a friend of mine.*

NOTE. The more usual verbs of this type are: **importar** *to matter,* **convenir** *to suit, be to one's advantage,* **bastar** *to suffice,* **doler, pesar** *to grieve, to be sorry for,* **suceder, ocurrir** *to occur, happen,* **resultar** *to turn out.*

b. **Me parece que tiene Ud. razón.** — *I think you are right.*
Me gusta leer en la cama. — *I like to read in bed.*
Le extrañó mi comportamiento. — *He was surprised at my conduct.* (My conduct surprised him.)

NOTE. **Ser** is always used to form impersonal phrases **(es lástima, es tarde,** etc.) except in the case of **está bien** *(it's) all right.*

EJERCICIOS

Sustitúyanse los verbos **gustar, parecer, importar, convenir, extrañar, pesar** por los verbos subrayados, haciendo los cambios necesarios en el verbo subordinado:

1. Nos parece que todos deben prestar atención.
2. Me gustaba que tuvieran encerrados a los insurgentes.
3. Le extraña que nadie lo reconozca.
4. ¿Te pesa que nos quedemos aquí?
5. Les importaba que el decano les escuchara.

139. Reflexive verbs as equivalent to intransitives

1. Reflexive verbs are much more frequent in Spanish than in English. Where English tends to create intransitives out of transitives, Spanish creates reflexives. Hence the Spanish equivalents of many English intransitives are reflexive.

TRANSITIVE		REFLEXIVE	INTRANSITIVE
acostar	*to put to bed*	**acostarse**	*to go to bed*
despertar	*to wake, rouse*	**despertarse**	*to awake*
levantar	*to raise*	**levantarse**	*to rise, get up*
alegrar	*to cheer, make glad*	**alegrarse**	*to rejoice, be glad*
adelantar	*to advance, put ahead*	**adelantarse**	*to advance, go ahead*
acercar	*to approach, bring up*	**acercarse**	*to approach, come up*
detener	*to stop, arrest*	**detenerse**	*to stop* (oneself)
casar	*to marry (off)*	**casarse**	*to marry, get married*

NOTE. The English *become (get, grow)* is often rendered in Spanish by the reflexive: **cansarse** *to become tired*, **enfriarse** *to grow (get) cold* (see §21).

2. A few verbs are always used reflexively in Spanish, *e.g.*, **atreverse (a)** *to venture, dare*, **arrepentirse (de)** *to repent*, **quejarse (de)** *to complain*, **desvivirse (por)** *to do one's utmost*, **dignarse** *to deign*, **preciarse (de)** *to pride oneself*, **jactarse (de)** *to boast.*

140. The "quasi-passive"

The English intransitive often approaches a passive in value, particularly in general statements. In such cases the Spanish again uses the reflexive.

La nieve se derrite.	*The snow melts* (is melted).
Las puertas se cierran a las once.	*The doors close* (are closed) *at eleven.*
Se rompió la cuerda.	*The rope broke* (was broken).

EJERCICIOS

Cámbiense los verbos siguientes al pasivo con **se**:

1. Rompieron las cuerdas.
2. Abren las tiendas a las nueve y media.
3. Tocan las campanas los días de fiesta.

141. The impersonal reflexive

1. The reflexive construction is further extended in Spanish *(a)* to transitive and intransitive verbs used impersonally, corresponding to the English use of *one, they, we, you* (indefinite), *people (b)* to form impersonal constructions similar to those treated in §**138**, but which indicate a fortuitous occurrence that affects someone. The person affected is the indirect object. *(c)* In general directions or announcements.

a. **¿Se fuma aquí?**	*Can one smoke here?*
Se come bien en este hotel.	*They serve good meals in this hotel.*
Se entra por aquí.	*You go in this way.*
Se hablaba agitadamente.	*They talked in great excitement.*
Se dice que habrá cambios en el Gobierno.	*It is said there will be changes in the Government.*
Esto no se hace.	*This isn't (can't be) done.*
b. **Se me figura.**	*I imagine.*
Se me olvidó.	*I forgot.*
Se le ocurrió una idea.	*An idea occurred to him.*
Se le rompió la pluma.	*His pen got broken.*
Se nos acabó el dinero.	*Our money ran out.*
Se nos murió el gato.	*Our cat died.*

NOTE. This construction is used to render the English construction of the type *I* (*i.e.*, to me) *was told that* **se me dijo que. . . .**

c. **Escríbase en español.**	*Write in Spanish.*
Se alquila.	*For rent.*
Se compran libros de texto.	*Textbooks bought.*

EJERCICIOS

Cámbiense las frases siguientes según el modelo: **Ganan mucho en esa fábrica. → Se gana mucho en esa fábrica.**

1. Venden autos de ocasión aquí.
2. Entran por la derecha.
3. Pagan bien por la mano de obra.
4. Cantan canciones populares.
5. Trabajan poco durante el verano.

Cámbiense las frases siguientes según el modelo: **El libro se rompió. → Se me (nos, te, le, les) rompió el libro.**

6. La gasolina se acabó.
7. Un incidente cómico ocurrió.

8. La botella se cayó.
9. El número se olvidó.
10. Los libros quedaron en casa.

TRANSLATION A

1. It rains a great deal in this part of the country. 2. Do you think it is going to snow?—I don't think **(parecer)** so. 3. It doesn't make any difference to me what they say. 4. I should like to meet your son-in-law. 5. It seems unbelievable that you should say that. 6. It is so cold in this room that it is impossible to study. 7. Is there [any] news?—No, I think it is too soon. 8. There were many people on the streets. 9. Where is my raincoat?—There it is, on the armchair. 10. There is no need to worry. 11. There were three men in the store. 12. Who is in the dining room?—There isn't anybody. 13. A very queer thing has happened to me. 14. It is my turn to talk. 15. It would interest me very much to read your essay. 16. It surprised us that he hasn't accepted the offer. 17. Are you getting tired?—Yes, I will take a bath now and go to bed. 18. I looked out of the window to see the parade. 19. Be careful, don't make a mistake. 20. It is strange that he hasn't telephoned me. 21. He didn't dare to give him the news. 22. Don't complain of your luck. It seems to me that you have been very fortunate. 23. This cloth tears (is torn) easily. 24. Water turns (is turned) to steam. 25. This can't be permitted. 26. How **(por dónde)** do you get out of this building? 27. A good idea occurs to me. 28. One travels comfortably in Spain. 29. May I (one) [come in]? 30. Don't forget to give her the candy. 31. Five years ago he did not have a cent. 32. How long have you been living here? 33. Umbrellas repaired. 34. Translate into English. 35. That is not said in Spanish. 36. In one room people were smoking and chatting; in another they were dancing.

II

142. Impersonal verbs used with personal subject

Impersonal verbs describing natural phenomena are sometimes used with the personal subject.

Anochecimos en La Mancha.	*It was nightfall when we entered La Mancha.*
Tronó la artillería.	*The artillery thundered.*

143. Impersonal *haber (cont.)*

1. **Haber** is occasionally used impersonally in *(a)* expressions of weather when the phenomenon is observed rather than felt **(hacer)** and *(b)* to express distance.

a. **Hay viento.** (observed) *It is windy.*	**Hace viento** (felt).
Hay sol. (observed) *It is sunny.*	**Hace sol** (felt).
Hay estrellas. (observed) *The stars are out.*	(No corresponding form with **hacer.**)
b. **¿Cuánto hay de aquí a Londres?**	*How far is it from here to London?*
But: **París está a 24 horas de Madrid.**	*Paris is 24 hours from Madrid.*

NOTE. **Haber** expressing lapse of time, as in **mucho tiempo ha** *a long time ago* is an archaism.

2. Personal **haber** is found as an archaic survival in certain set phrases.

Su padre, que santa gloria haya . . .	*His father, may his soul rest in peace . . .*
Tendrá que habérselas conmigo.	*He will have to fight it out with me.*
Hubieron de quedar sorprendidos.	*They were surprised.*[1]

144. Causative reflexives

A few reflexive verbs have causative meaning.

Voy a cortarme el pelo.	*I am going to have my hair cut.*

145. Impersonal pronouns

Impersonal **uno (una)** has a more colloquial flavor than the English *one.*

No para uno de trabajar.	*One never stops working.*
Una no puede estar en todas partes.	*One can't attend to everything.*

NOTE. The second person (including **usted**) may be used colloquially in the sense of the English impersonal *you* when the speaker wishes to dramatize his story: **Vas por la calle y de pronto se te acerca un individuo y te dice . . .** *You are* (one is) *going along the street and suddenly a fellow comes up to you and says to you . . .*

[1]In this case **haber de** merely reinforces the meaning of the preterit.

146. Impersonal construction with **there**

The English impersonal construction with the anticipatory *there* is rendered in Spanish *(a)* by merely postponing the subject, *(b)* by using **haber** with a noun object, or *(c)* by using the impersonal reflexive construction.

a. **Llegó un momento . . .**	*There came a moment . . .*
b. **Hubo gritos y tiros.**	*There was shouting and firing.*
c. **Por Navidad se come mucho.**	*There is a great deal of eating at Christmas time.*

147. Word order

Spanish word order is much less fixed than is English word order. Consequently, while in English the vast majority of sentences follow the order **Subject—Predicate (Verb—Object),** in Spanish the order **Predicate—Subject** is as frequently found as the reverse order. The choice of order seems to depend upon which element presents new information and is therefore stressed. Thus, **Juan vino** puts the emphasis on the verb, while **vino Juan** emphasizes the subject. For a simple rule to aid the student in deciding which order to use, one may ask which implied question is being answered by a simple declarative sentence. **Juan vino** is the answer to the implied question **¿ Qué hizo Juan ? Vino Juan** corresponds to the question **¿ Quién vino ?** This rule applies best to simple sentences and, of course, is only a rule of thumb, and not a complete analysis of Spanish sentence order. Factors of sentence stress, formalized order, etc. may complicate matters. The basic idea that new information comes last, however, seems to be a valid one.

In complex sentences, the predominant order is **Predicate—Subject** in the dependent clause, probably because the subject is usually the new information.

Ayer estábamos en casa, cuando llegó un telegrama urgente.	*Yesterday we were at home, when an urgent telegram arrived.*
Me di cuenta de que había ocurrido algo muy raro.	*I realized that something very strange had happened.*

TRANSLATION B

1. I woke up with a headache. 2. It is sunny but very windy. 3. There is moonlight. 4. How far is the Escorial from Madrid ? 5. I didn't think it was so near.

6. I am surprised to see him here. 7. The door opened and there entered the colonel. 8. There was complete silence. 9. Is there much game around here? 10. There will be [a] banquet and [a] dance. 11. There is much talking and little deciding. 12. It is a question of his future. 13. We would like to accept your invitation, but I don't think it will be possible. 14.[It] worried him what you told him. 15. It would be a good thing for you to learn to swim. 16. There is your friend. Shall I tell him to come in? 17. It seems unbelievable that there is no good hotel in this town. 18. The plan doesn't suit me. 19. It seems to me that we are never going to get there. 20. Don't forget to turn the lights out. 21. A great deal of time is lost discussing. 22. And now it turns out that they don't agree. 23. I don't like to have my picture taken. 24. It is hard for me to believe it. 25. One has too many worries.

III

VERBS AND IDIOMS

Haber (§246) *to be* (impersonal), *have* (in a few set phrases and as auxiliary to form compound tenses).
1. There are no stars [out]; the sky is very cloudy. 2. Were there many people at **(en)** the dance? 3. When **(al)** the speech was over, there were protests and hisses. 4. There will not be [enough] time for everything. 5. He must have come before. 6. Many thanks!—Don't mention it **(no hay de qué).** 7. What's the news **(de nuevo)**? 8. How are you? (**¿ Qué hay** ?—*informal*). 9. We are to sail next week. 10. I don't know why it has to be this way. 11. We *(impers.)* must get up earlier 12. You should **(habrá que)** hear him! 13. There was no reason **(para qué)** to hide it from (to) him. 14. How far is it from Bilbao to Barcelona? 15. My grandfather—may he rest in peace **(que santa gloria haya)**—always stopped at **(en)** this inn. 16. He will have to have it out **(habérselas)** with me.

Tener (§260) *to have, hold, be* (when followed by *nouns*, especially those referring to physical and emotional states, *e.g.*, **hambre, miedo**).
1. Here is (you have) the book you were looking for. 2. He was thirsty (hungry, sleepy, cold, warm, afraid). 3. I don't think you are right. 4. I don't know what is the matter with me (I have). 5. How old (**¿ Cuántos años** ?) were you then? 6. I don't feel like **(ganas de)** going out. 7. My feet were (I had) swollen. 8. We must *(impers.)* have pity on him. 9. We have to return tonight. 10. I had to dismiss the servant for [being] insolent. 11. We have no need **(por qué)** to hide it. 12. I have the letter written. 13. He has told me so many times. 14. The sickness had us quite worried. 15. The joke was not funny **(gracia)** 16. The scene takes place in the mountains of Asturias. 17. Hold the wheel while I light a cigarette.

chapter thirteen

The passive voice and related constructions

I

148. The passive voice ("*ser* passive")

1. The passive voice always involves action; it is used when the action is viewed from the standpoint, not of the subject acting, but of the object acted upon. In the sentence *the bridge was built by the Romans* the object of the action *(the bridge)* becomes the grammatical (or passive) subject, while the active subject *(the Romans)* becomes the agent.
2. The passive voice is formed in Spanish by **ser** with the inflected past participle, agreeing in gender and number with the passive subject. The agent (or instrument) is introduced by **por.**

El puente fue construído por los romanos.	*The bridge was built by the Romans.*
La aldea fue destruída por un incendio.	*The village was destroyed by (a) fire.*

NOTE. The "ser passive" is almost never found in the present tense, usually being replaced by other constructions **(§150).**

EJERCICIOS

Cámbiense las frases siguientes al pasivo con **ser:**

1. Las tropas rebeldes atacaron el cuartel.
2. El presidente alzó la bandera blanca.
3. Los tanques ganaron los objetivos.

4. El ministro nombrará un nuevo embajador.
5. El gobierno censuró la prensa.
6. Los empleados limpiaron la sala.

149. Expressions of resultant condition

1. English, in most cases, fails to distinguish (except by the context) between the passive voice and expressions of resultant condition (**§17,** 3*h*). But in Spanish the construction with **estar** (or its substitutes) is to be used, unless action is clearly performed, in which case the passive voice (or its equivalent) is called for.

El libro está bien escrito.	*The book is well written* (resultant condition).
La ventana estaba cerrada.	*The window was shut* (resultant condition).
La ventana fue cerrada por el viento.	*The window was (blown) shut by the wind* (action).

NOTE. That the imperfect is more frequent in resultant conditions (description), while the preterit is more frequent in the passive and its equivalents (action).

2. In expressions of resultant condition the instrument or agent *(with, by)* is usually expressed by **de.**

Las montañas cubiertas de nieve.	*The snow-covered mountains.*
La casa estaba rodeada de árboles.	*The house was surrounded by trees.*

EJERCICIOS

Cámbiense las frases siguientes según el modelo: **El libro fue escrito por él.** → **El libro está escrito.**

1. La calle fue iluminada.
2. Las tiendas fueron abiertas a las ocho.
3. La casa fue inundada por el agua del río.
4. El ministerio fue rodeado por las tropas.
5. Los documentos fueron firmados.

Cámbiense las frases del ejercicio de **§148** al pasivo con **se,** quitando el agente: e.g., **el hombre tocó la guitarra.** → **La guitarra fue tocada por el hombre.** → **Se tocó la guitarra.**

150. Spanish equivalents of the English passive

1. The passive voice is used much less in Spanish than in English. Even in cases where the agent is expressed, the active voice is often retained, especially when the passive subject is a pronoun. In such cases, the grammatical subject follows the verb.

Le detuvo un guardia. *He was arrested by a policeman.*

2. In English the passive voice is widely used, not only to express resultant condition but also action performed by an unnamed agent. This latter construction—the "impersonal construction"—is rendered in Spanish *(a)* by the reflexive (with the passive subject usually following the verb), especially if the subject is a thing, or *(b)* by the impersonal use of the third person plural of the active voice, especially if the passive subject is a living being. This latter construction *(c)* lays more stress on the action than does the more indefinite construction with the reflexive.

a. **Se prohibe fumar.** *No smoking (smoking is forbidden).*
Se sospechaba algo pero no se decía nada. *Something was suspected but nothing was said.*
Se suspendió la función. *The performance was called off.*
Se construyó la casa el año pasado. *The house was built last year.*
Las oficines se abren a las nueve. *Offices (are) open(ed) at nine.*

NOTE. That the reflexive construction is especially frequent with the present tense, and in announcements and general statements. (See §§**140, 141.**)

b. **Detuvieron al criminal.** *The criminal was arrested.*
Nombraron alcalde al Señor Montes. *Mr. Montes was appointed mayor.*

NOTE. This construction is used more frequently in Spanish than the indefinite *they* in English: **me han dicho que se marcha usted** *I am told you are leaving.*

c. **Cerraron la ventana.** *The window was shut.* (Somebody shut the window.)
Se cerró la ventana. *The window was shut* (mere statement of a fact).

NOTE. When the passive subject is a living being, the straight reflexive construction is not used to render the English passive because of confusion with the literal reflexive meaning. *The horses were killed* would not be **se mataron los caballos** *(the horses killed themselves)* but **mataron los caballos.**

EJERCICIOS

Sustitúyanse el pasivo con **se** por el pasivo con **ser**:

1. El palacio fue destruido.
2. Las comidas fueron preparadas.
3. El grupo fue organizado.
4. Los manuscritos fueron vendidos.
5. Las cartas fueron mandadas.
6. Las lecciones fueron entregadas.

Cámbiense las frases precedentes a la tercera persona del plural según el modelo: **El papel fue roto.** → **Se rompió el papel.** → **Rompieron el papel.**

151. Summary

The following summary may be helpful in determining the more usual Spanish equivalents of the English passive:

A. *Resultant Condition:* no action = **estar** + past participle.
B. *True Passive:* action performed with agent expressed or clearly implied = **ser** + past participle (passive voice).
C. "*Impersonal* construction": action performed but agent unnamed =
1) reflexive construction, especially in general statements of fact and if the subject is a thing.
2) third person plural active voice, especially if action is stressed, and passive subject is a living being.

TRANSLATION A

1. We were arrested, but when we showed our passports, we were set free. 2. The town was destroyed by an earthquake. 3. These books are not well bound. 4. When he was a student he was appointed president of the committee. 5. Spanish is spoken here. 6. The newspaper was suppressed by the government. 7. The streets were crowded and traffic (was) stopped. 8. All the furniture has been sold. 9. The ceremony has been postponed until tomorrow. 10. The damages are estimated at (in) a million (of) pesetas. 11. The house was very well built. 12. The travellers were robbed last night. 13. My friend the major was promoted yesterday. 14. At what time does the bank close?—It closes at three. 15. The

decision was made public. 16. In England tea is served every afternoon at five o'clock. 17. Eight bulls were killed at the bullfight. 18. An agreement was arrived at after a short discussion. 19. We are told that (the) tickets can be exchanged here. 20. The road was full of mud. 21. Energetic measures will be taken. 22. Foreign money is not accepted. 23. He was convinced by his friends. 24. Classes will be resumed after New Year's. 25. The mystery has been cleared up. 26. The mystery is cleared up. 27. The famous scientist was surrounded by his friends *(condition)*. 28. The famous scientist was surrounded by his friends *(action)*.

II

152. The reflexive passive ("*se* passive")

The Spanish use of the reflexive as equivalent to the English passive is fundamentally the same construction as the use of the reflexive as equivalent to the English intransitive (see §§**139–141**). In both cases the English omits entirely the unnamed element (the object, or the agent) whereas in Spanish the reflexive construction achieves grammatical completeness[1] without adding the unnamed element. The pronoun object **se** makes up, in a purely grammatical sense, for the absence of an active subject (*i.e.*, passive agent). This fact accounts *(a)* for the post-position of the grammatical subject, logically the object of the action, and *(b)* for the cases in which **se** has acquired the value (but not the construction) of an indefinite subject pronoun similar to the English *one*, *you*, *we*, *they*, *people* (see §**141**).

a. **Aquí se venden flores.** — *Flowers are sold here.*
Se levantó la sesión a las nueve de la noche. — *The meeting (was) adjourned at nine p.m.*

NOTE. In the true reflexive and the "quasi-passive" (§**140**) the grammatical subject normally precedes: **Concha se está peinando** *Concha is fixing her hair*, **esta tinta no se borra fácilmente** *this ink is not easily erased*. But in the impersonal passive, where the action is more prominent than the unnamed actor, the verb normally precedes.

b. **Se estaba muy bien junto al fuego.** — *It (one) was very comfortable by the fire.*
Cuando se es mal ciudadano, se es mal hombre. — *A bad citizen is a bad man.*

NOTE. A similar use of **se** is seen in the type **se fusiló al espía** *the spy was shot* (§**153**, 4).

[1]See §**56**.

153. Special variations in the use of the passive voice and related constructions

1. **De** occasionally introduces the agent when an emotional attitude (of love, hate, respect, etc.) rather than specific action is stressed.

Es respetado de amigos y enemigos.	*He is respected by friends and enemies.*
Fueron bien recibidos de todos.	*They were well* (courteously) *received by everybody.*

EJERCICIOS

Cámbiense las frases siguientes al pasivo con **ser**:

1. Todos estiman mucho a los que buscan la paz.
2. Sus amigos le aman.
3. Los soldados respetaron a la mujer del coronel.
4. Las mujeres admiran al actor famoso.
5. Los jornaleros odian a los terratenientes.

2. The passive voice is sometimes avoided in Spanish even when the agent is expressed, since the effect of the passive (that of stressing the object acted upon) can be obtained with the active voice by placing the object before the verb (**§150,** 1). When a noun object precedes it is recapitulated by the proper pronoun (**§48***a*).

La finca la compró mi padre.	*The estate was bought by my father.*

NOTE. That the Spanish change in word order attains the same result (and the same order of ideas) as the English change in construction.

3. The passive voice is frequently used in past tenses (especially in the present perfect) when the agent is not expressed, but clearly implied.

El baile ha sido suspendido.	*The dance has been called off* (*i.e.*, by the persons in charge).
El conferenciante fue muy aplaudido.	*The lecturer was greatly applauded* (*i.e.*, by the audience).

4. When the passive subject is a living being, the impersonal reflexive—always with the singular verb—may be used with the personal accusative. But in these cases the third person plural is a more graphic and colloquial alternative.

Se fusiló al espía.	*The spy was shot* (summary statement of fact).

Fusilaron al espía.	*The spy was shot* (graphic presentation of an act).
Se nombró alcalde al Sr. Montes.	*Mr. Montes was appointed mayor* (more formal).
Nombraron alcalde al Sr. Montes.	*Mr. Montes was appointed mayor* (more colloquial).

NOTE. When the passive subject is a pronoun **le** and **les** are the invariable forms: **se les trató muy mal (los trataron muy mal)** *they were very badly treated.*

EJERCICIOS

Cámbiense las frases siguientes según el modelo: **Fusilaron al espía. → Se fusiló al espía. → Se le fusiló.**

1. Detuvieron a muchos estudiantes.
2. Libertaron al prisionero.
3. Esperaron a la señora.
4. Eligieron presidente al señor Grandes.
5. Recibieron con entusiasmo a los astronautas.

5. The third person plural has a greater indefinite value in Spanish than in English. It is sometimes used when only one person is involved.

Llaman a la puerta. Abren y entra un desconocido.	*There is a knock at the door. It is opened and a stranger enters.*

EJERCICIOS

Cámbiense las frases siguientes según el modelo: **Alguien llamaba a la puerta. → Llamaban a la puerta.**

1. Alguien ha preguntado por Ud.
2. Alguien empezó a tirar piedras al ministro.
3. Alguien abrió las puertas.
4. Alguien rompió el paraguas.
5. Alguien iba cantando por la calle.

6. Spanish uses the resultant condition (with **resultar, salir, quedar** etc.) to render the English passive in the sense of "turn out."

El caballo resultó muerto pero el jinete salió ileso.	*The horse was* (resulted) *killed but the rider was* (turned out) *unhurt.*

7. The agent is occasionally added to the reflexive passive, thus resulting in a peculiar hybrid construction.

Los rumores se desmintieron por el gobernador.	*The rumors were denied by the governor.*

8. In addition to the guiding principles stated in **§151** the attitude of the speaker is an important factor in determining the choice between the various possibilities of rendering the English passive. Thus, in the example the *tourists were entertained* the statement may be presented from the viewpoint *(a)* of the tourists, *(b)* of the entertainers, or *(c)* objectively and impersonally.

a. **Los turistas fueron agasajados.**
b. **Agasajaron a los turistas.**
c. **Se agasajó a los turistas.**

154. The passive infinitive

The same distinctions apply to the passive infinitive as to the passive voice in general. It is used only *(a)* when the active or reflexive form cannot be employed. The English passive infinitive is usually rendered *(b)* by a noun clause with the indefinite third person plural, *(c)* by the active infinitive, *(d)* by **de**+the active infinitive after **ser** used impersonally (**§19,** 3), and *(e)* by **hay que** (**§127***c*).

a. **Más vale querer que ser querido.**	*It is better to love than be loved.*
b. **No quiero que me molesten.**	*I don't want to be bothered.*
c. **Hizo derribar la tapia.**	*He had the wall torn down.*
No es para leerlo en un día.	*It cannot be read in a day.*

NOTE 1. In certain set phrases with **para** the past participle alone is occasionally used: **no es para dicho en público** *it is not (a thing) to be said in public.*
NOTE 2. The English passive infinitive indicating action to be performed in the future is occasionally rendered in Spanish by a+the active infinitive: **las deudas a extinguir** *the debts to be liquidated.* **Por** in this construction (**§109,** 3*c*) would have the value of *still to be, yet to be.*

EJERCICIOS

Cámbiense las frases siguientes según el modelo:
Se construyó una casa nueva. → Mandaron construir una casa nueva; Juan construyó una casa. → Juan hizo (mandó) construir una casa.

1. Se terminó el trabajo.
2. Ramón vendió la colección de arte moderno.
3. Despidieron a los trabajadores.
4. Se suspendió el vuelo a Cuba.
5. El jefe del estado anunció el nuevo consejo de ministros.

Cámbiense las frases siguientes según el modelo: **Se teme que la paz no puede durar mucho. → Es de temer que la paz no puede durar mucho.**

6. Se cree que todavía hay esperanza.
7. Se esperaba que los enemigos llegaran a un acuerdo.
8. Se oía la melodía que hacían los pajarillos.
9. No se olvidaba que la guerra era una tragedia.
10. Se nota que no permiten conducta escandalosa en España.

TRANSLATION B

1. The watch was given to me by my uncle. 2. He will be given a banquet by his friends. 3. Samples will be sent on request. 4. The tennis court was rarely used. 5. Houses are being built along the road. 6. Free delivery. 7. The firemen were decorated before a numerous public. 8. We were overtaken by a motorcycle. 9. The enterprise is being financed by several bankers. 10. Constitutional guarantees have been suspended and martial law declared. 11. One cannot believe everything that is said. 12. People dine very late in Spain. 13. The governor is expected tonight. 14. They are accused of embezzlement. 15. I was received with (the) open arms. 16. We were not allowed to smoke. 17. You never hear him around the house. 18. His conduct is to be respected and admired. 19. His conduct is respected and admired by everybody. 20. What I am telling you is not to be repeated. 21. His orders are to be obeyed by all persons surrounding him. 22. Several appointments will be announced tomorrow. 23. We weren't at all bothered by the customs officials. 24. The astronauts were enthusiastically received. 25. They had the collection sold. 26. He is to be feared when he gets angry. 27. This play is rather to be read than to be performed. 28. Somebody was playing the piano in the next house. 29. It is preferable to suffer injustice rather than to be unjust.

III

VERBS AND IDIOMS

Ser (§259) *to be* (essentially) and **estar (§245)** *to be* (located, look, act, feel). *Review of Chapter I.*

1. The scene is (takes place) in Madrid. 2. What has become (been) of your brother? 3. It would be desirable **(de desear)** that they (should) come to an agreement. 4. The joke was your brother-in-law's idea **(cosa).** 5. It was not [any] thing to be taken **(tomarlo)** seriously. 6. It is not impossible, but it is rather difficult to do it. 7. The furniture in (of) the living room was (of) mahogany. 8. The

house was painted **(de)** yellow. 9. They are very good friends; they are always together. 10. He is very cultured; he is well informed about library matters.

Estar and **andar (§233)** *to walk*, *go around*, *go* (especially of mechanisms), *be* (moving about doing something). (Note that in sentences 1–8 **andar** may be used as a more graphic substitute for **estar**).

1. How's everything (are we)? 2. I am not in very good health **(bien de salud)**. 3. He is very much worried about **(por)** business. 4. He is (engaged in) writing a book. 5. I don't like to be always travelling **(de viaje)**. 6. These days we are having **(de)** examinations. 7. What is your friend doing now?—He has a job (is) as **(de)** steward on a boat. 8. I am wild; I have no (am without) money and I don't know what to do. 9. People are (going around) saying you are going to resign. 10. Why are you going around with such a serious look (face)? 11. He liked to walk about the streets at night. 12. How is the affair going? 13. Is your watch going? Mine has stopped. 14. This clock is slow (*or* fast). 15. We must *(impers.)* go very carefully. 16. Go (on)! I can't believe it. 17. Come (on), tell me now. 18. Let's get down to business **(vamos al asunto, al grano)**, don't beat about the bush **(andarse por las ramas, con rodeos)**.

chapter fourteen

The article

I

155. Forms of the article

1. See §§**1, 9, 10.**
2. The feminine singular has the special forms **el** and **un** before feminine nouns (not adjectives) beginning with a stressed **a** or **ha.** The plural forms are regular.

	el agua	*(the) water*	**las aguas**	*(the) waters*
	el hacha	*(the) axe*	**las hachas**	*(the) axes*
	un águila	*an eagle*	**unas águilas**	*(some) eagles*
But:	**la alta cima**	*the high peak*		

EXCEPTIONS: **la a** *the* (letter) *a,* **la hache** *the h,* **la Haya** *The Hague.*

156. Contraction of the definite article

1. See §3.
2. **El** does not contract with **a** and **de** when the definite article forms part of a name or title.

La finca de "El Encinar" pasó del padre al hijo.	*The estate of "El Encinar" passed from father to son.*
Fueron a El Escorial.	*They went to the Escorial.*

157. Uses of the definite article

1. The definite article is used more frequently in Spanish than in English. For the most important uses see §§**7, 73.**
2. The definite article is also used—in contrast to English: *(a)* with the names of all rivers and mountains (these are invariably masculine), *(b)* with the names of certain countries and cities, forming, especially in the case of certain cities, an integral part of the name *(c)* in apposition with personal pronouns, expressed or implied, *(d)* with nouns of weight and measure, *(e)* in set adverbial phrases.

a. **El Guadalquivir** *the Guadalquivir,* **el Misisipí** *the Mississippi,* **el Guadarrama** *the Guadarrama,* **los Alpes** *the Alps,* **los Pirineos** *the Pyrenees.*

b. **El Japón** *Japan,* **el Perú** *Peru,* **el Brasil** *Brazil,* **el Canadá** *Canada,* **la Florida** *Florida,* **la Habana** *Havana,* **la Argentina** *Argentina* (see Appendix, §**273**).

c. **(Nosotros) los españoles preferimos un desayuno ligero.** *We Spaniards prefer a light breakfast.*

NOTE. In such cases the pronoun may be omitted **a los hombres no nos gusta ir de compras** *we men do not like to go shopping.*

d. **Estas naranjas se venden a diez pesetas la docena.** *These oranges sell for ten pesetas a (the) dozen.*
Le costó la tela cincuenta pesetas el metro. *The cloth cost her fifty pesetas a meter.*

e. **Ir a la escuela (iglesia).** *To go to school (church).*
A las mil maravillas. *Wonderfully, perfectly.*

3. In contrast to the English usage the article is omitted in Spanish before the numerical designations of rulers.

Carlos Quinto *Charles the Fifth,* **Pío Once** *Pius the Eleventh.*

EJERCICIOS

Póngase el artículo definido en los espacios donde es necesario:

1. Vamos a aprender ______ portugués.
2. El pan se vende a veinte pesetas ______ kilo.
3. El año pasado cruzamos ______ Andes cuando fuimos de ______ Chile a ______ Argentina.
4. A ______ mujeres les encanta hablar por hablar.
5. ______ Montevideo, ______ Cairo, y ______ Nueva York son ciudades pintorescas.

6. Muchos cubanos que han venido de ______ Habana, ahora viven en ______ Miami en ______ Florida.
7. Alfonso ______ Trece fue el último rey de España.
8. ______ Canadá y ______ Haití son países de ______ habla francesa.
9. Vosotros ______ norteamericanos os preocupáis demasiado por la salud.
10. ______ Perú y ______ Ecuador reclaman el mismo territorio.
11. ______ plátanos cuestan veinte pesetas ______ docena.
12. ______ democracia es un ideal en muchos países.
13. ______ domingos vamos a ______ iglesia.
14. Don Quijote y Sancho Panza son símbolos de ______ humanidad.
15. A ______ buen callar llaman Sancho.
16. ______ pasearse es un placer.
17. ¿Vas a ponerte ______ americana?
18. ______ señorita Martínez tiene ______ ojos negros y ______ pelo castaño.
19. ______ general Prim fue ministro de Isabel ______ Segunda.
20. ______ hambre es mal consejero.

158. The indefinite article and its equivalents (§9)

1. **Uno** always retains *(a)* some of its basic numerical value *(one)*. As a consequence it is used much less frequently than the English indefinite article, which is *(b)* usually rendered in Spanish by the omission of the article, or *(c)* occasionally by the definite article.

a. **Tiene un hoyo en la barbilla.**	*She has a* (*i.e.*, one) *dimple in her chin.*
b. **Llevaba bastón.**	*He was carrying a cane* (not *one* cane).
¿Tiene Ud. fósforos?	*Have you a match?* (*i.e.*, any matches.)
Salió sin abrigo.	*He left without an overcoat.*

NOTE. This omission of the article is especially frequent in prepositional phrases.

c. **Tengo la garganta mala.**	*I have a* (*i.e.*, my) *sore throat.*

NOTE. A similar use of the definite article occurs in the type: **tiene el pelo negro y los ojos azules** *she has black hair and blue eyes.*

2. **Uno**—as a consequence of the preceding—is normally not used with the indefinites **otro** *another*, **cierto** *a certain*, **tal** *such a*, and **semejante** *such a* (see §**205**, 3).

Déme otra taza de café, haga el favor.	*Give me another cup of coffee, please.*

En cierto pueblo de Castilla . . . *In a certain town of Castile . . .*

NOTE. In spite of its numerical value **uno** is not used with **ciento** *one hundred* or **mil** *one thousand* (see §**207,** 1 *d, e*).

EJERCICIOS

Póngase el artículo indefinido en los espacios donde es necesario:

1. Mi tío es ______ abogado.
2. Entró jadeante sin ______ sombrero ni ______ chaqueta.
3. Linares es ______ ciudad.
4. Bilbao es ______ ciudad industrial.
5. ¿Tiene Ud. ______ cigarrillos?
6. Ayer nos encontramos con ______ cierto señor Zubizarreta que es ______ profesor simpático.
7. Nos contó algo de ______ otro profesor, ______ amigo suyo.
8. Nunca había oído ______ tal cosa en su vida.
9. El primer ministro es ______ católico democrático.
10. Más de ______ mil turistas fueron a la fiesta.
11. No tengo ______ enemigos.
12. El cantante tenía ______ cicatriz en la cara.
13. La criada era ______ andaluza muy joven.
14. La señorita llegó en ______ taxi.

TRANSLATION A

1. Hunger is a bad adviser. 2. García Gutiérrez is the author of *El Trovador.* 3. You Americans are not as fond of talking as we are. 4. His oldest son enters college next fall. 5. We always pay cash. 6. This store sells wholesale. 7. Pope Clement VII and King Henry VIII were contemporaries. 8. Don't go out without an umbrella. 9. I haven't a pen. 10. She had a headache. 11. He hasn't a telephone in his house. 12. I have very cold hands. 13. They have bought a country house in Florida. 14. We don't have a fireplace in our apartment. 15. Miss Helen went to church and then home. 16. Painting is one of the fine arts. 17. Fish is more expensive than meat. 18. There are some mines in Andalusia which produce silver, copper, and mercury. 19. Uruguay and Paraguay are on the same continent as Peru. 20. The Pyrenees separate Spain from the rest of Europe. 21. The Amazon is larger than the Plata. 22. Don Miguel is Dr. Gutiérrez's uncle. He is a Catholic and a Republican. 23. This food hasn't any salt. 24. We wanted to rent the house, but it doesn't have a garage. 25. A certain day, when I was in the country . . . 26. The dog has long legs and a short tail. 27. Green fruit is not good to eat. 28. Gold weighs more than iron. 29. Girls like to study more than boys.

30. What language is he speaking, Catalan or Portuguese? 31. Do you like Spanish bread? 32. Open your mouth and close your eyes. 33. He forgot (left forgotten) his briefcase. 34. Bring your notebooks to class. 35. Take your overcoat with you. 36. Mr. Gómez's pocketbook was stolen. 37. Our patience was exhausted. 38. Have (take) another cigar. 39. Have you ever seen such a blockhead? 40. Such ignorance left us amazed. 41. Veal sells at sixty pesetas the half kilo.

II

159. Further uses of the definite article

The definite article is further used *(a)* with proper and geographical names modified by an adjective, *(b)* in referring to feminine celebrities, and with the given names of women, in popular and colloquial style, and *(c)* with infinitives and noun clauses (§**107**).

a. **La España moderna** *modern Spain*, **la Gran Bretaña** *Great Britain*, **la Rusia Soviética** *Soviet Russia*, **el amigo Manso** *(our) friend Manso*, **la pobre Rita** *poor Rita*.

b. **La Pardo Bazán** *(Mrs.) Pardo Bazán*, **la Xirgu** *(Miss) Xirgu*, **la Pepa** *Jo*.

c. **El casarse es algo serio.** *Getting married is something serious.*

160. Omission of the article *(cont.)*

In general, the omission of the article gives to the expression the effect of a single concept, which in many cases acquires a generic and rhetorical value.

Perdió casa, fortuna y familia en aquel desastre.	*He lost his home, his fortune, and his family* (everything) *in that disaster.*
Casa y cortijo pertenecían a D. Juan.	*The house and the farm* (together) *belonged to Don Juan.*
Perro que ladra no muerde.	*A barking dog never bites.*
Con paciencia de bestia sumisa.	*With the patience of a long-suffering beast of burden.*

EJERCICIOS

Póngase el artículo definido en los espacios donde es necesario:

1. Hay mucha industria en ______ Italia septentrional.
2. Se enfermó ______ pobre Carlos.

3. El año pasado estudiamos ______ Europa medieval.
4. ______ Matute y otros novelistas han contribuido a ______ literatura contemporánea.
5. Raquel leyó algo de la historia de ______ México.
6. Muchos oficiales criollos participaron en la liberación de ______ América.
7. No podemos olvidar la importancia de ______ China comunista.
8. A ______ buen entendedor, pocas palabras.

161. Further uses of the indefinite article

1. When a predicate noun denoting a social, political, religious, or occupational group is used *(a)* without the indefinite article (§9), no idea of numerical differentiation is present and the predicate noun functions as an adjective denoting a general class, such as **rico, pobre, joven, viejo**.[1] But when such a predicate noun is used *(b)* with the indefinite article, some numerical value is present and the predicate functions as a noun.

a. **Es rico.**	*He is (a) rich (man).*
Es cobarde.	*He is cowardly (a coward).*
Es médico.	*He is (a) medical (man), (i.e.,* doctor).
Es artista.	*He is an artist* (by profession).
b. **Es un artista.**	*He is an artist* (by temperament).
Es un cobarde.	*He is a* (real) *coward.*

NOTE. The added stress given by the article in these examples.

2. The same principles hold true when the predicate noun has adjectival modifiers. If the predicate as a whole forms a general class concept, *(a)* the indefinite article is omitted. If the adjectival modifier is differentiating in force, *(b)* the infinite article is employed.

a. **Es buen sastre.**	*He is a good tailor* (differentiation unstressed).
Es mala persona.	*He is a bad sort* (single concept).
Es médico de fama.	*He is a well-known doctor* (general group).
b. **Es un sastre muy bueno.**	*He is a very good tailor* (differentiation stressed).
Es un español que conocí en San Luis.	*He is a Spaniard I met in St. Louis.*

NOTE. Augmentative and diminutive suffixes function as adjectival modifiers with differentiating force: **es un pintorcete** *he is a cheap painter.*

[1]In point of fact, the large majority of such predicate nouns are adjectival in origin (*e.g.*, **español, médico, militar, católico, socialista**—including all nouns ending in **-ista**).

3. When **uno** is used with **cierto** and **tal** they become more specific in value.

Cierto hombre.	*A certain* (indefinite) *man.*
Un cierto sabor.	*A special flavor.*
Tal cosa.	*Such a thing.*
Un tal Gómez.	*A certain Gómez.*

EJERCICIOS

Póngase el artículo indefinido donde es necesario en los espacios:

1. Mi primo era ______ novelista, pero no era ______ novelista muy conocido.
2. Es ______ buen profesor, a pesar de sus defectos.
3. Antonio Goicoechea es ______ vasco que vive en Guernica.
4. Me dijo que era ______ valiente.
5. No puedes darte cuenta de que es ______ poeta.

162. Emphatic uses of *uno*

Uno is used in exclamatory and elliptical expressions with the force of the English *such* (colloquially "some").

¡Había una (enormidad) **de gente!**	*There was such a crowd!* ("some" crowd!)
¡Tiene unos ojos! (más bonitos)	*She has such eyes!*

163. Use of the article in appositional phrases

(a) The definite article is used when the appositional or parenthetical phrase supplies information regarded as already familiar to the listener; *(b)* the indefinite article is omitted when the parenthetical fact is regarded as necessary to identify the noun; *(c)* the indefinite article is used only when the parenthetical information is stressed.

a. **Platón, el filósofo griego.**	*Plato, the Greek philosopher* (well-known fact).
b. **Platón, filósofo griego.**	*Plato, a Greek philosopher* (unstressed identification).
c. **Platón, un filósofo griego.**	*Plato, a Greek philosopher* (stressed identification).

164. Further uses of the neuter article

(See §§**10, 78, 126.**) The neuter article **lo** is used *(a)* with adverbs in expressions of sufficiency and possibility, *(b)* with adverbs and adjectives to form prepositional phrases, and *(c)* with **de** in prepositional phrases (see §78).

a. **lo antes (más pronto) posible**	*as soon as possible*
lo bastante para vivir	*enough to live (on)*
b. **a lo lejos**	*in the distance*
a lo largo de la costa	*along the coast*
a lo gitano	*in the gypsy style*

NOTE. This latter construction can be extended to nouns used adjectivally: **a lo siglo dieciocho** *in the eighteenth century style (spirit)*, **a lo Napoleón** *Napoleon-like* (in spirit). Contrast with the more specific **a la (manera) española** *in the Spanish fashion*: **Chocolate a la española** (made according to the Spanish recipe).

TRANSLATION B

1. Southern Spain produces wheat, grapes, and olives. 2. [Miss] Christie, [Miss] Taylor, and other movie actresses were staying in that hotel. 3. Typewriting tires me a great deal. 4. His cousin Elizabeth is a piano teacher. 5. My roommate is a real artist. 6. He is a brave [man]. 7. He was a good father and a good citizen. 8. He is a bad carpenter. 9. He is a man of great influence. 10. This girl is silly. 11. A certain Don Raimundo has been here to see you. 12. He says such things! 13. There was "some" shooting! 14. Zorrilla, the famous Spanish poet, died in poverty. 15. Havana, the capital of Cuba, has a magnificent harbor. 16. We arrived at Marbella, a town near Málaga. 17. Mr. Soler, a councilman, invited us to dinner. 18. We live here in student fashion. 19. Do you like rice Valencian style? 20. First of all let us have breakfast and then we'll talk. 21. She was talking in a low voice. 22. He is fifty years old at the utmost. 23. Evidently we will have to stay here. 24. I have "some" appetite! 25. The master and the servant sat at the same table. 23. I do not know him [well] enough to invite him. 27. He wrote the letter as (the) best he could. 28. He replied with the haughtiness of an old aristocrat.

III

VERBS AND IDIOMS

Quedar *to remain, be (have) left, turn out, become, etc.;* **quedar en** *to agree to;* **quedarse** *to stay, be* (stressing result, with participles and adjectival phrases); **quedarse con** *to keep (retain).*

1. Most of the guests had gone; only a few intimate friends were left. 2. Whatever is left will be for the poor. 3. He has nothing left (is left to him) of his immense fortune. 4. [There] remain a few details to **(por)** be finished. 5. Will you be much longer (have much left)?—No, I [will] finish right away. 6. We have "gotten in wrong" with **(quedar mal con)** those gentlemen. 7. He passed **(quedar bien en)** the examination. 8. They became *(result)* great friends. 9. How (**¿en qué?**) did (has) the argument turn out? 10. We agreed to meet **(vernos)** on the following day. 11. He went off to Barcelona and we stayed in Madrid. 12. Why don't you stay a few **(unos)** days with us? 13. Walk a little faster; don't lag (stay) behind. 14. I was astonished. 15. They remained silent. 16. Clean it with this and it will be like new. 17. He became blind. 18. Do you like it? Then keep it. 19. If you lend him a book he [will] keep it. 20. He lost his voice (became voiceless). 21. Sincerely yours **(Quedo suyo afectísimo)**.

Seguir (**§§228, 229**) *to follow, continue, keep on, be still* (in an act or state).
1. We will follow the course of the river. 2. Let's keep on going **(adelante)**. 3. Continue reading. 4. We *(impers.)* can't keep on this way. 5. We are still without news of him (his). 6. He is still as amusing as ever. 7. The strike is still [on]. 8. He still has **(sigue con)** his cough.

chapter fifteen

Nouns

I

165. Gender of nouns

1. See §2.
2. Nouns of Greek origin ending in **-a** (usually **-ma**) are masculine (for longer list see §274).

el poema	*poem*	**el tema**	*theme*
el drama	*drama*	**el telegrama**	*telegram*
el mapa	*map*	**el panorama**	*panorama*

NOTE. Nouns ending in **-ista** are masculine or feminine according to their meaning: **el (la) novelista.**

3. Nouns ending in **-ad, -ud, -ie, -ión,** and **-umbre** are feminine. Such nouns are usually abstract or collective in meaning.

la ciudad	*city*	**la especie**	*species, kind*
la libertad	*liberty*	**la nación**	*nation*
la juventud	*youth*	**la muchedumbre**	*multitude*

4. Many nouns denoting male beings have a corresponding feminine form in **-a.** (See, however, §2, 3.)

el tío	*uncle*	**la tía**	*aunt*
el estudiante	*student (m.)*	**la estudianta**	*student (f.)*
el general	*general*	**la generala**	*general's wife*

5. Certain nouns vary in meaning according to whether they are masculine or feminine.

el cura	*priest*	**la cura**	*cure*
el capital	*capital* (money)	**la capital**	*capital* (city)
el orden	*order* (arrangement)	**la orden**	*order* (command, rule)

NOTE. **Arte** is masculine in the singular and feminine in the plural: **el arte moderno** *modern art,* **las bellas artes** *fine arts.* **Mar** may be either masculine or feminine. **El mar** usually is more concrete, simply designating the sea, while **la mar** is more poetic and may be used figuratively, e.g., **la mar de gente** *crowd of people.*

6. The feminine of many nouns must be learned by use.

el poeta	*poet*	**la poetisa**	*poetess*
el conde	*count*	**la condesa**	*countess*
el emperador	*emperor*	**la emperatriz**	*empress*
el marido	*husband*	**la esposa**	*wife*
el yerno	*son-in-law*	**la nuera**	*daughter-in-law*

7. Phrases used as nouns are usually masculine. They may be *(a)* infinitives (**§108,** 2), *(b)* verb phrases (**§174,** 2), *(c)* other set phrases.

a. **el deber**	*duty*	**el poder**	*power*
b. **el pagaré**	*I.O.U., promissory note*	**el pésame**	*condolence*
un no sé qué	*a certain something*	**el cúmplase**	*approval; decree*
c. **el visto bueno (V.º B.º)**	*approval*	**el enhorabuena**	*congratulations*

EJERCICIOS

Póngase el artículo en los espacios:

______ clima, ______ bondad, ______ servidumbre, ______ periferia, ______ idioma, ______ costumbre, ______ atleta, ______ merced, ______ problema, ______ síntoma, ______ telegrama, ______ vanidad, ______ poeta, ______ dilema, ______ superficie, ______ cometa, ______ pesadumbre, ______ virtud, ______ sistema.

166. Plural of nouns

1. See **§§4, 5.**
2. Nouns ending in accented vowels—except **-é**—add **-es** to form the plural.

el bajá	*pasha*	**los bajaes**	**la o**	(letter) *o*	**las oes**
el rubí	*ruby*	**los rubíes**	**el tisú**	*tissue*	**los tisúes**

EXCEPTIONS: **el papá** *papa* **los papás; la mamá** *mama* **las mamás.**

3. Nouns ending in **-é** add **-s** to form the plural.

el pie	*foot*	**los pies**	**el café**	*coffee, café*	**los cafés**

EXCEPTION: **las ees** *the e's* (all letters of the alphabet are feminine).

4. The following words shift their accent in the plural:

el carácter	**los caracteres**	*characters*
el régimen	**los regímenes**	*régimes*

5. The following are unchanged in the plural: *(a)* patronymics with final unaccented syllable ending in **-z,** *(b)* nouns with final unaccented syllable in **-s,** *(c)* a few Latinisms.

a. **los Fernández**	*the Fernandezs*
b. **las crisis**	*(the) crises*
los lunes	*(the) Mondays*
c. **los déficit**	*the deficits*

NOTE. A few foreign importations drop a final consonant to form the plural: **el lord, los lores** *lords.* The majority, however, are regular: **el chófer, los chóferes** *chauffeurs,* **el mitin, los mítines** *(political) meetings.*[1]

167. Distributive plural and generic singular

1. The masculine plural of personal nouns may be used to designate both the male and female members of a pair (or group) possessing equal natural, hereditary, or occupational standing.

los hermanos	*brothers, brother(s) and sister(s)*
los señores Peña	*Mr. and Mrs. Pena*
los padres	*parents*
los porteros	*the janitor and janitress*
los reyes	*the king and queen*
But: **el doctor Núñez y señora**	*Dr. and Mrs. Núñez*

2. With parts of the body and articles of clothing, Spanish chooses between the generic singular and the distributive plural according to the exact shade of meaning involved.

Todos levantaron la mano.	*All raised their hands.* (Each raised one hand.)
Todas levantaron las manos.	*All raised their hands.* (Each raised both hands.)

[1]In some cases the foreign plural forms are retained: **los clubs** *clubs,* **los complots** *conspiracies,* **los jerseys** *sweaters,* **los sueters** *sweaters,* **los smokings** *tuxedos,* **los esnobs** *snobs,* plus many more less integrated Anglicisms like **films, flirts, gangsters, cocktails, gentlemans,** etc.

Las mujeres, con la mantilla puesta . . .	*The women, wearing the (typical) mantilla . . .*
Las mujeres, con las mantillas puestas . . .	*The women, wearing their mantillas . . .*

3. The same distinction applies to the use of singular or plural verbs with collective nouns.

La mayor parte llegó (llegaron) tarde.	*The majority arrived late.*
La mayor parte de los estudiantes se había(n) marchado ya.	*Most of the students had already left.*

EJERCICIOS

Cámbiense las frases siguientes según el modelo: **Andrés es el hermano y Pilar es su hermana. → Andrés y Pilar son hermanos.**

1. El rey era Fernando y la reina era Isabel.
2. La señorita Arregui es profesora y el señor Alcalá es profesor.
3. Margarita es mi prima y Jorge es mi primo.
4. Mi tío vive en Zaragoza y mi tía vive allí.
5. Eduardo era el hijo de doña Gertrudis y Lupe era su hija.

Póngase el singular o el plural de las palabras entre paréntesis en el espacio:

6. Vamos a ponernos ______ (el sombrero).
7. Se quitaron ______ (el zapato).
8. Se pusieron ______ (la corbata) y ______ (el guante).
9. Abren ______ (la boca) y comienzan a reír.
10. Hemos perdido ______ (la camisa).

168. Personal accusative

1. See **§§6, 99, 118.**
2. The use of the personal accusative gives to any noun the qualities of *(a)* definiteness and individuality, or *(b)* personification. Conversely, its absence has the opposite effect. Its use with numerals and the indefinites **uno, otro, ninguno, todo, cualquera,** etc., follows this principle.

a. **Busco a un amigo.**	*I am looking for a* (definite) *friend.*
Busco un amigo.	*I am looking for a* (any) *friend.*
He encontrado otro chófer.	*I have found another chauffeur* (undifferentiated).
He encontrado a mi chófer.	*I have found my chauffeur* (definite).
He encontrado a otro amigo.	*I have met another friend* (definite).

b. **Amar a la virtud y aborrecer al vicio.** — *To love virtue and hate vice.*
Llaman resignación a su cobardía. — *They call their cowardice resignation.*

NOTE. The personal accusative is not used with geographical names accompanied by the definite article: **atravesó el Ebro** *he crossed the Ebro,* **he visto la Coruña** *I have seen La Corunna.*

3. The personal accusative is not used with **tener,** except as an idiomatic equivalent to the verb *to be.*

Tengo tres hermanos. — *I have three brothers.*
But: **Tengo a un hermano en México.** — *I have a brother in Mexico.* (One of my brothers is in Mexico.)
Ahí tiene Ud. al Sr. Salas. — *There is Mr. Salas.*

EJERCICIOS

Póngase a delante de los objetos donde es necesario, sustituyendo las palabras entre paréntesis por las palabras subrayadas:

1. Veo el tranvía pero no veo a Manolo.
2. Saludaron a la muchacha.
3. ¿Han visto Uds. la televisión?

(el taxi, el chófer, el jardín, el jardinero, la cocinera, su hija, Carlos, sus amigos, la bandera, los soldados, el jefe, el turista, mi perro, su caballo, nuestro obispo, los periodistas).

169. Compound nouns

One of the outstanding characteristics of English is the ease with which two or more nouns may be combined to form compounds, such as *railroad* and *stock market.* To form similar compounds Spanish is *(a)* usually compelled to resort to prepositional phrases, chiefly with **de** and **para,** although *(b)* a few genuine compounds of the type **ferrocarril** *railroad* exist.

a. **la máquina de coser** — *sewing machine*
la bolsa de valores — *stock market*
abrigos para señoras — *ladies' coats*
neumático de repuesto — *spare tire*
el plan de abastecimiento de aguas — *water supply project*
la compañía de seguros contra incendios — *fire insurance company*

b. **la radiodifusión**	*broadcasting*
el electromagnetismo	*electromagnetism*
el telerreceptor	*television receiver*

NOTE. Abbreviations, such as **la radio** *radio* for **radiotelefonía, la mecano** *typist* for **mecanógrafa** retain their original gender.

EJERCICIOS

Contéstense:

1. ¿Qué es una estación donde venden gasolina? (Es una estación de gasolina.)
2. ¿Qué es un vaso del que bebemos agua? (Es un vaso para agua.)
3. ¿Qué es un asilo donde viven los huérfanos?
4. ¿Qué es una máquina que sirve para escribir?
5. ¿Qué es un agente que da publicidad?
6. ¿Qué es un campamento donde encierran a los prisioneros?
7. ¿Qué es una compañía que opera los tranvías?
8. ¿Qué es una declaración en la que se notan los ingresos?
9. ¿Qué es una fábrica donde hacen muebles?
10. ¿Qué es un hombre que se dedica a los negocios?
11. ¿Qué es un hombre que se dedica a la ciencia?

170. Diminutives and augmentatives

On the other hand, Spanish, unlike English, has great freedom in the formation of diminutives and augmentatives. The more frequent *(a)* diminutive suffixes are: **-ito (-cito, -ecito)** and **-illo (-cillo, -ecillo)**,[2] which imply small size or affectionate interest. The more frequent *(b)* augmentative suffixes are **-ón, -ote,** and **-azo,** which imply large size or comic effect. *(c)* Diminutives may be added to other parts of speech besides nouns and adjectives (see §**183**).

a. **caballo**	*horse*	**caballito**	*little horse*
chico	*small (boy)*	**chiquillo**	"*kid*"
viejo	*old (man)*	**viejecito**	*(nice) old man*
joven	*young (man)*	**jovencito**	*youngster*
b. **mujer**	*woman*	**mujerona**	*large (ungainly) woman*

[2]The suffix **-illo** generally implies a more subjective attitude than **-ito.** For general principles concerning the formation of diminutives, see Appendix, §§**275–277.**

perro	*dog*	**perrazo**	*big dog*
pajaro	*bird*	**pajarote**	*big bird*

NOTE. These forms are especially characteristic of colloquial speech, diminutives being used much more than augmentatives. They are very frequent with proper names: **Mariquita (María), Manolito (Manuel), Dolorcitas (Dolores),** and with adjectives and adverbs **(§183).**

c. **cerquita** *very near* **adiosito** *bye-bye*

EJERCICIOS

Fórmense los diminutivos de las palabras siguientes:

mesa, cuchara, libro, casa, mano, solo, amigo, perro, gato, muchacha, ventana, peseta, hombre, dolor, jardín.

II

171. Gender of cities and countries

Names of countries and cities are feminine when they end in **-a**; otherwise they are usually masculine.

la romántica Granada	*romantic Granada*
el montañoso Chile	*mountainous Chile*

NOTE. Even when the name of a city is feminine **todo, medio, un(o)** may be used to refer to the population rather than to the area: **todo Barcelona** *all Barcelona.*

172. Abstract nouns with concrete meaning

In keeping with the characteristic tendency of Spanish toward the graphic and the concrete, abstract nouns may be used to denote specific manifestations of the abstract idea.

Eso es una locura.	*That is a crazy idea* (or *act*).
Las ridiculeces de este señor.	*The absurd notions* (or *acts*) *of this gentleman.*

173. Personal accusative *(cont.)*

The personal accusative may be *(a)* used or *(b)* omitted in the interests of clearness. It is *(a)* used with non-personal objects in order to distinguish the object from the subject, and *(b)* may be omitted with personal objects in order to distinguish the direct from the indirect object.

a. **A la primavera sigue el verano.** *Summer follows spring.*
b. **Le mandé mi secretario a mi socio.** *I sent my secretary to my partner.*

TRANSLATION A

1. The general's wife is a very charming woman. 2. Two sisters of Charity were in the street car. 3. You can't see the Azores Islands on this map. 4. The fruit orchard belonged to the mayor of the town. 5. The postman kicked the gardener's dog. 6. Days of happiness are short. 7. The boys of the town serve as guides to tourists. 8. The Catholic Sovereigns are buried in Granada. 9. Mr. and Mrs. Aguilar are my friend's parents. 10. Yesterday I visited my uncle and aunt. 11. They have a nice little house near the river. 12. He went to the city to see his niece. 13. The robber killed a policeman. 14. The prisoner bribed the guards. 15. He was made knight of the Order of "Isabel la Católica". 16. The students raised their hands. 17. They all took off their hat[s] on entering the church. 18. We put on our overcoats and left. 19. Only fifty per cent of the workers went on (to the) strike. 20. That is the man to whom I sold my car. 21. The chief was scolding someone. 22. The orphan asylum is near a furniture factory. 23. I don't want to see anybody. 24. The colors of this steamship company are blue and white. 25. All the cars have eight-cylinder engines. 26. All sorts of things are sold in the store: typewriters, safety razors, ladies' silk stockings, children's clothes, writing paper. 27. What a huge man! 28. You have a very cute little daughter. 29. My mother is sick (*use* **tener**). 30. We saw many women working in the fields. 31. He called his children to his deathbed. 32. There you have the book you were looking for. 33. He admires England. 34. We visited all our friends. 35. My feet ache. 36. This street is full of cafés. 37. We saw the parade of the Moroccan troops. 38. I called the taxi driver a liar.

174. Compound nouns *(cont.)*

1. A special class of compounds in Spanish is that formed by combining the third person singular of the present indicative and a complement, usually a plural noun, e.g. **el cortaplumas** *penknife* (cf. English compounds like *breakfast*, *breakwater*, *cutthroat*, *sawbones*, etc.). There are hundreds of these compounds in Spanish and new ones can be formed at any time. They are frequently characteristic of popular speech, and are usually masculine.

Many of these compounds are used to indicate *(a)* instruments or gadgets, *(b)* occupations, *(c)* inferior or despised representatives of certain occupations, *(d)* persons with annoying characteristics.

a. **el sacacorchos**	*corkscrew*
el cuentakilómetros	*odometer; speedometer*
el paraguas	*umbrella*
el salvavidas	*life preserver*
el portaequipajes	*baggage rack*
el paracaídas	*parachute*
b. **el limpiabotas**	*bootblack*
el lavacoches	*car washer*
el guardagujas	*switchman*
el quitamanchas	*spotter (dry cleaner)*
c. **el matasanos**	*quack doctor*
el chupatinta	*office worker*
el buscapleitos	*shyster lawyer*
el manchacuartillas	*hack writer*
d. **el aguafiestas**	*killjoy*
el sábelotodo	*know-it-all*
el papanatas	*simpleton*
el correfaldas	*skirt chaser*
el perdonavidas	*bully*
el quitamotas	*flatterer*

2. Other verb phrases and set phrases may be used as compound nouns. These, too, are usually masculine (see §**165**).

el hazmerreír[3]	*laughing-stock*
el acabóse	*chaos*
dimes y diretes	*bickering*
el qué dirán	*gossip, public opinion*

3. The noun is occasionally used as an adjective in set appositional phrases, especially with proper names. In this construction the nouns **color, tipo,** or **marca** are often expressed or understood.

una esposa modelo	*a model wife*
un camión Ford	*a Ford truck*
una novela tipo Walter Scott	*a novel of the Walter Scott type*
un sombrero hongo	*a Derby hat*
un automóvil color cereza	*a cherry-colored automobile*
una carroza siglo dieciocho	*an eighteenth century* (style) *carriage*
el hombre masa	"*mass-man*"

[3]In compounds an original initial **r** is written **rr** to reflect the pronunciation, e.g. **prerromanticismo, iberorrománico, telerrecepción, puertorriqueño,** etc.

4. Very rarely two nouns are combined without one being considered an adjective.

la casatienda	*store and home in the same building*
el papel moneda	*paper money*
el maestrescuela	*schoolmaster*
la hoja-bloque	*souvenir sheet of postage stamps*

EJERCICIOS

Contéstense:

1. ¿Qué es un instrumento que apaga los incendios? (Es un apagaincendios.)
2. ¿Qué es un instrumento que corta tubos? (Es un cortatubos.)
3. ¿Qué es una cosa que cubre los platos?
4. ¿Qué es un hombre que cata los vinos?
5. ¿Qué es una caja en que se guardan joyas?
6. ¿Qué es un hombre que guarda un puente?
7. ¿Qué es un instrumento que limpia el parabrisas de un automóvil?
8. ¿Qué es un instrumento para matar las moscas?
9. ¿Qué es una cosa que sirve para pisar los papeles?

175. Suffixes

Suffixes play an important part in word formation in Spanish. The following uses of suffixes are worthy of note: *(a)* the diminutive suffixes **-ete, -cete, -ecete; -uelo, -zuelo, -ezuelo** indicate a depreciative or contemptuous attitude on the part of the speaker, *(b)* **-ote, -ejo, -ajo, -aco, -acho, -uco,** and **-ucho** give a stronger depreciative or contemptuous force;[4] *(c)* the suffix **-ada** indicates capacity (cf. English *-ful*), *(d)* **-ada** and **-azo** indicate a wound or blow, *(e)* **-al, -ar, -eda** indicate a collection or group; *(f)* **-dor** (cf. English *-or*) one who performs a certain action, *(g)* **-ero** (cf. English *-er*) one engaged in a certain occupation; *(h)* **-ería** a place where certain business or work is carried on. *(i)* **-ista** one who engages in a certain profession or occupation, or is the adherent of a doctrine (cf. English **-ist**), *(j)* **-ismo** a doctrine or ideology.

a. **el vejete**	*old man*
el mozuelo	*youngster*
b. **el caballejo**	*nag, hack*
la casucha	*small, ill-kept house*
el perrote	*big, clumsy dog*

[4]For a list of depreciative suffixes see Appendix, **§277**.

c. **una cucharada**	*a spoonful*
una manada	*a handful; flock, herd*
d. **la puñalada**	*dagger thrust*
un balazo	*a bullet wound* or *shot*
un portazo	*a door slam*
un cañonazo	*a cannon shot*
e. **el arenal**	*sandbank*
el pinar	*pine grove*
una arboleda	*a clump of trees*
una alameda	*poplar grove; tree-lined walk, mall*
f. **el cobrador**	*conductor, collector*
el vencedor	*winner, conqueror*
g. **el librero**	*book seller*
el portero	*doorman; janitor*

NOTE. A few common formations have a syllable between the base word and the suffix: **carnicero** *butcher,* **panadero** *baker.*

h. **la zapatería**	*shoe store*
la herrería	*iron works, smithy*
i. **la modista**	*dressmaker*
el cuentista	*story writer*
el militarista	*militarist*
el separatista	*separatist*
j. **el centralismo**	*centralism*
el marxismo	*Marxism*

EJERCICIOS

Contéstense, sustituyendo las palabras entre paréntesis por las palabras subrayadas:

1. ¿Qué es un rey despreciable?—Es un reyezuelo. (pintor, autor, mujer, dictador)
2. Si uno le da a Ud. un golpe con un bastón, ¿qué le da?—Me da un bastonazo. (botella, pelota, flecha)
3. ¿Qué es un hombre que vende cosas de papel?—Es papelero. (hace alfombras, hace pan, hace pasteles, hace la comida en la cocina)
4. ¿Qué es una tienda donde venden papel?—Es una papelería. (botones, sombreros, ropa, leche, muebles)
5. ¿Qué es un hombre que trabaja?—Es trabajador. (vende, acomoda a los espectadores en un teatro, alista reclutas para el ejército, doma caballos, educa, habla mucho, engaña, mata el toro en una corrida)
6. ¿Qué es una persona que pertenece a la izquierda?—Es izquierdista. (pertenece a la derecha, cree en el centralismo, cree en el comunismo, trabaja con la electricidad, es notado por su egoísmo)

TRANSLATION B

1. He gave me good advice *(pl.)*. 2. You are driving me crazy with your impatient [outbursts]. 3. I have very good friend[ships] here. 4. That was a rash act. 5. That bootblack used to own a shoe store in this town. 6. He hit the pickpocket with his cane. 7. He always wears a brown (coffee color) derby. 8. What a beautiful oak grove! 9. I have to buy something in the hardware store. 10. Our landlord is a very generous man. 11. My hands are full of scratches. 12. That poor, old, wrinkled woman is a chestnut vender. 13. Is there a pastry shop on this street?—Yes, there is one between the dairy store and the dry cleaner's. 14. I had to nudge him to keep quiet. 15. This is a vile low newspaper. 16. We prefer a foreigner to a native. 17. The committee discussed the problem of the unemployed. 18. He was the laughing-stock of the neighborhood. 19. This section [of the town] has a certain something which I like very much. 20. Paris is called the City [of] Light. 21. I introduced my friend to the young lady. 22. His speech preceded mine. 23. Toledo, the Museum City of Spain. 24. He does that for fear of public opinion. 25. Where is the loudspeaker? 26. The play is a historical drama of the Calderón type. 27. He wore a canary colored tie. 28. She has tiny little feet. 29. What an awful temper he has! 30. He is a grand actor. 31. Let us take this narrow little path.

III

VERBS AND IDIOMS

Ir (**§249**) *to go;* **irse** *to go away, go off;* **¡Vaya!** *Come now!* (coaxing), *What a . . . !* (approval or disapproval), *etc.*

1. This road leads to (the) town. 2. When is he going (away)? 3. Let's see. 4. I'll (go to) see. 5. No, don't say anything to him, lest you (don't go to) make him angry. 6. What can we do about it **(le)**?—It can't be helped. 7. What do you mean he is **(¿Qué va a ser?)** rich? 8. What do you bet **(va a que)** he shows up here tomorrow? 9. He was (went) looking for it everywhere. 10. I am arranging the apartment. 11. They all went [along] very happy. 12. You are very silent. 13. His affairs are not going very well (for him). 14. How are (goes it with) you? 15. This hat looks very well on you. 16. It annoys me to have to go shopping. 17. I have nothing at stake. **(A mí no me va nada en ello.)** 18. Don't pay any attention to him; that is not meant **(no va)** for you. 19. Don't go away without seeing (talking to) me. 20. Let's get out of here. 21. All his money goes **(se le va)** for **(en)** books. 22. Come now, come now, don't get angry. 23. What an answer!

Tardar *to be long (in).*

1. We are waiting for you. Don't be long. 2. How long does it take to go **(se tarda)** from Cadiz to Seville?—It takes *(refl. pl.)* about three hours. 3. It took him a long time **(mucho)** to **(en)** do it.

chapter sixteen

Adjectives

I

176. Gender of adjectives

1. See §**11.**
2. Adjectives (including those used as nouns) which end in **-án, -ón, -or, -ín** add **a** to form the feminine.

burlón	**burlona**	*mocking*
encantador	**encantadora**	*charming*
chiquitín	**chiquitina**	*tiny (person)*
holgazán	**holgazana**	*lazy (person)*

EXCEPTION: The comparative-superlatives **mejor, peor, mayor, menor (§196)** and the adjectives **interior, exterior, anterior, posterior, inferior, superior** are invariable.[1]

3. Adjectives (and nouns) ending in **-ete, -ote,** form the feminine by changing the final **-e** to **-a.**

feote	**feota**	*ugly*
pesadote	**pesadota**	*heavy, boring*
pobrete	**pobreta**	*wretch*

4. Adjectives of Greek origin ending in **-a,** including those formed with the suffix **-ista,** are invariable.

el arte indígena	*the native art*
el partido socialista	*the Socialist party*

[1]The above rule does not apply to the noun **superiora** *Mother Superior.*

177. Plural of adjectives

See §**4.**

178. Apocope of adjectives

See §**13.**

179. Agreement of adjectives

1. See §**12.**
2. An adjective modifying two or more nouns of different gender is *(a)* masculine, if plural, *(b)* if singular, in agreement with the nearest noun.

a. **El chófer y la cocinera eran muy divertidos.**	*The chauffeur and the cook were very amusing.*
Árboles, casas y puentes fueron arrastrados por la riada.	*Trees, houses, and bridges were carried away by the flood.*
b. **Se portó con toda justicia y decoro.**	*He acted with thorough justice and decorum.*

NOTE. That the adjective is used in the singular when the two nouns form a single concept.

EJERCICIOS

Pónganse las formas correctas de los adjetivos entre paréntesis en los espacios:

1. Elena y Concha son muchachas ______. (hablador, mandón, superior)
2. Los jefes se portaban de manera ______. (burlón, juguetón)

180. Position of adjectives

1. Determinative adjectives (articles, demonstratives, possessives, numerals, and indefinites) usually precede the noun they modify (see §**14**). But when they are stressed or used with differentiating force, they follow.

un amigo mío	*a friend of mine*
el hombre aquel	*that man*
sin dificultad alguna	*without any difficulty*

un hombre cualquiera	*an ordinary man*
la lección primera	*the first lesson (used as a title)*
Felipe Segundo	*Philip the Second* (and so all titles)

2. When the descriptive adjective serves to differentiate, distinguish, or in any way subdivide the group or concept expressed by the noun, it follows the noun; when the idea of differentiation is neither present nor stressed, the descriptive adjective becomes an epithet and precedes the noun. This occurs when the adjective denotes a characteristic of the noun taken as a whole, or a quality already established by previous statement or knowledge as a characteristic of the noun.

Viven en la casa amarilla.	*They live in the yellow house* (differentiation).
las blancas casas del pueblo andaluz	*the white houses of the Andalusian town* (characteristic)
sus parientes ricos	*his rich relatives* (those which are rich)
sus ricos parientes	*his rich relatives* (all known to be rich)
la España septentrional	*Northern Spain*
la Noruega meridional	*Southern Norway*
la meridional España y la septentrional Noruega	*southerly Spain and northerly Norway* (epithets)

NOTE. In general, the differentiating position of the adjective in Spanish corresponds to the heavy stress (and pause) in English: **sus parientes ricos** *his* **rich'** *relatives;* **sus ricos parientes** *his rich⁀relatives.*

3. As a consequence, certain adjectives have different meanings depending on whether they precede or follow the noun. (For a longer list see Appendix, §271.)

un pobre hombre	*a nonentity*
un hombre pobre	*a poor* (indigent) *man*
un discurso muy valiente	*a courageous speech*
¡Valiente discurso!	*What a speech!*
el español medio	*the average Spaniard*
medio español	*half Spanish*

EJERCICIOS

Contéstense según el modelo: **¿Qué es un hombre desgraciado? (pobre)—Es un pobre hombre. ¿Qué es un hombre que no tiene dinero y pocas esperanzas de tenerlo?—Es un hombre pobre.**

1. (viejo) ¿Qué es un amigo que conocemos desde hace mucho tiempo? ¿Qué es un amigo que tiene muchos años?

2. (nuevo) ¿Que es un coche que acaba de salir de la fábrica?
¿Qué es un coche que acabamos de comprar?
3. (único) ¿Qué es una pintura que no tiene igual?
¿Qué es una pintura que tengo, si tengo una sola?
4. (alto) ¿Qué es un oficial del gobierno en una posición muy elevada?
¿Qué es un oficial que mide dos metros de altura?
5. (grande) ¿Qué es un libro de dimensiones extraordinarias y que pesa mucho?
¿Qué es un libro clásico de alta calidad?
6. (cierto) ¿Qué es un informe ordinario sobre algo?
¿Qué es un informe que nos da datos absolutamente seguros?
7. (antiguo) ¿Qué es una residencia que antes era del rey?
¿Qué es una residencia que se construyó en la Edad Media?

4. When a noun is modified by two or more descriptive adjectives each is placed *(a)* according to the preceding principles. If *(b)* both adjectives precede or follow they are connected with **y**, unless *(c)* one of the two adjectives is so closely related to the noun as to form with it a concept equivalent to a compound noun.

a. **Velázquez y Goya son dos famosos pintores españoles.** — *Velasques and Goya are two famous Spanish painters.*
b. **una habitación grande y clara** — *a large, light room*
las estrechas y misteriosas calles de Toledo — *the narrow and mysterious streets of Toledo*
c. **el arte gótico español** — *Spanish Gothic art*

EJERCICIOS

Pónganse dos adjetivos de los adjetivos entre paréntesis con los sustantivos subrayados:

1. En Toledo se ven casas. (antiguo-pintoresco; famoso-antiguo; grande-medieval)
2. Cerca de Madrid hay montañas. (alto-verde; grande-empinado; seco-rocoso)
3. En Segovia conocí a unas muchachas. (bonito-español; simpático-atractivo; hermoso-hablador)
4. Fuimos a un hotel. (moderno-grande; viejo-pequeño; lujoso-turístico)
5. Miguel estudió las culturas. (francés-italiano; americano-indio)

181. Adjectives used as nouns

1. In Spanish, adjectives—and participles—are used as nouns when the noun they modify is deleted (see §§**67, 68**). English often supplies the nouns *man, woman,* or the pronoun *one.*

los vivos y los muertos	*the living and the dead*
la casa blanca y la amarilla	*the white house and the yellow one*
los versados en aquella ciencia	*those versed in that science*
los casados	*married people*

2. Predicate adjectives and participles are often used in Spanish as equivalent to adverbs or adverb phrases in English.

Vivían contentos.	*They lived contentedly.*
Corrimos veloces.	*We ran swiftly.*
Gritaron asustadas.	*They shouted in alarm.*

182. Adjective phrases

Spanish usually has recourse to prepositional phrases to render *(a)* adjectives of material, *(b)* the adjectival element in compounds of the type *sewing machine* (see §**169**).

a. **un banco de piedra**	*a stone bench*
un reloj de plata	*a silver watch*
b. **la telegrafía sin hilos**	*wireless telegraphy, radio*
una espada con puño de oro	*a gold-hilted sword*
un sombrero de ala ancha	*a broad-brimmed hat*

183. Diminutives

Diminutive endings may be used to strengthen adjectives, participles, and adverbs, especially in popular speech (see §**170**).

Vuelvo en seguidita.	*I am coming right back.*
El problema es dificililllo.	*The problem is difficult.*
Entraron callandito.	*They came in noiselessly.*
El niño estaba dormidito.	*The child was sleeping sweetly.*

TRANSLATION A

1. She is a dreamer. 2. The landlady of the boardinghouse was a very saving woman. 3. This theatre always presents the best pictures. 4. The dean and his wife were very courteous to us. 5. That child *(fem.)* is [an] awful **(muy)** cry-baby. 6. How handsome and healthy-looking she is. 7. The silk stockings were very inferior to the ones she bought the last time. 8. She belongs to one of the feminist associations. 9. Did you see him?—Whom?—That fellow who was looking for you. 10. The joke was not a bit funny. 11. The costumes and the scenery are splendid. 12. The high mountains of northern Spain are covered with snow the greater

part of the year. 13. Her black eyes and dark complexion made her pass for a Spanish woman. 14. The comical adventures of Don Quixote have inspired many great writers. 15. The blind man plays the piano in a downtown café. 16. The blue Mediterranean bathes the Valencian coast. 17. That yellow building is the town hall. The doorway is a good example of plateresque art. 18. The immense plains of Texas resemble greatly the landscape of central Spain. 19. Napoleon died in the remote island of Saint Helena. 20. Merry England, green Ireland, sweet France, and wide Castile have been sung by many poets. 21. Mr. and Mrs. Moncada have a fine collection of old tapestries. Their house is a real antique shop. 22. The excessive speed of the car was the cause of the collision. 23. Vast Russia is a country half European, half Asiatic. 24. Gothic architecture is the most glorious expression of the Middle Ages. 25. The comedy has three principal characters: a wealthy businessman, a clever stenographer, and a very funny newspaperman who comes to the office. 26. I want you to meet my new partner, Mr. Galindo. 27. It was a dark moonless night. After various incidents we finally arrived at the inn. 28. This blessed fireplace never works. 29. What a predicament! 30. Poor old man! 31. Cadiz and Malaga are the most ancient Spanish cities. 32. He is a tall, thin man with a blond mustache. 33. The solitary and melancholy moon shed its dim light on the rough stones of the old castle. 34. We were the last ones to (in) arrive. 35. Those favored by fortune seldom think of the less fortunate. 36. They were talking excitedly. 37. Have you any pipe tobacco? 38. Some of my travelling companions were Europeans; others, Americans. 39. I don't like fresh-water fish. 40. It was very cold. I had a couple of woollen blankets on my bed. 41. Let's go slowly *(dim)*. 42. They were waiting for me impatiently. 43. She is a very pretty little English girl.

II

184. Agreement of adjectives *(cont.)*

When two or more adjectives modify a plural noun in a distributive sense, they remain in the singular.

los tomos primero y segundo	*the first and second volumes*
las literaturas francesa y española	*French and Spanish literatures*

185. Apocope of adjectives *(cont.)*

Santo is not apocopated before names beginning with **To-** or **Do-**.

Santo Tomás[2]	*Saint Thomas*
Santo Domingo[2]	*Saint Dominick*

[2]The forms **San Tomás, San Tomé, San Domingo,** etc. are occasionally found as relics of a former usage.

186. Adjectives used as nouns *(cont.)*

Spanish uses the adjective as noun—in contrast to English—in the following constructions: *(a)* in partitive and superlative expressions of the type *one of the . . . and of the . . . kind (sort,* etc.), and *(b)* in appositional phrases introduced by **de** ("genitive of apposition"). This latter construction is much more frequent in Spanish than in English, and may be extended to nouns.

a. **una calle de las céntricas**	*one of the central streets*
un amigo de los que tengo en España	*of one of the friends I have in Spain*
vino del más caro	*wine of the most expensive kind*
de lo mejor y más granado	*of the finest and most select kind*

NOTE. This construction is often used as equivalent to the absolute superlative: **una noche de las más hermosas** *a most beautiful night.*

EJERCICIOS

Cámbiense las frases siguientes según el modelo: **Pasan por una calle de las calles céntricas.** → **Pasan por una calle de las céntricas.**

1. Fuimos a visitar un castillo de los castillos más antiguos.
2. El guardia era un hombre de los hombres que parecen ser parte del país.
3. Nos mostró un libro medieval de los libros que tenía en un aposento.
4. Luego nos invitó a probar un vino del vino típico de la región.
5. Regresamos por unas montañas de las montañas altas de la región.

b. **el bueno de D. Diego**	*good old D. Diego*
la tonta de mi suegra	*that fool of a mother-in-law of mine*
¡qué egoísmo de hijo!	*what a selfish son!*

EJERCICIOS

Cámbiense las frases siguientes según el modelo: **Mi suegra es tonta y no sabe nada.** → **La tonta de mi suegra no sabe nada.**

1. Román es pobre y tiene que trabajar todo el día.
2. La criada es chismosa y repite todo lo que oye.
3. Mi tío era un santo y no podía creer mal de nadie.
4. Carlos es un idiota y va a estropearlo todo.
5. La muchacha es un encanto y roba todos los corazones.

187. Position of adjectives *(cont.)*

1. Since the position of the adjective is so flexible in Spanish, it is frequently employed as a rhetorical device or stylistic weapon. Any displacement of the adjective from its normal position gives it a rhetorical or emotional stress, in short, a subjective value.

¡Terrible vicio es la ingratitud!	*Ungratefulness is a terrible vice.*
Asomaba el sol por el hispano horizonte.	*The sun was rising over the Spanish horizon.*
Una mirada de sus negros ojos y estoy perdido.	*A glance from her black eyes and I am lost.*
El dulce, amoroso, romántico canto del ruiseñor.	*The sweet, amorous, romantic song of the nightingale.*
La inglesa costumbre de tomar el té.	*The English custom of having tea.*
Paseaba dedicado a sus nocturnas meditaciones.	*He strolled along, wrapped up in his nocturnal meditations.*
Interrumpió su oficinesca labor.	*He interrupted his bureaucratic labors.*
Sus fieros bigotes y enorme calva producían cómico contraste.	*His fierce mustache and his enormous bald spot produced a comic contrast.*

188. Summary of adjective position

POST-POSITION	PRE-POSITION
Differentiation	No differentiation
Divided concept	Single (undivided) concept
Objective value	Subjective value (preconception; rhetorical, lyric, comic, etc., effect).

189. Compound adjectives

There are two general patterns for the formation of compound adjectives in Spanish: *(a)* the double adjective, the first part of which takes the Latin form ending in **o**, and *(b)* those compounded of a noun and adjective, in which the connecting vowel is **i**.

a. **anglosajón**	*Anglo-Saxon*
hispanoamericano	*Hispanic American*
francoitaliano	*Franco-Italian*
políticorreligioso	*politico-religious*

b. **ojinegro**	*black-eyed*
verdinegro	*black-green*
puntiagudo	*sharp-pointed*

190. Prefixes

The intensifying prefixes **re-** **(rete-,** **requete-)** and **archi-** are used colloquially with adjectives and participles: **re-** (etc.), is also used with adverbs.

¡Qué rebonito!	*How awfully cute!*
una cosa archisabidísima	*something absolutely everybody knows*
Habla muy requetebién.	*He is a perfectly marvellous speaker.*

TRANSLATION B

1. The nineteenth and twentieth centuries are the most interesting in human history. 2. It was a sailboat of the sort that are seen in the Mediterranean. 3. We went to one of those [country] town fairs. 4. This is one of the best of his descriptions. 5. He gave him a good, sound scolding. 6. The [old] gossip of a cook . . . 7. Poor D. Alejandro! 8. What a silly *(noun)* article! 9. What a charming *(noun)* girl! 10. It was a marvellous *(noun)* landscape. 11. The lonely, distant barking of a dog added a mysterious note to the scene. 12. The burning African sun blinded the weary travellers. 13. He has the disagreeable habit of talking in a very loud voice. 14. The wounded animal gave a sad cry. 15. This is an incredible thing *(reverse order)*. 16. Those were unforgettable days. 17. Who is that red-haired [girl]? 18. Medieval Hispano-Arabic literature was very rich in scientific and philosophic works. 19. The musical murmur of the pine trees calmed our spirits. 20. As we rested, we listened to the animated and graceful rhythm of Spanish folk music. 21. The repeated visits of his insistent creditors began to worry him. 22. The sweet, juicy, golden oranges of Valencia always remind me of my trip to the Levant. 23. The peasant wiped his sweaty brow. 24. In a quiet little town of the province, far from the noisy and feverish bustle of the city, not long ago there lived a strange old man.

III

VERBS AND IDIOMS

Venir (§263) *to come, suit, agree.* **¡Venga!** *Let's have it! Give (bring) it here!*
1. Don't come to me with gossip! 2. Come around (here) whenever you can! 3. It has to be done, come what may (come). 4. What is that for? (**¿a qué viene**

eso?) 5. The news is (comes) in today's paper. 6. He is (comes) very sick. 7. They were (came away) enthusiastic over **(con)** the speech. 8. He came in **(de)** uniform. 9. I have been telling you so for **(hace)** a long time. 10. Your present suits me to a T **(al pelo).** 11. Shake! **(¡venga esa mano!)** 12. Give the money [here]! 13. It amounts to **(viene a ser)** the same [thing]. 14. That's beside the point **(no viene a cuento).** 15. His family had come down in the world **(venir a menos).**

Traer(se) (§261) *to bring (with), carry (with), have.*
1. Bring me the coffee at once. 2. I didn't bring my bathing suit with me. 3. Bring your brother along. 4. They brought orders from the governor. 5. Does the dictionary have this word? 6. His conduct has me very worried. 7. The result doesn't worry me at all **(me trae sin cuidado).** 8. The problem is a real one **(se las trae).** 9. Do you have any money?

Constar (impers.) *to be known (clear) to one;* **constar de** *to consist of, be contained in.*
1. I want it known (let it be clear) that this plan is not mine. 2. I know *(impers.)* he is in Madrid. 3. The volume consists of some 400 pages. 4. These sentences are not (contained in) in the last edition.

chapter seventeen

Adverbs and expressions of comparison

I

191. Formation of adverbs and adverbial phrases

1. Adverbs of manner are formed by suffixing **-mente** (compare English suffix *-ly*) to the feminine singular of adjectives (**§16**). When two or more adjectives connected by a conjunction are so used, **-mente** is added only to the last adjective.

Trabajaba lenta y pacientemente.	*He worked slowly and patiently.*
Le contestó amable, pero enérgicamente.	*He answered him kindly but firmly.*

2. Equivalent to adverbs in **-mente** are adverbial phrases formed by *(a)* the preposition **con** (or **sin**)+noun and *(b)* the phrase **de una manera (modo)**+adjective.

a. **Viene a vernos con frecuencia.**	*He comes to see us frequently.*
b. **Habla de una manera muy confusa.**	*He talks in a very confused way.*

192. Position of adverbs

Adverbs usually stand close to the verb they modify. They come first in the sentence much more frequently in Spanish than in English.

Pronto sabremos el resultado.	*We shall soon find out the result.*
Después hablaremos de eso.	*We will talk about that later.*
Abajo está su hermano.	*Your brother is downstairs.*

193. Special uses of certain adverbs

1. **Ahora** means *(a) now*, while **ya** may mean *(b) now* or *already*—with present tenses, *(c) already* or *just*—with past tenses, *(d) later*—with future tenses. *(e)* **Ya** is used colloquially to indicate to someone that one understands or agrees with what is being said.

a. **Ahora viven en México.**	*They are now living in Mexico.*
b. **Ya vienen los bomberos.**	*The firemen are coming now.*
Ya están aquí.	*They are already here.*
c. **Ya se lo he dicho.**	*I have already told him.*
Ya he terminado.	*I have just finished.*
d. **Ya se lo contaré a Ud.**	*I will tell you later.*
Ya verá Ud.	*You'll see.*
e. **Tenemos que hacer lo que quiere. En fin, se trata de un amigo.—Ya, ya.**	*We have to do what he wants. After all, he's a friend.—Of course.*
Soy representante de la casa editorial.—¡Ah, ya!	*I'm a representative of the publishing house.—Oh, yes!*

NOTE. **Ya no** = *no longer:* **ya no viven aquí** *they no longer live here.*

2. **Todavía** and **aún** mean *yet, still.*

¿Todavía están Uds. aquí?	*Are you still here?*
No estoy bien aún.	*I am not well yet.*

NOTE. **Seguir (§133)** is often used in this sense: **sigue enfermo** *he is still sick.*

3. Equivalents of *Then.*

Entonces means *(a) then* in the sense of *at that moment* or *in that case;* **pues** (or **pues entonces**) means *(b) well then, in that case, but;* **luego** means *(c) immediately afterwards* or *consequently;* **después** *(d)* is *afterwards* (more general).

a. **Entonces oímos un gran ruido.**	*Then* (at the moment) *we heard a great noise.*
No me gusta ese ejemplo.—(Pues) entonces busca tú otro.	*I don't like that example.—Well, then you find another.*
b. **Pues no lo encuentro.**	*But I don't (can't) find it.*
c. **¿No resulta? Luego dejémoslo.**	*Doesn't it work? Then* (therefore) *let's abandon it.*
Luego salieron a la calle.	*Then* (thereupon) *they went out.*
d. **Y después se fueron al teatro.**	*And afterwards they went to the theatre.*

4. The noun **tiempo** *time* is usually expressed in Spanish when rendering the English *long (time)* and related expressions.

¿Se queda Ud. aquí (por) mucho tiempo?	*Are you going to be there long?*
más tiempo	*longer*
demasiado tiempo	*too long*
¿cuánto tiempo?	*how long?*
But: **hace poco**	*a short while ago, (for) a short time*

NOTE. **Rato** *while* (duration not exceeding a few hours) is similarly used: **¿Lleva Ud. aquí mucho rato?** *Have you been here long?*

194. The general or absolute superlative

An indefinite or general degree of superlativeness, corresponding to the English *a* (not *the*) *most*, *very*, *highly*, *exceedingly*, is expressed in Spanish by suffixing **-ísimo, -ísima** to adjectives and adverbs. This usage is very frequent in Spanish. **Muchísimo** (not **muy mucho**) is the regular form for *very much.*

unos montes altísimos	*some very high mountains*
una función aburridísima	*a most tiresome performance*
lentísimamente	*most (exceedingly, very) slowly*

NOTE. Adjectives and adverbs ending in **-co, -go,** and **-z** show the requisite orthographic changes: **cerquísima** *very near*, **larguísimo** *very long*, **felicísimo** *most happy*; those ending in **-ble** retain the **i** of the original Latin: **noble, nobilísimo.**

195. The specific or comparative superlative

The definite or specific comparison of superiority or inferiority between two or more members of the same class is rendered in Spanish by placing the adverbs **más** *more, (the) most* and **menos** *less, (the) least* before adjectives and adverbs.

Ella es más lista que él.	*She is more clever than he.*
Él es el menos inteligente de la familia.	*He is the least intelligent of the family.*
Iban más de prisa que nosotros.	*They were going faster than we.*

EJERCICIOS

Combínense las frases siguientes según el modelo: **María es lista pero Luis es más listo. → Luis es más listo que María.**

1. Paco es rico pero Rafael es más rico.
2. Nuestra destinación está lejos pero la suya está más lejos.
3. Este país está atrasado pero aquel país está más atrasado.
4. El texto de José es interesante pero nuestro texto es más interesante.

Sustitúyanse las palabras entre paréntesis por las palabras subrayadas:

5. Jorge[a] es el más inteligente[b] de la clase[c].

a. (Josefa, tú y Carlos, Roberto, las dos amigas)
b. (rico, divertido, serio, alegre)
c. (familia, mundo, grupo, escuela)

196. Irregular forms of the comparative superlative

The following forms show irregularities:

mucho—más	*more, (the) most*
poco—menos	*less, (the) least*
bueno, bien—mejor	*better, (the) best*
malo, mal—peor	*worse, (the) worst*
grande—más grande or mayor	*larger, (the) largest; older, (the) oldest*
pequeño—más pequeño or **menor**	*smaller, (the) smallest; younger, (the) youngest*

Más grande and **más pequeño** refer strictly to size, while **mayor** and **menor** usually, although not exclusively, refer to age (of persons).

Habla inglés mejor que yo.	*He speaks English better than I.*
Su mujer es mayor que él.	*His wife is older than he.*

NOTE. **Más bien** means *rather.*

197. Uses of *que* and *de* in comparisons

1. *Than* introducing a phrase or clause not containing a finite verb is rendered *(a)* by **que,** or *(b)* by **de** before numerals.

a. **Más vale reír que llorar.**	*It is better to laugh than to cry.*

b. **Este cuadro vale más de cinco mil dólares.** — *This picture is worth more than five thousand dollars.*

NOTE. **No . . . más que** = *only* (with verb expressed): **no tiene más que doce años** *he is only twelve years old.* It may replace **sólo** or **solamente,** except when the verb is not expressed.

EJERCICIOS

Sustitúyanse las palabras entre paréntesis por las palabras subrayadas:

Alberto gastó[a] más (menos) de cien dólares[b].
a. (ganar, perder, tener)
b. (mil pesetas, cincuenta pesos, quinientos francos)

2. But when the *than* clause contains a finite verb, *than* is rendered in Spanish by the full forms *(a) than what* **de lo que** or (*b*) *than that (those, the ones) which* **del que, de la que,** etc. **De lo que is** used when the antecedent is an adjective or adverb; the inflected forms are used when it is a noun.

a. **Las dificultades eran más serias de lo que habíamos creído.** — *The difficulties were more serious than we had thought.*
Tiene más de lo que necesita. — *He has more than he needs.*
Tiene más de lo (que es) necesario. — *He has more than (what is) necessary.*

b. **El asunto tiene más dificultades de las que habíamos previsto.** — *The affair has more difficulties than* (the specific ones which) *we had foreseen.*

3. In superlative expressions Spanish uses **de** where English uses *in.* In this type of sentence **mejor, peor, mayor** and **menor,** like **bueno, malo,** etc., always precede the nouns they modify, except when they stress differentiation.

Es el peor estudiante de la clase. — *He is the worst student in the class.*
La mayor alegría de su vida. — *The greatest joy in his life.*
But: **Mi hija menor.** — *My youngest daughter.*

EJERCICIOS

Sustitúyanse las palabras entre paréntesis por las palabras subrayadas:

Mi padre nos dio más libros[a] de los que queríamos[b].
a. (dinero, pesetas, carne, pesos)
b. (pedir, hacernos falta, anticipar)

198. Comparisons of equality

Comparisons of equality are rendered by **tanto** and **como** according to the following scheme: *(a)* **tanto como** *as much as* after verbs, *(b)* **tan . . . como** *so, as . . . as* with adjectives and adverbs, *(c)* **tanto** (inflected) . . . **como** *as much (many) . . . as* with nouns, expressed or understood.

a. **Gasta tanto como gana.**	*He spends as much as he earns.*
b. **Es tan generoso como su padre.**	*He is as generous as his father.*
Tan pronto como posible.	*As soon as possible.*
c. **Este piso tiene tantas habitaciones como el otro.**	*This apartment has as many rooms as the other one.*

EJERCICIOS

Sustitúyanse las palabras entre paréntesis por las palabras subrayadas:

1. Aquella iglesia[a] no es tan grande[b] como la otra.
   a. (casa, museo, pueblo, lugar)
   b. (antiguo, interesante, pintoresco, hermoso)
2. A mí me hace falta tanto dinero como a Ud. (plata, libertad, suerte, pesetas, vino)
3. Tomás toca la guitarra tan bien como los gitanos. (mal, admirablemente, delicadamente, seriamente)

TRANSLATION A

1. We were all talking rapidly and heatedly. 2. He expressed himself very accurately. 3. Then she entered noiselessly. 4. We are going to the fair tomorrow. 5. I have all my books upstairs. 6. What are you going to do now? 7. The show has already begun. 8. The parade is starting now. 9. Are you coming with us?—No, I can't now. I'll see you later in the café. 10. He no longer writes to us. 11. Are you still living in the same house?—Yes, we haven't moved yet. 12. I don't want to stay too long in this town.—Well, then, we will leave whenever you want. 13. Have you been here long?—Only ten minutes. 14. It was an extremely hot day. 15. She has the **(unos)** blackest eyes! 16. My brother is [a] better mechanic than I. 17. He likes cats better **(más)** than dogs. 18. I have paid more for the furniture than it is worth. 19. He has more than five thousand dollars (of) income. 20. There are more students in the course than we had anticipated. 21. He buys more books than he can read. 22. He is kind as [he is] intelligent. 23. She is younger than her sister. 24. They have only a daughter. 25. This desk is larger than mine.

26. These mountains are not so high as those in the West. 27. Have you seen many plays this season?—Not as many as I should like. 28. There were more than one hundred guests at the wedding. 29. The weather was exceedingly fine. 30. In the morning we went to the bank, then to the consulate, and afterwards to the station.

II

199. Special uses of certain adverbs *(cont.)*

1. Adverbial phrases of time and direction usually follow nouns. The English *-wards* is usually rendered by **hacia**+adverb. (Occasionally **para** is also found.)

años después	*years after(wards)*	**calle abajo**	*down the street*
hacia atrás	*backwards*	**hacia aquí**	*this way* (towards here)
hacia adelante	*forward*		
para adelante	*forward*	**cuesta arriba**	*up (the) hill*

EJERCICIOS

Pónganse las palabras entre paréntesis en los espacios en las frases siguientes:

1. El viejo seguía ______.
2. Los guardias corrieron ______.
3. Alfredo fue ______.

(hacia adelante, para atrás, hacia abajo, calle abajo, cuesta arriba, hacia aquí)

2. Adverbial phrases of manner may be formed *(a)* by **a la**+feminine adjectives of nationality (**§164,** note) and *(b)* by **a**+the feminine plural of adjectives and participles.

a. **a la francesa**	*in the French style*
b. **a ciegas**	*blindly*
a sabiendas	*wittingly*
a gatas	*on all fours*
a escondidas	*on the sly*
a hurtadillas	*stealthily*
a oscuras	*in the dark*
a solas	*alone*
a pie juntillas	*with feet together; firmly*
(a pie juntillo, a pies juntillos)	

EJERCICIOS

Sustitúyanse las palabras entre paréntesis por las palabras subrayadas:

Me gusta la carne[a] a la francesa[b].
a. (el chocolate, la ensalada, el postre, el pescado)
b. (española, italiana, alemana, mexicana)

3. Certain adverbs may be used as nouns.

en aquel entonces	*at that time*

4. **Recientemente** *recently, newly* is shortened to **recién** before past participles.

el recién llegado	*the newcomer*
los recién casados	*the newlyweds*

200. Intensification

Following are some of the more frequent means of intensifying words and phrases in Spanish: *(a)* by the adverbs **ya, mismo, bien, tan,** and **puro;** *(b)* by repetition of adverbs; *(c)* by the absolute superlative and, in colloquial speech, by the diminutive of adverbs; *(d)* by introducing phrases with **si** (§123, 3), **que, sí que,** or **es que.**

a. **¡Ya caigo!**	*I see!*
¡Ya lo creo!	*I should say so!*
ahora mismo	*right now*
ayer mismo	*just yesterday*
Bien creí que me moría.	*I surely thought I was dying.*
¡Y ellos tan contentos!	*And weren't they happy!*
No me puedo mover de puro cansado.	*I can't move for sheer exhaustion.*
b. **casi casi**	*almost*
así así	*so-so*
c. **lejísimos**	*very far*
en seguidita	*right away*
¡callandito!	*hush! hush!*
d. **¡Si ya lo sé!**	*Why, of course, I know it!*
¡Que no he sido yo!	(I insist) *it wasn't I!*
¡Entonces sí que nos lucíamos!	*We certainly would be in a fix then!*
¡Eso sí que no!	*By no means that!*
¿Es que no le gusta?	*But don't you really like it?*

NOTE. In Spanish America **no más** is frequently used as an intensifier *(just, right)*: **¡Pase Ud. no más!** *Come (go) right in!*

EJERCICIOS

Intensifíquense las palabras subrayadas según el modelo: **Vamos ahora.** → **Vamos ahora mismo. Trabajamos mucho.** → **Sí que trabajamos mucho.**

1. Nos vio y entonces empezó a correr.
2. Margarita habla mucho.
3. Fui a verlo ayer.
4. No fue él quien lo hizo.
5. Me llamó aquí.

201. Absolute superlative *(cont.)*

There are certain irregular forms of the absolute superlative, relics of the original Latin. (For a complete list, see Appendix, §**272**.)

202. The comparative superlative *(cont.)*

1. No formal distinction exists in Spanish between the comparative and superlative degrees.[1] The context suffices to show the meaning. The definite article is used only when necessary for the meaning, *i.e.* in certain cases of apposition.

El hombre de más mérito.	*The man of most merit.*
¡Pero yo . . . criatura más inútil!	*But I am such a (the most) useless creature!*
Mi hija la menor.	*My younger—or youngest—daughter* (lit. my daughter the youngest one of the lot).

2. The following special uses should be noted: *(a)* **más bueno** and **más malo** are used when moral qualities are involved, *(b)* they may also be used as substitutes in exclamations for the absolute superlative; *(c)* **lo** is used with the superlative of adverbs when followed by an expression of possibility; *(d) most of* is either **la mayor parte de** or **los (las) más de** (see §**167**); *(e)* **nada más** is used colloquially as equivalent to **no más . . . que.**

a. **Es más bueno que el pan.**	*He is as good as gold.*
Es más malo que Barrabás.	*He is more wicked than Barabbas.*
b. **¡Es el (un) hombre más bueno!**	*He is such a kind man!*

[1]Compare the perfectly natural tendency to say in colloquial English *the least of the two.*

c. **Lo más pronto posible.** — *As soon as possible.*

d. **La mayor parte (los más) de los turistas desembarcaron en Cádiz.** — *Most of the tourists landed in Cadiz.*

NOTE. **Los más** may also be used adjectivally: **las más veces** *most of the time.*

e. **Tiene doce años nada más.** — *He is only twelve years old.*

NOTE. In Spanish America the colloquial form is **no más,** which is used very frequently.

203. Than *(cont.)*

1. The **de lo que, del que,** etc., construction[2] offers the following special cases: *(a)* **de lo que** may be used instead of the inflected forms in order to impart an indefinite value to the noun antecedent; *(b)* if the antecedent of **el que** is the subject, not the object, of the preceding verb, **que,** not **de,** is used for *than; (c)* sometimes especially in colloquial and proverbial expressions, **que** alone is used, if the two finite verbs are directly contrasted.

a. **Este asunto tiene más importancia de lo que se creía.** — *This affair has more importance than was thought.*

b. **Este plan ofrece más ventajas de las que se ven.** — *This plan offers more advantages than can be seen.*

Este plan ofrece más ventajas que el que nos propuso ayer. — *This plan offers more advantages than the one which you proposed yesterday.*

Esta revista es más interesante que la que leímos ayer. — *This magazine is more interesting than the one we read yesterday.*

c. **Pescador de caña, más pierde que gana.** — *The man who fishes with a rod loses more than he gains.*

Peor está que estaba. — *He's worse off than he was before.*

2. **Que que** *than that* may be *(a)* amplified to **que el que** or **que no que,** or *(b)* reduced to simple **que** (since both **que's** are conjunctions).

a. **Es mejor que lo piense que que** (or **que el que, que no que**) **lo diga.** — *It's better for you to think so than to say so.*

NOTE. **Que no que** is used only when direct contrast is involved, as above.

b. **¡Qué más quisiera yo que me dejaran la criatura!** — *What more could I ask for than that they should let me have the child?*

[2]These forms are used instead of simple **que** when the finite verb is expressed because **que** cannot function both as the conjunction *than* and as the relative pronoun object of the verb, since the relative cannot be omitted, as in English.

204. *Tanto*, *cuanto*, and other expressions of comparison

1. Following are some special uses of **tanto, cuanto,** and related forms: *(a)* **tanto** (not **tan**) is used with comparatives, *(b)* **tan** may be omitted in combination with **como,** *(c) as, like,* is **como,** while *the same as, just like* is **lo mismo que, igual que,** *(d)* **tanto como** is occasionally replaced by **tanto cuanto,** *(e)* **cual** is found for **como** only in archaic or poetic style.

a. **Tanto peor para ellos.**	*So much the worse for them.*
b. **Es claro como el agua.**	*It is (just as) clear as water.*
c. **El enfermo está lo mismo que ayer.**	*The patient is just the same as yesterday.*
d. **Gasta tanto cuanto gana.**	*He spends as much as (all that) he earns.*
e. **Su frente cual borrascoso cielo . . .**	*His brow, like a tempestuous sky . . .*

2. *(a) The more . . . the more* is expressed in Spanish by **cuanto más . . . (tanto) más,** *(b) more and more* by **cada vez más,** and *(c) all the more . . . because* by **tanto más . . . cuanto que.**

a. **Cuanto más se habla, menos se piensa.**	*The more one talks, the less one thinks.*

NOTE. **Mientras** may be substituted for **cuanto: mientras más estudio, más aprendo** *the more I study the more I learn.*

b. **Estaba cada vez más preocupado.**	*He became more and more worried.*
Hablaba cada vez más confusamente.	*He spoke more and more confusedly.*
Andaba cada vez más lentamente.	*He walked slower and slower.*
c. **Es Ud. injusto para con él, tanto más cuanto que no sabe Ud. nada de cierto.**	*You are all the more unjust toward him because you know nothing certain.*

TRANSLATION B

1. We were walking uphill. 2. I had seen him two weeks before. 3. We were going half and half in the purchase. 4. I don't know his name; they simply call him John. 5. Here I have a few books just published. 6. I will surely write to them tomorrow. 7. Her hair seemed blue from sheer black(ness). 8. The bullring is quite near.—Well, then, let's go on (a) foot. 9. That certainly would be difficult. 10. Unless the express is late we are going to miss it.—Then we certainly shall miss

it. 11. He has gone *(refl.)* to live in the country as far as possible away from business. 12. He has more pride than it seemed. 13. This map has more details than the one I have just bought. 14. It is better for him to stay than to come with us. 15. If they don't want to accept, so much the worse for them. 16. He is [as] tame as a lamb. 17. Everything was the same as when we left. 18. The more I hear this music, the more I like it. 19. The more you think about it, the more difficult it will seem to you. 20. He is getting fatter and fatter.—Well, I haven't noticed it. 21. The sea was getting rougher and rougher. 22. I think all this is inopportune, all the more because we haven't been invited to express our opinion. 23. The apartment is much larger than the one we had last year. 24. The morning train doesn't make as many stops as the evening train. 25. This bulb doesn't give as much light as the other one.

III

VERBS AND IDIOMS

Llevar *to take (to), bear, wear, have, be* (indicating duration of time); **llevarse** *to take away, carry off, get along together.* **(Llevar** implies **ir, traer** implies **venir,** while **tomar** implies either reception or choice.)

1. Take me to the circus! 2. He has taken my overcoat [away with] him. 3. The flood carried away the bridge. 4. He leads a very healthful life. 5. He was wearing a top hat and [carrying a] cane. 6. The job took me two hours. 7. The author has already written two acts. 8. How many years have you been here? 9. My brother is **(me lleva)** four years [older than I]. 10. He carried out **(a cabo)** the orders of the general. 11. You are always opposing **(llevar la contraria)** me. 12. The two get along very well together. 13. I was greatly disappointed **(llevarse un gran chasco).**

Subir *to go (come, carry, bring, take, put) up, rise, get on* (a train, etc.); **bajar** *to go (come, carry, bring, take, put) down, lower, get off* (a train, etc.). (Note that these two verbs (also **entrar**) are both transitive and intransitive.) (When used intransitively and without adverb complement, **subir arriba** and **bajar abajo** are heard colloquially.)

1. Go up (down) to my room and bring my my hat. 2. The price of commodities has gone up (come down) recently. 3. The car went up (down) the hill in high **(directa).** 4. Please tell them to bring (up, down, in) my breakfast. 5. We will have to *(impers.)* call a porter to carry (bring, take) our baggage (up, down). 6. This year they have raised (lowered) his (the) salary (for him) twice. 7. We must get on (off) the **(al, del)** train now. 8. The tide is coming in (going out). 9. We climbed the tower to see the view. 10. Success has gone to his **(subírsele)** head. 11. Lower your voice[s]; there is someone **(un)** sick in the house.

chapter eighteen

Indefinites and numerals

I

205. Indefinites

Following are the more common indefinites in Spanish:

1. **Alguien, alguno, algo; nadie, ninguno, nada**—see §§**98, 99.**
2. **Mucho** *much* (sing.), *many* (pl.) and **poco** *little* (sing.), *few* (pl.) are both adjectives and pronouns. *A little (of)* is **un poco (de).** *Very much (many)* is **muchísimo.** These forms are likewise used as adverbs. **Mucho** is shortened to **muy** before adverbs and adjectives. *Too, too much (many)* is **demasiado.**

Tengo muchos libros pero pocos buenos.	*I have many books but few good ones.*
Tenía poco dinero pero mucha suerte.	*He had little money but a great deal of luck.*
Déme Ud. un poquito de eso.	*Give me a little of that* (kind).
Es demasiado caro.	*It is too expensive.*

NOTE. **Mucho,** not **muy,** is used when it stands alone: **¿Está muy ocupado?—Sí, mucho.** *Is he very busy?—Yes, very.*

3. **Otro** *another, other, else,* and **tal** *such (a)* are both adjectives and pronouns, but **cierto** *a certain* and **semejante** *such (a)* are always adjectives.

otra vez	*another time, again.*
otra cosa	*another thing, something else*
¿Qué dicen los otros?	*What do the others say?*
esto y lo otro	*this and that*

NOTE. *Nothing else* is **nada más.** *The others* in the sense of *the rest, the remaining* is **los (las, lo) demás, los restantes.**

No hay tal cosa.	*There is no such thing.*
Cierta persona de influencia.	*A certain influential person.*
¿Ha visto semejante majadero?	*Have you ever seen such a blockhead?*
una cosa cierta	*an assured thing*
una locura semejante	*such a piece of folly*

NOTE. The indefinite article is used with **cierto** and **semejante** when they follow the noun.

4. **Cada** *each* is an invariable adjective, but **ambos** (or **los dos**) *both* and **todo** *every, all* are both adjectives and pronouns. *Everybody* is **todo el mundo** and *everything* is **todo** (neuter). **Todo** in the sense of *all* requires the definite article between it and the noun; when **todo** is direct object of the verb the pronoun **lo** must also be used.

cada semana	*each week*
cada uno, cada cual	*each one*
Esto basta para los dos.	*This is enough for both (of us).*
Tiene ambas piernas rotas.	*He has both legs broken.*
todo hombre	*every man*
todas las mujeres	*all the women*
todo el día	*all day (long)*
Hay para todos.	*There is enough for all.*
Lo tengo todo aquí.	*I have everything here.*

NOTE. In translating *every* in time expressions, **todos** is collective and **cada** is distributive and more emphatic: **cada noche** *every night (night after night)*, **todas las noches** *every night (all the nights)*. The latter construction is the more frequent.

5. **Cualquiera** *any, anyone, anybody (whatsoever, at all)* is both adjective and pronoun. It loses its final **-a,** when it precedes; when it follows, the indefinite article is used with the noun. The plural is **cualesquier(a).**

cualquier cosa	*anything (at all)*
una persona cualquiera	*anybody (at all)*
¿Cuál prefiere Ud.?—Cualquiera.	*Which one do you prefer?—Any one.*
Eso cualquiera lo sabe.	*Anybody knows that.*

NOTE. The ordinary English pronoun *whatever* is either **lo que** (with subjunctive) or **cualquier cosa que** (emphatic): **haré lo que (cualquier cosa que) Vd. me diga** *I will do whatever (thing) you say.* The **que** is always required to introduce the following clause. The indicative is used when the meaning requires it: **cualquier cosa que hace, la hace bien** *whatever thing he does (do), he does well.*

6. *Somewhere, anywhere,* is **alguna parte** *nowhere,* **ninguna parte,** *everywhere* **todas partes.** Note that in Spanish the proper preposition must always be used with these forms.

La encuentro en todas partes.	*I meet her everywhere.*
No voy a ninguna parte.	*I am not going anywhere.*

NOTE. In conversation especially, **lado** and **sitio** are sometimes used instead of **parte.**

EJERCICIOS

Sustitúyanse las palabras entre paréntesis por las palabras subrayadas:

1. Tiene bastantes libros. (pocos, muchos, demasiados)
2. No me traiga Ud. tales cuentos. (semejante, este)
3. Trabajo en la biblioteca todas las tardes. (cada, cualquier, mucho)
4. A él le gusta cualquier cosa. (todo, mucho, tal, poca)
5. Las llaves estarán en alguna parte. (ninguno, todo, cualquiera)
6. Todo el día jugamos al tenis. (tarde, mañana, semana)

206. The partitive or appositional *de*

In certain set expressions with the verbs **haber** and **tener,** a partitive or appositional **de** is introduced between the indefinites **algo, mucho, nada, ¿qué?, lo que,** and the adjective which follows.

¿Qué hay de nuevo?—Nada de particular.	*What's up?—Nothing special.*
Tiene algo (mucho) de inglés.	*He has something (a great deal) of the Englishman about him.*
lo que hay de dramático en ello	*the dramatic elements in the matter*

NOTE. Similarly, **hay de todo** *there are all kinds.*

EJERCICIOS

Sustitúyanse las palabras entre paréntesis por la palabra subrayada:

Hay algo de interés en este asunto. (poco, mucho, nada, ¿qué?)

207. Numerals

For a list of the cardinal and ordinal numerals, see **§279.**

1. The following peculiarities of the cardinal numbers are to be noted: *(a)* the composite forms **(dieciséis, veintiuno,** etc.) are more frequent in rendering 16 through 19, 21 through 29, while the compound forms **(treinta y**

uno, etc.) prevail from 31 on; *(b)* the irregular forms **quinientos, setecientos,** and **novecientos;** *(c)* **veintiuno, treinta y uno,** etc., and **doscientos, trescientos,** etc., are inflected for gender; *(d)* **un(o)** is omitted before **cien(to)** and **mil;** but *(e)* not before **millón** *million,* which, like **par** *pair* and **docena** *dozen,* is a noun and is construed with **de.**

a. **Veintidós hombres y treinta y tres mujeres.**	*22 men and 33 women*

NOTE. A written accent is required on **dieciséis, veintidós, veintitrés,** and **veintiséis.**

b. **Lo vendí en quinientas pesetas.**	*I sold it for 500 pesetas.*
c. **veintiuna páginas**	*21 pages*
novecientas libras	*900 pounds*
d. **cien soldados**	*100 soldiers*
¡Mil gracias!	*A thousand thanks!*
ciento cincuenta páginas	*150 pages*

NOTE. In colloquial speech **cien** is heard as a noun: **tengo unos cien** *I have about a hundred.*

e. **quinientos millones de pesetas**	*500,000,000 pesetas*
un millón de dólares	*a million dollars*

EXCEPTIONS: **millón y medio** *a million and a half;* **miles de personas** *thousands of people.*

2. The ordinals are inflected for gender and number. Above *tenth* they are usually replaced by the cardinals. Both ordinals and cardinals follow the noun if they indicate an individual member of an established series.

Leí las cien primeras páginas.	*I read the first hundred pages.*
Leí hasta la página ciento once.	*I read as far as page 111.*
Felipe Segundo; Alfonso Doce	*Philip II; Alfonso XII.*
el capítulo segundo	*the second chapter*

3. In dates the cardinals are regularly used with one exception: **primero.** In writing full dates the preposition **de** may be omitted.

¿Cuál es la fecha de hoy? **¿Qué fecha es hoy?** **¿A cuántos estamos?**	*What date is today?*
Hoy es el cinco de septiembre. **Estamos a cinco de septiembre.**	*Today is the 5th of September.*
But: **el primero de marzo**	*the first of March*
5 (de) septiembre (de) 1982.	*September 5, 1982.*

NOTE. In oral dates and in counting **mil** is always used: **mil ochocientos cincuenta** *1850.*

EJERCICIOS

Léase el párrafo siguiente y después contéstense las preguntas:

Simón acaba de recibir 2.500 pesetas de su padre. Luego vendió a su amigo Diego tres libros que ya no quería a 250 pesetas cada uno. En la Caja de Ahorros tenía depositadas 4.795 pesetas. Por la tarde fue al centro a comprar un regalo para su novia. Quería comprar a plazos un collar de perlas por 3.100 pesetas y dejó como depósito 900 pesetas. Al salir de la tienda vio que le habían multado en 150 pesetas por haber aparcado su auto en una zona azul.

1. ¿Cuánto dinero recibió por los libros?
2. ¿Cuánto tenía después de venderlos?
3. Cuánto tenía después de hacer el primer pago por el collar?
4. Al fin del día, ¿cuánto dinero tenía?
5. ¿Cuánto debía Simón?

Contéstense:

6. ¿Qué fecha es hoy? ¿A cuántos estamos?
7. ¿Cuál es la fecha del cumpleaños de Ud.?
8. ¿Cuál es la fecha del nacimiento de su padre?

TRANSLATION A

1. They were walking very slowly. 2. Give me a little water. 3. They have many relatives in Havana. 4. Do you like this suit?—Very much. 5. Let us talk about something else. 6. Ring again. 7. Do you want anything else?—No, thanks, nothing else. 8. Don't come to me with such stories. 9. I'll send you a check every month or if you prefer, every other month. 10. Each time the telephone rings, I have to go downstairs to the living room. 11. We have been playing tennis the whole morning. 12. I work every afternoon in the library. 13. He is satisfied with anything. 14. I'll bet you anything. 15. He'll arrive here any day. 16. This train doesn't stop anywhere until we get to Madrid. 17. The key must be here somewhere. 18. Have you any cigarettes left?—Yes, I have some. 19. Buy me [some] sugar and [some] coffee at the store. 20. Which one do you want?—Any one. 21. Come to see us any evening. 22. He has something of [the] missionary [about him]. 23. The little there is [in the way] of dialogue is the best thing in the book. 24. We translated the first two hundred lines without making a single mistake. 25. He had some five hundred dollars left after paying a few bills. 26. The feast of St. John is the 21st of June.

II

208. Indefinites *(cont.)* except those of quantity

1. *(a)* **Otro** usually precedes other adjectives, except **alguno**; *(b)* **ajeno** *of others, other people's* is the possessive corresponding to **otro**; *(c)* **sendos** (pl.) is the distributive adjective corresponding to **cada uno**; *(d)* **uno y otro (ni uno ni otro)** *both, either (neither)* are distributive, referring to a pair.

a. **esto y otras muchas cosas**	*This and many other things*
otros cien soldados	*another hundred soldiers*
algún (que) otro	*some (one or) other*
Viene por aquí alguna que otra vez.	*He drops in once in a while.*
b. **lo propio y lo ajeno**	*one's own property and that of other people*
c. **Los dos ancianos, sentados en sendas mecedoras . . .**	*The two old men, each seated in a rocking chair . . .*
d. **una y otra ribera del río**	*both (either) bank(s) of the river*
ni uno ni otro partido	*neither (of the two) party(ies)*

2. In colloquial speech *(a)* **cada** has acquired iterative—and hence emphatic —value and *(b)* **cualquiera** has taken on negative force.

a. **¡Le dió cada golpe . . .!**	*He gave him such a beating!* (blow after blow)
¡Oye uno cada historia!	*One hears all kinds of stories!*
¡Metiste cada pata!	*You really put your foot in it!*
b. **¡Cualquiera le hablaba!**	*Nobody could talk to him.*

NOTE. **Un cualquiera** (pl. **unos cualquieras**) is *an ordinary person, a nobody.*

3. Similar to **cualquiera** in meaning and form, but much less frequently used are the very emphatic *(a)* **quienquiera** *whoever*, *(b)* **dondequiera** *wherever* *(c)* **cuandoquiera** *whenever*, and *(d)* **comoquiera** *since, as* (see also **siquiera, §103**). The **que** must be used to introduce the following clause, which takes the indicative or the subjunctive according to the rules for adjective clauses.

a. **Diga a quienquiera que sea que no estoy en casa.**	*Tell whomever it may be that I am not at home.*

NOTE. *Whoever* is ordinarily **el que (quien)** followed by the subjunctive **(§118)**. *Whoever* in the sense of *every one who* is **todo el que: todo el que se encuentre en esas circunstancias** *whoever finds himself in that situation.*

b. **Por dondequiera que vamos.**	*Wherever we* (do) *go.*
Por dondequiera que vaya.	*Wherever he* (may) *goes.*
c. **Cuandoquiera que lo necesite.**	*Whenever you* (may) *need it.*
Tráigalo comoquiera que esté.	*Bring it just as it is* (may be).

4. Both *(a)* **un tal** *a certain* and *(b)* **el tal** *the aforesaid* are used of persons;[1] *(c)* **dicho** or **el referido** *said* and **determinado** *(a) certain* (known but unmentioned) are used of both persons and things; *(d)* **un no sé qué de** means *a certain* (indefinable) *air* (or *quality*) *of.*

a. **Hablamos con el dueño del garaje, un tal D. Facundo.**	*We had a conversation with the owner of the garage, a certain D. Facundo.*
b. **El tal señor era un hombre de muy mal humor.**	*The aforesaid gentleman was a very ill-humored man.*
c. **dicha señora**	*the said lady*
los referidos artículos	*the above-mentioned articles*
Anoche nos refirió determinada persona . . .	*Last night a certain party told us . . .*
d. **Esta música tiene un no sé qué de exótico.**	*This music has a certain exotic quality.*

5. Spanish possesses the following characteristic indefinite pronouns referring to persons: **Fulano** *Mr. So-and-so*, which may be used as a noun, and **Zutano, Mengano,** and **Perengano,** which are used only in series after **Fulano.**

Don Fulano de Tal y don Mengano de Cual	*John Doe and Richard Roe*
Fulano, Zutano y Mengano	*Tom, Dick, and Harry*
¿Quién es ese fulano?	*Who is that fellow?*

EJERCICIOS

Sustitúyanse las palabras entre paréntesis por las palabras subrayadas:

1. Ayer vimos la catedral y muchas otras <u>cosas</u>. (iglesias, lugares, puntos de interés)
2. Alguno que otro <u>muchacho</u> venía a saludarnos. (mujer, turista, guía, amigo)
3. <u>El tal</u>[a] <u>sujeto</u>[b] venía preparado a reñir.
   a. (dicho, referido)
   b. (señor, guardia, mujer)
4. ¿Conoce Ud. a Fulano, el que <u>fue a América</u>? (mató a su mujer, ganó el premio gordo en la lotería, vivía en la otra calle)

[1]**El tal** may be used in humorous style referring to things.

209. Indefinite expressions of quantity

1. In general, it may be said that the Spanish indefinites present more precise shades of meaning than their English equivalents (compare the different ways of rendering the vague and general English *some*, *any*, *certain*, *such*, *said*, etc.). This is especially true of indefinite expressions of quantity such as *(a)* **unos, unos cuantos, algunos,** and **varios,** *(b)* **unos pocos, un poco (poquito) de, un (algún) tanto, bastante.**

a. **Conocimos a unos españoles.**	*We met some Spaniards* (very general).
Conocimos a unos cuantos españoles.	*We met some* (a small number of) *Spaniards.*
Conocimos a algunos españoles.	*We met some* (a few) *Spaniards.*
Conocimos a varios españoles.	*We met several Spaniards.*

NOTE the decreasing order of indefiniteness in the above examples.

b. **¿Tiene Ud. muchos libros en su despacho?—Unos pocos.**	*Do you have many books in your study?—Just a few.*
Écheme un poquito más de café.	*Pour me a little more coffee.*
El artículo era un tanto insolente.	*The article was a bit* (somewhat) *insolent.*
Suspendieron a bastantes.	*Quite a few were "flunked".*

NOTE. In certain expressions **cuatro** (and less frequently **dos**) is used with indefinite value: **¡Señorito, cuatro palabras nada más!** *Please, sir, just a few words.* **Dos palabras al lector** *Preface* (a few words to the reader).

2. Indefinite expressions of collective meaning are **una porción de** *some, a number of,* **(una) gran parte, (un) gran número** *a great many,* **una serie de** *a series (collection) of.*

He comprado una porción de cosas antiguas.	*I have bought a number of antiques.*
En el andén había un gran número de extranjeros.	*A great many foreigners were on the platform.*
Gran parte de los pasajeros perecieron en el naufragio.	*A great many of the passengers perished in the shipwreck.*
¡Qué serie de disparates!	*What a mass of nonsense!*

NOTE. **Una barbaridad, la mar,** and similar expressions are used colloquially: **me gustó una barbaridad (la mar)** *I liked it immensely;* **tiene la mar de gracia** *it's awfully funny;* **una barbaridad de gente** *an awful crowd.*

3. **Tanto** and **mucho** may be used collectively in the singular (see **§167**, 2).

No se podía andar con tanto automóvil y tanto autobús.	*You couldn't walk for the mass of automobiles and busses.*
Hay mucha piedra por aquí.	*There is an abundance of stone(s) around here.*

4. **Cosa** is used in several indefinite expressions: *(a)* **una cosa** (also **alguna, ninguna cosa**) as emphatic equivalents of **algo** (or **nada**); *(b)* **gran cosa** (in negative sentences) as an emphatic variant of **poco**; *(c)* **cosa de,** *about, approximately, some.*

a. **Voy a decirle una cosa.**	*I'm going to tell you something.*
b. **No me importa gran cosa.**	*It makes but little difference to me.*
c. **Tengo cosa de cuatrocientos dólares en el banco.**	*I have about (some) 400 dollars in the bank.*

5. Other expressions of approximation are **unos** *some;* **cerca de** *about, around;* **como** *about, as if;* **(poco) más o menos,** *approximately, more or less;* **y pico** *a little over (after)*. **A eso de** *about* and **sobre** *around* are used only of time.

Un hombre de unos cuarenta años. **Un hombre como de cuarenta años.** **Un hombre de cuarenta años, (poco) más o menos.**	*A man about forty years old.*
Tiene cerca de un millón.	*He has almost (close to) 1 million.*
La finca tiene ciento y pico de hectáreas.	*The estate contains a little over a hundred hectares.*
Vino a eso de (sobre) las ocho.	*He came around eight o'clock.*

NOTE. **Tantos** may be added to *twenty, thirty* (up to *ninety*) to express approximation: **tiene veintitantos (treinta y tantos) años,** *he is some twenty (thirty) years old.*

EJERCICIOS

Sustitúyanse las palabras entre paréntesis por las palabras subrayadas:

1. Aprendí unas palabras de francés. (algunas, unas cuantas, varias, bastantes, unas pocas, cuatro)
2. Había una porción de pinturas interesantes en la tienda. (gran número, una serie, una barbaridad)
3. Esta es mucha casa para mí. (automóvil, trabajo, dinero)

210. Numerals *(cont.)*

1. English *half* is *(a)* as a noun, **la mitad (de)** *(b)* as an adjective **medio** (with no accompanying article).

a. **Perdí la mitad de mi dinero.**	*I lost half my money.*
b. **media docena**	*a half dozen*
año y medio	*a year and a half*
a las cinco y media	*at half past five.*

NOTE. **Medio** may also mean *average;* **el hombre medio** *the average man.* (*Average* as a noun is **media.**) **Medio** is also used adverbially: **medio muertos** *half dead* (pl.), **está a medio hacer** (or **hecho a medias**) *it is half done.* **Medio** as a noun means *middle:* **en medio de la calle** *in the middle of the street.* It must not be confused with **medio** *means.*

2. Arithmetical fractions have cardinals as numerator and ordinals as denominator. In non-technical language the construction with **parte** is usually employed.

Seis es dos tercios de nueve, pero la mitad de doce.	*Six is two-thirds of nine, but half of twelve.*
Perdí la tercera parte de mi dinero.	*I lost a third of my money.*

3. Collectives are usually formed by the suffixes **-ena** and **-ar.** In some cases these collectives have an indefinite value.

docena	*dozen*
una decena, veintena, centena	*some ten, twenty, hundred*
La huerta tiene un centenar de manzanos.	*The orchard has about a hundred apple trees.*

4. For expressions of price, rate, and measure, see §§**157***d*, **211,** 2*c*. Time rate is usually expressed by an adjective.

seis pesetas diarias (por día)	*six pesetas a day*

Also **semanales (por** or **a la semana), mensuales (al mes)** and **anuales (al año)**

NOTE. In expressions of amount, size, or price **ser** is usually followed by **de: el precio (total) será de unos doscientos dólares** *the (total) price will be around 200 dollars.*

5. Dimensions may be expressed according to the following scheme of possibilities:

La torre tiene (or **es de**)	**una altura de cien metros.** / **cien metros de altura** or **de alto.**	*The tower is* 100 *meters high.*

El tamaño que busco es cuatro centímetros de largo por tres de ancho.	*The size I want is four centimeters long by three wide.*

EJERCICIOS

Contéstense en frases completas:

1. Gregorio tenía dieciocho libros y vendió la tercera parte de ellos. ¿Cuántos le quedaban?
2. Ana tenía veinticuatro pesetas y gastó la mitad de ellas. ¿Cuántas tenía entonces?
3. Un rascacielos tiene 900 metros de altura. ¿Cuántos metros hay en la cuarta parte de él? ¿En la quinta parte? ¿En la sexta parte?
4. Felipe gana 1.750 pesetas cada semana y trabaja cinco días a la semana. ¿Cuánto gana por día? Si trabaja siete horas por día, ¿cuánto gana por hora? ¿Cuánto gana al mes? ¿Al año?
5. Varios amigos hacen una colección de libros usados para venderlos. Uno da cincuenta libros de a un dólar cada uno, otro da sesenta y cinco libros de a dos dólares cada uno, y un tercer amigo da cinco libros de a tres dólares y medio cada uno. ¿Cuánto recibirán por todos los libros? Si dividen el dinero igualmente, ¿cuánto recibirá cada amigo?

TRANSLATION B

1. He always keeps other people's books. 2. I have told you once and again not to do it. 3. They drew their pistols *(each one drew a pistol)*. 4. He used to give **(echar)** him such sermons! 5. She gave him such looks! 6. He smokes such [big] cigars. 7. Whoever has said that doesn't know what he is talking about. 8. Wherever you go you will find good friends. 9. Last night I met a certain D. Gregorio, a countryman of yours. 10. The said town is about twenty-two miles from Cordova. 11. The whole scene had the tone of a painting by (of) Goya. 12. We saw each other a few times. 13. There were several misprints in a few (small number of) pages. 14. It was an informal dinner. A few **(cuatro)** friends, that was all. 15. Where do you keep the back numbers of *ABC?*—There you have a few, the rest are on the shelf. 16. Drop **(poner)** me a line **(unas letras)**. 17. I have a great many things to discuss with you. 18. These people are awfully serious. 19. She was about sixty years old when she died. 20. We arrived a little after nine o'clock. 21. We made an average of thirty miles an (by) hour. 22. We will leave Algeciras at half past one. 23. The average Eskimo cares little for comfort. 24. The Mulhacén in [the] Sierra Nevada is over three thousand meters high.

25. There were about one hundred people on the beach. 26. I have translated a fourth of the lesson. 27. The lake is more than two miles wide.

III

VERBS AND IDIOMS

Salir(se) (§258) *to leave* (intrans.), *come out, go out, turn out, etc.*
1. I am leaving tomorrow for Europe. 2. What time does the boat sail? 3. The servant told us that the master and mistress had gone out for a **(de)** walk. 4. Come out to the window. 5. How are we going to get out of the difficulty? 6. They all came out unhurt. 7. You are the one who will be the loser **(perdiendo)**. 8. He came forth with a silly remark. 9. How **(¿por dónde?)** do you *(indef.)* get out of this building? 10. He is very headstrong; he always gets his own way. 11. Almost all the students passed the examinations. 12. This pitcher leaks. 13. The deal did not turn out right **(bien)** for him. 14. The photographs have turned out very well. 15. His hair has turned gray **(salirle canas)**. 16. Two contracts have turned up for us today. 17. A wheel came off **(salírsele)** the car. 18. He took off like a shot **(salir disparado; como alma que lleva el diablo)**.

Entrar *to enter, come in, bring in, get (afraid, sleepy,* etc.)
1. Four steamers have entered (in) the port. 2. Come in this way. 3. This key does not fit. 4. Have **(que)** them bring my breakfast in. 5. I see he doesn't understand **(entrarle)**. 6. I am getting sleepy *(noun)*. 7. We got afraid.

Ocurrir *to occur, happen;* **ocurrírsele a uno** *to come to one's mind.*
1. What's the matter (goes on)?—An accident has occurred. 2. Let this not happen again. 3. Many things happened to us on the trip. 4. I have an idea. 5. He thinks of very amusing things [to say].

chapter nineteen

Prepositions and conjunctions

I

211. Simple prepositions

The most frequently used are **de, a, en, con, por,** and **para.** The following brief treatment of each (except **por** and **para**; see §§**107, 109**), is, of course, far from complete.

1. **De** has a very wide range of uses. It corresponds, in general, to the English *(a) from, of* (except as dative of separation; §**53**), *(b) with* or *in* (in the sense of *from, of, with regard to)*, and *(c) as (in the capacity of)*. It is used *(d)* in many adverbial expressions.

   a. **Soy de Madrid** *I am from Madrid;* **abrigo de pieles** *fur coat;* **el dueño de la casa** *the owner of the house;* **máquina de escribir** *typewriter.*
   But: **se lo robaron al viejo** *it was stolen from the old man.*
   b. **Loco de alegría** *mad with joy;* **el hombre de la capa** *the man with (in) the cloak;* **vestido de negro** *dressed in black;* **ciego del ojo derecho** *blind in the right eye.*
   c. **Vestido de paisano** *dressed as a civilian;* **servía de guía** *he served as a guide;* **estuvo allí de embajador** *he was there as ambassador.*
   d. **De buena gana** *willingly;* **de oídas** *on hearsay;* **de prisa** *rapidly.*

2. **A** also has a very wide range of uses. It corresponds, in general, *(a)* to the English *to, at*, denoting motion or direction, or location in space or time with reference to motion or direction. **A** also expresses *(b)* manner, *(c)* price or rate, *(d) on* or *in* (in the sense of *to, at, like*).

a. **Llegó a Barcelona** *he arrived at (in) Barcelona;* **echó a correr** *he started to run;* **a la derecha** *to (on) the right;* **a dos kilómetros de aquí** *two kilometers from here;* **asomado a la puerta** *standing at (looking out of) the door;* **sentado a la mesa** *seated at the table;* **a las dos de la tarde** *at two o'clock in the afternoon.*

b. **A la francesa** *in the French style;* **poco a poco** *little by little;* **a toda prisa** *in all haste.*

c. **A peseta el kilo** *a peseta a (the) kilo;* **a 90 kilómetros por hora** *at 90 kilometers an hour.*

d. **A la mañana siguiente** *on the following morning;* **a bordo del vapor** *on board the steamer;* **al contrario** *on the contrary;* **a gatas** *on all fours* (**§199,** 2); **a tiempo** *on (in) time;* **a su alcance** *within his reach;* **a su servicio** *at (in) his service.*

3. **En** corresponds in general *(a)* to English *in* or *at* (place where or state in which), *(b)* to English *in=within* (time and place), *(c)* to English *into* (after certain verbs), *(d)* to English *on.*

a. **en Madrid** *in (at) Madrid,* **en casa** *in the house, at home,* **en mangas de camisa** *in shirt sleeves.*

NOTE. In translating English *at,* **en** indicates rest, **a** motion: **llegamos al hotel** *we arrived at the hotel,* **estamos en casa** *we are at home.*

b. **en el verano** *in (the) summer,* **en dos semanas** *in two weeks.*

NOTE. *Within is* **dentro de: dentro de la casa** *inside the house,* **dentro de poco tiempo** *within a short while.*

c. **Entramos en la casa** *we entered the house* (also with **meter, penetrar, introducir,** etc.).

d. **en la mesa** *on the table,* **en la isla** *on the island.*

4. **Con** corresponds in general, *(a)* to the English *with* (accompaniment, instrument, manner); *(b)* it occasionally has concessive force.

a. **Estaba en el café con sus amigos.**	*He was in the café with his friends.*
Lo he visto con mis propios ojos.	*I have seen it with my own eyes.*
con rapidez	*rapidly*
b. **Con todo su dinero no tenía un solo amigo.**	*With (in spite of) all his money he did not have a single friend.*

5. For a list of the more common verbs construed with prepositions see Appendix **§269.**

EJERCICIOS

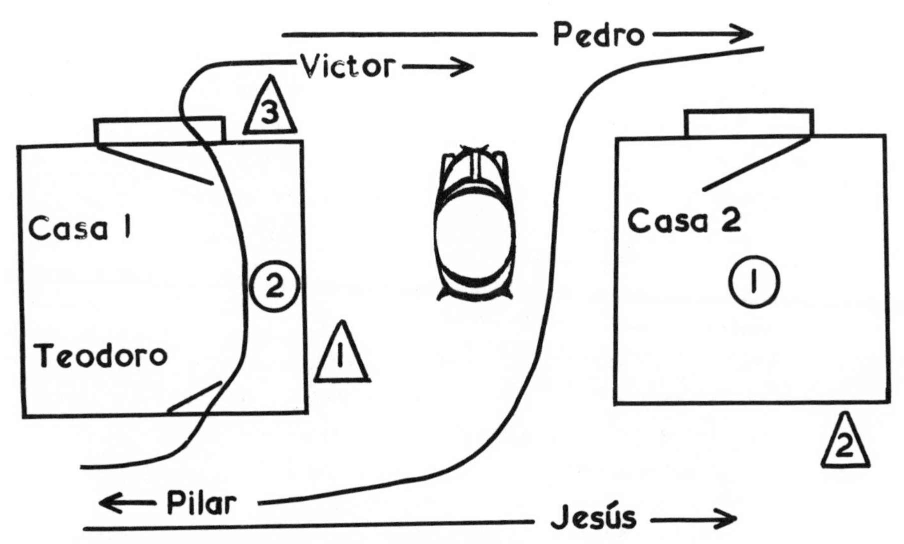

Aquí vemos dos casas vistas desde el aire.

Contéstense:

1. ¿Dónde está el árbol?
2. ¿Dónde está el autómovil?
3. ¿Dónde está Teodoro?
4. ¿Dónde está el círculo número 1?
5. ¿Dónde está el círculo número 2?
6. ¿Dónde está el triángulo número 1?
7. ¿Dónde está el triángulo número 2?
8. ¿Dónde está el triángulo número 3?

212. Compound prepositions

Compound prepositions are usually formed *(a)* chiefly from adverbs and adverbial phrases by the addition of **de,** *(b)* sometimes from adjectives, participles, and nouns, by the addition of **a.**

a. **antes de** *before* (time, order); **después de** *after* (time, order); **delante de** *before* (place); **detrás de** *behind, after* (place); **dentro de** *within;* **fuera de** *outside of;* **cerca de** *near;* **encima de** *over, on top of.*

b. **conforme a** *according to;* **(con) respecto a** *with respect (regard) to;* **tocante a** *touching, concerning;* **junto a** *close to, beside;* **frente a** *opposite to.*

213. Coördinate conjunctions

The coördinate conjunctions are: *(a)* **y** *and* (**e** before words beginning with **i** or **hi**), *(b)* **o** *or* (**u** before words beginning with **o** or **ho**) and **ni** *nor* (see §**103**), *(c)* **pero** *but (nevertheless)*, *(d)* **sino** *but (on the contrary*—direct contrast to preceding negative).

a. **España e Italia**	*Spain and Italy*
madre e hija	*mother and daughter*

EXCEPTIONS: Before the diphthong **ie: sangre y hierro** *blood and iron;* before questions: **¿y Isabel?** *and what about Isabel?*

b. **siete u ocho**	*seven or eight*
mujer u hombre	*man or woman*
c. **El pueblo es grande, pero sucio.**	*The town is large, but dirty.*
No queríamos ir, pero fuimos.	*We didn't want to go, but we went.*

NOTE. **Mas** *but* (equivalent to **pero**) is archaic and rhetorical.

d. **No parece española, sino inglesa.**	*She doesn't look Spanish, but English.*
No les gusta salir, sino quedarse en casa.	*They don't like to go out, but to stay home.*

NOTE. When two finite verbs are directly contrasted, **sino que** is used: **no hace falta que venga, sino que escriba** *it isn't necessary for him to come, but to write. But* in the sense of *only* is either **no . . . más que (§197)** or **no . . . sino: no hace (nada) sino comer y dormir** *he does nothing except eat and sleep.*

214. Subordinate conjunctions

1. Many of the subordinate conjunctions have already been treated. The simple subordinate conjunctions are *(a)* **que** *that,* **como** *as, since* (causal), **cuando** *when,* **mientras (que)** *while* **pues (que)** *for, since* (cause) and **si** *if.* The compound subordinate conjunctions are usually formed *(b)* by adding **que** to adverbs, prepositional phrases and prepositions, chiefly the latter.

a. **Como no sé alemán no pude hacerme entender.**	*Since (as) I don't know German I couldn't make myself understood.*

b. **Antes (de)**[1] **que** *before* (time); **después (de)**[1] **que** *after* (time); **hasta que** *until;* **mientras (que)** *while;* **así que** *as soon as, so that;* **luego que** *as soon as;* **desde que** *since* (time); **aunque, bien que** *although*; **con tal (de)**[1] **que** *provided;* **(en) caso (de)**[1] **que** *in case;* **para que, a fin de que** *in order*

[1]This **de** has entered by analogy to the construction with the infinitive. In **antes (de) que** and **(en) caso (de) que** the **de** form is the more common.

that; **de modo (manera, suerte, forma) que** *so that;* **pues (que), puesto que** *for, since* (cause); **ya que** *now that, since* (cause); **sin que** *without;* **a medida que** *(according, in proportion) as.*

2. **Que** *that* is ordinarily not omitted in noun clauses, and is even required after verbs of saying and thinking when followed by **sí** or **no** or when used parenthetically.

Creo que sí.	*I think so.*
Dice que no.	*He says not (no).*
¡Ya lo creo que sí!	*I should certainly say so!*
Fue a casa, me parece que por su abrigo.	*He went home for his overcoat, I think.*

TRANSLATION A

1. The city of Granada was the last capital of the Moors in Spain. 2. Fashionable beaches are found on the Costa Brava. 3. A velvet rug covered the floor. 4. The girl with the red hat was wearing a bikini on the beach. 5. He dressed in [a] tuxedo. 6. The child was pale from fear. 7. I have a mahogany table. 8. He was blind with rage. 9. I have him here as [my] secretary. 10. He died of hunger. 11. I know the book by heart. 12. I have received a letter from your cousin. 13. We went out to the street. 14. Turn to the left. 15. They started to laugh. 16. The steamer was going at full speed. 17. She likes to ride horseback. 18. He finished the short story in three days. 19. I will see you at the office. 20. I will be there within half an hour. 21. They entered the cathedral. 22. I met her on the boat. 23. I cannot eat this with a fork. 24. In spite of all that I can't make up my mind to buy it. 25. Put the lights out before you go to bed. 26. There is an avenue of trees in front of the house. 27. We all sat around the bonfire. 28. The station is far from the village. 29. We haven't decided anything in regard to that matter. 30. He doesn't know how to swim, but he wants to learn. 31. She does nothing but read. 32. Her eyes aren't black, but blue. 33. He didn't say that he didn't want to, but that he couldn't. 34. I will tell him when I see him. 35. Stay here until we come back. 36. We'll wait for you provided you don't take long. 37. His ambitions and ideals are exceptional for someone his age. 38. The *Poem of the Cid* has (a) great literary and historical importance. 39. Do you think he will be successful?—I hope so. 40. I'll change it, since you insist.

II

215. Simple prepositions *(cont.)*

(a) The English *of* is sometimes rendered by **a** (in the sense of **por** or **hacia**); *(b)* **en** is sometimes used to express estimate or price; *(c)* **sin**

sometimes corresponds to the English prefix *un-* or suffix *-less; (d)* **hasta** means *as far as, even; (e)* **cuando** and **mientras** are occasionally used as prepositions; *(f)* **según** may be used as an adverb.

a. **su amor a la patria**	*his love for his country*
b. **Lo tasaron en cien mil pesetas.**	*They appraised it at 100,000 pesetas.*
Lo compramos en un duro.	*We bought it for a duro.*
c. **una noche sin luna**	*a moonless night*
un hombre sin cultura	*an uncultured man*
d. **Esto lo saben hasta los niños de pecho.**	*Even babes in arms know this.*
e. **cuando la visita del Presidente**	*at the time of the President's visit*
f. **¿Piensas contestar?—Según.**	*Do you intend to answer?—That depends.*

EJERCICIOS

Sustitúyanse las palabras entre paréntesis por las palabras subrayadas:

1. El coche[a] lo vendí[b] en 70.000 pesetas.
   a. (los muebles, la ropa, los trajes de luces, los tres toros)
   b. (comprar, obtener)
2. Conoció a su mujer cuando la fiesta nacional. (la exposición internacional, la huelga general, la caída del dictador, la muerte del jefe)

216. Compound prepositions *(cont.)*

Note the following peculiarities: *(a)* **por** and **de** combine with other prepositions after verbs of motion: *(b)* **para con** as equivalent of the English *to, towards* (*i.e.*, attitude towards persons); *(c)* **de a** in adjectival phrases of set price, manner, or size.

a. **Los trenes pasan por debajo del río.**	*The trains go under the river.*
Un hombre salió de entre los árboles.	*A man came out from among the trees.*
b. **las atenciones que tuvo para conmigo**	*his kindness to (towards) me*
c. **puros de a diez pesetas**	*ten peseta cigars*
los de a caballo y los de a pie	*those on horseback and those on foot*

EJERCICIOS

En los dibujos de §**211**, contéstense:

1. ¿Por dónde va Jesús?
2. ¿Por dónde va Víctor?
3. ¿Por dónde va Pedro?
4. ¿Por dónde va Pilar?

Sustitúyanse las palabras entre paréntesis por las palabras subrayadas:

5. Le sorprendió su actitud[a] para con sus padres[b].
   a. (atenciones, falta de respeto, desprecio)
   b. (hermanos, profesores, amigos)

217. Distinctions between related prepositions

The following groups of related prepositions require careful differentiation: *(a)* **antes de** refers to time and order, **delante de** to place, and **ante** means *in the presence of; (b)* **bajo** is used figuratively, **debajo de** literally; *(c)* **cerca de** refers to location or approximation, **acerca de** means *about, concerning; (d)* **desde** and **hasta** are used both of time and place; *(e)* **después de** refers to time, **detrás de** to position and **tras** to succession; *(f)* **en** is usually *on*, **sobre** *upon, above* and **encima de** *on top of, above, over.* **Sobre** also means *concerning* and *in addition to.*

a. **antes de salir**	*before leaving*
delante de la casa	*before (in front of) the house*
ante el tribunal	*before the court*
b. **debajo de la mesa**	*under the table*
bajo un cielo estrellado	*under a starry sky*
c. **cerca del pueblo**	*near the town*
cerca de dos mil	*nearly, about 2,000*
acerca del caso	*concerning the matter*
d. **desde aquí**	*from this point*
desde aquí en adelante	*from now on*
hasta la esquina	*as far as, up to the corner*
hasta mañana	*until tomorrow*
e. **después de cenar**	*after supper*
detrás del Ayuntamiento	*behind the City Hall*
tras la tormenta viene la calma	*after the storm comes fine weather*
uno tras otro	*one after another*
f. **en la pared**	*on the wall*
sobre la mesa	*upon the table*
encima de la cómoda	*on top of the bureau*

Sobre (por encima de) el interés personal está el deber.	*Duty is above personal gain.*
sobre el asunto	*about the affair*
Sobre no tener salud, no tiene dinero.	*In addition to having bad health he has no money.*

NOTE. The adverbs **delante, encima,** etc., are used instead of the corresponding prepositions when the object of the latter would be a personal pronoun: **la casa que tenía delante** *the house which was (I had) in front of me;* **el árbol le cayó encima** *the tree fell on top of him.* Note the use of the dative pronoun of reference **le** in the second example. (No such pronoun is required in the first because the person concerned is the subject of the verb.)

218. Coördinate conjunctions *(cont.)*

Y when beginning a question or an exclamation frequently has ponderative value.

Pero ¿y usted?	*Yes, but what about you?*
¡Y los tíos sin saber nada!	*Just think of it! Aunt and Uncle didn't suspect a thing.*

NOTE. **Pero** may be used in repetitions for emphasis: **¡Muy bien, pero que muy bien!** *Very well, very well indeed.*

219. Subordinate conjunctions *(cont.)*

Como, cuando, and **si** clauses—and other indirect questions—may be construed as noun clauses and be introduced by prepositions or the article **el** (§§**104,** 5; **108,** 1).

Me enteré de cómo ocurrió.	*I learned how it happened.*
En cuanto a si acepta o no . . .	*As to his accepting or not . . .*
No me explico el por qué de todo eso.	*I can't understand the reason for all that.*

NOTE. **Como** in certain cases loses most of its interrogative force and becomes equivalent to **que** (compare English *how = that*), in which case it bears no written accent: **me habló de como había cambiado de opinión** *he told me how he had changed his opinion.*

220. Special constructions with *que*

1. **Que** introducing a noun clause after verbs of saying or requesting is occasionally omitted, chiefly *(a)* in correspondence and *(b)* to avoid the cacophony that would result from the juxtaposition of several **que's.**

a. **Le ruego se sirva informarme.** — *I beg you please to inform me.*
b. **Las cosas que supongo te habrá dicho.** — *The things I suppose he has told you.*

2. Similar to the use registered in §**214,** 2, **que** is widely employed as a connective (for which there is no equivalent in English) carrying the force of a verb or expression of affirmation: *(a)* after any word or phrase of exclamation or asseveration, expressed or implied, *(b)* before the answer to a question beginning with **¿qué?**, *(c)* as an intensifier to introduce exclamations or commands.

a. **¡Claro que lo hará!** — *Of course he'll do it.*
La señorita, que vayas en seguida. — *The mistress wants you to come right away.*

NOTE. A further extension of this use may be seen in the introductory conjunctions of the type **sólo que, ahora que** *only, but,* **por cierto que** *to be sure,* **de aquí que** *hence* and **sobre que**[1] *besides* used in coördinate or pseudo-principal clauses: **acabo de ver a D. Jorge, por cierto que no me dijo nada del asunto** *I have just seen D. Jorge—to be sure, he said nothing about the matter.*

b. **¿Qué ha dicho?—Que te presentes en seguida.** — *What did he say?—For you to come at once.*
c. **¡Que me matan!** — *They are killing me!*
¡Que vienen ahora! — *They're coming now!*
¡Que sí! — *Yes, indeed!* (In answer to a negative statement.)

3. In other cases the general connective **que** has the force of a mild causal conjunction equivalent to the English *for, as.* This **que** is particularly frequent after exclamations and imperatives.

Vamos, que ya son las seis. — *Come along, it's already six o'clock.*
Abra Ud. la ventana, que hay mucho humo aquí. — *Open the window, (for) there is (too) much smoke here.*

NOTE. The relative **que** is similarly used as a loose connective (see §**94**).

4. The general connective **que** occasionally has the value of *(a)* result, *(b)* purpose (equivalent of **para que, a fin de que, de modo que**), *(c)* manner.[2] This latter type of **que** is also used *(d)* as an intensifier in repetitions.

a. **¿Donde estás que no te veo?** — *Where are you, (that) I don't see you?*

[1]The **que** in **sobre que, además de que, fuera de que** *besides* introducing a pseudo-principal clause may be relative, as it is in the introductory conjunction **con que** *so then.*

[2]Of course, **que** by itself possesses no meaning of cause, result, purpose manner, concession, etc. It is the context which imparts the special meaning to the general connective.

b. **Acércate que te oiga mejor.**	*Come closer so I can hear you better.*
c. **Escribe que da gusto.**	*He writes splendidly.*
d. **¡Mejor que mejor!**	*So much the better!*
Venía silba que silba.	*He came along whistling merrily.*
Estaban fuma que (te) fuma.	*They were smoking incessantly.*

NOTE. In these expressions the graphic verbs **estar, ir,** etc., are either expressed or implied. A similar use of the intensifying repetition may be seen in the rare **en llegando que llegó (llegue)** *as soon as he arrived (arrives)* and **llegado que hubo (§133)** types.

221. Correlative conjunctions

Following are some of the more usual correlatives: **ni . . . ni** *neither . . . nor* (see §103); **o (bien) . . . o (bien)** *either . . . or;* **ya . . . ya, sea . . . sea** *whether . . . or* (see §117); **así . . . como, tanto . . . como, lo mismo . . . que** *both . . . and, as well as;* **apenas . . . cuando, no bien . . . (cuando)** *scarcely . . . when, no sooner . . . than, as soon as.*

Apenas había salido él cuando llegó ella.	*He had scarcely left when she arrived.*
No bien nos acercamos cuando comprendimos la causa del tumulto.	*As soon as we drew near we understood the cause of the uproar.*
Lo mismo el padre que el hijo son buenos músicos.	*Both father and son are good musicians.*

NOTE. In conversation **que** may be used as a substitute for correlative **ora, ya, sea,** etc.: **Cuando uno sale de noche es para algo divertido, que el café, que el teatro, que los amigos. . . .** *When one goes out at night it is for entertainment: the café, the theatre, friends, etc.*

TRANSLATION B

1. They got him out from under the car. 2. We passed behind the factory. 3. His name appeared in letters a palm's length high. 4. Under Charles III the Enlightenment came to Spain. 5. There is a large square in front of the church. 6. I will do it before I go out. 7. The case was discussed before the board of directors. 8. They live near us. 9. Do you know anything about this? 10. I will accompany you as far as the station. 11. I will wait for your reply until next week. 12. I can't see it from here. 13. After some unsuccessful experiment . . . 14. I will let you know after consulting with my partner. 15. I have left my gloves on the counter 16. It is **(hace)** five degrees below zero. 17. There was a bronze figure on top of the bookcase. 18. [Be sure you] don't fail to write. 19. She plays the piano [in

such a way] that it is glorious to hear **(que da gloria)**. 20. I had no sooner arrived at the hotel than I received your telegram. 21. He writes a great deal in Spanish as well as in English. 22. And [there] I [was] without a penny. 23. She sings very well indeed. 24. Find out if (the) dinner is ready. 25. They told us how the flood had destroyed everything. 26. Please (I request you to) answer at your earliest convenience. 27. [I should like you to] write to me often. 28. These oranges surely are good.—They certainly are. 29. Go to the kitchen and [tell] them to make some sandwiches for us. 30. What did he say?—[He said] he would give it to us to-morrow. 31. Don't be long I am in a hurry. 32. They were talking and talking.

III

VERB AND IDIOM DRILL

Pasar *to pass (by, through, along, in, to, for), spend, happen, suffer, etc.;* **pasarse** *to pass (off, beyond), surpass, etc.*
1. Some policemen passed on bicycles. 2. Shall we go through this town? 3. We spent the morning playing golf. 4. We have had a splendid time in Santander. 5. What is the matter? 6. What happens is that we have a puncture. 7. What is the matter with you? 8. He went by **(de largo)** without speaking to me. 9. The bullet pierced the wall. 10. We ordered a couple of boiled **(pasados por agua)** eggs. 11. Come in. 12. They went into the office. 13. Send me the bill at the end of the month. 14. Drop around to **(por)** my house this afternoon. 15. He has suffered many hardships in his youth. 16. I cannot stand for such a thing. 17. He passed for a man of great influence. 18. Let us pass over **(por alto)** his defects. 19. Let it pass this time but let it not be repeated. 20. We have missed (gone beyond) our **(de)** station. 21 Have you gotten over (has it passed off) your headache? 22. He was too smart **(pasarse de listo)**. 23. I can't do without my pipe. 24. This fruit is spoiled *(condition)*.

Tratar *to treat, address* (by pronoun or title), *speak to, be intimate with;* **tratar de** *to deal with, to try to;* **tratarse de** *to be a question of, etc.*
1. They treated me as [one] of the family. 2. The children addressed their grand-parents as **(de)** Ud. and their parents as **tú**. 3. Do you know the mayor?—I know him, but not to speak to (but I do not, etc.). 4. The two families did not speak to each other. 5. Try to convince him. 6. The board of directors dealt with various matters. 7. That's not the point.

Valer (§262) *to be worth, be of avail, etc.;* **valerse de** *to avail oneself of, make use of.*
1. How much is this worth? 2. Excuses are of no avail. 3. It is not worth while **(la pena)** to stay here a week. 4. He makes use of all kinds of tricks to get what he wants. 5. This time the prestige of his name will not help him. 6. His scientific work has brought him the Nobel Prize. 7. God help me! 8. Don't say anything.

It is best **(más vale)** to keep quiet. 9. It would be better for you to mind your own business **(ocuparse de lo suyo)**. 10. It is not that nor anything like it **(cosa que lo valga)**. 11. There is no but about it **(no hay pero que valga)**. 12. He is a young lawyer of great promise **(que vale mucho)**.

Caber (§235) *to be contained (in), be room for (in), hold, be possible.*
1. There is not [enough] room for me in this bed; it is too narrow. 2. One of us will have to stay ashore; there is not [enough] room for all of us. 3. How many people does this bus hold? 4. It is possible to indicate other reasons besides the ones already mentioned. 5. I have no doubt (no doubt is possible to me) that things happened that way.

Cumplir(se) *to carry out, fulfil, reach one's birthday;* **cumplir con** *to perform* (one's duty), *keep* (one's promise).
1. The order has not been carried out. 2. His hopes were not fulfilled. 3. Isabel is just twenty years [old]; yesterday was her birthday. 4. Let us do our duty. 5. I am going to live up to what [I] promised. 6. Let's not stand on **(andar con)** ceremony **(cumplidos)**. 7. He is a very polite person.

Faltar *to be lacking, fail, etc.*
1. Here is the baggage, three pieces **(bultos)**; one is missing. 2. He lacks two months, of **(para cumplir)** twenty-one (years). 3. I am five dollars short; I must have lost a bill. 4. I [will] expect you at five o'clock; don't fail. 5. Don't miss the **(al)** banquet. 6. You will stay to dinner (dine) with us, will you not?—I should say so! Of course! **(¡No faltaba más!)** 7. After we had waited for several hours, the mechanic told us he couldn't fix the car until the next day. That was the last straw! **(¡No faltaba más!)**.

Bastar *to suffice, be enough (for), have enough (with);* **bastarse** *to be self-sufficient.*
1. He is so ambitious that nothing satisfies (suffices) him. 2. The arrival of the police was enough to quell the riot. 3. How many actors do we have (count with)? (With) Five.—That's (they are) not enough. 4. That's enough **(¡Basta de!)** talk **(discusión)**. 5. It should be enough for (let it suffice) you to know that there will be no meeting. 6. Here are the stamps, take all you want.—One is enough (I have enough with one). 7. Your saying so is enough for me (I have enough with, etc.). 8. One must be self-sufficient (to oneself).

Sobrar *to be (have) more than enough, left over, superfluous, etc.*
1. With his income he has more than enough to live well. 2. I have two tickets left over for this evening's performance. Do you want them? 3. How many are there? —Twelve.—Then that's two too many. 4. There is more than enough time.

Acabar[1] *to finish, end, be over;* **acabar de** *to finish, have just;* **acabarse** *to give out, be finally over.*
1. This book has just been published. 2. Wait a moment, I [will] finish right away.

[1]**Terminar** (and **concluir**) may be used in sentences 2–8. These uses of **terminar** (but not of **concluir**) are on the increase.

3. Finish dressing and we will go out together. 4. He ended by **(por)** going to sleep. 5. Our provisions gave out. 6. Is the writing paper all gone? 7. It's all over now **(¡ya se acabó!)** 8. No more **(se acabaron)** foolishness *(pl.)*. [Get] to work! 9. This is the limit **(el acabóse)**! 10. He died and was buried and that was all there was to that **(sanseacabó)**.

COMPOSITION

Tema primero

La travesía

(En el aeropuerto de Kennedy.) 25 de junio.

Hoy, el día de mi partida, hace un tiempo espléndido. Ayer el tiempo estuvo tan malo que las líneas aéreas se vieron obligadas a cancelar todos los vuelos de Nueva York. Afortunadamente las tormentas pasaron, y el cielo está muy azul, sin una nube. Pronto subiremos al avión con esperanzas de llegar a España sin contratiempos. ¡Tanto mejor! El aire no es precisamente mi punto fuerte, y aunque no lo paso mal en los aviones, confieso que desearía verme en tierra cuanto antes.

Los viajes aéreos difieren mucho de las travesías en barco. Cuando se pasa varios días en compañía de otros viajeros forzosamente la gente llega a conocerse y sin duda se forman verdaderas amistades. En cambio, en los aviones de chorro (de reacción) modernos, los viajes son tan breves que difícilmente puede uno entablar una conversación con el compañero de asiento sin interrupciones de las azafatas que nunca quieren dejar en paz a los pasajeros. — ¿Quieren los señores chicles? ¿Una bebida? ¿Una revista que leer? ¿Una almohada? — Y luego apenas se encuentra un momento de tranquilidad y es la hora de comer. Entonces después de una siesta brevísima, ya estamos al otro lado del océano, preparándonos para aterrizar. Forzoso es reconocerlo, los medios modernos de transportación tienen bastantes inconvenientes a pesar de todas sus ventajas.

(En el avión.) Después de todas mis dudas sobre el vuelo, tengo que confesar que las cosas han ido mucho mejor de lo que había esperado. Al abordar el avión tropecé con un compañero de clase de la universidad, un español que estudia ingeniería en los Estados Unidos y vuelve a España para pasar las vacaciones de verano. Me invitó a sentarme con él. Inmediatamente nos pusimos a charlar en castellano y al oirnos varios otros jóvenes cerca de nosotros nos saludaron en la misma lengua. Resulta que hemos formado un grupo animado. Me felicito de haber tomado un avión español. Hay un ambiente de cordialidad y de llaneza que me encanta. Además, las azafatas se desviven por servirnos. Son unas chicas encantadoras. Me pregunto si es verdad eso de ser todas ellas de familias nobles. ¡Qué más da! A mí todas me parecen princesas reales.

Ahora lamento que el viaje sea tan corto. Dentro de una hora estaremos sobre Lisboa (es lástima que no hagamos escala) y pocos minutos después empezaremos a bajar para aterrizar en el aeropuerto de Barajas. Espero que después de nuestra llegada mi amigo Peña y yo no nos perdamos de vista. Ojalá me presente a algunos amigos suyos. Así podré conocer mejor a España, conociendo primero a unos españoles.

Theme 1

On the airplane Duque de Alba, June 25.

Dear Joe,

Today, having had an excellent Spanish meal, I finally find time to write you a few lines. You know how I am; I would rather talk to my friends than write to them.

The flight, although short, has been most enjoyable. I haven't had a single moment of boredom. The weather has been splendid and we have had some magnificent views of the Atlantic. There were some clouds and some turbulence shortly after we left New York, but it did not amount to anything **(no pasó de ahí).** So much the better. Which means I was afraid of getting airsick. Air travel isn't exactly my strong point.

I'm glad I took a Spanish plane. What an atmosphere of cordiality on the part of everybody! The hostesses outdo themselves to please us.

My seat companion is very likeable and through him I have met some Spaniards who are returning to Spain. Spaniards are excellent travelling companions. A conversation can be started on **(con)** the slightest pretext and soon everybody is acquainted. So far I have had a wonderful time **(divinamente, a las mil maravillas).**

At this moment the captain has just announced that (with)in a few minutes we will be over Lisbon, to(wards) the right. I am too excited to write any more. It is thrilling to think that I shall soon see the heart of Spain. I am anxious to land and begin to get acquainted with everything.

Goodbye until my next **(Hasta la próxima).**

Your (good) friend,
FRANK

Tema segundo

En Madrid

(En el cuarto del hotel.)
(Suena el teléfono. Frank descuelga el receptor.)

Frank. Diga.

Conserje. Hay un señor aquí que pregunta por usted.

Frank. ¿Por mí? ¿Está usted seguro?, porque no conozco a nadie en Madrid. ¿Ha dado su nombre?

Conserje. No, no ha querido. Dice que quería sorprenderle.

Frank. ¡Ah, vamos! Bueno, dígale que haga el favor de subir. Aunque no, mejor será que baje yo.

Conserje. Está bien, señor. Se lo diré.

Criada. (Llamando a la puerta.) ¿Se puede?

Frank. ¡Adelante!

Criada. ¿Quería el señor alguna cosa?

Frank. Muchas gracias, ahora no. Aunque si no es mucha molestia podría usted traerme una pastilla de jabón.

Criada. Con mucho gusto, señor.

(En el hall del hotel.)

Frank. ¡Hombre! ¡Peña! ¡Usted por aquí! ¡Qué sorpresa tan agradable! Creía que me había dicho que su familia vive en Murcia. Íbamos a vernos allí.

Diego. Sí, era lo convenido, y en efecto allí viven mis padres. Pero resulta que en este momento están en Madrid visitando a mi hermano mayor y a mis tíos que viven aquí. Por eso decidí quedarme con ellos y reunirme con usted inmediatamente. Quizá podré pedir prestado el coche a mi padre y así podemos ver algunos de los puntos de interés cerca de Madrid. ¿Le parece bien?

Frank. ¡Ya lo creo! ¡Magnífico!

Diego. Bueno. Y, a propósito, puesto que vamos a ser compañeros de viaje, ¿qué le parece que nos hablemos de tú? Así será más cómodo.

Frank. ¡Pues, sí! Con mucho gusto. Es que no quería ofenderte.

Diego. ¿Ofenderme? ¡Qué va! Ni por pienso. Todos los estudiantes se tutean. Y ahora, ¿qué planes tienes? Porque estoy a tu entera disposición.

Frank. Tú dirás. Hagamos lo que quieras. Estoy seguro de que cualquier cosa me va a encantar. Estoy dispuesto para todo.

Diego. Te veo entusiasmado.

Frank. Sí que lo estoy. Hace tantos años que leo de España que me es difícil creer que realmente estoy aquí.

Diego. ¡Vaya! Entonces, con todos tus estudios a lo mejor sabrás más que yo de las cosas de Madrid.

Frank. ¡Hombre! No exageres. Escoge tú lo que veremos primero.

Diego. Muy bien, pero ¿no quieres descansarte un poco después de tantas horas de vuelo?

Frank. ¿Descansarme? ¿Yo? Sería imposible ahora.

Theme 2

(Diego Peña, an old friend of Frank's, presents himself at the latter's hotel. He goes up to the office.)

—Is an American gentleman by the name of Frank Wilbur staying here?—Yes, sir.—Is he [in]?—I think so.—Will you please inform him that a friend is waiting [to see] him?—The gentleman's name, please?—It does not matter. I wish to surprise him.—Well, all right.

(The concierge calls the room.)—Mr. Wilbur, there is a gentleman here (who is) asking for you. [Shall] I tell him to go up?—Very well.

(Diego goes up in the elevator and knocks on the door of Frank's room.) May I come in?

Frank. Come in! Man alive! Peña! You here? This *is* a surprise! So this is why you did not wish to give your name?

Diego. Of course. I knew that you were not expecting to meet me until you arrived in Murcia. That was what was agreed upon. But it turns out that my parents are visiting some of my relatives here in Madrid so I thought it would be pleasant to join you here for a while. Maybe I can borrow my father's car and we can see some interesting places together. What do you say?

Frank. Great! A thousand thanks for your kindness.

Diego. Not at all, not at all. What are your plans?

Frank. Whatever you wish. I'm ready for anything.

Diego. Fine! By the way, what do you say we say *tú* to each other?

Frank. I agree. It will be nicer that way. Well, where shall we go? I'm very enthusiastic **(me tiene)** [about it].

Diego. I see you are. **(Ya lo veo.)** You probably know more about Madrid than I do.

Frank. Don't exaggerate. Let's go anywhere. It would be impossible for me to rest now.

Tema tercero

Impresiones de Madrid

28 de junio.

Varios paisanos míos me habían asegurado que Madrid no tenía carácter alguno, que era una ciudad moderna como otra cualquiera, que una vez visto el Museo del Prado no valía la pena quedarse aquí. No, no es verdad. Madrid es muy bonito. Tiene un gran número de parques, paseos y jardines. Sus plazas son muy hermosas, especialmente la Cibeles con su gran fuente en el medio, y la Plaza Mayor con sus viejos soportales; aquélla, moderna, ésta, del siglo XVII. El extremo occidental de la capital es francamente bellísimo, lo mejor de Madrid. Velázquez y Goya han pintado muchas veces este mismo paisaje como fondo de sus cuadros. Por encima de la espesa arboleda de la Casa de Campo y el Pardo, antiguas posesiones reales, se divisa con toda claridad la Sierra de Guadarrama, a una distancia de veintitantas millas.

El centro de Madrid es la Puerta del Sol, plaza relativamente pequeña donde desembocan unas once o doce calles, entre ellas la de Alcalá, que es la principal de la población. Esto dará idea de la extraordinaria animación que hay siempre en este sitio.

Los edificios que pudiéramos llamar antiguos son escasos. Casi todo lo importante, por ejemplo, el Palacio Nacional, el Prado, data a lo sumo del siglo XVIII. Ese "old Madrid" de que se habla en algunas canciones norteamericanas es una pura leyenda. En realidad Madrid no es más viejo que, digamos, Boston. Y, como todas las ciudades modernas, tiene un gran número de edificios del último estilo.

Esta noche voy a asistir a una de esas famosas tertulias de café. Peña va a presentarme a sus amigos. El consejo que acaba de darme me hace mucha gracia.—Tendrás que hablar más y más de prisa que tu contrario; si no, vas a producir una mala impresión.—¿Mi contrario? No tengo la menor intención de meterme con nadie.—¿Que no? Ya lo verás. Al cabo de un cuarto de hora estarás gritando con toda la fuerza de tus pulmones.—Bueno, ¿y tú qué piensas hacer mientras tanto? le pregunté yo.—¿Yo? Gritar más que tú, naturalmente.

Theme 3

Several of his fellow-countrymen had assured Frank that the only thing in Madrid worth while was the Museo de Prado, and that, as for the rest of the city, he would find it without any character at all, a modern city, [just] like any other.

But once he had seen the city, he changed his (of) opinion completely. Madrid seemed to him very beautiful and very attractive, with its fine buildings and its many gardens, boulevards, and parks. Everything seemed bright and neat under the brilliant sun and the blue sky. The splendid landscape at the western edge of the city—(which was) often used by Velázquez and Goya as background for their paintings—struck him [as] frankly the best thing in Madrid. Over the thick groves of the Casa de Campo and El Pardo—former royal property—the Guadarrama mountains stand out in all clearness, some twenty miles away.

The two most interesting squares are the Cibeles and the Plaza Mayor, the former modern and imposing, the latter ancient and picturesque with its numerous shops under the old arcades. But where there is the greatest animation, what we might call the center of Madrilian life, is the Puerta del Sol, where some eleven or twelve streets converge, among them the most important ones in the city.

Most of the important monuments of the city, for example, the National Palace, the Prado, the City Hall, date from the eighteenth century. Madrid is not an old city. It is modern, with an atmosphere of culture, leisure, and cosiness that give it a special character, a charm [all] its own. It is at one and the same time a cosmopolitan capital and a Spanish town.

Diego had planned to take Frank to a typical café gathering, where he was going to introduce the latter to some of his friends. Apropos of this, he said: I am going to give you a [piece of] advice. You will have to talk louder and more rapidly than your opponent.—Than my opponent? That strikes me as amusing. I haven't the slightest intention of quarrelling with anybody.—You haven't, haven't you? I'll bet anything that at the end of half an hour you will be shouting at the top of your lungs.—We'll see about that. And you, what do you intend to do in the meantime?—Shout more than the others, of course.

Tema cuarto

A. Escriba Ud. varios párrafos, utilizando para cada frase las palabras y modismos indicados. Por ejemplo, de *yo/salir/antes/ver/amigo* se podría formar una frase sencilla como: *yo salí antes de ver a mi amigo.* O si se quiere, se produce una frase un poco más complicada: *yo saldré de la estación antes de ver a mis amigos*, o *yo salía mucho antes, pero no veía a tu amigo*, o *salí antes que me viera mi amigo.*

El viaje

1. aeropuerto/animado/yo/tomar/avión
2. avión/no salir/la gente/echar la culpa/línea aérea
3. azafata/echar una mirada/compañero de viaje/cuando/oirnos/hablar español
4. compañeros/echarse a reír/cuando/avión/temblar
5. yo/no querer/perder/vista/Lisboa
6. yo/contar con/ayuda/amigos/para ver/cosas/interés

La llegada

7. avión/aterrizar/8:30/mañana
8. oficiales de inmigración/pedirnos/pasaporte
9. oficiales de aduana/pedirme/abrir/maletas
10. después/revisarme la ropa/permitirme/salir
11. yo/salir/aeropuerto/coger/autobús/ciudad
12. yo/no tener dinero español/tener que/cambiar

En el hotel

13. yo/bajar del autobús/el centro/ir al hotel
14. dejar caer/maleta/al entrar
15. botones/tomarme/maleta/sonrisa
16. yo/firmar/tarjeta/presentar/pasaporte
17. yo/subir/habitación/dar propina/botones

Un paseo

18. en el hotel/yo/descansar/unas horas
19. luego/lavarme la cara/cambiarme de ropa
20. yo/bajar/empezar/dar un paseo
21. después/andar/media hora/sentarme/café
22. yo/pedir/café cortado/sentirme/a gusto

B. Escriba Ud. un diálogo entre Ud. y el conserje de un hotel. Ud. le pregunta si hay una habitación libre y cuánto cuesta por día. El conserje le dice que hay varias habitaciones disponibles y que una exterior costará 400 pesetas diarias pero que si Ud. quiere una habitación más razonable hay una para una persona que da al patio por 300 pesetas por día. Ud. le dice que se quedará con la habitación más barata. El conserje pide que Ud. firme la tarjeta y entregue su pasaporte. Ud. quiere saber por que quiere el pasaporte. El conserje le explica que es necesario que los hoteles den a la policía todos los días una lista de los nombres de todos los que se alojan en el hotel, y que tienen que poner también el número del pasaporte de todos los extranjeros en el hotel. A Ud. le parece un poco extraño pero le da el pasaporte. El conserje dice que le de volverá el pasaporte en unos minutos, y entonces llama al botones y le dice que suba el equipaje.

C. Escriba Ud. un diálogo entre Ud. y un amigo con que se encuentra en una terraza. Ud. le dice cuanto le gusta verle después de tanto tiempo y el amigo dice que a él también le agrada muchísimo verle a Ud. Ud. le cuenta algo de lo que ha visto, qué tal fue el viaje, qué es lo que espera ver durante su visita, etc. El amigo se ofrece como guía a algunos puntos de interés. Luego le invita a Ud. a una tertulia que se reúne esa noche en un café muy cerca del hotel. Le explica cómo se ha de portar en una tertulia y cómo serán los que van a esta tertulia que se compone de un grupo de jóvenes con aspiraciones literarias.

Tema quinto

Un paseo por la Castellana

Diego. Vamos a tomar un taxi. Aquí cerca, en la esquina, hay un punto.

Frank. ¿Por qué no ir a pie? Desde que estoy aquí no hago ningun ejercicio. No juego al *golf*, ni al tenis, ni siquera ando. Vamos a todas partes en taxi o en autobús. Y, además, hay tantos coches que es casi más rápido ir a pie.

Diego. Pues vamos a pie. A mí lo mismo me da.

Frank. ¡Qué hermoso es este paseo! ¡Qué ancho! La Castellana, ¿verdad?

Diego. Aquí no. Hemos empezado en la Castellana que va desde la Plaza de San Juan de la Cruz hasta la plaza de Colón. Este trozo, entre Colón y la Cibeles, se llama Paseo de Calvo Sotelo, antiguamente de Recoletos. De la Plaza de San Juan de la Cruz al norte era antiguamente también la Castellana pero ahora se llama la Avenida del Generalísimo Franco. Y todavía tiene un cuarto nombre entre la Cibeles y la Estación de Atocha.

Frank. El Paseo del Prado, ¿no?

Diego. Eso es. Como ves, es la misma avenida con cuatro nombres distintos. Ese edificio que ocupa toda una manzana es la Biblioteca Nacional. Tiene una colección riquísima de manuscritos y libros raros.

Frank. Casi todos estos son edificios oficiales, ¿no es eso?

Diego. Sí, muchos de ellos. Mira. Allí ves la Presidencia del Gobierno. Luego, en la Plaza de la Cibeles están el Palacio de Comunicaciones, o sea el Correo, el Ministerio del Ejército y el Banco de España.

Frank. ¿Hay muchas industrias aquí?

Diego. Ahora hay bastantes, sobre todo la industria ligera, especialmente la de automoción y la de construcción. Madrid empezó siendo ante todo una ciudad oficial, el centro de la vida política, pero con el desarrollo industrial se ha hecho uno de los cinco primeros centros industriales del país.

Frank. Hay más centros industriales en las provincias, ¿no?

Diego. Sí. Además de los centro antiguos en Bilbao y Barcelona, ahora hay lo que llaman polos de fomento industrial, o sea, ciudades donde el gobierno quiere que se desarrollen más industrias, como Vigo, Burgos, Valladolid, Sevilla y otras.

Frank. ¡Tanta actividad!

Diego. Es verdad. A principios del siglo veinte España era todavía un país exportador de primeras materias, pero en años recientes ha venido industrializándose extraordinariamente.

Frank. Lo que puede parecerles a los turistas una desventaja porque aquí encuentran muchas de las mismas cosas y los mismos problemas que en todos los países modernos, como, por ejemplo, el mucho tránsito que vemos en estas calles.

Diego. ¿Ah, sí? Pues, allá ellos. Yo no soy de esos españoles que se contentan con una España anticuada y pintoresca, una España de museo.

Frank. Me parece muy justo que pienses así. Ahora que yo, como turista, no puedo compartir tu opinión.

Diego. Te aseguro que España no ha perdido su encanto y su carácter distintivo por haber adquirido algunas de las ventajas del mundo moderno, y por haber dejado de ser tan pobre como antes.

Frank. Oh, no. Nadie puede lamentar que el país tenga más prosperidad ahora. Pero me pregunto si España realmente ha quedado la misma con todos los cambios que han ocurrido en este siglo.

Diego. Pues, yo creo que sí, a pesar de que los españoles tenemos ahora un problema que antes sólo teníais los americanos: el de no poder hallar donde aparcar el coche.

Theme 5

Diego asked Frank which he preferred, to take a taxi or go on foot, adding that it was immaterial to him. Frank said that he preferred to walk. Since he had been in Madrid, he had gone everywhere in [a] car, on the bus or in the subway. He had not taken any exercise, not even walking, even though he was accustomed to play golf and tennis regularly.

The two were [standing] on a corner of the Calle de Alcalá. They went down the street as far as the Plaza de la Cibeles—so called on account of the statue of the goddess Cybele (which is) in the center. Surrounded by some of the largest and finest buildings in Madrid—the Central Post Office, the Ministry of the Army, the Bank of Spain—this huge square is the most imposing in the city. It is crossed by (crosses it) one of the broadest and most beautiful boulevards in Europe, the Paseo de Calvo Sotelo, which to the south becomes the Paseo del Prado. Frank and Diego walked up **(subir por)** Calvo Sotelo as far as the Plaza de Colón. Near this square are also many handsome and important buildings, for instance, the Presidency of the Government, the Mint, and the National Library. The latter occupies a whole block, and has a [very] fine collecton of manuscripts and rare books. Along the boulevard, which from Colón on is called the Castellana, up to the Plaza de San Juan de la Cruz, are many other public and private buildings, the finest in Madrid. In this part of Madrid is revealed better than anywhere else (in any other) its character as a (of) national capital.

It reminded Frank, in [a] certain sense, of Washington. He then realized that Madrid, like Washington, is an official rather than a natural capital, while Paris and London, on the other hand, have been political and economic centers from the beginning. Frank asked Diego if he shared his opinion.

Diego. Of course, of course. Only I, being a Spaniard, prefer Madrid. But don't think for that [reason] that I am one of those Spaniards who are contented with the picturesque and the old-fashioned. Don't forget that for us Spaniards the industrial and the commercial [sides] are much more important than (they are) for tourists.

Frank. Of course. I realize that. I suppose (that) Barcelona and Bilbao are the industrial cities of Spain?

Diego. Yes, those and to a lesser extent Valencia, Seville and Málaga are the cities which have traditionally been industrial centers. But these days one sees industrial development in many places that before our war were only provincial towns, like Burgos, Valladolid, Vigo, and others.

Frank. Modern progress seems to have transformed the country in many ways.

Diego. Not really. In my opinion the soul of Spain has not changed, even though we now share many of the problems of other industrialized countries.

Tema sexto

Una tertulia de café

4 de julio

Después de cenar—en Madrid se cena muy tarde, entre nueve y media y diez y media—nos fuimos a un café de la calle de Alcalá donde se reunen Peña y sus amigos. En la terraza no había una sola mesa vacía. Entramos; el interior estaba lleno también. Tuvimos que esperar unos minutos de pie y al fin conseguimos sitio en el rincón del fondo. El calor, las luces, el ruido, y la atmósfera espesa de tabaco me dejaron aturdido; sin embargo, la confusión no parecía molestar a nadie. Todo el mundo se hallaba a su gusto, charlando, fumando y saboreando despacio el vaso de café. Poco a poco fueron llegando los amigos de la tertulia. Ésta se componía en total de unas diez o doce personas, gente joven en su mayoría; algunos estudiantes de derecho y de medicina, un periodista, un pintor, y otros más que no sé lo que eran. La conversación se generalizó desde el primer momento en un tono de franqueza y cordialidad típicamente español. Dar idea de todos los incidentes sería cosa punto menos que imposible. Baste decir que se habló apasionadamente de todo lo humano y lo divino: de política, de literatura, de teatro, de cine. Por mi parte yo estaba asombrado. Aquello era un verdadero derroche de ingenio. Hubo un momento en que trataron de envolverme en una discusión sobre un asunto de política internacional, pero yo, recordando el consejo de Peña, decidí seguirlo al revés, y salí del paso como pude. Para mí era mucho más divertido dejar que hablaran ellos que no hacerlo yo. A la una, ya un poco fatigado, me levanté para despedirme, pero acababan de llegar otros amigos, y la reunión continuó durante un buen rato. Cuando salimos a la calle aun había gente paseando por la acera, sin gran prisa por volver a casa.—Pero ¿a qué hora se levanta toda esta gente? le pregunté a Peña.—Depende. Hay muchos, como esos estudiantes, que están ahora de vacaciones y se levantan a la hora que quieren; pero los que tienen que trabajar se levantan entre ocho y nueve o quizá antes.—Yo no podría hacer eso a diario. Me pondría enfermo.

—Es que vosotros, los anglosajones, os preocupáis de la salud mucho más que nosotros. Probablemente vivís más tiempo, pero yo creo que mientras dura, nosotros lo pasamos mejor.

Theme 6

One evening after dinner—in Madrid people do not dine until ten o'clock or even later—Diego took Frank to the café where he and his friends had their *tertulia.*

It was around eleven o'clock, the hour they were accustomed to meet. The café was full; there wasn't a single free table on the sidewalk nor even on the inside. To get a seat seemed practically impossible. After standing [and] waiting some time, they were able to install themselves in a corner in the rear.

The noise, the heat, the bright lights, and the thick tobacco smoke did not seem to disturb anybody. Everybody was enjoying himself smoking, talking, or slowly sipping his glass of coffee. For Frank the whole thing formed **(aquello era)** a confusion which at first made **(dejar)** him dizzy, but he gradually became accustomed [to it].

The ten or twelve friends who composed the *tertulia* were chiefly young people: a few law and medical students, a journalist, an artist, and others, whose occupation —if they had any—Frank did not get to know. The conversation became general from the start; everything under the sun was discussed—literature, politics, the theatre, moving pictures—with great feeling, but with a frankness and cordiality typically Spanish. It is enough to say that it was a veritable feast of wit.

There was a moment in which someone tried to involve Frank in an argument. The latter did not fail to recall Peña's advice, but he decided to follow it contrariwise and got out of the difficulty as [best] he could. For his part he thought it more amusing to let the others talk than to talk himself.

At one o'clock Frank, being a bit tired, rose to leave. Peña was in no great hurry to go because [some] other friends had just arrived. When they finally went out on the street, there were still some people strolling along the sidewalk.—What time do all these people get up? he asked Peña.—That depends. Those who have to work get up early, but all regularly go to bed late.—I couldn't do that without getting sick—I know. [The trouble] is that you Americans worry too much about your health. You may live longer than we, but I believe we have a better time while it lasts.

Tema séptimo

En el museo del Prado

Diego. Te advierto que no podremos verlo todo en una mañana. Habrá que elegir ciertos pintores, los que te interesen más, y dedicarnos a ver sus obras despacio y sin prisa.

Frank. De acuerdo. Empecemos por la pintura española y si queda tiempo veremos lo demás.

Diego. Ésta es la sala de Velázquez. Ahí tienes sus famosos bufones, sus bobos, y sus reyes de la casa de Austria.

Frank. ¡Qué realismo tan despiadado! Velázquez no parece preocuparse mucho de favorecer a sus modelos.

Diego. No, y eso que era pintor de la Corte.

Frank. ¿Dónde está el cuadro de *Las Meninas?* No lo veo por ninguna parte.

Diego. Está en una sala especial. Ven por aquí.

Frank. Ah, aquí está. Voy a sentarme un rato. Quiero contemplarlo detenidamente.

Frank. ¡Qué lástima que no hayamos podido ver toda la pintura española, Ribera, Zurbarán, Morales! Tenemos que volver otro día.

Diego. Me parece notar que Murillo y el Greco no te han hecho gran impresión.

Frank. Desde luego no me gustan tanto como Velázquez y Goya. Estos dos son mis pintores favoritos.

Diego. Y el Greco, ¿no te gusta?

Frank. No he dicho que no me guste. El colorido de sus cuadros es muy bello, muy original; pero, francamente, ese tipo de pintura no me emociona. Será falta de apreciación por parte mía.

Diego. Estoy seguro de que has de cambiar de opinión. Al Greco lo comprenderás no aquí en el Museo, sino en Toledo.

Frank. ¿Por qué? ¿Es que éstos no son sus mejores cuadros?

Diego. No, no es eso. Es que hay algo extraño en el alma de Toledo, en su paisaje, en sus colores, en su mismo aire, que el Greco, utilizó como punto de partida para sus imaginaciones pictóricas. Sin conocer el ambiente toledano es bastante difícil llegar a comprender su arte. ¿Por qué te sonríes?

Frank. No sé. Todo eso me parece demasiado sutil. En fin, ya veremos si logras convencerme.

Diego. No, eso sí que no. De convencerte, tendrás que hacerlo solito. Yo no pienso obligarte.

Frank. Bueno, bueno, no hay que enfadarte. Iremos a Toledo, y si cambio de opinión te lo diré con toda sinceridad.

Theme 7

Diego. I have already warned you that one morning will not be enough to see everything. It will be necessary to choose the painters that interest you most and leave the rest for another time.

Frank. All right. Let's devote the time we have left to the works of the Spanish painters, beginning with those of Velázquez. But how do we get **(¿por dónde se va?)** to the Velázquez room?

Diego. Come this way. You have made a good choice (chosen well). Velázquez is the most realistic of our painters, the one most easily appreciated by foreigners, and perhaps for that reason the most famous.

Frank. This must be the Velázquez room. I recognize his celebrated idiots, buffoons, and princes of the House of Austria. What marvellous realism! But how pitiless! I am going to sit down a while to look at it all slowly and carefully.

Diego. That's right. Take your time (don't hurry). In this room you have Velázquez's best [work].

Frank. All this is magnificent! Better than I expected. But where is the most famous picture of all, *Las Meninas?* I don't see it anywhere.

Diego. It is in the next room. Let's go there.

Frank. What a pity we haven't had more time! Only enough to see Velázquez, Goya, el Greco, and Murillo. We shall have to come back another do to see the paintings of Ribera, Zurbarán, and the others.

Diego. Which painters made [the] greatest impression on you today?

Frank. Velázquez and Goya, of course. They are so different, yet so alike in their frank, sincere realism. Neither (of the two) bothered to flatter his models—even though they were both court painters.

Diego. I suppose you found Murillo and el Greco [too] unrealistic for your taste?

Frank. Frankly, yes. Murillo too sentimental and el Greco too fantastic. It may be lack of appreciation on my part. After all, I don't pretend to be an art critic.

Diego. I understand. But you have a right to say what you think. Only, I am sure you will change your opinion when we go to Toledo. El Greco must be seen, not here but in Toledo, to be appreciated. Don't smile. You will see [for yourself].

Frank. But (it is that) all this is too subtle for me. And I doubt if (that) you [will] succeed in convincing me.

Diego. That's not the point at all! If [it's a question of] being convinced, you will have to do it all by yourself. I don't intend to compel you.

Frank. All right, all right. No need to get angry. If I change my opinion, I'll tell you so in all sincerity.

Tema octavo

En Toledo

10 de julio.

La Ciudad Imperial, la antigua capital de España, es hoy una tranquila capital de provincia. Asentado sobre una alta roca y casi completamente circundado por el río Tajo, Toledo presenta el aspecto de una fortaleza. El paisaje, de tonos rojos, grises y amarillos, es adusto, severo; paisaje que invita a la meditación, a la quietud, más bien que al movimiento. Todo es antiguo, lejano. Los automóviles y autocares llenos de turistas que suben penosamente por las callejuelas en cuesta parecen absurdos anacronismos.

Podría decirse de Toledo que más que una ciudad histórica es la ciudad histórica por excelencia, la Historia misma. Y, en efecto, ha sido declarado monumento nacional. Aquí, una iglesia gótica del siglo XIII o del siglo XV; más allá, una antigua sinagoga; en esta calle, una bella fachada plateresca; en aquel callejón, una casa mora. Romanos, godos, árabes, judíos y cristianos han dejado las huellas de sus distintas culturas en estas viejas piedras.

Cada rincón evoca una multitud de recuerdos poéticos: leyendas de Bécquer y de Zorrilla, romances del Duque de Rivas, escenas de las comedias de capa y espada, Garcilaso de la Vega, el Greco, Cervantes.

Los nombres de las calles suenan a cuentos maravillosos: calle del Pozo Amargo, calle del Taller del Moro, calle del Hombre de la Pata de Palo.

¡Qué lejos estamos de nuestro modo diario de vida! Toledo dista de Madrid menos de 50 millas, pero habría que medir la distancia no en el espacio, sino en el tiempo, no en millas, sino en siglos.

Toledo es inagotable. No hemos parado ni un solo instante y sin embargo no hemos visto ni la mitad de lo que quisiéramos ver. Aparte de los monumentos mayores, como la Catedral, San Juan de los Reyes, el Alcázar—ahora completamente reconstruido después de haber sido casi totalmente destruido durante su heroica defensa en la Guerra Civil—hemos visitado otros muchos lugares de interés. La cervantina Posada de la Sangre tiene un carácter de época delicioso.

No quiero dejar de mencionar dos obras de arte que por sí solas merecerían un viaje a Toledo: la estatua yacente del Cardenal Tavera, por el gran Berruguete, y el *Entierro del Conde de Orgaz*, famosísimo cuadro del Greco.

Theme 8

Toledo, a city already famous in Roman times, the capital of Visigothic Spain, a center of Moorish, Jewish, and Castilian cultures, the imperial city of the great Charles V, is today a quiet, isolated provincial capital. And precisely for that reason it has been able to retain its historic character so completely as to (that it has come to) merit the title of Museum City of Spain. But this does not mean that Toledo is something artificial or dead. On the contrary, what happens is that in Toledo the present does not exist because the past is still alive.

Although Toledo is less than fifty miles from Madrid, the distance between the two cities should be measured in time rather than in space. Madrid represents almost exclusively the Spain of the nineteenth and twentieth centuries, the spirit and strength of modernity; Toledo embodies the living past, the glories of history, and the force of tradition. Thus it might be said that these two cities—so close and yet so far apart—symbolize a fundamental, vital aspect of Spanish reality: the coexistence of the present and the past.

Perched on a high rock, almost surrounded by the Tagus river, Toledo looks like a medieval fortress. Medieval and ascetic is the bare, harsh landscape with its red, gray, and brown tones. Medieval and Moorish, too, are the steep, winding, narrow streets with their picturesque and romantic names. Every house seems to breathe mystery; every corner evokes historic and exotic memories. Romans, Goths, Moors, and Jews have left the marks of their different cultures on the walls, the gates, and the temples. But the greatest glories of Toledo are genuinely Spanish: artistic and religious. The magnificent Cathedral, the richest in all Spain, the beautiful church of San Juan de los Reyes. the hospitals of Santa Cruz and of Tavera, the innumerable churches and convents make (of) Toledo the religious city *par excellence* of Spain. Toledo recalls the learning of Alfonso el Sabio, the realism of *Lazarillo de Tormes* and of the great Cervantes, the romanticism of the Duque de Rivas, of Zorrilla, of Bécquer. But the spirit of Toledo—medieval and oriental, Catholic and exotic, harsh and mystic—is best expressed in the paintings of El Greco, especially in the famous *Burial of the Count of Orgaz*, which for its own sake is worth (merits) a trip to Toledo.

Tema noveno

A. Escriba Ud. un párrafo de unas setenta a ochenta palabras sobre un paseo por un lugar favorito de Ud. Al escribir, conteste Ud. las preguntas siguientes:

1. ¿Dónde y cuándo empezó el paseo?
2. ¿Por qué medio de transportación fue Ud.?
3. ¿Qué le atrae a Ud. más en aquel lugar?
4. ¿Qué hay de interés allí?
5. ¿Es un lugar muy recorrido o es Ud. uno de pocos que lo visitan?
6. ¿Qué cosas suele Ud. hacer allí?
7. ¿Tiene Ud. amigos que también van allí o prefiere ir solo?
8. ¿A qué clase de personas le gusta ese lugar?

B. Escriba Ud. un párrafo de unas setenta a ochenta palabras sobre el artista favorito de Ud. Puede ser artista en cualquier arte, la pintura, la escultura, la arquitectura, la literatura o la cinematografía. Al escribir, conteste Ud. las preguntas siguientes:

1. ¿Dónde y cuándo vivió este artista?
2. ¿Cuáles son sus obras más importantes y conocidas?
3. ¿Cuáles son las obras que más le agradan a Ud.? ¿Por qué?
4. ¿Cuáles son los rasgos más notables del arte de este artista?
5. ¿Cuáles han sido los rasgos más apreciados por los conocedores del arte?
6. ¿Qué importancia tuvo este artista en la historia de su arte?

7. ¿Qué influencia ha tenido en otros artistas?
8. ¿Quisiera Ud. ser artista?

C. Escriba Ud. un párrafo de unas setenta a ochenta palabras sobre la ciudad favorita de Ud. Conteste las preguntas siguientes:

1. ¿Dónde se halla esta ciudad?
2. ¿Cómo es la región en que se halla?
3. Describa Ud. lo más notable de su apariencia física, su población, etc.
4. ¿Cómo son los habitantes?
5. ¿Tiene esta ciudad alguna importancia histórica?
6. ¿Qué es lo que más le gusta de esta ciudad?
7. ¿Viviría Ud. allí si pudiera o sólo le gusta para visitar?
8. ¿Qué debe tener una ciudad para que sea un buen lugar para vivir?

Tema décimo

Diversiones españolas

Diego. ¡Valiente semana de agitación! Estoy rendido. Teatros, cines, corridas de toros, partidos de fútbol . . . Podrías escribir todo un libro acerca de las diversiones de los españoles.

Frank. No, escribir un libro, no; pero me parece que no he perdido el tiempo. Después de todo, la mejor manera de conocer a un pueblo es estudiar sus diversiones. Un español, un francés, y un norteamericano podrán diferenciarse bastante en sus métodos de trabajo, pero esta diferencia se agranda todavía más cuando llega el momento de divertirse. ¿No crees?

Diego. Sin duda, sin duda. ¿Y qué has sacado en limpio de esos estudios? Me gustaría conocer tu opinión.

Frank. Pues te diré. Al español le interesa principalmente el espectáculo, no el deporte.

Diego. Eso será verdad en los toros, pero en otras cosas . . .

Frank. Creo que en otras cosas también. En los partidos de fútbol y de pelota que hemos visto, la atención del público parece concentrarse siempre en el gesto individual, en el momento brillante, más bien que en la actuación del equipo. Un deporte como el *football* norteamericano no gustaría nada aquí.

Diego. No; tienes razón. Requiere demasiada organización, demasiada técnica, para nuestro gusto. En cambio, un partido de pelota vasca, ¡eso sí que es bonito! Rápido, gracioso, elegante. Los jugadores, de blanco, con sus fajas rojas y azules . . . Es casi como un baile.

Frank. ¿Ves? Volvemos a lo que yo decía antes, al espectáculo.

Diego. Bien, ¿pero tú concibes el interés de un deporte en el que no haya nada artístico, aunque sea de un modo inconsciente? Yo no.

Frank. Yo sí. No creo que eso sea absolutamente necesario.

Diego. Bueno, no discutamos. Tú tomas un punto de vista, yo tomo otro, y se acabó. En el fondo se trata de la diferencia entre dos civilizaciones.

Frank. Y naturalmente cada uno cree que lo suyo, por ser suyo, es siempre lo mejor.

Diego. Claro, eso ni que decir tiene.

Theme 10

Madrid, July 20.

Dear Joe,

What a busy week this has been! I am worn out from so much going to theatres, movies, bullfights, etc. I could write you a whole book on the amusements of the Spaniards. But don't think I have wasted time. After all, it seems to me that one of the best ways of getting to know the Spaniards is to study their amusements. A Spaniard and an American may be quite different in their methods of work, but in their amusements this difference becomes still greater. Don't you think so?

You will doubtless ask me to what conclusions I have come [as a result] of my observations. I shall tell you, because I should like to know your opinion in (about) the matter.

The Spaniard is chiefly interested in spectacle, not in sport. This is true, not only in bullfights, but in other things also: for example, in soccer and in *pelota vasca*. The public seems always to prefer a brilliant individual stroke to team play. I am sure that our American football or baseball would not go at all here. They require too much organization, too much technique for the Spanish taste. On the other hand, a game of *pelota vasca*, that's what they like! They find it speedy, graceful, elegant, in a word "pretty." For us it would be too simple, too much like a dance.

Diego says that in every sport there should be some artistic element, even if it be unconscious(ly); otherwise he does not understand the interest it could have for anybody. Do you agree with him? I don't. But we haven't argued as violently [about] this as [about] some other things. He takes one point of view, I another, and that's all there is to it. At bottom it is a question of the difference between two civilizations. And naturally each one thinks that what is his, just because it is his, is the best. That goes without saying.

Well, enough for the present. I will write you soon again.

Yours as always **(tuyo afectísimo),**

FRANK

Tema once

Teatros y corridas

23 de julio

Yo, que soy hombre casero más que nada, aquí me paso el día en la calle. Por las mañanas suelo dar un paseo por el Retiro o entro en la Biblioteca Nacional a leer un rato hasta la hora de almorzar. Comer, como siempre fuera, cada vez en un sitio distinto. Vuelvo al hotel a recoger el correo; me refresco un poco, y otra vez a la calle. Por las noches voy siempre al teatro. He asistido a varios estrenos, y con una sola excepción las obras fueron muy bien recibidas, y los autores salieron a escena al final de cada acto. Del repertorio clásico he visto solamente *El alcalde de Zalamea.* Las obras antiguas, según me dicen, no se representan con toda la frecuencia que sería de desear. Esto para mí ha sido una gran desilusión, porque yo venía entusiasmado con la idea de ver muchas de las comedias del Siglo de Oro. Pero, en fin, si no he visto teatro clásico, en cambio no me he perdido ninguna de las zarzuelas antiguas anunciadas en las carteleras. ¡Qué tipo de teatro tan español, tan castizo! *La Revoltosa* y *La verbena de la paloma*, modelos del género, me han gustado a más no poder.

Como todo el mundo, yo había leído algo, lo mismo en pro que en contra de la llamada fiesta nacional, esto es, las corridas de toros; sin embargo, no había llegado a formar una idea justa de tal espectáculo. Me había figurado a los toreros como una especie de fuertes atletas que luchaban con el toro casi a brazo partido. Nada de esto. Con gran sorpresa por mi parte me encuentro con que los toreros son muchachos jóvenes, delgados, que no tienen en absoluto nada de atléticos. La corrida de toros no es un espectáculo de fuerza bruta, ni mucho menos; al contrario, lo que el público busca en ellas es el valor sereno, la gracia, la ligereza, el encanto de líneas. En ciertos momentos toro y torero, solos en el ruedo de arena amarilla, forman un grupo escultórico de emoción y belleza insuperables. Esto es solo un aspecto, claro está. Hay otros, por ejemplo la suerte de varas, francamente desagradables, penosos.

Si me preguntaran de buenas a primeras, "¿Le gustan a Ud. o no las corridas de toros?", yo contestaría, "Me gusta un cinco por ciento del total". Y por lo que me dice Peña, a la mayoría de los españoles les pasa lo mismo.

Theme 11

In Spain, social life—for men especially—takes place outside the home, in the café, the club, the theatre, or on the street. The result was that Frank, being a homebody, would often spend the whole day in the open air, taking walks through the streets or the Retiro, or seated in the *terraza* of a café. Sometimes he would go to the National Library in the mornings, to read until lunch time. [As for] eating, he always ate out, each time in a different place. After lunch he would go back to his hotel to get his mail, freshen up a bit, and [go] out again. In the evenings he usually went to the theatre, preferably to the opening night of a play, whenever there was one. If the plays were well received the authors would come out on the stage at the end of each act. The kind of show he liked most was (were) the old *zarzuelas*, which he found so thoroughly—and—typically Spanish, and he did not miss a one of the ones advertised on the billboards. But he was able to see only one *comedia* of the Golden Age—*La vida es sueño*—one of the most famous of all Spanish plays. That was a disappointment for him, since he had come to Madrid full of enthusiasm at at the idea of seeing the greatest number possible of plays of the classical repertory.

Frank had never managed to get a fair idea of the so-called national sport—that is [to say], of bullfighting—although, like everyone [else], he had read a great deal (both) pro and con this spectacle. He had always thought of bullfighters as strong athletes who fought almost hand to hand with the bull. To his great surprise he found that a (the) bullfight is by no means an exhibition of brute strength and that bullfighters do not look at all like athletes, but are **(siendo)**, on the contrary, slender young men, since what the public looks for is not strength, but calm courage, agility, grace, and plastic beauty. He realized that at certain moments [the] bull and bullfighter, alone in the ring of yellow sand, form a sculptural group full of beauty, color, and emotional appeal. Nevertheless, this was the only aspect that pleased him. There were others that were frankly disagreeable and painful. He felt that, if he were asked point blank if he liked bullfights, he would have to answer that he liked about five per cent of the whole [spectacle]. And [judging] by what Peña told him, many Spaniards feel the same way.

Tema doce

Planeando una excursión

Diego. ¿Qué te pasa, hombre, con ese aire tan preocupado? ¿Estás enfermo? ¿Has recibido alguna mala noticia?

Frank. No, nada de eso, afortunadamente. Es que me he pasado la mañana planeando una de esas excursiones de que hemos hablado, y por más cambios que hago en el itinerario no me sale como yo quisiera.

Diego. Pues no será por falta de sitios interesantes, porque hay muchísimos a poca distancia de Madrid.

Frank. Ahí está lo malo. Me gustaría ir a todas partes, recorrerlo todo, pero no puede ser. No hay tiempo. Aquí tengo el mapa. He señalado con lápiz rojo los lugares que me gustaría visitar.

Diego. A ver. ¡Pues no te has quedado corto señalando! Apenas si has dejado nombre de ciudad o pueblo sin su correspondiente señal. Desde luego no vamos a poder recorrerlos todos.

Frank. Claro está que no. Por eso quisiera que me ayudaras a elegir la mejor ruta. Está visto que yo no puedo hacerlo.

Diego. Hazme el favor del lápiz. Mira Tomando a Madrid como centro y en un radio de unos 150 kilómetros se pueden hacer cuatro excursiones de gran interés: dos por el sur, y dos por el norte. Aquí tienes una: Aranjuez, Toledo, Talavera de la Reina, el monasterio de Guadalupe y Ciudad Real.

Frank. Sí, eso estaría muy bien, pero como ya he visto Toledo preferiría un paisaje de otro tipo distinto.

Diego. Aquí tienes otra ruta: por Aranjuez a Cuenca, que es una ciudad bellísima, mal conocida aún de los mismos españoles.

Frank. Tú has estado allí, ¿no?

Diego. Sí, por una rara casualidad.

Frank. Bueno, sigamos.

Diego. Por el norte tienes este magnífico itinerario: Madrid, Segovia, la Granja con sus palacios, fuentes y jardines, y luego a la vuelta Ávila, el Escorial, y el Valle de los Caídos. Además, con las magníficas autopistas que tenemos ahora, se puede hacerlo todo en un fin de semana.

Frank. ¿De veras? Pero, como no tengo coche tendré que ir en autobús.

Diego. Hombre, no hay para qué. Si no te molesta mi compañía, puedo pedir prestado el coche de mi hermano ya que mis padres han vuelto a Murcia.

Frank. Ahí hablas como un español moderno. Pero no quiero molestar a tu hermano.

Diego. No te preocupes. Es sólo por un par de días. A ver si podremos ir este fin de semana.

Theme 12

Diego. Why that worried look? You look like a sick man or a person who has just received some bad news.

Frank. There's nothing like that the matter with me, fortunately. The fact is my head is in a whirl with this [business] of making plans for a trip through Castile. I have spent the entire morning studying the map and the bus timetable, and no matter how many combinations I try, none of them turns out as I should like.

Diego. But why (**¿a qué vienen?**) all those red marks on the map? You have scarcely left without a mark any of the cities and towns within a **(a)** short distance of Madrid.

Frank. That's true. I know I didn't limit myself in marking. But all those places are very interesting, and if I have to leave any [of them out], it won't be for lack of wanting to see them. Of course, I'd like to cover them all, but that can't be [done].

Diego. Of course not. You haven't enough time.

Frank. That's [just] the trouble. Unless you help me to make a choice, I'm not going to be able to go anywhere.

Diego. Let's see. Please [give] me the map. Look here. Here is a good trip to the south: Cuenca, a very interesting city, not very well known even to Spaniards, Aranjuez, a bit of France in the middle of the Castilian desert, Toledo, the monastery of Guadalupe, and Ciudad Real. In short, a large part of La Mancha and New Castile.

Frank. As I have already seen Toledo, I should prefer a trip to the north.

Diego. All right. Let's continue. Here is another [and] shorter one: Madrid to Segovia, by way of the Guadarrama range and the royal residence of La Granja, then, on the way back, Ávila, El Escorial, and the Valley of the Fallen. Since there are such good highways now, you can see all of that in a weekend.

Frank. I could if I had a car, but since I don't I'll go by bus.

Diego. Don't worry! My parents have gone back to Murcia, but I can borrow my brother's car.

Frank. Now you talk like a modern Spaniard who prefers to travel by car.

Diego. Why not? It's much more convenient. Let's go this weekend.

Tema trece

Ávila y Segovia

31 de julio.

Hemos hecho una excursión formidable en sólo dos días. Tanto como mi visita a Toledo, el viaje a Ávila y Segovia fue un viaje por la historia. El contraste entre las dos ciudades no podría ser mayor.

Ávila, tierra de cantos y de santos, dice una frase proverbial. La ciudad mística, la ciudad de Santa Teresa, vive aparte del mundo, encerrada en sus murallas medievales. Aquí todo es gravedad, reconcentración, piedra gris. Para mi gusto, sin embargo, no puede compararse con Segovia. La situación topográfica de ésta, alzada soberbiamente sobre una alta roca, su color cálido, su gracia y armonía espirituales, la hacen destacar entre sus hermanas castellanas. En cuanto a riqueza artística y monumental, Segovia ofrece una gran variedad de formas y estilos, desde las sólidas y macizas construcciones romanas, como el famoso Acueducto, hasta los exquisitos palacios del Renacimiento, pasando por el románico y el gótico en sus diferentes períodos. Hasta se podría decir que Segovia está llena de colores y música, tan alegres si Castilla pudiera ser alegre.

No hay en toda España, quizá en toda Europa, nada tan grandiosamente sencillo como el Monasterio del Escorial. La roca brava, a impulso del espíritu, se ha convertido en masa arquitectónica. Es la sierra castellana hecha pensamiento. Fundado y aún dirigidas las obras personalmente por Felipe II, el Monasterio—inmensa mole de granito—encarna la voluntad, el sueño de dominio universal de un rey y de un pueblo. Para mí ha sido la impresión más fuerte que he recibido hasta ahora.

El panteón de los Reyes de España, la Biblioteca de manuscritos, las Salas Capitulares con su magnífica colección de pinturas, pueden servir como ejemplos particulares del interés excepcional que ofrece este lugar único.

Por fin, como todos los turistas, fuimos a visitar la magnífica iglesia esculpida en la roca viva de una montaña en el Valle de los Caídos. Allí están enterrados muchos de los combatientes muertos en la Guerra Civil. Es verdaderamente impresionante aquella iglesia que sirve como triste recuerdo eterno del momento más trágico de la historia de la España moderna. Volví a Madrid muy callado, lleno de pensamientos y emociones.

Theme 13

One day, early in the morning, Frank and Diego began their trip. They drove across the mountains to Ávila, the mystic walled city, as the tourist posters customarily proclaim in flowery language. The highway ran across vast moors surrounded by mountains and scattered with gigantic boulders—a fitting homeland for **(tierra de)** warriors and saints. The city, with its perfectly preserved walls, its fortress cathedral, its many Romanesque churches, its convents and lordly mansions with coats-of-arms carved over the doorway, is an evocation of medieval Castile, of the glory and the greatness of the *conquistadores* and the mystics, crusaders of the faith.

Frank, however, preferred Segovia. The massive Roman aqueduct, the golden Gothic cathedral, the Plaza Mayor, similar to the Zocodover of Toledo, the winding streets with their Romanesque churches, old houses, Renaissance mansions, and picturesque little squares—all this gives the city an air of richness, variety, and color that fascinated him. And from the Alcázar, the finest medieval castle in Spain, perched on the tip of the rock on which the city is located, he saw an unforgettable view of the city and of the multicolored Castilian plain which it dominates.

There was nothing in all he had seen that impressed Frank so profoundly as the Escorial, the huge monastery-palace built by Philip II on the edge of the Guadarrama. On one side the mountains rise precipitously, on the other the Castilian plain stretches away seemingly to infinity. And the palace—an immense mass of gray granite cast into the most severe of architectural styles—harmonizes perfectly with the landscape to express not only the religious spirit of its founder and of his work—the Catholic Counter-Reformation—but also the solid but solitary grandeur, the austere majesty of the Castilian soul.

These severe walls hold a rich and varied treasure of priceless books and manuscripts, of paintings and tapestries. The rooms of Philip II—preserved just as he left them—reveal the almost ascetic simplicity in which this monkish despot lived and died.

Last of all, Frank and Diego visited the Valley of the Fallen, whose church reminds visitors of the bare simplicity of the Escorial. It is one of the most modern of the monuments of Spain, and will stand as a permanent reminder of the tragedy of modern Spain.

Tema catorce

Por tierras de Castilla

14 de agosto.

Mi amigo Peña tuvo que ir a Murcia porque había quedado en Madrid más tiempo de lo que había pensado y sus padres le esperaban en casa. Nuestro viaje a Ávila y Segovia había despertado en mí el deseo de ver más de Castilla. Así que antes de ir a visitar a Diego en Murcia, emprendí un viaje por autobús a varias ciudades del norte.

La excursión ha sido para mí una experiencia valiosísima. Esta tierra castellana, parda, sin árboles, que al principio casi repele al extranjero con su aridez y sequedad, finalmente se adueña de nuestro espíritu. El interés histórico de esta región es imposible de exagerar. Aquí, en la alta meseta castellana, es donde hay que buscar el secreto de España, los motivos de su actuación política en el mundo, de su arte y su literatura. Castilla, tierra de guerreros, conquistadores y santos, es la madre de España.

Alcalá de Henares, bello ejemplo del Renacimiento español, me ha interesado especialmente por este motivo: presenta, no edificios aislados de carácter renacentista como pueden hallarse en Toledo, en Sevilla, y en otros muchos lugares, sino un conjunto armónico, de clásicas proporciones, difícil de encontrar en la Península. La Universidad, fundada en 1508 por el Cardenal Cisneros, Regente de Castilla a la muerte de Fernando el Católico, fue uno de los más famosos centros de cultura de Europa. Se estima que en su época de esplendor llegó a sentar en sus aulas unos 12,000 estudiantes.

Guadalajara con su maravilloso Palacio del Infantado, de estilo plateresco; Sigüenza, con su curiosa catedral románica, abundante en escultura; Soria, cuyas desoladas cercanías evocan las correrías del Cid y de sus compañeros de destierro; Valladolid, antigua capital de España, rica en gótico y en plateresco, con su magnífico museo de escultura española antigua, son verdaderas ciudades tesoro, cada una de las cuales bien merece larga y detenida visita. Al salir de Valladolid llegué a los campos llanos de la provincia de Salamanca. Pasamos unas cuantas estaciones sin importancia, y al fin divisamos la torre de la catedral en la lejanía.

Salamanca. El nombre es ya de por sí una evocación de grandeza intelectual. La Universidad, fundada en el siglo XIII, fue la rival de Oxford y París, y en ella han enseñado los hombres más eminentes de España, sea un Fray Luis de León en el siglo XVI o Don Miguel de Unamuno en nuestros días.

Todavía más que Alcalá de Henares, Salamanca es puro clasicismo: elegancia de forma, belleza intelectual, armonía.

Salamanca es toda dorada, de una suavidad de color maravillosa. ¡Qué bien me encontraba allí! Si yo viviera en España ésa sería mi ciudad. Y pienso una vez más, "¡Qué variedad infinita la de España! ¡Qué difícil llegar a conocerla!"

Theme 14

The trip through the historic lands of Castile was for Frank a most valuable experience. He visited nine or ten cities of the Castilian plateau, going as far as Soria and Burgos, and returning by way of Valladolid and Salamanca. All that he saw had for him an interest impossible to exaggerate. The Castilian landscape at first repelled him, as it does almost every foreigner, but it soon took possession of his spirit. He came to the conclusion that the secret of Spain, the mainsprings of her literature, her art, and her rôle in history, must be sought in these Castilian lands, harsh, dry, austere, the home of warriors and of mystics.

Our traveller first stopped at Alcalá de Henares less than two hours from Madrid, the city where, in 1547, Cervantes was born. The famous University, founded in 1508, was transferred in 1837 to Madrid, and Alcalá is now only a small provincial town. But, like its older sister Salamanca—also a university city—it still bears throughout **(en todo)** the stamp of the Renaissance, not so much in the individual buildings—the University is the only one of pure Renaissance style—as in the general atmosphere of tranquillity, grace, and harmony.

Next he visited Guadalajara, with its plateresque palace, Sigüenza, with its fortress cathedral, and Soria, with its blood colored landscape and its Romanesque ruins. He was now in heroic Castile, the heart of Spain.

Through epic lands that recalled the deeds of the *Romancero* and the wars between Moors and Christians he went on to Burgos, the home of the Cid and the first capital of Castile, a city famous for its magnificent Gothic Cathedral,—one of the most beautiful in the world. On the way he passed through the vast, monotonous plain of Western Castile, staying one night in Valladolid and then going to Salamanca.

In a plain to the west of Madrid lies Salamanca, the city of scholars and poets, the Oxford of Spain; Salamanca the golden, so called because of the marvellous golden color which the stone in (of) all the old buildings has. Not even Toledo has more artistic monuments than Salamanca, with its two cathedrals—the old Cathedral is a real gem of Romanesque art—its magnificent University, its many churches, convents, and palaces, examples all of them, of the finest plateresque style. Toledo belongs to all ages, Salamanca to only one. It embodies the beauty and the strength of the Renaissance and of the Golden Age of Spain's intellectual and artistic life. No city in Spain has such an air of classic harmony, which is perfectly expressed in its monumental Plaza Mayor—the finest in all Spain—which is still the center of the city's life. Seville and Salamanca are two cities which have been able to harmonize modern life with the spirit of tradition.

Tema quince

A. Escriba Ud. un párrafo de unas ochenta palabras sobre el deporte favorito de Ud. Conteste Ud. las preguntas siguientes:

1. ¿Cómo se organiza este deporte?
2. ¿Es un deporte que sólo juegan los profesionales o hay también aficionados que lo juegan?
3. ¿Le gusta a Ud. (o le gustaría) participar en el deporte?
4. ¿Es un deporte muy popular y suele haber muchos espectadores en los partidos?
5. ¿Es un deporte que requiere mucha preparación y entrenamiento?
6. ¿Puede Ud. comparar el deporte con la corrida de toros?
7. ¿Cree Ud. que los deportes reflejan el carácter nacional? ¿Cómo y por qué?

B. Escriba Ud. unas cien palabras sobre la época histórica que más le interesa a Ud. o algún acontecimiento histórico que le atrae, p. ej. la guerra de la independencia de los Estados Unidos o de España o de las repúblicas hispanoamericanas; la conquista de Granada o de América; el descubrimiento de América, etc. Conteste Ud. las preguntas siguientes:

1. ¿Cuál es la época (o el acontecimiento) de la historia humana que más le atrae a Ud.?
2. ¿Qué hay en esta época o acontecimiento que le suscita más interés?
3. ¿Quiénes son los personajes históricos que tuvieron más influencia en este periodo?
4. ¿Qué hicieron estas personas que fue importante?
5. ¿Qué impresión hicieron en sus contemporáneos?
6. ¿Cuál ha sido el juicio de la historia sobre estos personajes y la importancia de este acontecimiento?
7. ¿Qué efecto tuvo esta época en el desarrollo del mundo moderno?
8. ¿Qué sería diferente hoy si este acontecimiento hubiera sido diferente?
9. ¿Sería mejor el mundo entonces?

C. En unas cien palabras describa Ud. lo que Ud. entiende por la palabra "industrialización". En su respuesta conteste las preguntas siguientes:

1. ¿Qué se necesita para que un país se industrialice?
2. ¿Cuáles son algunos de los efectos en la vida pública, en la educación, en los medios de transportación, en la vida privada?
3. ¿Qué queremos decir cuando decimos que un país está atrasado o que es un país subdesarrollado?
4. ¿Es la industrialización una señal del progreso?

Tema dieciseis

De Madrid a Murcia

20 de agosto.

Después del recorrido por las tierras de Castilla la Vieja, dejé Madrid para ir a visitar a Diego y su familia en Murcia. Una mañana muy temprano el autobús salió de la ciudad. Pasamos por Aranjuez y dentro de poco llegamos a La Mancha.

La carretera atraviesa, monótonamente, la vasta llanura. Van quedando atrás dehesas y campos de cultivo. Aparece la torre cuadrada de una iglesia con su pueblecito de adobe agrupado en torno. Y luego, sembrados, rastrojos, más campo amarillo.

Casi puedo imaginar en la distancia infinita las solitarias figuras de Don Quijote y Sancho Panza que siguen su búsqueda eterna. Hasta vi un par de molinos de viento al lado de la carretera, no muy lejos del Toboso.

Al anochecer llegué a Murcia donde me esperaban Diego y su padre. Me saludaron calurosamente y casi inmediatamente me sentía un pariente cercano. Tienen una casa cómoda en los arrabales de la ciudad. Murcia no es muy grande ni muy famosa, pero tiene su propio encanto. Las calles estrechas de la típica ciudad provinciana me atraen. La comarca alrededor de Murcia se llama "La Huerta" por ser tan famosas sus naranjas. Para mí pueden competir con las de Valencia.

Un día Diego me llevó a la Cresta del Gallo, una montaña no muy lejos de la ciudad. Según la fama, la desolación de ese lugar se parece a la de la luna. Y es verdad. Uno muy fácilmente puede ver la semejanza con las fotografías hechas por los exploradores de la luna. Hay una extraña hermosura en esa desolación que contrasta con la riqueza vegetal de la Huerta.

Dentro de algunos días Diego y yo vamos en coche a visitar dos de las ciudades más famosas de Andalucía, Sevilla y Granada. ¡Qué lástima que no tengamos tiempo para ver más!

Theme 16

At last I began the journey to the south which I had been planning all summer. Very early one morning our bus left Madrid and in a couple of hours we were crossing the vast treeless plain of La Mancha. The road crossed a typical landscape of yellow and reddish fields. Occasionally there were pasture lands, and in the distance there would stand out the square tower of a church with its adobe village huddled around it. Except for an occasional **(alguna que otra)** flock of sheep much of La Mancha seems to be empty of all life. I could easily imagine the figures of Don Quixote and Sancho moving across the barren ground.

I found that Murcia is a pleasant city. It is not very big by American standards, and not well known except for its oranges, but there is a certain charm in its narrow streets. One day Diego took me to the Cresta del Gallo, a desolate mountain peak which is said to resemble the moon. In a way it does look like the pictures made by the men who explored the moon. It contrasts strongly with the richness of the country around Murcia.

Diego's parents live in a comfortable house on the outskirts of the city. In the evening Diego and I and his parents often go walking through the town. I find it fascinating to go up and down the winding streets. One never knows what surprises he may find: a small shop where all kinds of things are sold, like tiles, old pictures, and objects that in the United States would be sold at high prices in antique stores. Here one can buy such things for almost nothing.

Soon Diego and I are going to go by car to the most famous cities of Andalusia, Seville and Granada. I wish I had time to see more of this region. What a pity I can't spend more time in Spain.

Tema diecisiete

En Sevilla

(En un café céntrico.)

Diego. ¿Qué, te has cansado ya de ver cosas y de dar vueltas por las calles?

Frank. ¡Ca, hombre! ¡Ni mucho menos!

Diego. ¿Qué es lo que más te ha gustado hasta ahora?

Frank. No sé. Es muy difícil de decir. Me ha gustado todo. La catedral es verdaderamente magnífica. Tengo entendido que es la mayor de España. ¿Es verdad eso?

Diego. Sí, es verdad. Pero supongo que no te parecerá admirable por el solo hecho de ser la mayor.

Frank. Tú, como siempre, dispuesto a empezar una disputa. Pues lo que es esta tarde no vas a salirte con la tuya. Di todo lo que quieras, porque yo no he de llevarte la contraria.

Diego. Bueno, hablando en serio ahora. ¿Qué hacemos esta tarde?

Frank. Una cosa que me gustaría mucho es subir a la Giralda.

Diego. ¿Sí? Pues andando. En cuanto termines de tomarte la cerveza, vamos allá.

(Desde la Giralda.)

Frank. ¡Qué vista tan espléndida! ¡Y qué cielo tan claro! Es curiosísimo este panorama de azoteas. No había visto nunca una cosa asi.

Diego. Mira por este lado, hacia el río. ¿Reconoces esos edificios?

Frank. Claro que sí. Aquella torre redonda, amarilla, es la Torre del Oro. Más allá la Plaza de Toros. A lo lejos, en la otra orilla del Guadalquivir, el barrio de Triana.

Diego. Ven aquí ahora. ¿Qué ves?

Frank. Debajo de nosotros, el Alcázar, con los jardines que me han gustado tanto. Ahí enfrente, el Archivo de Indias. Aquellos son los edificios de la Exposición Hispano-Americana, ¿verdad?

Diego. Sí. La Exposición y el Parque de María Luisa. Todo eso fue construido para la Exposición Hispano-Americana en 1929.

Frank. ¿Tienes la hora? A mí se me ha parado el reloj.

Diego. Son las cuatro y veinte. ¿Te parece que bajemos y demos un paseo por el centro?

Frank. Encantado.

Diego. Y luego, esta noche, te llevaré a casa de unos amigos míos para que veas por dentro una casa sevillana típica.

Frank. Hombre, no podías sugerir nada que me gustara más.

Theme 17

Diego and Frank, tired for the moment of walking around the streets, stopped at one of the downtown cafés in (de) Seville to take some refreshment **(algo fresco).** While they were sitting (seated) there, Frank noticed that his watch had stopped and asked his friend: Do you have the time?

Diego. Yes, it's quarter to five. What [is the matter]? Have you had enough sightseeing for this afternoon?

Frank. I should say not! Not at all. [What] do you say we climb the Giralda? I'd like to see the view from there.

Diego. So? Well, then [let's get] going. *(He stands up.)*

Frank. Wait a moment until I finish my beer. I won't be long.

Diego. All right, I'll sit down again. Only I thought you, like [a] typical American tourist, would be in a hurry to see everything.

Frank. So you're ready to start an argument as usual. But for this afternoon, I am (have) determined you won't have your way. Say anything you want. I won't contradict you.

Diego. Oh, don't take it so seriously. I was [only] kidding.

From the top of the Giralda (the old Moorish bell tower which forms part of the magnificent Gothic cathedral of Seville) Frank was able to recognize most of the buildings he had seen before. Below was the Alcázar, whose interior is like a palace from the *Arabian Nights.* Toward the river he could see the Torre del Oro, another Moorish relic, with the suburb of Triana in the distance, on the other bank. Toward the opposite side were the buildings of the Exposition of 1929. But what pleased Frank more than anything [else] was the panorama of the housetops.

At night Frank and Diego took a walk through the picturesque Santa Cruz quarter, with its narrow and winding streets, its white houses, grilled windows, cool patios, and perfumed air. Frank was delighted. He had never seen anything like [that]. He then wanted to see a typical Sevillian house on the inside and Diego took him to a friend's (house). Frank began to understand why to a Sevillian everything Sevillian seems the best in the world, just because it is Sevillian.

Tema dieciocho

En Granada

España es el país de la variedad. Cada ciudad, cada pueblo, cada paisaje, tiene su propio espíritu, su propio estilo. ¡Qué diferencia entre Sevilla y Granada! Son dos mundos distintos. Sevilla es una ciudad de llanura; Granada, ciudad de colinas, rodeada de altas sierras cubiertas de nieves perpetuas. Sevilla, sin dejar de ser antigua, castiza, es una ciudad moderna, emprendedora, la más importante de Andalucía; Granada, aunque en cierto modo modernizada, sigue siendo la capital de un reino histórico, perdido para siempre. Aquélla es la ciudad de la gracia, de la alegría; ésta, la ciudad del misterio, del ensueño. Sólo en una cosa se parecen, en la claridad del cielo, siempre limpio y azul.

Hemos estado dos veces en la Alhambra; una por la mañana y otra por la tarde. ¡Ojalá pudiera verla de noche! Debe de ser una cosa fantástica a la luz de la luna.

¡Qué maravilla de ornamentación la de estas salas! Los complicados y bellísimos arabescos de las paredes, los azulejos de reflejos metálicos, las bóvedas con sus estalactitas de colores, son de una riqueza decorativa indescriptible.

El Patio de los Leones me desilusionó bastante. Es mucho más pequeño de lo que me había imaginado. En cambio, el Patio de los Arrayanes me parece una de las cosas más encantadoras que he visto en mi vida.

De todas las vistas granadinas hay dos que se me han quedado fuertemente grabadas en la memoria. Una es la perspectiva desde lo alto de la Alhambra, desde el Peinador de la Reina, por ejemplo. Desde allí se abarca el Generalife, el estrecho valle del Darro que forma la parte central de la ciudad, el Sacro Monte, con sus cuevas donde viven los gitanos, y en el fondo la famosa vega y los picos de Sierra Elvira. La otra es la vista de la Alhambra desde abajo. Sobre la colina inaccesible se alzan las torres de color rosado anaranjado, y detrás, el muro de Sierra Nevada con sus crestas blancas.

Theme 18

August 27.

Dear Joe,

You're probably wondering what has happened to me in Spain. I finally have a few minutes to write you **(poner)** these lines from Granada, as I had **(tener)** promised you.

At last I am in Andalusia after having visited Madrid and as much of Castile as I could.

I don't know which city I like better (more), Seville or Granada. They are so different. In Spain each city, each region has its own spirit, its own character, which is revealed in the buildings, in the landscape, in the general atmosphere, and in the people.

Seville lies in a broad, open plain, Granada in the narrowest [part] of a valley, surrounded by mountains. In Seville, in spite of the many imposing monuments, it is the air of the city [as a] whole that impresses one more than anything [else]. In Granada it is (are) the concrete sights and memories (the ones) which remain engraved in one's (the) mind: the Court of the Lions, the Court of the Myrtles, the gardens of the Generalife, the caves of the gypsies, the music of the fountains, and, above all, the many magnificent panoramas that take in the green *vega*, the steep green cliff crowned by the orange-rose colored walls of the Alhambra, with the white peaks of [the] Sierra Nevada in the distance.

Seville has the grace, the elegance, the charm of many centuries without bearing the [particular] stamp of any [one of them]. There the old and the new live together in a perfect harmony, which is (something) peculiarly Sevillian. On the other hand, Granada has a (the) divided soul. It is at one and the same time the city of the Catholic Sovereigns, who lie buried in the Royal Chapel of the Cathedral, and of the conquered Moors whose spirit pervades the ruined splendor of the Alhambra. The city itself belongs to the descendants of the former, the glory and the beauty to the memory of the latter.

But Seville and Granada are alike in that they both express, in **(de)** different ways, the spirit of Andalusia. The only thing in Granada that disappointed me was the gypsies. I found them less picturesque than I had imagineed.

I must close now. Regards to all our (the) friends and for you a cordial embrace from

FRANK

Tema diecinueve

De compras

Diego. ¿Dónde te metes? No te he visto durante toda la mañana.
Frank. He estado de compras.
Diego. ¿Por qué no me lo dijiste? Te hubiera acompañado.
Frank. No, ya he abusado bastante de tu amabilidad para obligarte encima a ir de tienda en tienda hasta volverte loco. Esto de los regalos es todo un problema. Nunca se sabe qué llevar.
Diego. Pues a juzgar por el montón de cajas y paquetes que tienes ahí, te has debido de portar muy bien.
Frank. Te enseñaré lo que he comprado. Un par de mantillas antiguas, una para mi cuñada y otra para mi hermana. Esto era un encargo que no tenía más remedio que cumplir.
Diego. Perdona la indiscreción, pero, ¿te han costado mucho?
Frank. Tres mil pesetas cada una.
Diego. ¡Hombre! Deben ser piezas de museo a ese precio.
Frank. Pues, sí que son caras pero ves lo hermosas que son. Y son antiguas, hechas de una tela riquísima.
Diego. En ese caso, fue una ganga.
Frank. Aquí tengo unos cuantos objetos de damasquinado toledano: un cortapapel, una pitillera, un encendedor, pulseras...
Diego. ¿Y esos tres grandes paquetes?
Frank. Son alfombras. Con éstas me quedo yo. Las voy a poner en mi habitación.
Diego. Milagro será que no te hayas comprado también un traje de luces.
Frank. No sé qué es un traje de luces.
Diego. Un traje de torero.
Frank. Pues te diré en secreto que llegué a preguntar el precio de uno, pero era demasiado caro.
Diego. ¿Qué más tienes ahí?
Frank. La mar de cosas. Azulejos de Segovia, unos collares muy bonitos de filigrana de Salamanca, varios objetos de cuero de Córdoba, y por último una buena colección de discos.
Diego. Hombre, eso me interesa. A ver, a ver.
Frank. Creo que darás el visto bueno a mi selección. Música de Albéniz, de Falla, de Turina; varias zarzuelas antiguas; todas las canciones populares que he podido encontrar; y ¡asómbrate!, un album entero de cante flamenco.
Diego. ¡Muy bien, pero que muy bien! Veo que eres gran perito en materia de

música española. Yo no lo hubiera hecho mejor. ¿Y cómo vas a enviar todo esto?

Frank. Las cosas menudas las meteré en la maleta, y el resto lo mandaré embalar. Ya he avisado a un mozo de cuerda para que las lleve a casa del embalador.

Diego. ¿Entonces insistes en marcharte mañana?

Frank. Sí, el avión sale el cinco de setiembre y quiero pasar unos días con mis padres antes de volver a la universidad.

Diego. Sí, el tiempo vuela. Muy pronto tendré yo también que tomar el avión a Nueva York. Nos veremos cuando la apertura de clases a fines del mes.

Theme 19

Frank was absent when Diego got up and no one knew where he had gone. Later Frank walked in loaded with packages. Diego asked: Where have you been keeping yourself?

Frank. I've been shopping.

Diego. I'm sorry you didn't let me know. I would have liked to go with you.

Frank. No, that would be abusing your kindness too much. This business of buying presents is [enough] to drive you crazy. You never know what to take to your (the) friends and relatives. It's a real problem.

Diego. Well, judging by that pile of boxes and packages, they won't have any right to complain. You must have spent the entire morning going from store to store. Pardon me if I'm being indiscreet, but would you mind showing me some of the things you bought?

Frank. On the contrary. I'd like you to give your O.K. to the whole collection. Here's a pair of genuine old mantillas that cost me three thousand pesetas each.

Diego. Wow! They must be museum pieces.

Frank. Well, they *were* expensive, but they're old and made of very fine cloth.

Diego. In that case, it was a bargain.

Frank. They're for my mother and sister—a commission I simply had to fulfill. But those large packages I'm going to keep myself. They are rugs for my room at home.

Diego. It's a wonder you didn't buy a bullfighter's costume.

Frank. [To tell you] the truth, I did go as far as to ask the price of one, but it was too expensive.

Diego. What else do you have there?

Frank. Lots of typically Spanish things: some articles of Toledan damascene—a paper knife, a cigarette case and lighter—Segovia tiles, necklaces of Salamanca filigree, articles of Cordovan leather, Talavera pottery. . . . Some of these things I'm going to give to my friends. By the way, here is something that will interest you, a collection of records: selections from Falla, Albéniz, Turina, and other composers, several old *zarzuelas*, a great many folk songs, and a whole album of *cante flamenco.*

Diego. I'm really (you leave me) astonished. Congratulations! I didn't suspect you were such an expert on Spanish music. You've chosen well, very well indeed.

Frank. Thanks. You embarrass me. What's worrying me now is how to send all this [stuff].

Diego. The small things you can put in your suitcase. The rest you can have crated. I'll send for a porter right away to carry them to the packer's. And so you still insist on leaving tomorrow?

Frank. It can't be helped. The plane leaves Madrid on the fifth.

Diego. Anyway, we'll see each other soon when classes begin at the end of September.

Tema veinte

Madrid, 5 de septiembre.

Querido amigo:

Ante todo quiero expresarte de nuevo mi profundo agradecimiento por las continuas amabilidades que has tenido para conmigo durante mi estancia en España. Como te dije de palabra al despedirnos y te repito ahora por escrito, sin tu buena amistad y tus generosos servicios de *cicerone* mis apreciaciones de las cosas españolas se hubieran reducido simplemente a impresiones superficiales y deficientes de turista, careciendo de ese no sé qué íntimo que sólo nace de la verdadera comprensión y que tú has sabido comunicarme. Espero que algún día—ojalá sea pronto—te decidas a pasar el verano en los Estados Unidos y me proporciones el placer de pagarte esta grata deuda.

Volveré cuando pueda, quizá el año que viene. Me queda tanto por ver que todavía necesitaré un par de viajes más para llegar a conocer España tan bien como quisiera. ¡Figúrate! No he visto nada de la parte de Levante, ni las islas Baleares, ni Aragón, ni la costa del Cantábrico, ni las Provincias Vascongadas, ni Asturias, ni Galicia.

Y además me gustaría volver a muchos de los sitios que ya conozco. Se me ha despertado tanto el interés por el mundo hispánico que quiero ir también a la América Española para conocer todas las facetas de lo hispánico.

El mundo es un pañuelo, amigo Peña. ¿Quieres creer que uno de mis compañeros de viaje en el autobús de Murcia a Madrid, vive en Nueva York y a dos pasos de mi casa? Es un muchacho español, agente de una casa importadora, que vuelve frecuentemente a España en viaje de negocios. Por cierto que aunque paramos en el mismo hotel no volví a verle más. Probablemente andaba el hombre muy atareado con sus asuntos. ¿Qué te parece el encuentro?

No puedo escribir más ahora porque el avión sale esta tarde. Espero que sabrás comunicar a tus padres el agradecimiento que siento por sus bondades para conmigo. Si algún día vienen a los Estados Unidos tendrán que ir a mi casa a conocer a mis padres. Estoy seguro que simpatizarán inmediatamente.

Dentro de pocos días nos veremos otra vez en la universidad y te contaré más de mis impresiones de mi estancia en España. Es verdad que tú has pasado más tiempo en mi patria que yo en la tuya, y así conoces bien a los norteamericanos. Pero todavía no has viajado mucho por los Estados Unidos y te queda mucho por ver.

Hasta muy pronto con un fuerte apretón de manos de tu buen amigo

FRANK

Theme 20

Madrid, September 5.

Dear Diego,

First of all I want to tell you again how deeply I appreciate the many kindnesses you have shown me during my stay in Spain, and to repeat in writing what I tried to say verbally when we parted in Murcia. Thanks to your kind friendship and generous services as guide my trip has not been limited to the superficial impressions of a tourist. Thanks to you my judgment of things Spanish does not lack completely that indefinable intimate [quality] which comes only from a genuine understanding, [such] as (the one) you were able to give me. I realize each day more and more how much I owe to you. May you decide to spend your summer vacation in the United States some day so that I can have the pleasure of repaying this kind debt!

Just imagine! In spite of all I say, I'll need a couple of trips more to Spain in order to get to know the country as I want to. I haven't seen anything of the north, the Levant, Catalonia, Asturias, Galicia. And now I'm interested in seeing Spanish America in order to see the Hispanic world in all its many facets.

The world is a small place after all. Will you believe that on the way to Madrid I had the good fortune of meeting a young Spaniard who lives in New York, and [only] a short distance from my house? [Just] imagine [it]! He is an agent for a firm of importers and has to make frequent business trips to Spain. And by the way, I didn't see any more of him—although we were staying at the same hotel. His business affairs must have kept him engaged. What do you think of this [chance] encounter?

In a few days we'll see each other at the university and can continue to exchange impressions of our two countries. Of course, you've spent more time in my country than I have in yours, so you already know a lot about Americans. However, you haven't travelled much so you still have a lot to see.

Until then, most cordial greetings from your sincere friend

FRANK

Tema veintiuno

A. Escriba Ud. un párrafo sobre una visita a un castillo viejo. Empiece con las frases siguientes: "La solitaria y melancólica luna derramaba su débil luz sobre las toscas piedras del castillo. El lejano ladrar de un perro añadía una nota de misterio a la escena."

B. Describa Ud. un viaje por las montañas. Empiece con la frase siguiente: "Las altas montañas de la España septentrional están cubiertas de nieve la mayor parte del año."

C. Describa Ud. un personaje raro. Empiece con las frases siguientes: "En un pueblecito tranquilo de la provincia lejos del ruidoso y febril bullicio de la ciudad, hace poco que vivía un viejo loco. ¡Pobre de don Alejandro!"

D. Escriba Ud. un diálogo entre dos amigos que discuten las diferencias entre la vida española y la vida norteamericana. Los amigos hablan de los deportes, la vida de todos los días, las actitudes hacia el mundo, etc.

E. Escriba Ud. un diálogo entre un estudiante y un profesor viejo. Hablan de lo que quieren los jóvenes modernos.

APPENDIX

Verbs

Regular verbs

222. Simple Tenses

INFINITIVE

hablar *to speak*	vender *to sell*	vivir *to live*

PRESENT PARTICIPLE

hablando	vendiendo	viviendo

PAST PARTICIPLE

hablado	vendido	vivido

INDICATIVE MOOD

Present

hablo	vendo	vivo
hablas	vendes	vives
habla	vende	vive
hablamos	vendemos	vivimos
hablais	vendeis	vivís
hablan	venden	viven

Imperfect

hablaba	vendía	vivía
hablabas	vendías	vivías
hablaba	vendía	vivía

Imperfect

hablábamos	vendíamos	vivíamos
hablabais	vendíais	vivíais
hablaban	vendían	vivían

Preterit

hablé	vendí	viví
hablaste	vendiste	viviste
habló	vendió	vivió
hablamos	vendimos	vivimos
hablasteis	vendisteis	vivisteis
hablaron	vendieron	vivieron

Future

hablaré	venderé	viviré
hablarás	venderás	vivirás
hablará	venderá	vivirá
hablaremos	venderemos	viviremos
hablaréis	venderéis	viviréis
hablarán	venderán	vivirán

Conditional

hablaría	vendería	viviría
hablarías	venderías	vivirías
hablaría	vendería	viviría
hablaríamos	venderíamos	viviríamos
hablaríais	venderíais	viviríais
hablarían	venderían	vivirían

Imperative (intimate)

habla	vende	vive
hablad	vended	vivid

SUBJUNCTIVE MOOD

Present

hable	venda	viva
hables	vendas	vivas
hable	venda	viva
hablemos	vendamos	vivamos
habléis	vendáis	viváis
hablen	vendan	vivan

Imperfect, **-ra** *Form*

habl**ara**	vend**iera**	viv**iera**
habl**ara**s	vend**iera**s	viv**iera**s
habl**ara**	vend**iera**	viv**iera**
habl**ára**mos	vend**iéra**mos	viv**iéra**mos
habl**ara**is	vend**iera**is	viv**iera**is
habl**ara**n	vend**iera**n	viv**iera**n

Imperfect, **-se** *Form*

habl**ase**	vend**iese**	viv**iese**
habl**ase**s	vend**iese**s	viv**iese**s
habl**ase**	vend**iese**	viv**iese**
habl**áse**mos	vend**iése**mos	viv**iése**mos
habl**ase**is	vend**iese**is	viv**iese**is
habl**ase**n	vend**iese**n	viv**iese**n

Future

habl**are**	vend**iere**	viv**iere**
habl**are**s	vend**iere**s	viv**iere**s
habl**are**	vend**iere**	viv**iere**
habl**áre**mos	vend**iére**mos	viv**iére**mos
habl**are**is	vend**iere**is	viv**iere**is
habl**are**n	vend**iere**n	viv**iere**n

223. Compound tenses of *hablar*

PERFECT INFINITIVE

haber hablado

PERFECT PARTICIPLE

habiendo hablado

INDICATIVE MOOD

Present Perfect

he hablado
has hablado
ha hablado
hemos hablado
habéis hablado
han hablado

Pluperfect

había hablado
habías hablado
había hablado
habíamos hablado
habíais hablado
habían hablado

Preterit Perfect

hube hablado, *etc.*

Future Perfect

habré hablado, *etc.*

Conditional Perfect

habría hablado, *etc.*

SUBJUNCTIVE MOOD

Present Perfect

haya hablado, *etc.*

Pluperfect

hubiera hablado, *etc.*
hubiese hablado, *etc.*

Future Perfect

hubiere hablado, *etc.*

224. Progressive tenses

These tenses are formed regularly with **estar (ir,** *etc.*—**§§20, 132)** and the invariable present participle (gerund).

225. Passive voice

The passive voice is formed regularly with **ser** and the inflected past participle **(§148)**. In the compound tenses **sido** is invariable: **habían sido castigadas** *they* (fem.) *had been punished.*

Radical- (or stem-) changing verbs

(Radical-changing verbs are indicated as such in the Vocabulary. They must be learned by observation.)

226. Class I (*contar-perder* type)

There are three classes of radical- (or stem-) changing verbs in Spanish. Class I comprises verbs of the first **(-ar)** and second **(-er)** conjugations, in which the stem-vowels **e** and **o** change when stressed to **ie** and **ue** respectively.

These changes occur only in the present tenses (indicative and subjunctive) throughout the singular and in the third person plural, and in the intimate imperative, singular.

contar *to tell*

PRES. IND. **cue**nto, **cue**ntas, **cue**nta, contamos, contáis, **cue**ntan
PRES. SUBJ. **cue**nte, **cue**ntes, **cue**nte, contemos, contéis, **cue**nten
IMPERATIVE **cue**nta, contad

perder *to lose*

PRES. IND. **pie**rdo, **pie**rdes, **pie**rde, perdemos, perdéis, **pie**rden
PRES. SUBJ. **pie**rda, **pie**rdas, **pie**rda, perdamos, perdáis, **pie**rdan
IMPERATIVE **pie**rde, perded

227. Class II (*sentir-dormir* type)

This class comprises verbs of the third (**-ir**) conjugation in which the stem-vowels **e** and **o** not only change when stressed to **ie** and **ue** respectively, but also to **i** and **u** respectively in the present participle, the first and second persons plural of the present subjunctive, the third person singular and plural of the preterit, and throughout the imperfect subjunctive (both forms) and the future subjunctive.

sentir *to feel*

PRES. IND. **sie**nto, **sie**ntes **sie**nte, sentimos, sentís, **sie**nten
PRES. SUBJ. **sie**nta, **sie**ntas, **sie**nta, s**i**ntamos, s**i**ntáis, **sie**ntan
IMPERATIVE **sie**nte, sentid
PRES. PART. s**i**ntiendo
PRETERIT sentí, sentiste, s**i**ntió, sentimos, sentisteis, s**i**ntieron
IMPERF. SUBJ. (**-ra**) s**i**ntiera, *etc.* IMPERF. SUBJ. (**-se**) s**i**ntiese, *etc.*
FUT. SUBJ. s**i**ntiere, *etc.*

dormir *to sleep*

PRES. IND. d**ue**rmo, d**ue**rmes, d**ue**rme, dormimos, dormís, d**ue**rmen
PRES. SUBJ. d**ue**rma, d**ue**rmas, d**ue**rma, d**u**rmamos, d**u**rmáis, d**ue**rman
IMPERATIVE d**ue**rme, dormid
PRES. PART. d**u**rmiendo
PRETERIT dormí, dormiste, d**u**rmió, dormimos, dormisteis, d**u**rmieron
IMPERF. SUBJ. (**-ra**) d**u**rmiera, *etc.* IMPERF. SUBJ. (**-se**) d**u**rmiese, *etc.*
FUT. SUBJ. d**u**rmiere, *etc.*

228. Class III (*pedir* type)

This class comprises verbs of the third (**-ir**) conjugation in which the stem-vowel **e** changes to **i** both when stressed and in all cases indicated in Class II.

pedir *to ask for*

PRES. IND. p**i**do, p**i**des, p**i**de, pedimos, pedís, p**i**den
PRES. SUBJ. p**i**da, p**i**das, p**i**da, p**i**damos, p**i**dáis, p**i**dan
IMPERATIVE p**i**de, pedid
PRES. PART. p**i**diendo
PRETERIT pedí, pediste, p**i**dió, pedimos, pedisteis, p**i**dieron
IMPERF. SUBJ. (**-ra**) p**i**diera, *etc.* IMPERF. SUBJ. (**-se**) p**i**diese, *etc.*
FUT. SUBJ. p**i**diere, *etc.*

Orthographic-changing verbs

229.

Many verbs present certain regular changes in orthography (spelling) in order to reflect the pronunciation accurately.

1. Verbs ending in **-car** and **-gar** change **c** and **g** to **qu** and **gu** respectively before **e** (*i.e.*, in the first person preterit and throughout the present subjunctive).

buscar *to look for*

PRETERIT **busqué,** buscaste, buscó, buscamos, buscasteis, buscaron
PRES. SUBJ. **busque, busques, busque, busquemos, busquéis, busquen**

llegar *to arrive*

PRETERIT **llegué,** llegaste, *etc.*
PRES. SUBJ. **llegue, llegues,** *etc.*

2. Verbs ending in **-guar** change **gu** to **gü** before **e** (in the same cases as in 1).

averiguar *to find out, ascertain*

PRETERIT **averigüé,** averiguaste, *etc.*
PRES. SUBJ. **averigüe, averigües,** *etc.*

3. Verbs ending in **-zar** change **z** to **c** before **e** (in the same cases as in 1).

empezar *to begin*

PRETERIT **empecé,** empezaste, *etc.*
PRES. SUBJ. **empiece, empieces,** *etc.*

4. Verbs ending in **-cer** or **-cir** preceded by a consonant change **c** to **z** before **a** and **o** (*i.e.*, in the first person present indicative and throughout the present subjunctive).

convencer *to convince*

PRES. IND. **convenzo,** convences, convence, *etc.*
PRES. SUBJ. **convenza, convenzas, convenza,** *etc.*

5. Verbs ending in **-ger** and **-gir** change **g** to **j** before **a** and **o** (*i.e.*, in the same cases as in 4).

dirigir *to direct*

PRES. IND. **dirijo,** diriges, *etc.*
PRES. SUBJ. **dirija, dirijas,** *etc.*

6. Verbs in **-guir** change **gu** to **g** before **a** and **o** (in the same cases as in 4).

seguir *to follow*

PRES. IND. **sigo,** sigues, sigue, seguimos, seguís, siguen
PRES. SUBJ. **siga, sigas,** *etc.*

7. Verbs whose stems end in **ll** or **ñ** drop the **i** of the diphthongs **ie** and **io.**

reñir *to scold, quarrel*

PRES. PART. **riñendo**
PRETERIT reñí, reñiste, **riñó,** reñimos, reñisteis, **riñeron**
IMPERF. SUBJ. **(-ra) riñera,** *etc.* IMPERF. SUBJ. **(-se) riñese,** *etc.*

NOTE. All verbs in **-eñir** are radical-changing (Class III).

bullir *to bubble*

PRES. PART. **bullendo**
PRETERIT bullí, bulliste, **bulló,** bullimos, bullisteis, **bulleron**
IMPERF. SUBJ. **(-ra) bullera,** *etc.* IMPERF. SUBJ. **(-se) bullese,** *etc.*

8. **Oler** *to smell* is a radical-changing verb of Class I. Wherever the diphthong **ue** appears initially, the form in which it appears is written with **h-.**

PRES. IND. **huelo, hueles, huele,** olemos, oléis, **huelen**
PRES. SUBJ. **huela, huelas, huela,** olamos, oláis, **huelan**
IMPERATIVE **huele,** oled

9. **Errar** *to err*, and any radical-changing verb in which the diphthong **ie** appears initially, spells the diphthong **ye-**. (See **erguir** [§244].)

PRES. IND. **yerro, yerras, yerra,** erramos, erráis, **yerran**
PRES. SUBJ. **yerre, yerres, yerre,** erremos, erréis, **yerren**
IMPERATIVE **yerra,** errad

230. Verbs of the *-er* and *-ir* conjugations whose stem ends in a vowel

Verbs like **creer, leer,** etc. always spell the unstressed **i** with the letter **y.** Stressed **i** always bears the written accent.

creer *to believe, think*

PRES. PART. **creyendo** PAST PART. **creído**
PRETERIT creí, creíste, **creyó,** creímos, creísteis, **creyeron**
IMPERF. SUBJ. **(-ra) creyera,** *etc.* IMPERF. SUBJ. **(-se) creyese,** *etc.*

NOTE. **Oír (§251),** and **caer (§236),** and their compounds show the above changes.

231. Verbs in *-eír* are radical-changing verbs of Class III (*pedir* type).

Stressed **i** always bears the written accent. Two contiguous **i**'s are reduced to one.

reír *to laugh*

PRES. PART. riendo PAST PART. reído
PRES. IND. **río, ríes, ríe,** reímos, reís, **ríen**
PRETERIT reí, reíste, **rió,** reímos, reísteis, **rieron**
IMPERATIVE **ríe, reíd**
PRES. SUBJ. **ría, rías, ría, riamos, riáis, rían**
IMPERF. SUBJ. **(-ra) riera,** *etc.* IMPERF. SUBJ. **(-se) riese,** *etc.*

Irregular verbs

232. Principal and derived parts

1. From the five principal parts of the Spanish verb (infinitive, present participle, past participle, present indicative, and preterit) all other moods and

tenses may be derived, according to the scheme printed below. The principal parts are consequently very useful in learning the conjugation of irregular verbs.

INFINITIVE	PRES. PART.	PAST PART.	PRES. IND.	PRETERIT
tener	**teniendo**	**tenido**	**tengo**	**tuve**
IMPERF. IND.	PROGRESSIVE TENSES	COMPOUND TENSES	PRES. SUBJ.	IMPERF. SUBJ.
tenía	**estoy,** *etc.* **teniendo**	**he,** *etc.* **tenido**	**tenga**	**tuviera** **tuviese**
FUT.			IMPERAT.	
tendré			**ten** **tened**	FUT. SUBJ. **tuviere**
CONDIT.				
tendría				

2. In the preceding table, all forms except **tendré** and **tendría** are derived regularly from the principal parts. Consequently, in the following synopses of Spanish irregular verbs, only the principal parts and those forms not regularly derived therefrom are given. No separate mention is made of the conditional (which is always similar to the future) nor of the imperfect and future subjunctive unless these forms show special irregularities. The irregular forms, together with radical and orthographic changes, are printed in bold-faced type.

233.

andar *to walk, go*

PRIN. PARTS andar, andando, andado, ando, **anduve**

234.

asir *to seize*

PRIN. PARTS asir, asiendo, asido, **asgo,** así
PRES. IND. **asgo,** ases, ase, asimos, asís, asen
PRES. SUBJ. **asga, asgas,** *etc.*

235.

caber *to be contained in*

PRIN. PARTS caber, cabiendo, cabido, **quepo, cupe**
PRES. IND. **quepo,** cabes, cabe, cabemos, cabéis, caben
PRES. SUBJ. **quepa, quepas,** *etc.*
FUT. IND. **cabré,** *etc.*

236.

caer *to fall*

PRIN. PARTS caer, **cayendo,** caído, **caigo,** caí
PRES. IND. **caigo,** caes, cae, caemos, caéis, caen
PRES. SUBJ. **caiga, caigas,** *etc.*
PRETERIT caí, caíste, **cayó,** caímos, caísteis, **cayeron**
IMPERF. SUBJ. **cayera,** *etc.*; **cayese,** *etc.*
FUT. SUBJ. **cayere,** *etc.*

237.

concluir *to conclude*

(All verbs whose infinitive ends in **-uir** [except **-guir** and **-quir**] and **üir** insert **y** between the **u** and the ending in the singular and third person plural of the present tense and the familiar imperative. Unstressed **i** is also spelled **y** in other forms [see §**230**].)

PRES. PART. **concluyendo** PAST PART. concluido
PRES. IND. **concluyo, concluyes, concluye,** concluimos, concluís, **concluyen**
PRETERIT concluí, concluiste, **concluyó,** concluimos, concluisteis, **concluyeron**
IMPERATIVE **concluye,** concluid
PRES. SUBJ. **concluya, concluyas,** *etc.*
IMPERF. SUBJ. **(-ra) concluyera,** *etc.* IMPERF. SUBJ. **(-se) concluyese,** *etc.*

238.

conducir *to conduct*

(All verbs in **-ducir** are conjugated similarly.)

PRIN. PARTS conducir, conduciendo, conducido, **conduzco, conduje**
PRES. IND. **conduzco,** conduces, conduce, conducimos, conducís, conducen
PRES. SUBJ. **conduzca, conduzcas,** *etc.*
PRETERIT **conduje, condujiste, condujo, condujimos, condujisteis, condujeron**
IMPERF. SUBJ. **condujera,** *etc.*; **condujese,** *etc.*
FUT. SUBJ. **condujere,** *etc.*

239.

conocer *to know, be acquainted with*

(All verbs in **-ecer, -ocer, -ucir** insert **z** before **c** in the first person present indicative and throughout the present subjunctive.)

PRES. IND. **conozco,** conoces, conoce, *etc.*

PRES. SUBJ. **conozca, conozcas, conozca,** *etc.*

NOTE. Irregular verbs in **-ducir (§238)** show the above changes, but **hacer, decir, cocer, mecer** and their compounds do not.

240.

continuar *to continue*

(Verbs in **-uar** [except **-guar**] regularly have stress, and a written accent, on the **u** throughout the singular and in the third person plural of the present tense.)

PRES. IND. **continúo, continúas, continúa,** continuamos, continuáis, **continúan**

PRES. SUBJ. **continúe, continúes, continúe,** continuemos, continuéis, **continúen**

IMPERATIVE **continúa,** continuad

241.

dar *to give*

PRIN. PARTS dar, dando, dado, **doy, di**

PRES. IND. **doy,** das, da, damos, dais, dan

PRES. SUBJ. **dé,** des, **dé,** demos, deis, den

IMPERF. SUBJ. **diera,** *etc.*; **diese,** *etc.*

FUT. SUBJ. **diere,** *etc.*

242.

decir *to say, tell*

PRIN. PARTS decir, **diciendo, dicho, digo, dije**

PRES. IND. **digo, dices, dice,** decimos, decís, **dicen**

PRES. SUBJ. **diga, digas,** *etc.*

IMPERATIVE **di,** decid

PRETERIT **dije, dijiste, dijo, dijimos, dijisteis, dijeron**
IMPERF. SUBJ. **dijera,** *etc.*; **dijese,** *etc.*
FUT. SUBJ. **dijere,** *etc.*
FUT. IND. **diré,** *etc.*

243.

enviar *to send*

(Some other verbs in **-iar** stress the **i** through the singular and the third person plural of the present tense.)

PRIN. PARTS enviar, enviando, enviado, **envío,** envié
PRES. IND. **envío, envías, envía,** enviamos, enviáis, **envían**
PRES. SUBJ. **envíe, envíes, envíe,** enviemos, enviéis, **envíen**
IMPERATIVE **envía,** enviad

244.

erguir *to raise, lift up*

PRIN. PARTS erguir, **irguiendo,** erguido, **yergo (irgo),** erguí
PRES. IND. **yergo, yergues, yergue, erguimos, erguís, yerguen**
(alternate) **irgo, irgues, irgue,** erguimos, erguís, **irguen**
PRES. SUBJ. **yerga, yergas, yerga, irgamos, irgáis, yergan**
(alternate) **irga, irgas, irga, irgamos, irgáis, irgan**
PRETERIT erguí, erguiste, **irguió,** erguimos, erguisteis, **irguieron**

245.

estar *to be*

PRIN. PARTS estar, estando, estado, **estoy, estuve**
PRES. IND. **estoy, estás, está,** estamos, estáis, **están**
PRES. SUBJ. **esté, estés, esté,** estemos, estéis, **estén**
IMPERATIVE **está,** estad

246.

haber *to have* (impers. *to be*)

PRIN. PARTS haber, habiendo, habido, **he, hube**
PRES. IND. **he, has, ha** (impers. **hay**), **hemos,** habéis, **han**
PRES. SUBJ. **haya, hayas,** *etc.*
FUT. IND. **habré,** *etc.*

247.

hacer *to do, make*

PRIN. PARTS hacer, haciendo, **hecho, hago, hice**
PRES. IND. **hago,** haces, hace, hacemos, hacéis, hacen
PRES. SUBJ. **haga, hagas,** *etc.*
IMPERATIVE **haz,** haced
PRETERIT **hice, hiciste, hizo, hicimos, hicisteis, hicieron**
FUT. IND. **haré,** *etc.*

248.

inquirir *to inquire*

PRIN. PARTS inquirir, inquiriendo, inquirido, **inquiero,** inquirí
PRES. IND. **inquiero, inquieres, inquiere,** inquirimos, inquirís, **inquieren**
PRES. SUBJ. **inquiera, inquieras, inquiera,** inquiramos, inquiráis, **inquieran**
IMPERATIVE **inquiere,** inquirid

249.

ir *to go*

PRIN. PARTS **ir, yendo,** ido, **voy, fui**
PRES. IND. **voy, vas, va, vamos, vais, van**
PRES. SUBJ. **vaya, vayas,** *etc.*
IMPERATIVE **ve,** id.
IMPERF. IND. **iba, ibas,** *etc.*
PRETERIT **fui, fuiste, fue, fuimos, fuisteis, fueron**
IMPERF. SUBJ. **fuera,** *etc.*; **fuese,** *etc.*
FUT. SUBJ. **fuere,** *etc.*

250.

jugar *to play* (a game)

PRIN. PARTS jugar, jugando, jugado **juego, jugué**
PRES. IND. **juego, juegas, juega,** jugamos, jugáis, **juegan**
PRES. SUBJ. **juegue, juegues, juegue,** juguemos, juguéis, **jueguen**
IMPERATIVE **juega,** jugad
PRETERIT **jugué,** jugaste, jugó, jugamos, jugasteis, jugaron

251.

oír *to hear*

PRIN. PARTS oír, **oyendo,** oído, **oigo,** oí
PRES. IND. **oigo, oyes, oye,** oímos, oís, **oyen**
PRES. SUBJ. **oiga, oigas,** etc.
IMPERATIVE **oye,** oíd
PRETERIT oí, oíste, **oyó,** oímos, oísteis, **oyeron**
IMPERF. SUBJ. **oyera,** *etc.*; **oyese,** *etc.*
FUT. SUBJ. **oyere,** *etc.*

252.

placer *to please* (used as impersonal verb and in third pers.)

PRIN. PARTS placer, placiendo, placido, place, **plugo** (*or* plació)
PRES. SUBJ. **plega, plegue,** *or* **plazca**

253.

poder *to be able*

PRIN. PARTS poder, **pudiendo,** podido, **puedo, pude**
PRES. IND. **puedo, puedes, puede,** podemos, podéis, **pueden**
PRES. SUBJ. **pueda, puedas, pueda,** podamos, podáis, **puedan**
FUT. IND. **podré,** *etc.*

254.

poner *to put, place*

PRIN. PARTS poner, poniendo, **puesto, pongo, puse**
PRES. IND. **pongo,** pones, pone, ponemos, ponéis, ponen
PRES. SUBJ. **ponga, pongas,** *etc.*
IMPERATIVE **pon,** poned
FUT. IND. **pondré,** *etc.*

255.

querer *to wish*

PRIN. PARTS querer, queriendo, querido, **quiero, quise**
PRES. IND. **quiero, quieres, quiere,** queremos, queréis, **quieren**

PRES. SUBJ. **quiera, quieras, quiera,** queramos, queráis, **quieran**
IMPERATIVE **quiere,** quered
FUT. IND. **querré,** *etc.*

256.

raer *to scrape*

PRIN. PARTS raer, rayendo, raído, **raigo (rayo),** raí
PRES. IND. {**raigo** / **rayo**} raes, rae, raemos, raéis, raen
PRES. SUBJ. **raiga, raigas,** *etc.*; **raya, rayas,** *etc.*

257.

saber *to know*

PRIN. PARTS saber, sabiendo sabido, **sé, supe**
PRES. IND. **sé,** sabes, sabe, sabemos, sabéis, saben
PRES. SUBJ. **sepa, sepas,** *etc.*
FUT. IND. **sabré,** *etc.*

258.

salir *to go out*

PRIN. PARTS salir, saliendo, salido, **salgo,** salí
PRES. IND. **salgo,** sales, sale, salimos, salís, salen
PRES. SUBJ. **salga, salgas,** *etc.*
IMPERATIVE **sal,** salid
FUT. IND. **saldré,** *etc.*

259.

ser *to be*

PRIN. PARTS ser, siendo, sido, **soy, fui**
PRES. IND. **soy, eres, es, somos, sois, son**
PRES. SUBJ. **sea, seas, sea, seamos, seáis, sean**
IMPERATIVE **sé,** sed
IMPERF. IND. **era, eras, era, éramos, erais, eran**

PRETERIT **fui, fuiste, fue, fuimos, fuisteis, fueron**
IMPERF. SUBJ. **fuera,** *etc.*; **fuese,** *etc.*
FUT. SUBJ. **fuere,** *etc.*

260.

tener *to have*

PRIN. PARTS tener, teniendo, tenido, **tengo, tuve**
PRES. IND. **tengo, tienes, tiene,** tenemos, tenéis, **tienen**
PRES. SUBJ. **tenga, tengas,** *etc.*
IMPERATIVE **ten,** tened
FUT. IND. **tendré,** *etc.*

261.

traer *to bring*

PRIN. PARTS traer, **trayendo,** traído, **traigo, traje**
PRES. IND. **traigo,** traes, trae, traemos, traéis, traen
PRES. SUBJ. **traiga, traigas,** *etc.*
PRETERIT **traje, trajiste, trajo, trajimos, trajisteis, trajeron**
IMPERF. SUBJ. **trajera,** *etc*; **trajese,** *etc.*
FUT. SUBJ. **trajere,** *etc.*

262.

valer *to be worth*

PRIN. PARTS valer, valiendo, valido, **valgo,** valí
PRES. IND. **valgo,** vales, vale, valemos, valéis, valen
PRES. SUBJ. **valga, valgas,** *etc.*
IMPERATIVE **val,** valed
FUT. IND. **valdré,** *etc.*

263.

venir *to come*

PRIN. PARTS venir, **viniendo,** venido, **vengo, vine**
PRES. IND. **vengo, vienes, viene,** venimos, venís, **vienen**
PRES. SUBJ. **venga, vengas,** *etc.*
IMPERATIVE **ven,** venid.
FUT. IND. **vendré,** *etc.*

264.

ver *to see*

PRIN. PARTS ver, viendo, **visto, veo,** vi
PRES. IND. **veo,** ves, ve, vemos, veis, ven
PRES. SUBJ. **vea, veas,** *etc.*
IMPERF. IND. **veía, veías, veía, veíamos, veíais, veían**

265.

yacer *to lie*

PRIN. PARTS yacer, yaciendo, yacido, **yazco (yazgo,** *or* **yago), yací**

PRES. IND. { **yazco** / **yazgo** / **yago** } yaces, yace, yacemos, yacéis, yacen

PRES. SUBJ. **yazca, yazcas,** *etc.*; **yazga, yazgas,** *etc.*; **yaga, yagas.** *etc.*
IMPERATIVE **yaz** (*or* yace), yaced

266. Irregular past participles

Certain regular verbs have (with their compounds and analogues) irregular past participles.

abrir, abierto *opened*
cubrir, cubierto *covered*
escribir, escrito *written*
freír, frito *fried*
imprimir, impreso *printed*
morir, muerto *dead*
proveer, provisto *provided*
resolver, resuelto *resolved*
romper, roto *broken*
ver, visto *seen*
volver, vuelto (*re*)*turned*

NOTE. All verbs ending in **-scribir** have the irregular past participle in **-scrito**:
adscribir, adscrito *ascribed*
circumscribir, circumscrito *circumscribed*
describir, descrito *described*
inscribir, inscrito *inscribed*
prescribir, prescrito *prescribed*
proscribir, proscrito *proscribed*
suscribir, suscrito *subscribed*

Regimen of verbs

267. Common verbs of differing regimen

Following is a list of frequently used verbs in Spanish whose construction differs from that of their English equivalents.

acercarse a *approach*
acordarse (ue) de *remember*
agradecer *be thankful for*
aguardar *wait for*
apostar (ue) a *bet (that)*
aprovechar *take advantage of*
buscar *look for*
cambiar de (tren *etc.***)** *change*
carecer de *lack*
conseguir (i) *succeed in (doing)*
cuidar (de) *care for, take care of*
cumplir con *fulfil*
disfrutar de *enjoy* (a thing)
entrar en (in America also **a**) *enter*
escuchar *listen to*
esperar *wait for*
fijarse en *notice*
gozar de *enjoy*
influir en *influence*
jugar a *play* (a game)
mirar *look at*
oponerse a *oppose*
pagar a *pay* (a person)
pagar *pay for* (a thing)
pedir (i) *ask for* (a thing)
renunciar a *renounce, give up*
reparar en *notice, observe*
resistir a *resist*
salir de *leave*
tirar de *pull*

268. Verbs governing direct infinitive

Following is a list of frequently used verbs in Spanish which, being transitive, are followed by the direct infinitive (see §**104**, 6).

aconsejar *advise*
advertir (ie, i) *warn*
afirmar *declare, affirm*
ansiar *be anxious*
asegurar *assure, declare*
bastar *be enough*
celebrar *rejoice, be glad*
confesar *confess*
convenir *be suitable* (impersonal)
creer *believe, think*
deber *ought, must*
decidir *decide*
declarar *declare*
dejar *let, permit*
descuidar *neglect*
desear *desire*
determinar *determine*
dignarse *deign*
dudar *doubt, hesitate*
elegir (i) *choose*

encargar *order, entrust*
esperar *hope*
evitar *avoid*
figurarse (impersonal) *it seems*
fingir *pretend, feign*
gustar *please, like*
hacer *make, cause, have*
imaginarse *imagine*
impedir (i) *prevent*
importar *matter*
intentar *attempt*
jurar *swear*
lograr *succeed in, manage*
mandar *cause, have, order*
merecer *deserve*
mirar *watch*
necesitar *need*
negar *deny*
ocurrirse (impersonal) *occur (to one)*
ofrecer *offer*
oír *hear*
olvidar *forget*
ordenar *order*
parecer *seem*
pensar (ie) *intend*
pesar *grieve*
permitir *permit*
poder (ue) *can, be able*
preferir (ie, i) *prefer*
pretender *claim*
procurar *try*
prohibir *forbid*
prometer *promise*
proponer *propose*
querer (ie) *want, wish*
reconocer *admit, acknowledge*
recordar (ue) *remember*
rehusar *refuse*
repugnar *find repugnant*
resolver (ue) *resolve*
rogar (ue) *beg, ask, request*
saber *know (how)*
sentir (ie, i) *be sorry, regret*
servirse (i) *please*
soler (ue) *be in the habit of, used to*
sostener *maintain*
suplicar *beg*
temer *fear*
tocar (impersonal) *be one's turn*
valer más (impersonal) *be better*
ver *see*

269. Verbs governing prepositions

Following is a list of frequently used verbs in Spanish which are construed with prepositions.

abandonarse a *give oneself up to*
acabar de *finish, have just;* **— con** *finish, exhaust;* **— por** *end by*
acertar (ie) a *chance to, manage to; succeed in*
acordarse (ue) de *remember*
acostumbrarse a *be accustomed, get used to*
aguardar a *wait for, until*
alegrarse de *be glad to*
alejarse de *go away from*
amenazar con *threaten to,* or *with*
animar a *encourage to;* **—se a,** *make up one's mind to*
aprender a *learn to*
apresurarse a *hasten to, hurry to*
apurarse por *worry about*
arrepentirse (ie, i) de *repeat of, be sorry for*
arriesgarse a *risk*
asomarse a *appear at, look out of*
asombrarse de *be astonished at*

aspirar a *aspire to*
asustarse de *be frightened at*
atreverse a *dare*
autorizar a *or* **para** *authorize to*
avenirse a *agree to, consent to*
aventurarse a *venture*
avergonzarse (üe) de *be ashamed of*
ayudar a *help to, aid to*
bastar para *or* **a** *be sufficient to;* **— con** *have enough with*
burlarse de *make fun of*
cansarse de *grow tired of*
carecer de *lack*
casarse con *marry*
cesar de *cease to, stop*
comenzar (ie) a *commence to*
complacerse en *take pleasure in*
comprometerse a *obligate oneself to*
concluir de *finish,* **— por** *(or (ger.) end by*
condenar a *condemn to*
confiar en *trust*
conformarse a *conform to*
consagrarse a *devote oneself to*
consentir (ie, i) en *consent to*
consistir en *consist of*
contar (ue) con *count on, rely on*
contentarse con *content oneself with*
contribuir a *contribute to*
convenir en *agree to*
convertirse (ie, i) en *become*
convidar a *or* **para** *invite to*
cuidar de *take care of (to)*
dar a *open on, face;* **— con** *come upon;* **— en** *persist in*
decidirse a *make up one's mind to,* **— por** *decide on*
dedicarse a *devote oneself to*
dejar *let, allow, permit;* **— de** *stop, fail to*
desafiar a *dare to, challenge to*
despedirse (i) de *take leave of*
destinar a *or* **para,** *destine to, assign to*
desvivirse por *do one's utmost to*
determinarse a *make up one's mind*
disculparse de *excuse oneself for*
disfrutar de *enjoy* (a thing)
disponerse a *get ready to*
divertirse (ie, i) en *or* **con** *(or ger.) amuse oneself by*
dudar de *doubt;* **— en** *hesitate to*
echarse a *begin to*
empeñarse en *insist on*
empezar (ie) a *begin to*
enamorarse de *to fall in love with*
encargarse de *undertake to, take charge of*
encontrarse (ue) con *find, meet with, come upon*
enseñar a *teach (how) to*
enterarse de *find out*
entrar en *enter;* **— a** *enter, enter on*
entretenerse en, con *(or ger.) entertain oneself by* or *with*
enviar a *send to*
equivaler a *be equivalent to*
esforzarse (ue) a, para, por *or* **en,** *strive to*
esmerarse en *take pains in*
esperar *hope, expect, wait;* **— a** *wait for, until*
estar para *be about to;* **— por** *be in favor of, be inclined to*
exponerse a *expose oneself to*
extrañarse de *be surprised at (to)*
faltar a *be absent from, fail to (do)*
felicitarse de *congratulate oneself on*
fijarse en *notice*
gozar de *enjoy;* **—se en, con** *(or ger.) enjoy*
guardarse de *take care not to*

gustar de *be fond of*
haber de *have to, be going to;* **— que** (impersonal) *be necessary*
hacer por *try to;* **estar hecho a** *be accustomed to*
hartarse de *have one's fill of*
huir de *flee from, avoid*
impacientarse por *grow impatient for (to)*
incitar a *incite to*
inclinarse a *be inclined to*
incomodarse con *be annoyed at;* **— por** *put oneself out to*
inducir a *induce to*
insistir en *insist on*
inspirar a *inspire to*
instar a *or* **para** *urge to*
invitar a *or* **para** *invite to*
ir a *go to;* **—se de** *leave*
jactarse de *boast of*
limitarse a *limit oneself to*
llegar a *come to, go so far as; chance to*
luchar por *or* **para** *struggle for (to)*
maravillarse de *marvel at*
marcharse de *leave*
meterse a *take up;* **— en** *become involved in;* **— con** *provoke* (a person)
molestarse en *take the trouble to*
morirse (ue) por *be dying for (to)*
negarse (ie) a *refuse*
obligar a *oblige to*
obstinarse en *persist in*
ocuparse de *pay attention to, mind;* **— en** *busy oneself at*
ofrecerse a *offer to, promise to*
olvidarse de *forget to*
oponerse a *be opposed to, oppose*
optar por *choose (to)*
parar de *stop, cease;* **— se a** *stop to;* **— se en** *stop at, bother to*
parecerse a *resemble*
pasar a *proceed to, pass on to*
pensar (ie) de *think of* (have an opinion concerning); **— en** *think of*, (have in mind)
persistir en *persist in*
persuadirse a *persuade oneself to;* **estar persuadido de** *be convinced of*
ponerse a *set oneself to, begin to*
preciarse de *boast of*
prepararse a *or* **para** *prepare oneself to*
prescindir de *do without, neglect*
prestarse a *lend oneself to*
principiar a *begin to*
probar (ue) a *try to*
quedar en *agree to;* **— por** *remain to be;* **—se a** *or* **para** *remain to*
quejarse de *complain of*
rabiar por *be crazy about (to)*
rebajarse a *stoop to*
recrearse en *(or ger.)* *amuse oneself by*
reducirse a *bring oneself to*
renunciar a *renounce, give up*
resignarse a *resign oneself to*
resistirse a *resist, refuse to*
resolverse (ue) a *resolve to*
retirarse a *retire, withdraw*
reventar por (ie) *be bursting to*
romper a *begin (suddenly) to;* **— con** *break off relations with*
sentarse (ie) a *or* **para** *sit down to*
separarse de *leave*
servir de (i) *act as;* **— para** *be of use for;* **— se de** *use*
soñar (ue) con *dream of*
sorprenderse de *be surprised to*
subir a *go up to, climb, get on*
tardar en *take along to*
terminar por *(or ger.)* *end by;* **— de** *finish*
tornar a *return to; (do) again*

trabajar por *or* **para** *work to, strive to;* **— en** *work at*
tratar de *try to; address as;* **—se de** *be a question of*
tropezar (ie) con *come upon*
vacilar en *hesitate to*
valerse de *avail oneself of*
venir a *come to, amount to*
ver de *see to, look to, try to*
volver (ue) a *return to; (do) again*

270. Adjectives and participles that vary in meaning when used with *ser* and *estar*

Many adjectives and participles can be used with both **ser** and **estar**, with variations in meaning according to the principles laid down in §§**17, 20, 149.** In a number of cases these variations in meaning are so considerable as to be rendered by separate English equivalents.

	WITH *ser*	WITH *estar*
aburrido	*boring*	*bored*
agarrado	*stingy*	*clinging to, fastened to*
alto	*tall, high*	*tall* (for one's age), *high* (location)
ancho	*broad, wide*	*too broad, wide*
bajo	*low, short*	*too low, short; low* (location)
bueno	*good, kind*	*in good health; tasty*
callado	*silent* (taciturn)	*silent* (quiet)
cansado	*tiresome*	*tired*
casado	(a) *married* (person)	*married*
católico	*Catholic*	(look, feel, taste) *sound*
ciego	*blind*	*blinded*
débil	(a) *weak*(ling)	*weak, weakly*
delicado	*delicate*	*in delicate health*
despierto	*wide-awake, clever*	*awake*
distraído	*absent-minded*	*inattentive, confused*
divertido	*amusing*	*amused*
estrecho	*narrow*	*too narrow*
grande	*large, great*	*too large*
imposible	*impossible*	*unendurable*
inquieto	*restless*	*worried*
interesado	*mercenary*	*interested*
joven	*young*	(look, feel, act) *young*
justo	*just, fair*	*exact, fitting*
limpio	*cleanly*	*clean*
listo	*clever, bright*	*ready*
maduro	*mature*	*ripe*
malo	*bad, evil*	*sick, bad condition*
nuevo	*new, another*	*brand-new*

pequeño	*small*	*too small*
rico	(a) *rich* (person)	*tasty*
sano	*healthful*	*healthy*
verde	*green* (color)	*green* (unripe)
viejo	*old*	(look, feel, act) *old*
vivo	*lively*	*alive*

271. Adjectives that vary in meaning according to position

Following is a list of the more frequent adjectives which vary in meaning according to their position:

	AFTER NOUN	BEFORE NOUN
alto	*high, tall*	*exalted*
antiguo	*ancient*	*old, former*
bajo	*low, short*	*vile*
cierto	*sure*	*certain* (indefinite)
determinado	*determined*	*certain* (indefinite)
grande	*large*	*great*
malo	*wicked*	*bad*
medio	*average*	*half*
menudo	*small*	*what a!* (exclam.)
mismo	*self*	*very, same*
nuevo	*new*	*another*
pobre	*poor* (indigent)	*poor* (pitiable)
propio	(one's) *own*	*very, same*
único	*unique*	*only, single*
valiente	*brave*	*what a!* (exclam.)
viejo	*aged, worn*	*old*

272. Irregular absolute superlatives

1. Those having their origin in the irregular Latin superlative are: **óptimo** *very (most) excellent*, **pésimo** *very (most) bad*, **máximo** *very (most) great*, **ínfimo** *very (most) low*, **supremo** *supreme*, *very (most) high*.
2. Those preserving the Latin root are: **bonísimo** *very (most) good*, **fortísimo** *very (most) strong*, **novísimo** *very (most) new*, **fidelísimo** *very (most) faithful*, **amabilísimo** *very (most) kind*, **afabilísimo** *very (most) affable*, **nobilísimo** *very (most) noble*. **Buenísimo** and **fuertísimo** are also used.
3. Those preserving the Latin suffix are: **acérrimo** *very (most) vigorous*, **aspérrimo** *very (most) harsh*, **celebérrimo** *very (most) celebrated*, **libérrimo** *very (most) free*, **misérrimo** *very (most) miserable*, **paupérrimo** *very (most poor)*, **pulquérrimo** *very (most) beautiful*, **salubérrimo** *very*

(most) healthful, **ubérrimo** *very (most) fertile.* **Asperísimo** and **pobrísimo** are also used.

273. Definite article with place names

1. The definite article is used with the names of the following countries, although in some cases it is omitted in local or journalistic usage: **(la) Argentina, el Brasil, el Canadá, el Congo, (la) China, el Ecuador, (los) Estados Unidos, la Gran Bretaña, la Guayana, (la) India, (la) Indo-China, el Japón, el Líbano, (el) Paraguay, el Perú, el Senegal, el Transvaal, (el) Uruguay.**
2. With names of many regions and cities, *e.g.*, **la Alcarria** (province of Guadalajara, Spain), **el Callao** (city in Peru), **el Cairo, la Coruña, el Ferrol** (city in Galicia, Spain), **la Florida, la Habana, la Haya** (The Hague), **el Havre** (Le Havre), **la Mancha** (region southeast of Madrid), **la Montaña** (province of Santander, Spain), **la Rioja** (province of Logroño, Spain), **el Rosellón** (the Rousillon), **el Yucatán.**

274. Gender of nouns

1. Following are some of the more frequent masculine nouns of Greek origin ending in **-a: axioma, clima, cometa, dilema, diploma, drama, enigma, epigrama, fantasma** *(phantom)*, **idioma** *(language)*, **lema** *(motto)*, **mapa, melodrama, panorama, poema, poeta, planeta, problema, programa, síntoma, sistema, telegrama, teorema.**
2. All nouns ending in **-is** are feminine, except **el análisis, el cutis** *(skin)*, **el éxtasis, el iris** *(of the eye)*, and **el paréntesis.**

275. Augmentative suffixes

Augmentative suffixes are **-ón, -azo, -acho, -ote,** and **-arrón,** *e.g.*, **sillón** *armchair*, **manaza** *huge hand*, **ricacho** *(small-town) rich person*, **librote** *big book, tome*, **nubarrón** *dark (threatening) cloud.*

276. Diminutive suffixes

1. The choice of diminutive suffixes depends not only on the meaning of the suffix (**§170**) but also on the structure of the root word. Instead of the usual **-ito, -illo,** and **-uelo,** the following special forms are used:

   -cito, -cillo, -zuelo are applied to words of two or more syllables ending in **-n** or **-r**: **mujercita** *little woman, darling*, etc., **corazoncito** *sweet (little) heart.*

-ecito, -ecillo, -ezuelo, -achuelo, -ichuelo are applied *(a)* to monosyllables ending in a consonant, including **y**: **vocecita** *thin little voice*, **reyezuelo** *petty king; (b)* to words to two syllables containing in the first syllable the diphthongs **ei, ie, ue**: **cuerpecito** *tiny body; (c)* to words of two syllables ending in the diphthongs **-ia, -io, -ua**: **bestiecilla** *little beast; (d)* to some words of two syllables ending in **-ío**: **riachuelo** *small stream; (e)* to all words of two syllables ending in **-e**: **pobrecito** *poor fellow.*

-ececito, -ececillo, -ecezuelo are applied to monosyllables ending in a vowel: **piececito** *tiny little foot.*

2. Some of the more frequent exceptions are: **Juanito, Luisito, agüita.**
3. The suffixes **-ico (-cico, -ecico, -ececico), -ín, -ino, -iño,** are specially characteristic of regional usage.
4. The suffixes **-ón** and **-ote** may serve to form diminutives as well as augmentatives: **callejón** *alley*, **ratón** *mouse*, **islote** *islet.*
5. It is possible to combine various diminutive and augmentative suffixes: **chiquitito** *tiny*, **plazoletilla** *small square*, **corpachón** *big body*, **saloncito** *small parlor.*

277. Depreciative suffixes

1. Following is a list of depreciative suffixes: **-ete, -ote, -ajo, -ejo, -ijo, -aco, -uco, -acho, -ucho, -uza, -orrio, -orro, -ato, -astro, -alla: pobrete (pobre), feota (feo), libraco (libro), caballejo (caballo), casucha (casa), mujeruca (mujer), poetastro (poeta), villorrio (villa), gentuza (gente).**
2. With depreciatives (and augmentatives) there is often a change in gender: **el familión (familia), la peseta (peso), el tenducho (tienda), la lagartija (lagarto), el caserón (casa).**

278. Interjections

Interjections are used much more frequently in Spanish than in English.

1. The more common interjections are:

¡Oh! (surprise)	*Oh!*
¡Ah! (surprise)	*Ah!*
¡Alto!	*Halt!*

¡Ay! (lamentation)	*Oh! Alas! Ouch!*
¡Bah! (contempt incredulity)	*Bah!*
¡Ea! (encouragement)	*Come!*
¡Ea, ea! (impatience)	*Come on!*
¡Hola! (greeting, discovery)	*Hello!*
¡Huy! (disgust, admiration)	*Ouch! Gee!*
¡Ole! *or* **¡olé!** (applause)	*Bravo! "Attaboy"!*
¡Ca! (incredulity, denial)	*Nonsense! No!*
¡Chitón!	*Hush!*
¡Ya!	*I see!*
¡Zás!	*Crash!*
¡Arre!	*Giddap!*
¡So!	*Whoa!*

2. Imperatives are frequently used as interjections:

¡Anda! *or* **¡Ande!** (incredulity, importunity)	*Go on! Come on!*
¡Calla! *or* **¡Calle!** (silence, incredulity)	*Keep quiet! Nonsense!*
¡Diga! *or* **¡Mande!** (reply to call)	*Yes, sir! (what is it?)*
¡Oye! *or* **¡Oiga!**	*Listen! Look here! Say!*
¡Mira! *or* **¡Mire!**	*Look (here)!*
¡Quita! *or* **¡Quite!** (incredulity, annoyance)	*Oh, no! Stop!*
¡Toma! (agreement)	*Of course!*
¡Vamos!	*Come on! Come! Well!*
¡Vaya!	*Well! What a . . .! Of course!*
¡Viva!—¡Muera!	*Long live! Hurrah!—Down with (kill) him!*

3. Nouns and adjectives are frequently used as interjections: **¡Bravo!** *Bravo!*, **¡Claro!** *Of course! Sure!*, **¡Cuidado!** *Take care! Look (watch) out!*, **¡Firme!** *Steady!*, **¡Ojo!** *Attention! With care!*, **¡Socorro!** *Help!*
4. Divine names carry no implication of blasphemy when used as interjections: **¡Por Dios!** *For Heaven's sake!*, **¡Dios mío!** *Heavens!*, **¡Válgame Dios!** *Mercy me!*, **¡Jesús!** *Heavens!*, **¡Jesús, María y José!** (after a sneeze), **¡Virgen Santísima!** *Goodness gracious!* Similarly, **¡Demonio!**, **¡Diablo!** *the deuce!*
5. **Hombre, mujer, chico, hijo, hija** are frequently used in conversation for emphasis or expostulation. **¡Hombre!** and **¡señor!** are used addressing either men or women.
6. A number of words having the initial syllable **ca-** are used as interjections to express surprise or annoyance: **¡caramba! ¡caray! ¡caracoles! ¡canastos! ¡cáspita!** *Gosh! Gee!*

279. Numerals

CARDINALS

0 cero
1 un(o), una
2 dos
3 tres
4 cuatro
5 cinco
6 seis
7 siete
8 ocho
9 nueve
10 diez
11 once
12 doce
13 trece
14 catorce
15 quince
16 dieciséis, diez y seis
17 diecisiete, diez y siete
18 dieciocho, diez y ocho
19 diecinueve, diez y nueve
20 veinte
21 veintiún(o), veinte y un(o)
22 veintidós, veinte y dos
30 treinta
31 treinta y un(o)
32 treinta y dos
40 cuarenta
50 cincuenta
60 sesenta
70 setenta
80 ochenta
90 noventa
100 cien(to)
200 doscientos, -as
300 trescientos, -as
400 cuatrocientos, -as
500 quinientos, -as
600 seiscientos, -as
700 setecientos, -as
800 ochocientos, -as
900 novecientos, -as
1000 mil
2000 dos mil
1.000.000 un millón (de)
2.000.000 dos millones (de)

ORDINALS

1st primer(o)
2d segundo
3d tercer(o) (tercio)
4th cuarto
5th quinto
6th sexto
7th séptimo
8th octavo
9th noveno (nono)
10th décimo
11th undécimo
12th duodécimo
13th décimo tercio (tercero)
14th décimo cuarto
15th décimo quinto
16th décimo sexto
17th décimo séptimo
18th décimo octavo
19th décimo noveno (nono)
20th vigésimo
21st vigésimo primero (primo)
22d vigésimo segundo
23d vigésimo tercero (tercio)
30th trigésimo
40th cuadragésimo
50th quincuagésimo
60th sexagésimo
70th septuagésimo

80th octogésimo
90th nonagésimo
100th centésimo
101st centésimo primero (primo)
129th centésimo vigésimo noveno
200th ducentésimo
300th tricentésimo
400th cuadringentésimo
500th quingentésimo
600th sexcentésimo
700th septingentésimo
800th octingentésimo
900th noningentésimo
1000th milésimo
1.000.000th millonésimo

280. Days of the week and months of the year

Days: **lunes, martes, miércoles, jueves, viernes, sábado, domingo.** *Months:* **enero, febrero, marzo, abril, mayo, junio, julio, agosto, se(p)tiembre, octubre, noviembre, diciembre.** (The names of the days and months are not capitalized.)

VOCABULARY

Spanish–English

A

a to, at, for, after
abajo below, downstairs
abarcar take in, comprehend
abogado *m.* lawyer
abordar approach; board
abrigo *m.* overcoat; shelter
absolutamente absolutely
absoluto: en ____ absolutely not, not at all
absurdo absurd
abuelo, -a *m.f.* grandfather; grandmother
abundante abundant
aburrido bored; boring
aburrir bore; **____se** become bored
abusar de abuse
acabar finish, end; **____ de** have just; **se acabó** that's all there is to it (Ch. 19)
accidente *m.* accident
aceituna *f.* olive
acera *f.* sidewalk
acerca de about
acercar(se) approach
acomodador, -a *m.f.* usher
acomodar place
acompañar accompany
acontecimiento *m.* event
acordarse de remember
actitud *f.* attitude
actividad *f.* activity
acto *m.* act
actuación *f.* rôle; **____ del equipo** team play
acudir come (rush) to
acueducto *m.* aqueduct
acuerdo *m.* agreement; **llegar a un ____** come to an agreement, agree; **de ____** in accord, agreed, all right
adelante: ¡____! come in!
además besides, moreover
adiós good-bye, farewell
adjetivo *m.* adjective
admirable admirable
admiración *f.* admiration
adobe *m.* adobe
adquirir (ie, i) acquire, purchase
aduana *f.* customs
adueñarse (de) take possession of
adusto austere
advertir (ie, i) warn
aeropuerto *m.* airport
afable affable
aficionado *m.* fan; amateur
afirmar affirm
afortunadamente fortunately
agente *m.* agent
agitación *f.* activity
agosto *m.* August
agradable pleasant
agradar please
agradecimiento *m.* gratitude
agrandarse become greater
agrupado grouped, huddled
ahí there
ahora now; **por ____** for the present; **____ mismo** right away; **____ que** but, only; now that
ahorrar save
aire *m.* air
aislado isolated, single
Albéniz, Isaac *(1860–1909) founder of modern Spanish piano music*

álbum *m.* album
(El) Alcalde de Zalamea *The Mayor of Zalamea (title of a famous play of Calderón (1600–1681)*
Alcalá de Henares *former university town near Madrid*
Alcázar *m. Alcazar (royal palace in Seville, Toledo, and Segovia)*
alegrarse de be glad about
alegre joyful
alegría *f.* joy
alemán German
alfombra *f.* carpet, rug
alfombrero *m.* carpet maker
Alfonso el Sabio Alfonso X, the Learned *(King of Castile and León (1252–1284), founder of Castilian prose literature)*
alistar enlist; recruit
alistador recruiter
alforjas *f. pl.* saddlebags
algo something; somewhat, rather
alguno any, some; no, none
Alhambra *f.* Alhambra *(famous Moorish palace overlooking Granada)*
alma *f.* soul
almohada *f.* pillow
almorzar (ue) have lunch
alojarse lodge
alrededor de around
alto high, tall; **lo ___** the top
altura *f.* height
aluminio *m.* aluminium
alumno, -a *m.f.* student
alzar *raise*
allá there; **más ___** beyond, further on; **___ ellos** so much for them
amabilidad *f.* kindness
amanecer dawn
amargo bitter
amarillo yellow
ambiente *m.* atmosphere
americana *f.* sack coat
amigo, -a *m.f.* friend
amistad *f.* friendship
amistoso friendly
ampliación *f.* enlargement
anacronismo *m.* anachronism
anaranjado orange-colored
ancho broad, wide
Andalucía *f.* Andalusia *(southern part of Spain)*
andaluz Andalusian
andante walking; errant
andanza *f.* wandering
andar walk, be, go; **¡andando!** let's get going! **¡ande!** come! *(coaxing)* (Ch. 13)
anglosajón Anglo-Saxon
animación *f.* animation
anochecer become night
ante before (in presence of); **___ todo** above all
anteojos *m.pl.* eyeglasses
antes before, formerly; **cuanto ___** as soon as possible
anticipar anticipate
anticuado antiquated
antiguo old, ancient
anunciar advertise
año *m.* year
apagaincendios *m. sing.* fire extinguisher
apagar extinguish; put out *(light)*
aparato *m.* apparatus
aparcar park
aparecer appear, look
apariencia *f.* appearance
aparte apart; **___ de** besides
apasionadamente with great feeling
apenas (si) scarcely
apertura *f.* opening, beginning
apoderarse de seize, take possession of
aposento *m.* room, chamber
apreciación *f.* appreciation
apreciar appreciate
apresurarse hurry
apretón de manos *m.* handshake
apunte *m.* note; **sacar ___s** take notes
aquí here; **por ___** (around) here, this way
árabe Arab, Arabic
arabesco *m.* arabesque
Aragón *m.* Aragon *(region, and ancient kingdom, of Spain; capital: Zaragoza)*
Aranjuez *fertile spot on the Tagus near Madrid, former royal residence*
árbol *m.* tree
arboleda *f.* (grove of) trees
arcada *f.* arcade
archivo *m.* archive; **___ de Indias** Archives of the Indies *(containing a vast library of documents concerning Spanish America)*
arena *f.* sand
aridez *f.* aridity

aristócrata *m.* aristocrat
arma *f.* weapon
armar arm; *colloq.* cause, start
armonía *f.* harmony
armónico harmonious
arquitecto *m.* architect
arquitectónico architectural
arquitectura *f.* architecture
arrabal *m.* suburb; **___es** outskirts
arrayán *m.* myrtle
arreglar arrange, fix
arrogancia *f.* arrogance
arruga *f.* wrinkle
arte *m.* (pl. *f.*) art
artículo *m.* article
artista *m.* artist
artístico artistic
ascender ascend
asegurar assure
asentado perched
así so; **___ es que** so that; **una cosa ___** such a thing
asiento *m.* seat
asilo *m.* asylum
asistir (a) attend
asombrar astonish
aspecto *m.* look, aspect, appearance
aspiración *f.* aspiration
astronauta *m.* astronaut
Asturias *f.* *region, and province, on the northern coast of Spain*
astuto astute
asunto *m.* affair, matter, subject; *pl.* business
asustar frighten; **___se** become frightened
atacar attack
atardecer become late afternoon
atareado busy
atención *f.* attention
aterrizar land
atleta *m.* athlete
atlético athletic
atmósfera *f.* atmosphere
atractivo attractive
atraer attract
atrás behind
atrasado slow, backward
atravesar (ie) cross
atreverse dare
atribuir attribute
aturdido bewildered, stunned, dizzy
aula *f.* classroom
aun (aún) still, yet; even
aunque although; **___ no** but wait
Austria Austria; **casa de ___** the Hapsburg dynasty *(which reigned in Spain from 1516–1700)*
autobús *m.* motor-bus
autocar *m.* bus, tourist bus
automoción *f.* automotive manufacture
automóvil *m.* automobile
autopista *f.* turnpike, freeway
autor *m.* author
autorzuelo *m.* wretched author
avenida *f.* avenue
avergonzarse (de) (ue) be ashamed (of)
Ávila *f.* *city in Old Castile*
avión *m.* airplane; **___ de chorro, de reacción** jet plane
avisar to notify, warn, tell, let know
ayer yesterday
ayuda *f.* help
ayudar help
ayuntamiento *m.* city council, town hall
azafata *f.* airline hostess, stewardess
azotea *f.* open housetop *(in Andalusian houses)*
azul blue
azulejo *m.* tile

B

bahía *f.* bay
bailar dance
baile *m.* dance
bajar go (carry, come, bring) down (Ch. 17)
Baleares *f.* Balearic Islands *(group of islands off the eastern coast of Spain; capital: Palma de Mallorca)*
banco *m.* bank
bandera *f.* flag
banquero *m.* banker
barato cheap
barbaridad *f.* *colloq.* huge amount; **¡qué ___!** How awful!
Barcelona *f.* Barcelona *(second largest city in Spain, capital of Catalonia)*
barco *m.* ship, boat, steamer
barrio *m.* quarter, district, suburb
bastante enough, rather, considerable, considerably
bastar be enough, suffice (Ch. 19)
bastón *m.* cane
bastonazo *m.* blow with a cane

basura *f.* garbage, trash
batalla *f.* battle
baúl *m.* trunk
bebida *f.* drink
Bécquer, Gustavo Adolfo *(1836–1870) Spanish Romantic poet*
belleza *f.* beauty
bello beautiful
Berruguete, Alonso *(1480?–1561) famous painter and sculptor*
biblioteca *f.* library
bibliotecario *m.* librarian
bicicleta *f.* bicycle
bien well, good; **está** ___ all right; **más** ___ rather; ___ . . . ___ either . . . or
Bilbao *m.* Bilbao *(important port and industrial center, on the northern coast of Spain)*
billete *m.* ticket; bill *(money)*
blanco white
blancura *f.* whiteness
bobo *m.* fool, idiot
boca *f.* mouth
bola *f.* ball
bombero *m.* fireman
bombón *m.* bonbon
bonito pretty
bordo: a ___ on board
bosque *m.* woods
botella *f.* bottle
botellazo *m.* blow with a bottle
botón *m.* button
botonería *f.* button maker's shop
botones *m. sing.* bellboy
bóveda *f.* vaulted ceiling
bravo bare
brazo: a ___ **partido** hand to hand
brillante brilliant
brillar shine
bruto brute
bueno good, kind; *excl.* well, all right; **de** ___**as a primeras** point blank
bufón *m.* buffoon
Burgos *m.* *city in Old Castile*
burlón mocking
buscar seek, look for
búsqueda *f.* search

C

¡ca! not at all!
caballo *m.* horse
caber fit, be contained in (Ch. 19)
cabeza *f.* head
cabo: al ___ **(de)** finally, at the end of
cada each
Cádiz Cadiz *(important port on southwest coast of Spain)*
caer fall (Ch. 3)
café *m.* coffee; café; ___ **cortado** expresso coffee with some milk
cafetería *f.* café
caída *f.* fall
caja *f.* box; ___ **de ahorros** savings bank
calabazas: dar ___ jilt
calcetín *m.* sock
calentar (ie) heat
cálido warm
califa *m.* Caliph
calor *m.* heat
caluroso warm
Calvo Sotelo: Paseo de *(part of the Paseo de la Castellana, formerly called Paseo de Recoletos)*
callado silent
callarse keep silent
calle *f.* street; ___ **abajo** down the street; ___ **arriba** up the street
callejón *m.*, **callejuela** *f.* narrow street alley
camarero *m.* waiter
camarón *m.* shrimp
cambiante changing
cambiar (de) change
cambio *m.* change; **en** ___ on the other hand
caminar walk
camisa *f.* shirt
campana *f.* bell
campesino *m.* peasant
campo *m.* field; ___ **de cultivo** cultivated fields
canasto *m.* basket
cancelar cancel
canción *f.* song
cansar tire; ___**se** tire, become tired
Cantábrico Cantabrian *m.* Bay of Biscay
cantante *m.* singer
cantar sing
cante flamenco *m.* *Andalusian folk songs of strong oriental character, especially associated with the gypsies*
cantidad *f.* quantity
canto *m.* rock, boulder

capital *f.* capital
capitán *m.* captain
cara *f.* fade
carácter *m.* character
cárcel *f.* jail
cardenal *m.* cardinal
carecer de lack
cargado laden
carne *f.* meat, flesh
caro expensive
carretera *f.* highway
cartel *m.* poster
cartelera *f.* (bill)board
cartero *m.* mailman
casa *f.* house, home; firm
Casa de Campo *park across the river from the royal palace in Madrid*
Casa de la Moneda *f.* mint
casado married
casamiento marriage
casarse marry
casero domestic, home loving
casi almost
caso *m.* case
(la) Castellana *Madrid boulevard*
castellano Castilian
Castilla *f.* Castile
Castilla la Nueva *f.* New Castile *(Central Spain, south of the Guadarrama Mts.)*
castillo *m.* castle
castizo traditional, thoroughly Spanish
casualidad *f.* chance
catalán Catalán, Catalonian
Cataluña *f.* Catalonia *(region in the northeast of Spain; capital: Barcelona)*
catar sample, examine
catavinos *m.* winetaster
catedral *f.* cathedral
causa *f.* cause; **a ___ de** because of
céltico Celtic
cenar dine
censurar censor
central central
centralista centralist
céntrico downtown *(adj.)*
centro *m.* center, downtown
cerca near
cercanía *f.* surrounding territory
cercano nearby
ceremonia *f.* ceremony
ceremoniosamente ceremoniously
Cervantes, Miguel de *(1547–1616) greatest figure in Spanish literature, author of Don Quixote*
cervantino Cervantian
cerveza *f.* beer
Cibeles *f.* Cybele *(Mother Earth, mother of Jupiter, Neptune, Pluto, etc.; fountain and statue (18th cent.) in the Plaza de Castelar, Madrid)*
cicatriz *f.* scar
(el) Cid Ruy Díaz de Bivar ("*el Cid Campeador*" *(1030?–1099) Spanish national hero)*
cielo *m.* sky
ciencia *f.* science; **hombre de ___** scientist
ciento hundred; **por ___** per cent
cierto certain; **por ___ que** and by the way, to be sure
cigarrillo *m.* cigaret
cine *m.* moving pictures
cinematografía *f.* cinematography
círculo *m.* circle
circundado surrounded
Cisneros, Francisco Jiménez de *(1437–1517) archbishop of Toledo*
ciudad *f.* city
Ciudad Real *city of New Castile, capital of province of same name*
ciudadano *m.* citizen
civil civil
civilización *f.* civilization
claridad *f.* clarity
claro clear; of course; **¡ ___ que sí!** of course!
clasicismo *m.* classicism
clásico classic
clima *m.* climate
cocinero, -a *m.f.* cook
coche *m.* car (automobile)
coger gather, pick (Ch. 2)
colección *f.* collection
colina *f.* hill
Colón *m.* Columbus
color *m.* color
colorido *m.* color(ing)
collar *m.* necklace
comandante *m.* commander; major
comarca *f.* region, area
combatiente *m.* combatant
combinación *f.* combination
comedia *f.* comedy; play; **___ de capa y espada** "cloak and sword" play

comentario *m.* comment
comer eat
cometa *m.* comet
comida *f.* meal, food
como as, since, as if, like
comodidad *f.* comfort
cómodo comfortable
compañero *m.* companion, comrade; **—— de cuarto** room mate
compañía *f.* company
comparar compare
compartimiento *m.* compartment
compartir share
complacer please
completamente completely
completo complete; **por ——** completely
complicado complicated
componer compose
compra *f.* purchase; **ir (estar) de ——s** go shopping
comprar buy
comprender understand
comprensión *f.* understanding
comprometerse a to promise to
comunicar communicate, give
comunista communist
con with
concebir (i) conceive
concentrar concentrate
concierto *m.* concert
conde *m.* count
condenar condemn
conducta *f.* conduct
conferencia *f.* lecture, talk
confesar (ie) confess
confesor *m.* confessor
confusión *f.* confusion
conjunto *m.* whole; **en ——** all in all, by and large
conocer know, meet
conquista *f.* conquest
conquistador *m.* conquistador, conqueror
conseguir (i) get, obtain, succeed in
consejero *m.* counselor
consejo *m.* advice; council
conserje *m.* concierge
considerar consider
consistir en consist of
constar be known; **—— de** consist of (Ch. 16)
construcción *f.* construction
construir build
contar (ue) tell, relate (Prelim. Les. 2)
contemplar contemplate
contemporáneo contemporary
contender contend
contendiente contending
contener contain
contentar content
contento happy
contestar answer
continuar continue
continuo continual, continuous
contrario contrary; *m.* opponent; **llevarle la contraria (a uno)** oppose, contradict
contraste *m.* contrast
contratiempo *m.* misfortune
contrato *m.* contract
convencer convince
convenir agree; **lo convenido** the plan (Ch. 11)
conversación *f.* conversation
copa *f.* wineglass
corazón *m.* heart
corbata *f.* necktie
cordialidad *f.* cordiality
Córdoba *f.* Cordova *(capital of the Western Caliphate 756–1031; one of the principal cities of Andalusia)*
cordobés: lo —— the (spirit) of Cordova
coronel *m.* colonel
correo *m.* mail
correr run
correría *f.* raid
correspondiente respective
corrida (de toros) *f.* bullfight
corriente usual, ordinary, current
cortapapel *m.* paper cutter
cortar cut
cortatubos *m. sing.* pipecutter
corte *f.* court, capital
corto short; **quedarse ——** restrain oneself
La Coruña *f.* La Corunna *(most important city and port in Galicia)*
cosa thing
costa *f.* coast
Costa Brava *f.* Spanish Riviera *(coastal area north of Barcelona)*
costar (ue) cost; **—— trabajo** be hard, difficult
costumbre *f.* custom

creer believe, think; **¡ya lo creo!** I should say so! of course!
cresta *f.* crest
Cresta del Gallo *f.* *(mountain near Murcia)*
criado, -a servant
criollo native American
crisis *f.* crisis
cruz *f.* cross
cruzar cross
cuaderno *m.* notebook
cuadrado square
cuadro *m.* picture, painting
cual: el ___ *etc.* which
cualquiera any (at all, whatsoever)
cuando when
cuanto as much as, all that; **en ___** as soon as; **en ___ a** as for, as regards; **unos ___s** a few
cuartel *m.* barracks
cuarto *m.* room; fourth, quarter
cuatro four
cubano Cuban
cubierto covered
cubreplatos *m. sing.* dish cover
cuchara *f.* spoon; **meter la ___** butt in
Cuenca *f.* *city of New Castile, famous for its picturesque location*
cuenta: darse ___ realize
cuentista *m.* story writer
cuento *m.* tale, story; **___ de nunca acabar** endless story
cuero *m.* leather
cuesta *f.* hill; **en ___** steep; **___ arriba** uphill; **___ abajo** downhill
cueva *f.* cave
cuidado care; **tener ___** be careful
culpa *f.* blame
culpar blame
cultivar cultivate
culto cultured, cultivated
cultura *f.* culture
cumpleaños *m. sing.* birthday
cumplir fulfil, execute (Ch. 19)
cuñado, -a *m.f.* brother-, sister-in-law
curiosísimo very curious
curso *m.* course

CH

chaqueta *f.* jacket
charlar chat
chicle *m.* chewing gum
chico small; **-o, -a** *m.f.* boy; girl
chino Chinese
chisme *m.* gossip
chismoso gossipy
chocolate *m.* chocolate
chófer *m.* driver
chorro jet, stream; **avión de ___** jet plane
churro *m.* long thin fritter

D

damasquinado *m.* damascene work *(gold inlaid on black steel, a typical Toledan art)*
daño *m.* damage; **hacer ___** harm
dar give; **me da lo mismo** it makes no difference to me; **___ se cuenta (de)** realize (Ch. 6)
Darro *one of the two rivers of Granada*
datar date
de of, from, with
debajo de beneath, underneath
deber owe, ought, must; *m.* duty
debido fitting, proper
decano *m.* dean
decidir decide; **___(se)** decide, make up one's mind
décimo tenth
decir say; **querer ___** mean (to say); **ni que ___ tiene** it goes without saying (Ch. 10)
decisión *f.* decision
declaración *f.* declaration
decorativo decorative
dedicar devote
defecto *m.* defect
defensa *f.* defense
deficiente deficient
definir define
dehesa *f.* pasture land
dejar leave, make; let; **___ de** fail to; stop (Ch. 10)
delante in front of, ahead of
delgado thin
delicado delicate
delicioso delicious
demás: el ___ *etc.* the rest
demasiado too (much, many)
democracia *f.* democracy
democrático democratic

dentro: por ___ on the inside; **___ (de)** within
depender depend
deporte *m.* sport
depositar deposit
derecha *f.* right wing *(politics)*
derechista *m.* right winger
derecho right; *m.* right; law
derroche *m.* lavish expenditure
desagradable unpleasant
desaparecer disappear
desarrollar develop
desarrollo *m.* development
descansar rest
descolgar (ue) take down, unhook
desconocido unknown, strange
descripción *f.* description
descubrimiento *m.* discovery
desde from; **___ que** since (time)
desembarcar disembark
desear desire, wish, like
desembocar run (empty) into
desesperado desperate
designado chosen
desilusión *f.* disappointment
desmayado faint
desnudo bare, naked
desolación *f.* desolation
desolado desolate
despacio slowly
despacho *m.* study
despedirse (i) take leave (of)
despertarse (ie) awaken
despiadado pitiless
despierto awake
desprecio *m.* scorn
destacar stand out
destierro *m.* exile
destinación *f.* destination
desvivirse por outdo oneself to
detener(se) stop
detenidamente carefully
detenido detailed
detrás behind
deuda *f.* debt
devolver (ue) return
día *m.* day
diablo *m.* devil; **qué diablos** what the devil
diálogo *m.* dialogue, conversation
diario daily; *m.* diary; daily newspaper
dictador *m.* dictator
dictadorzuelo *m.* petty dictator
Diego James
diez ten
diferencia *f.* difference
diferenciarse be different
diferente different
diferir (ie) differ
difícil difficult, hard
dificultad *f.* difficulty
dignidad *f.* dignity
dilema *m.* dilemma
dimensión *f.* dimension
dineral *m.* large amount of money
dirigir direct; **___ la palabra** address
disco *m.* disk, record
discreto discreet
discusión *f.* argument
discutir argue
disponible available, useable
disposición *f.* disposal
dispuesto ready
disputa *f.* argument
distancia *f.* distance
distar be distant
distintivo distinctive
distinto different
diversión *f.* amusement, sport
diversos various
divertido amusing
divertir (ie, i) amuse
divisar descry
doce twelve
docena *f.* dozen
documento *m.* document
dólar *m.* dollar
domador *m.* tamer
domar tame
dominio *m.* dominion
Don Quijote *m.* Don Quixote
donde where
dorado golden
dormir (ue, u) sleep
dos two
dotado gifted
drama *m.* drama
dramaturgo *m.* dramatist
duda *f.* doubt
Duero *m.* Douro *(important river in Old Castile and Portugal)*
dulce sweet, soft
durante during, for
durar last
duro *m.* five pesetas

E

e and
echar throw; **___se (a)** begin to, burst out (Prelim. Les. 1)
edificio *m.* building
educación *f.* good breeding, politeness; education
educador *m.* educator
educar educate; bring up
egoísta *m.* egoist
ejemplo *m.* example
ejercicio *m.* exercise
electricidad *f.* electricity
electricista *m.* electrician
elegancia *f.* elegance
elegante elegant
elegir (i) choose, pick out, elect
elevado high, elevated
ello it
elogiar praise
embajada *f.* embassy
embajador *m.* ambassador
embalador *m.* packer
embalar crate
embarcar embark
embargo: sin ___ nevertheless
embrujamiento *m.* eeriness
eminente eminent
emoción *f.* emotion, emotional appeal
emocionante exciting
emocionar move, stir, appeal to
empezar (ie) start, begin
empinado high, lofty
empleado *m.* employee
empobrecer impoverish, become poor
emprendedor enterprising
emprender undertake
en in, on
enamorarse fall in love
encantador charming, delightful
encantar delight
encanto *m.* charm
encargar order
encargo *m.* errand, order, commission
encarnar *embody*
encendedor *m.* cigarette lighter
encender (ie) light
encerrado (en) shut up in
encerrar (ie) shut in
encima in addition; **(por) ___ de** above, on top of
encomendar (ie) commend
encontrar (ue) find, meet; **___se con** find
encuentro *m.* meeting
enfadar(se) make (get) angry
enfermarse become ill
enfermedad *f.* illness
enfermo ill
enfrente across the way, opposite
enfriar cool, chill, grow cold
engañador deceiving
engañar deceive
enojado angry
enojarse become angry
enormemente immensely
enriquecer grow rich
enrojecer redden
ensalada *f.* salad
enseñar show; teach
ensueño *m.* reverie
entablar start
entendedor *m.* understanding person
entender (ie) understand, make out; **___se** get along together (Ch. 1)
enterarse (de) find out
entero entire
enterrar (ie) bury
entierro *m.* burial
entonces then, that time
entrar enter; **___ le a uno sueño** *(etc).* to get (become) sleepy *(etc.)* (Ch. 18)
entre among, between
entregar deliver, hand over
entrenamiento *m.* training
entretener entertain
entristecer sadden, become sad
entusiasmado enthusiastic
enviar send, ship
envolver (ue) involve
enzarzarse (en) become involved in
época *f.* time, period
equipaje *m.* baggage
equipo *m.* team
errar (ie) err, wander
escala: hacer ___ call at (of a boat or airplane)
escandaloso scandalous
escaso few, rare
escena *f.* scene, sight, view; stage
esclarecer brighten, grow light
(el) Escorial *m.* the Escurial *(famous monastery-palace in the foot-hills of the Guadarramas)*

escribir write
escrito: por ___ in writing
escritor *m.* writer
escuchar listen
esculpir carve
escultórico sculptural
escultura *f.* wood carving, sculpture
esforzarse (ue) strive
esfuerzo *m.* effort
eso that; **por ___** therefore, that's why; **a ___ de** about *(time)*; **¡eso es!** that's it (right)!; **___ sí que no** that's not the point at all; **y ___ que** although, even if
espacio *m.* space
espantar frighten
España *f.* Spain
español Spanish, Spaniard
especial special
especialmente especially
especie *f.* kind
espectáculo *m.* spectacle
espectador *m.* spectator
espejo *m.* mirror
esperar hope; expect; wait (for)
espeso thick
espíritu *m.* spirit
espiritual spiritual
espléndido splendid, magnificent
esplendor *m.* splendor
esquiador *m.* skier
esquiar ski
esquina *f.* (street) corner
estación *f.* station; season, **___ de Atocha** *(railroad station in Madrid)*
Estados Unidos *m.* United States
estalactita *f.* stalactite
estancia *f.* stay
estar be, stand, lie; look, feel, act (Ch. 13)
estatua *f.* statue
este this
estilo *m.* style; **por el ___** of the sort, kind
estimar calculate
estimulante stimulating
estirar stretch
esto this; **___ de** this business of
estrecho narrow
estreno *m.* first performance, *première*
estrepitoso noisy, boisterous
estropear spoil
estudiante *m.* student
estudiar study
estudio *m.* study
eterno eternal, everlasting
Europa *f.* Europe
evocación *f.* evocation
evocar evoke
exagerar exaggerate
excelencia: por ___ *par excellence*
excelente excellent
excepción *f.* exception
excepcional exceptional
exceptuar except
excesivo excessive
excursión *f.* trip
excusar excuse, avoid
existencia *f.* existence
existente existing
éxito *m.* success
explorador *m.* explorer
explorar explore
explosión *f.* explosion
exportador exporting
Exposición *f.* Exposition
expresar express
exquisito exquisite
extender (ie) stretch
extenso wide
extranjero *m.* foreigner
extrañar surprise
extraño strange
extraordinario extraordinary
extremo *m.* end

F

fábrica *f.* factory
faceta *f.* facet
fácil easy
fachada *f.* façade
faja *f.* sash; strip (of land, etc.)
Falla, Manual de *(1876–1946) leading 20th-century composer*
falta *f.* lack; **hacer ___** be necessary
faltar be lacking (Ch. 19)
familia *f.* family
familiar familiar
famoso famous
fantástico fantastic
faro *m.* light(house)
fastidiar annoy, bore
fatigado tired
favor *m.* favor; **haga el ___ (de)** please (give)

favorecer flatter
favorito favorite
felicitar(se) congratulate
Felipe II Philip II *(1527–1598)*
fenicio Phoenician
fenómeno *m.* phenomenon
fiesta *f.* feast, holiday; sport
figura *f.* figure
figurarse imagine, think of
fijarse (en) notice
filigrana *f.* filigree
fin *m.* end; **al ___** finally; **en ___** after all, in short, well
final *m.* end
firmar sign
físico physical
fisonomía *f.* appearance
flecha *f.* arrow
flechazo *m.* arrow shot; *colloq.* sudden passion, love at first sight
flor *f.* flower
fomento *m.* fomentation, promotion
fondo *m.* background, rear; **en el ___** at bottom
fondos *m. pl.* funds
forastero *m.* stranger
formar form
formidable formidable, "swell"
fortaleza *f.* fortress
fortuna *f.* fortune
forzoso: es ___ it is necessary, it must
foto *f.* photograph
fotografía *f.* photograph
fracasar fail
fragmento *m.* fragment
francamente frankly, really
francés French, Frenchman
franco *m.* franc
Franco, Avenida del Generalísimo *Name of the Paseo de la Castellana north of the Plaza de San Juan de la Cruz*
franqueza *f.* frankness
frase *f.* phrase, sentence
frecuencia *f.* frequency
frecuentemente frequently
frente *f.* forehead; front
fruta *f.* fruit
fuente *f.* fountain, spring
fuera outside; **comer ___** dine out
fuertemente strongly
fuerza *f.* strength
fugaz fleeting
fugitivo *m.* fugitive
fumador smoker
fumar smoke
función (de teatro) *f.* performance, show
fundar found
furioso furious
fusilar shot (execute)
fútbol *m.* soccer
Galicia *f.* *province in the northwest corner of Spain*
gallego Galician
galleta *f.* cracker
gana *f.* desire; **darle a uno la ___ de, tener ___s de** feel like
ganar earn, win
ganga *f.* bargain
gasolina *f.* gasoline
gastar spend
gato *m.* cat
general general; **por lo ___** in general
Generalife *m.* Generalife *(Moorish palace famous for its gardens)*
generalizarse become general
generalmente generally
género *m.* type, genre
generosidad *f.* generosity
generoso generous
geniazo *m.* strong temper
genio temper; character
gente *f.* people
geográfico geographical
gerente *m.* manager
gesto *m.* stroke
(la) Giralda *the Moorish bell-tower of the Seville cathedral*
girar turn; **___ alrededor de** center on
gitano,-a gypsy
gobernación *f.* governing; **Ministerio de ___** Department of the Interior
gobierno *m.* government
godo Goth
gótico Gothic
Goya y Lucientes, Francisco de *(1746–1828) one of Spain's greatest painters*
gozar de enjoy
grabado engraved
gracia *f.* grace; wit; **hacer ___** amuse, strike as funny; **tener ___** be amusing; **caerle a uno en ___** charm someone

gracioso graceful
Granada *f.* Granada *(last capital of the Moors in Spain)*
granadino Grenadine
gran(de) great, large, big
grandeza *f.* grandeur, greatness
grandiosamente grandly
granito *m.* granite
granizar hail
grano *m.* grain; **ir al ___** come to the point
(la) Granja *former royal country seat near Segovia*
grato pleasant
grave grave, serious
gravedad *f.* gravity, sternness
(el) Greco, Domenico Theotocopouli *(1548–1625) famous Spanish painter, born in Crete*
gris gray
gritar shout
grupo *m.* group
Guadalajara *city in New Castile, capital of province*
Guadalquivir *m.* Guadalquivir *(the most important river in Andalusia)*
Guadalupe *mountain range in Extremadura;* **monasterio de ___** *monastery famous for its art treasures*
Guadarrama *m.* *mountain range northwest of Madrid, dividing Old and New Castile*
guante *m.* glove
guapo good looking
guardajoyas *m.* jewel case
guardapuente *m.* bridge guard
guardia *m.* policeman
guerra *f.* war
guerrero *m.* warrior
guía *f.* guide
guitarra *f.* guitar
gustar like (be pleasing)
gusto *m.* taste; pleasure; **hallarse a ___** be at ease, enjoy oneself

H

haber have (auxiliary); **hay, había** *etc.* there is, was; **he de,** *etc.* I am to, shall *etc.;* **hay que** it is necessary, one (we) must (Ch. 12)
hablador talkative
hablante *m.* speaker
hablar talk, speak
hacer do, make; **hace** it is *(of weather);* **desde hacía tiempo** for some time; **___se** become (Ch. 9)
hacia toward
hada *f.* fairy
hallar find; **___se** be
hambre *f.* hunger
hasta until, up to, as far as; **___ ahora** so far
hecho *m.* fact
helado *m.* ice cream
helar (ie) freeze
hermano, -a *m.f.* brother, sister
hermoso beautiful
heroico heroic
hispanoamericano Hispanic American
hispánico Hispanic
historia *f.* history
histórico historic, historical
hombre *m.* man; **¡___!** man (alive)!
holgazán lazy
honor *m.* honor
hora *f.* hour; **tener ___** have the time
horario *m.* schedule
hospitalidad *f.* hospitality
hotel *m.* hotel
hoy today
huelga *f.* strike
huella *f.* mark
huérfano *m.* orphan
huerta *f.* struck-farm
huir flee
humanidad *f.* humanity
humano human; **lo ___ y lo divino** everything under the sun
humo *m.* smoke
humor *m.* humor

I

idea *f.* idea
ideal ideal
idiota *m.* idiot
iglesia *f.* church
ignorar be ignorant of, not know
iluminar illuminate
imaginación *f.* imagination, imagining
imaginar(se) imagine
imperial imperial
impermeable *m.* raincoat

imponente imposing
importador importing
importante important
importar matter, be of consequence (importance)
imposible impossible
impresión *f.* impression
impresionante impressive
impresionar impress
impulso *m.* driving force
inaccessible inaccessible
inagotable inexhaustible
inatención *f.* inattention
incendio *m.* fire
incidente *m.* incident
inconsciente unconscious
inconveniente *m.* difficulty, disadvantage
increíble incredible
independencia *f.* independence
indescriptible indescribable
indicar indicate
indio Indian
indiscreción *f.* indiscretion
individual individual
individuo *m.* person, fellow
industria *f.* industry
industrial industrial
industrialización *f.* industrialization
industrializar industrialize
infinito infinite
información *f.* information
informe *m.* notice, report
infracción *f.* infraction, violation
ingeniería *f.* engineering
ingeniero *m.* engineer
ingenio *m.* wit
inglés English, Englishman
ingreso *m.* receipts; **___s** income
injusticia *f.* injustice
inmenso immense
inmigración *f.* immigration
innato innate
inolvidable unforgettable
insistir insist
insultante insulting
insultar insult
insuperable insuperable
insurgente insurgent
intelectual intellectual
intención *f.* intention
intentar try, attempt
interés *m.* interest
interesante interesting
interesar interest
interior *m.* interior
interminable endless
internacional international
íntimo intimate; **lo más ___** the innermost (part)
intrigar intrigue
inundar inundate, flood
invitar invite
ir go; **___se** go, go away, leave; **vamos a** let's; **¡Ah, vamos!** Oh, I see! **¡Qué va!** Nonsense! (Ch. 15)
irónico ironical
itinerario *m.* itinerary
izquierda *f.* left wing *(politics)*
izquierdista *m.* left winger
izquierdo left

J

jabón *m.* soap
jadeante panting
jardín *m.* garden
jefe *m.* chief, boss
jersey *m.* sweater
jornalero *m.* day laborer
jota *f.* *Aragonese folk dance in 3/8 time*
joven young
joya *f.* jewel
judío Jew, Jewish
juez *m.* judge
jugador *m.* player
jugar (ue) play (game) (Ch. 2)
juguetón playful
juicio *m.* judgement
julio *m.* July
junio *m.* June
justo fair, just, proper
juventud *f.* youth
juzgar judge

K

kilo *m.* kilo *(kilogram, 2.2 lbs.)*
kilómetro *m.* kilometer *(approximately five-eights of a mile)*

L

lado *m.* side
lamentar lament
lápiz *m.* pencil
largo long

lástima *f.*: **es ___** it is a pity; **dar ___** be pitiful
lata: dar la ___ bore
lavar wash
lección *f.* lesson
lectura *f.* reading
leche *f.* milk
lechería *f.* dairy, creamery
leer read
lejanía *f.* distance
lejano remote
lejos far; **a lo ___** in the distance
lengua *f.* tongue, language
león *m.* lion
León *m.* *capital of the ancient kingdom of León*
León, Fray Luis de *(1537–1591) famous mystic writer, poet, and scholar*
levantarse rise, get up
Levante *m.* Levant (*eastern coast of Spain)*
leyenda *f.* legend
liberal liberal
libertad *f.* liberty
libertar liberate
librería *f.* bookstore
libro *m.* book
liebre *f.* hare
ligereza *f.* agility
ligero light
limitar(se) limit
limpiaparabrisas *m. sing.* windshield wiper
limpiar clean
limpio clean, pure
línea *f.* line; **___ aérea** airline
Lisboa Lisbon *(capital of Portugal)*
lista *f.* list
listo ready; clever
literario literary
literatura *f.* literature
lo it; **___ que es** as for
loco mad, wild, crazy
lograr attain, succeed in
lotería *f.* lottery
luchar struggle, fight
luego then, later; thereupon, therefor; **desde ___** of course
lugar *m.* place; **tener ___** take place
lujoso luxurious
lunes *m.* Monday
luz *f.* light

Ll

llamado so-called
llamar call, knock
llaneza *f.* informality
llano flat
llanura *f.* plain
llegar arrive, come to
lleno full
llevar take; wear; have; **___(se)** take away with; **___se bien** get along well together (Ch. 17)
lloviznar drizzle

M

macizo massive
madre *f.* mother
Madrid *m.* Madrid
maduro ripe, mature
magnífico magnificent, splendid, wonderful
mal badly, not very well
Málaga *f.* Malaga *(most important port in southern Spain)*
maldecir curse
maldiciente slanderous, cursing
maleta *f.* suitcase
malo bad; **lo ___ es que** the trouble is that
mañana *f.* morning
(la) Mancha *f.* La Mancha *(south-eastern part of New Castile)*
mandar order, have
mandón bossy
manera *f.* manner, way, fashion; **de ___ que** so that
manía *f.* mania
manifestación *f.* manifestation
mano *f.* hand; **___ de obra** manual labor
mantener maintain
mantequilla *f.* butter
mantilla *f.* mantilla *(lace shawl worn as head-dress by Spanish women on ceremonial occasions)*
manuscrito *m.* manuscript
manzana *f.* block (of houses); apple
mapa *m.* map
máquina *f.* machine; **___ de escribir** typewriter
mar *m.* and *f.* sea; **la ___ de** lots of

maravilla *f.* marvel; **a las mil ___s** wonderfully
maravilloso marvellous
marcha: estar en ___ be moving; **ponerse en ___** start off
marcharse leave
margen *m.f.* margin
María Luisa *sister of Isabel II, who gave the park bearing her name to the city of Seville*
marido *m.* husband
más more
masa *f.* mass, pile
matador *m.* bullfighter
matamoscas *m.* fly swatter
matar kill
materia *f.* matter; **primera ___** raw material
material *m.* material
mayor larger, largest
mayordomo *m.* chief steward
mayoría *f.* majority
mecánico *m.* mechanic
medicina *f.* medicine
médico *m.* physician
medio half; **quitar (algo) de en ___** get (something) out of the way)
medieval medieval
medir (i) measure
meditación *f.* meditation
mejor better; **tanto ___** so much the better
melancólico melancholy
melodía *f.* melody
melón *m.* melon
memoria *f.* memory
mencionar mention
menear shake
(las) Meninas *(fr. Portuguese* **menina** *girl) The Maids of Honor (famous painting of Velázquez)*
menor smaller, smallest; slightest
menos less, least; **ni mucho ___** not in the least, by no means
mente *f.* mind
mentir (ie, i) lie
menudo small
mercader *m.* trader
merced *f.* favor, grace
merecer deserve
mesa *f.* table
meseta *f.* table-land, plateau
metálico metallic
meter put, place (into); **___se con** quarrel with; **___se** keep oneself (Ch. 7)
método *m.* method
metro *m.* meter *(39.37 in.)*
Mezquita *f.* Mosque *(of Cordova, at present a cathedral)*
mi my
mí me
mientras (que) while; **___ tanto** in the meantime
mil (one) thousand
milagro *m.* miracle, wonder
milla *f.* mile
ministerio *m.* ministry
ministro *m.* minister
mío my, of mine
mirador *m.* *in Cadiz, a turret, in the rest of Spain a glass-enclosed balcony*
mirar look (at)
mismo same, very; self
misterio *m.* mystery
misterioso mysterious
místico mystic
mitad *f.* half
mitin *m.* political rally
modelo *m.* model
modernizado modernized
moderno modern
modo way, fashion, manner
mole *f.* mass
molestia *f.* annoyance, bother
molestar annoy, disturb, bother
molino *m.* mill; **___ de viento** windmill
momento *m.* moment
monasterio *m.* monastery
mono cute, nice
monótonamente monotonously
montaña *f.* mountain
montón *m.* pile
monumental monumental, of (in) monuments
monumento *m.* monument
Morales, Luis "el divino" *(1509–1586) Spanish painter*
moro Moorish, Moor
motivo *m.* reason
mozo *m.* youth; servant; **___ de cuerda** street porter
muchacho *m.* young man, lad
mucho much; long (time)
mueble *m.* piece of furniture

mueblería *f.* furniture store
muerte *f.* death
mujer *f.* woman
mujerzuela *f.* low woman
multitud *f.* multitude
multar fine
mundial world
mundo *m.* world; **todo el ___** everybody
municipio *m.* municipality
muralla *f.* wall
Murcia *city in southeastern Spain*
Murillo, Bartolomé Esteban *(1619–1682) Spanish painter*
muro *m.* wall
museo *m.* museum
música *f.* music
músico *m.* musician
muy very

N

nacer be born
nacimiento *m.* birth
nación *f.* nation
nacional national
nadie nobody, no one, anybody, anyone
naipe *m.* playing card
naranja *f.* orange
naranjo *m.* orange tree
natural natural
naturaleza *f.* nature
naturalmente naturally, of course
necesario necessary
necesitar need
negocio business; **hombre de ___s** businessman
nevar (ie) snow
ni neither, nor
nieve *f.* snow
ninguno no, none; any
niño *m.* boy
no no, not
noble noble
noche *f.* night; **de ___** at night; **esta ___** tonight
nombre *m.* name
norte *m.* north
norteamericano (North) American
norteño northern
nosotros we
nota *f.* note; grade; **sacar buenas (malas) ___s** get good (bad) grades
notar note
noticia *f.* news
novela *f.* novel
novelista *m.* novelist
noveno ninth
novio, -a *m.f.* sweetheart, fiancé(e)
nube *f.* cloud
nublado overcast
nuestro our
Nueva York *f.* New York
nueve nine
nuevo new; **de ___** again
número *m.* number
nunca never, ever

O

o or
obedecer obey
objetivo *m.* objective
objeto *m.* object
obligar compel
obra *f.* work (of art, etc.); **mano de ___** manual labor
obrero *m.* work
observación *f.* remark
obtener obtain
ocasión *f.* occasion, opportunity; **de ___** second hand
océano *m.* ocean
occidental western
octavo eighth
ocupar occupy
ocurrir(se) occur, think of (Ch. 18)
odiar hate
ofender offend
oficial official, (of) government
ofrecer offer
¡ojalá! I wish (would) that!
ojo *m.* eye; **costar un ___ de la cara** cost a great deal
olivar *m.* olive orchard
olvidar forget
once eleven
opinión *f.* opinion
oportunidad *f.* opportunity
opuesto opposite
organización *f.* organization
oriental oriental
original original
orilla *f.* bank (river)
ornamentación *f.* decoration
oro *m.* gold

oscurecer darken, grow dark
oscuro dark
otro other, another: **___s dos** two more

P

paciencia *f.* patience
pagar pay
país *m.* country, land
paisaje *m.* landscape
paisano *m.* fellow countryman
pajarillo *m.* little bird
pájaro *m.* bird
palabra *f.* word; **de ___** verbally
palacio *m.* palace; **___ Nacional** *royal palace in Madrid;* **___ de Comunicaciones** *Central Post Office (Madrid)*
palmera *f.* palm tree
pan *m.* bread
panadero *m.* baker
panorama *m.* view, panorama
pantalones *m.pl.* trousers
panteón *m.* mausoleum
pañuelo *m.* kerchief; **el mundo es un ___** the world's a small place
papel *m.* paper
papelero *m.* stationer, papermaker
paquete *m.* package
par *m.* pair, couple
para for, in order to, to; **___ con** toward, to
parador *m.* wayside inn, hostelry
paraguas *m.* umbrella
parar(se) stop
pardo brown
(el) Pardo *town and former royal country-seat outside Madrid*
parecer seem, appear, look (like); **¿qué le parece?** what do you think of?; **¿le parece (bien)?** what do you say?; **___se** resemble (Ch. 5)
pared *f.* wall
pariente *m.* relative
parque *m.* park
parroquiano *m.* parishioner; customer
parte *f.* part; **a todas ___s** everywhere; **(por) ninguna ___** nowhere
participante participant
participar participate
particular specific
partida *f.* departure
partido *m.* game
pasado mañana day after tomorrow
pasajero *m.* passenger
pasar pass, spend; happen, feel, be the matter with; **___ a** shift to; **___lo bien (mal)** to have a good (bad) time (Ch. 19)
pasear(se) walk, take a walk
paseo *m.* walk; boulevard; **dar un ___** take a walk
pasillo *m.* corridor
paso step, pace; **dos ___s** short distance
pastel *m.* pastry
pastelería *f.* pastry shop
pastelero *m.* pastry cook
pastilla *f.* tablet, cake
pastor *m.* shepherd
pata *f.* paw, leg; **___ de palo** wooden leg
patio *m.* patio
patria *f.* native country, birthplace
patrón *m.* master, boss
paz *f.* peace
pedir (i) ask for, request; **___ prestado** borrow (Ch. 1)
pegar strike (Ch. 2)
Peinador de la Reina Queen's boudoir *(room in the Alhambra)*
peligro *m.* danger
pelo *m.* hair
pelota *f.* (hand) ball; **___ vasca** Basque handball, *jai alai*
pelotazo *m.* blow with a ball
pena *f.*: **valer la ___** be worth while
penetrante penetrating
penetrar penetrate
península *f.* peninsula
penosamente painfully
penoso painful
pensamiento *m.* thought
pensar (ie) think (over)
peñasco *m.* rock, boulder
pequeño small
perder (ie) lose, miss, waste; **___ de vista** lose sight of (Prelim. Les. 2)
perdonar pardon
perfeccionarse improve
perfectamente perfectly
periferia *f.* periphery

periodista *m.* journalist
periodo *m.* period
perito *m.* expert
perla *f.* pearl
permiso *m.* permission; **con ___** excuse me
pero but
perpetuo perpetual
perro *m.* dog
persona *f.* person, people
personaje *m.* personage, character
personalmente personally
perspectiva *f.* prospect, view
pertenecer belong
pesado heavy; boring
pesar weigh; grieve
pescado *m.* fish
peseta *f.* peseta *(Spanish monetary unit, worth 1.58 cents; 63.29 pesetas to $1.00 in 1973)*
peso *m.* weight; *(monetary unit in some Spanish American countries)*
pestaña *f.* eyelash
pianista *m.* pianist
pico *m.* peak
pictórico pictoric
pie *m.* foot; **de pie** standing
piedra *f.* stone
pierna *f.* leg
pieza *f.* piece
pinar *m.* pine forest
pintar paint
pintor *m.* painter
pintoresco picturesque
pintorzuelo *m.* wretched painter
pintura *f.* painting
pisapapeles *m. sing.* paperweight
pistola *f.* pistol
pitillera *f.* cigarette case
pitillo *m.* cigarette
placer *m.* pleasure
plan *m.* plan
planchar iron
planear plan
plantado: dejar ___ stand up
plantar plant
plata *f.* silver
plátano *m.* banana
plato *m.* plate, dish
plateresco plateresque *(style of Spanish architecture in 16th century)*
plaza *f.* (town) square; **___ de toros** bull ring; **___ Mayor** main square
plazo *m.* term, time limit; **a ___s** on credit, on time
pluma *f.* pen
población *f.* population; town
poco little, few; **___ a ___** little by little, gradually; **___ más o menos** more or less
poder (ue) be able, can, may; **¿se puede?** may I come in?; **como pude** as best I could; **a más no ___** to the utmost (Ch. 11)
poesía *f.* poem, poetry
poético poetic
política *f.* politics
político political
polo *m.* pole
poner place, put; **___se** become, get; put on (Ch. 7)
Pontevedra *f.* *city in Galicia*
popular popular, folk
por for, by, through, along, about, by way of
porque because
portarse behave, do
portero, -a *m.f.* doorkeeper; janitor
Posada de la Sangre *(formerly Mesón del Sevillano) inn in Toledo mentioned by Cervantes*
posesión *f.* possession, property
posición *f.* position
postre *m.* dessert
potente powerful
pozo *m.* well
(el) Prado *m.* the Prado *(wide boulevard in Madrid)*; **Museo del ___** Prado Art Gallery
prado *m.* meadow
precisamente precisely, just
precisión *f.* accuracy
preciso: es ___ it is necessary
precio *m.* price
preferir (ie, i) prefer
pregunta *f.* question
preguntar ask (inquire); **___se** wonder
prejuicio *m.* prejudice, preconceived notion
premio *m.* prize; **___ gordo** first prize
prensa *f.* press
preocuparse worry, bother
preparar prepare
presentar present, introduce

Presidencia del Gobierno *f.* *Office of the Chief of State*
presidente *m.* president
prestar lend; **pedir prestado** borrow
primer ministro *m.* prime minister
primo, -a *m.f.* cousin
princesa *f.* princess
principal principal, main
principio *m.* beginning; **al** ___ at first; **en un** ___ at first
prisa *f.* hurry; **de** ___ quickly
pro: en ___ **y en contra** pro and con
probablemente probably
probar test, try
problema *m.* problem
producir produce
producto *m.* product
profesor *m.* teacher
profesional professional
profundo profound, deep
programa *m.* program
pronto quickly, soon; **¡hasta muy** ___**!** See you soon!
propio own
proponer propose
proporción *f.* proportion
proporcionar give
propósito *m.* purpose; **a** ___ apropos, by the way
prosperidad *f.* prosperity
protestante Protestant
proverbial proverbial
provincia *f.* province
provinciano provincial
publicar publish
público *m.* public
pueblecito *m.* village
pueblo *m.* people, town
puente *m.* bridge
puerta *f.* door, gate; ___ **del Sol** *main square in Madrid (originally eastern gate to the city)*
puerto *m.* port
pues well (then); ___ **bien** well, then
puesta de sol *f.* sunset
puesto que since, as
pulmón *m.* lung
pulsera *f.* bracelet
punto *m.* point; (vehicle) stand; ___ **fuerte** strong point, forte; ___ **menos que** practically
puro pure, sheer

Q

que which, who; that; than; **qué** *excl.* what (a), how!
quedar(se) stay, remain, be, be left; ___**se con** keep (Ch. 14)
quejarse complain
querer (ie) wish, want, be willing (Ch. 11)
quietud *f.* quietude
quince fifteen
quinientos five hundred
quinto fifth
quitar take away; ___**se** take off (Ch. 5)
quizá perhaps

R

radical radical
radio *m.* radius; *f.* radio
ramplón coarse, vulgar
rapidez *f.* rapidity, speed
rápido speedy
raro rare, strange; ___**as veces** seldom
rascacielos *m. sing.* skyscraper
rastrojo *m.* stubble-field
rato *m.* while; **al poco** ___ after a while
razón *f.* reason; **tener** ___ be right
reacción *f.* reaction; **avión de** ___ jet plane
reaccionario reactionary
real royal; real
realismo *m.* realism
realmente really
rebelde rebel
recado *m.* message; **dejar** ___ leave word
receptor *m.* telephone receiver
recibir receive
reclamar claim
recluta *m.* recruit
recoger get
Recoletos *the central portion of the great north-south boulevard in Madrid, now called Paseo de Calvo Sotelo*
recomendar (ie) recommend
reconcentración *f.* immersion in oneself
recóndito hidden

reconocer recognize, admit
recordar (ue) remember, recall, remind one of
recorrer cover, visit
recorrido *m.* trip, tour
rector *m.* president *(of a university)*
recuerdo *m.* memory, remembrance; souvenir
redondo round
reducir reduce, limit
reflejo *m.* reflection
refrescarse wash up, freshen up
regalo *m.* gift
región *f.* region
regresar return
reina *f.* queen
reino *m.* kingdom
relación *f.* relation, account
relacionarse con be connected with
relativamente relatively
reloj *m.* watch, clock
remedio *m.*: **no tengo más ___ I** can't help, I simply have to
renacentista Renaissance *(adj.)*
Renacimiento *m.* Renaissance
rendido worn out
rendirse surrender; become exhausted
reparar repair
repeler repel
repente: de ___ suddenly
repertorio *m.* repertory
repetir (i) repeat
representante representative
representar play
reproche *m.* reproach
república *f.* republic
republicano republican
requerir (ie, i) require
residencia *f.* residence
resignarse resign oneself
resolver (ue) resolve
respetar respect
respeto *m.* respect
respirar breathe
resto: el ___ de the rest of
resultado *m.* result
resultar result, turn out, happen, be
resumen *m.* résumé, account
Retiro *m.* *a large public park in Madrid*
retórica *f.* rhetoric
reunión *f.* gathering, meeting
reunirse (con) meet, gather, join
revés: al ___ contrariwise
revisar check
revista *f.* magazine
(La) Revoltosa *title of a zarzuela by Chapí (1851–1909)*
revolucionario revolutionary
rey *m.* king
reyezuelo *m.* petty king
Ribera, José "el Españoleto" *(1588–1656) Spanish painter*
rico rich
rincón *m.* corner
río *m.* river
riqueza *f.* richness, wealth
rival rival
Rivas, Ángel de Saavedra, duque de *(1791–1865) Spanish Romantic poet and playwright*
robar rob, steal
roca *f.* rock
rocoso rocky
rodeado surrounded
rodear surround
rodeos: andar con ___ beat about the bush
rodilla *f.* knee
rogar (ue) beg
rojo red
romance *m.* ballad
románico Romanesque
romano Roman
ropa *f.* clothing
ropería *f.* clothing store
rosado rose
rubio blond
ruedo *m.* (bull) ring
ruido *m.* noise
rumbo *m.* course, tack
ruta *f.* route

S

saber know, be able; **no sé qué de** indefinable, certain something (Ch. 3)
sablazo *m.* sabre cut; **dar un ___** ask for a loan
saborear sip
sacar take out; **___ en limpio** deduce (Ch. 8)
saco *m.* bag
sacerdote *m.* priest
Sacro Monte *gypsy suburb of Granada*
sala *f.* room; **___s capitulares** chapter rooms

Salamanca *famous university city, once part of the kingdom of León*
salida *f.* departure
saliente projecting, salient
salina *f.* salt pit
salir leave, go out, turn out; **___se con la suya** have one's way (Ch. 18)
saltar: ___ a la vista be immediately evident *or* obvious (Prelim. Les. 1)
salud *f.* health
saludar speak to, greet
San Juan de los Reyes *Gothic church in Toledo built by the Reyes Católicos*
sanseacabó that's an end to it! Finished!
Santiago de Compostela St. James of Campostella *(city and famous medieval shrine in Galicia)*
santo saint
sección *f.* section
seco dry
secretario *m.* secretary
secreto *m.* secret
seda *f.* silk
Segovia *f.* *city in Old Castile*
seguida: en ___ immediately, at once
seguir (i) follow, keep on, continue (Ch. 14)
según according to, as
segundo second
seguro sure
selección *f.* selection, choice
sello *m.* stamp
semana *f.* week
sembrado *m.* ploughed field
semejante similar
sencillo simple
sentado seated
sentar (ie) seat (Prelim. Les. 2)
sentir (ie, i) feel, regret, be sorry
señal *f.* signal, mark
señalar mark
señor Mr.; *m.* gentleman
septentrional northern
séptimo seventh
sequedad *f.* dryness
ser be; **es que** (but) the fact is that; **sea** for example, that is; **sea como sea** be that as it may (Ch. 13)
sereno serene
serie *f.* series
serio serious; **en ___** seriously
servicio *m.* service
servidumbre *f.* servitude; servants
servir (i) serve, help (Ch. 1)
severo severe
Sevilla Seville *(largest city in southern Spain)*
sevillano Sevillian
si if
sí yes; **¿___?** is that so?
sí themselves, *etc.;* **de por ___** of itself
siempre always, ever
sierra *f.* mountain range
Sierra Morena *the range separating Andalusia and New Castile*
Sierra Nevada *highest range in Spain*
siesta *f.* siesta, rest after eating
siglo *m.* century; **___ de Oro** Golden Age *(of Spanish literature, in 16th and 17th centuries)*
Sigüenza *city in the province of Guadalajara*
siguiente following
silbar whistle
silla *f.* chair
simpático pleasant, likeable
simpatizar be congenial
sin (que) without
sinagoga *f.* synagogue
sinceridad *f.* sincerity
sino but
síntoma *m.* symptom
siquiera: ni ___ not even
sistema *m.* system
sitio *m.* place
situado situated, located
soberbiamente proudly
sobrar be left over (Ch. 19)
sobre on, upon
sobrino, -a *m.f.* nephew, niece
socialista Socialist
sociedad *f.* society
soler (ue) be accustomed to, usually (do a thing) (Prelim. Les. 2)
solicitud *f.* application, request
solidez *f.* solidity
sólido solid
solitario solitary
solo mere, single, only *(adj.);* alone, by oneself
sólo only
soltero single, unmarried
solución *f.* solution
sombrerería *f.* hat store
sombrero *m.* hat

sonar (ue) sound; ___ **a** evoke (by sound)
sonreír(se) (i) smile
sonriente smiling
sonrisa *f.* smile
soportal *m.* arcade
Soria *city in Old Castile*
sorprender surprise
sorprendiente surprising
sorpresa *f.* surprise
sospechar suspect
sostener maintain
su its, his, her, their, your
suave soft, gentle
suavidad *f.* softness
subdesarrollado underdeveloped
subir come (go, carry, bring) up (Ch. 17)
subrayar underline
suegro, -a *m.f.* father-, mother-in-law
suelo *m.* floor, soil, land
sueño *m.* sleep, dream
suerte de varas *f.* *the picador's act in a bullfight*
suficiente sufficient
sugerir (ie, i) suggest
sumo: a lo ___ at the most
superficial superficial
superficie *f.* surface
suponer suppose
suprimir suppress
sur *m.* south
surcado lined
suscitar provoke
sustantivo *m.* substantive, noun
sutil subtle
suyo his, her, its, their, your

T

tabaco *m.* tobacco
tacita *f.* *(dim.* **taza***)* little cup
Tajo *m.* Tagus *(most important river of Central Spain and Portugal)*
tal such (a); **¿qué ___?** How (is) . . .? How are you?
Talavera de la Reina *city in the province of Toledo, famous for its pottery*
taller *m.* workshop
también also
tan so
tanque *m.* tank
tanto so much, so many
tardar delay, be (take) long (Ch. 15)
tarde late; *f.* afternoon
tarea *f.* task
tarjeta *f.* card
Tavera, Juan Pardo de *(1472–1545) Spanish cardinal and patron of the arts*
taxi *m.* taxi
taza *f.* cup
teatro *m.* theatre, drama
técnica *f.* technique
técnico technical
tecnología *f.* technology
tela *f.* cloth
telefonear telephone
teléfono *m.* telephone
televisión *f.* television
tema *m.* theme
temblar (ie) tremble
temer fear
temor *m.* fear
temporada *f.* period (of time); **pasar una** ___ spend some time
temprano early
tendido: largo y ___ at full length, in detail
tener have; ___ **que** have to (Ch. 12)
tenis *m.* tennis
tercero third
Teresa (de Jesús), Santa *(1515–1582) Spain's most famous mystic writer and reformer*
terminante final, definitive
terminar (de) finish
término *m.* end
terrateniente *m.* landholder
terraza *f.* sidewalk in front of a café
tertulia *f.* (informal) gathering *(a typical feature of Spanish social life)*
tesis *f.* thesis
tesoro *m.* treasure
tiempo *m.* time; weather; **más** ___ longer
tienda *f.* store, shop
tierra *f.* land; **en** ___ ashore
timbre *m.* bell
tío *m.* uncle
típicamente typically
típico typical, traditional
tipo *m.* type, kind
tirante tense
tirantez *f.* tension, reserve, aloofness
tirar throw (Prelim. Les. 1)
tocadiscos *m.* phonograph

tocar ring (bell), play (instrument); touch (Ch. 2)
todavía yet, still
todo all
toledano Toledan
Toledo *m.* Toledo *(former Visigothic and imperial capital of Spain)*
tolerar tolerate
tomar take (Ch. 8)
tono *m.* tone
tonto foolish
topográfico topographic
torero *m.* bullfighter
tormenta *f.* storm
torno: en ___ (de) around
toro *m.* bull
toronja *f.* grapefruit
toros *m. pl.* bullfight
torre *f.* tower; **___ del Oro** *old Moorish tower on the Guadalquivir in Seville*
tostado sunburned
total total
trabajador *m.* worker
trabajar work
trabajo *m.* work
tradición *f.* tradition
tradicional traditional
traer bring (Ch. 16)
trágico tragic
traición *f.* treason
traje *m.* suit; **___ de luces** bullfighter's costume *(of silk and gold or silver braid)*
trajín *m.* round (of amusements, occupations, etc.)
tranquilo quiet, calm, tranquil
tránsito *m.* traffic
transportación *f.* transportation
tranvía *m.* trolley, street car
tras behind, after
tratar treat; **___ de** try to; **___se** to be (a question of) (Ch. 19)
trato *m.* association
travesía *f.* crossing
trayecto *m.* journey
tren *m.* train
Triana *suburb across the river from Seville, famous for gypsies, bullfighters, etc.*
triángulo *m.* triangle
trigo *m.* wheat
triste sad
tronar (ue) thunder
tropa *f.* troop
tropezar (ie) meet (with)
trozo *m.* fragment, part
Turina, Joaquín *(1882–1949) 20th century Spanish composer*
turista *m.* and *f.* tourist
turístico tourist
tutear use the familiar form of address with someone

U

último last; **por ___** finally
Unamuno, Miguel de *(1864–1936) one of the leading writers and thinkers of 20th century Spain*
único only, unique
unido joined
universal universal
universidad *f.* university
uno one, a
unos some
útil useful
utilizar use

V

vacaciones *f.* vacation
vacío empty
vagamente vaguely
Valencia *f.* *region on the eastern coast of Spain*
valer be worth, avail (Ch. 19)
valiente brave, courageous; **¡___!** what a!
valioso valuable
Valladolid *m.* *city in Old Castile*
valle *m.* valley
Valle de los Caídos Valley of the Fallen *cemetery and church north of Madrid built to honor the dead of the Spanish Civil War, 1936–1939*
vanidad *f.* vanity
valor *m.* courage
variedad *f.* variety
varios several
vasco Basque
Vascongado Basque; **Provincias ___as** Basque country *(region in the north of Spain)*
vaso *m.* glass
vega *f.* plain
vegetal vegetal

veinte twenty
veintitantos some twenty
Velázquez, Diego Rodríguez de Silva y *(1599–1660) one of Spain's most famous painters*
vendedor *m.* seller
vender sell
ventaja *f.* advantage
ventanilla *f.* window (of vehicle)
venir come; **que viene** next (time) (Ch. 16)
ver see; **¡a ___!** let's see; **___se** be; **está visto** it is clear
(La) verbena de la paloma *title of a zarzuela by Bretón (1850–1923)*
verdad *f.* truth; **es ___** it is true; **¿___?** is it not?
verdaderamente truly, really
verdadero real, true, genuine
verde green
verificarse take place
verso *m.* verse; line of poetry
vestido *m.* costume, dress
vestir dress
vez *f.* time; **de ___ en cuando** from time to time; **una ___** once; **otra vez** once more
viajar travel
viaje *m.* trip, voyage; **___ por mar** sea trip
viajero *m.* traveller
vida *f.* life
(La) vida es sueño *famous play by Calderón (1640)*
viejo old
Vigo *m.* *important port (and bay) in Galicia*
viñedo *m.* vineyard
vino *m.* wine
violinista *m.* violinist
virtud *f.* virtue
visita *f.* visit
visitar visit
vista *f.* sight; **a la ___** in sight
visto bueno (V.ºB.º) official approval, "O.K."
vitamina *f.* vitamin
vivir live
volar (ue) fly
voluntad *f.* will
volver (ue) return, go (come) back; drive; **___ a** + *inf.* do again (Prelim. Les. 2)
vuelo *m.* flight
vuelta *f.* return; **dar ___s** stroll, walk

Y

y and
ya already, now
yacente lying; **estatua ___** tomb (with statue)
yo I

Z

Zamora *f.* *city in the old kingdom of León*
zapato *m.* shoe
Zaragoza Saragossa *(capital of the old kingdom of Aragon)*
zarzuela *f.* *Spanish light opera*
Zocodover *a square in Toledo, center of city life*
zona *f.* zone; **___ azul** *zone where parking is by permit only*
Zorrilla, José *(1817–1893) Spanish Romantic poet and playwright*
Zurbarán, Francisco *(1598–1662) Spanish painter*

English–Spanish

A

ability talento *m.*
able: be ___ to poder
about *(concerning)* de acerca de; *(approximately)* cerca de, cosa de, unos; **be ___ to** estar para
above sobre, por encima de
abroad el extranjero
absent ausente
absent-minded distraído
absurd absurdo
abuse abusar de
academy academia *f.*
accept aceptar
accident accidente *m.*
accustomed acostumbrado; **be ___ to** acostumbrarse, tener la costumbre de, soler (ue)
account cuenta *f.*
account: on ___ of a causa de, por; **on my ___** por mí
accurately: very ___ con gran precisión
accusation acusación *f.*
accuse acusar
ache doler (ue)
acquaintance conocido
acquainted: become ___ conocer, llegar a conocer
across al otro lado (de), tras
act acto *m.;* *v.* obrar, estar
action acción *f.*
actor actor *m.*
add añadir
addition: in ___ to además de
address señas, dirección *f.;* *v.* dirigir, dirigirse a
admiration admiración *f.*
admire admirar
admit admitir, reconocer
adobe adobe *m.*
advantage ventaja *f.;* **to be to one's ___** convenirle a uno
adventure a ventura *f.*
advertise anunciar
advice consejo *m. (usu. pl.)*
advise aconsejar
adviser consejero,-a
affair asunto *m.*
affliction aflicción *f.*
afraid: be ___ of tener miedo de, temer(se); **feel ___** darle miedo a uno
African africano
after después de, tras; después (de) que; **___ all** en fin
afternoon tarde *f.*
afterwards después, luego
again otra vez, de nuevo; **do ___** volver (ue) + *inf.*
against contra
age edad, época *f.;* **Golden ___** Siglo de Oro *m.*
agent agente *m.*
agility agilidad, ligereza *f.*
ago: a year ___ hace un año
agree convenir (en), ponerse (estar) de acuerdo
agreement acuerdo *m.;* **come to an ___** ponerse de acuerdo
ahead (de) delante
air aire, ambiente *m.*
airsick mareado (en el aire)
album álbum *m.*

alike parecido; **be ___** parecerse
alive: be ___ vivir
all todo; **___ in ___** en conjunto; **(not) at ___** nada, en absoluto; de nada
allow dejar, permitir
almost casi
alms limosna *f.*
alone solo
along a lo largo de, por
already ya
although aunque; y eso que
always siempre
amateur aficionado,-a
amaze asombrar
Amazon el Amazonas
ambassador embajador *m.*
ambition ambición *f.*
ambitious ambicioso
America América *f.*
American americano; norteamericano
among entre
amount to ascender (ie) a
amusement diversión *f.*
amusing divertido
ancient antiguo
Andalusia Andalucía *f.*
Andalusian andaluz
angry enfadado; **make ___** enfadar; **get ___** enfadarse
animal animal *m.*
animated animado
animation animación *f.*
announce anunciar
annoy molestar
answer contestación *f.*; *v.* contestar
anticipate prever
antique shop tienda de antigüedades *f.*
anxious: be ___ desear
any algun(o), cualquiera; *(neg.)* ningun(o)
anyone alguien; *(neg.)* nadie
anything algo, cualquier cosa, *(neg.)* nada
anywhere en (a, por) cualquier (ninguna) parte
apart: far ___ distante
apartment piso *m.*, apartamiento *m.*
apiece cada uno
apparently por lo visto, parecer + *inf.*
appeal (to one) emocionar
appear parecer, aparecer
appetite apetito *m.*
apple manzana *f.*
appointment nombramiento *m.*
appreciate apreciar
appreciation apreciación *f.*
approach acerarse a
approve aprobar (ue)
approximating tirando a
April abril
apropos (of) a propósito (de)
aqueduct acueducto *m.*
Arab árabe
Arabian Nights Las mil y una noches
Aragon Aragón *m.*
Aragonese aragonés
arcade soportal *m.*; **___d** con soportales
architectural arquitectónico
architecture arquitectura *f.*
argue discutir
argument discusión, disputa *f.*
aristocrat aristócrata
arm brazo *m.*
armchair sillón *m.*, butaca *f.*
around por; alrededor de; en torno; a eso de *(time)*
arrange arreglar
arrest detener
arrival llegada *f.*
arrive llegar
arrogance arrogancia *f.*
art arte *m.* *(pl. f.)*; **fine ___s** bellas artes
article artículo *m.*
artificial artificial
artist artista; pintor *m.*
artistic artístico
as como; *(while)* mientras; *(according as)* según, conforme, a medida que; **___ for** en cuanto a, lo que es; **___ if** como si, **just ___** tal (y) como
ascetic ascético
ashtray cenicero *m.*
ashamed: make one feel ___ darle vergüenza a uno
ashore en (a) tierra
Asiatic asiático
aside from aparte de
ask *(inquire)* preguntar; **___ a question** hacer una pregunta; *(request)* pedir (i); **___ for (to)** pedir (i)

aspect aspecto *m.*
assembly asamblea *f.*
association asociación *f.*
assure asegurar
astonish asombrar
astonishing sorprendente
astronaut astronauta *m.*
asylum asilo *m.*
at a, en
athlete atleta *m.*
atmosphere ambiente *m.*
attend to ocuparse de
attention atención *f.;* **pay ___ to** hacer caso de, a *(of persons)*
attitude actitud *f.*
attract tirar, atraer
attractive simpático; agradable
aunt tía *f.*
austere austero
author autor *m.*
authorization autorización *f.*
avenue avenida *f.*
average *adj.* medio; *n.* media *f.*
aviator aviador *m.*
avoid evitar
awake despierto
away: be ___ estar ausente, fuera; *(distance)*, a una distancia de
awfully la mar de

B

back espalda *f.*
back *adj.* atrasado; **be ___** estar de vuelta
background fondo *m.*
bad malo; **___(ly)** mal
baggage equipaje *m.*
Balearic balear
ballads romancero *m.*
bank banco *m.*; ___ *(river)* orilla *f.*
banker banquero *m.*
banquet banquete *m.*
bare desnudo
bargain ganga *f.*
bark ladrar; *n.* **(bark, barking)** ladrar *m.*
barren árido, yermo
baseball baseball, béisbol
basket cesto, canasto *m.*
Basque vasco
bath baño *m.;* **take a ___** bañarse
bathe bañar(se)
bay bahía *f.*
be ser, estar; haber *(there is);* **llevar** *(spend time)*
beach playa *f.*
bear llevar
beaten vencido
beautiful hermoso
beauty belleza *f.*
because porque; **___ of** por, a causa de; **just ___** por el solo hecho de
become hacerse; ponerse; llegar, venir, a ser; volverse; convertirse (ie, i) en; ser de
bed cama *f.;* **go to ___** acostarse (ue); **stay in ___** guardar cama
bedroom alcoba *f.*, dormitorio *m.*
beer cerveza *f.*
beet remolacha *f.*
before *adv.* antes, ante; *prep.* antes de, ante; *conj.* antes (de) que; **___ I** antes que yo
beg rogar (ue), pedir (i)
beggar mendigo *m.*
begin empezar (ie), comenzar (ie)
beginning principio *m.*
behind detrás (de); atrás
Belgium Bélgica *f.*
believe creer
bell campana, campanilla *f.*
bellboy botones *m. sing.*
bell tower torre *f.*, campanario *m.*
belong to ser de, pertenecer a
below debajo (de), abajo, bajo
belt cinturón *m.*
besides además (de)
best mejor; **to do one's ___** hacer lo posible (por)
bet apostar (ue)
better mejor; **I had better** mejor será
between entre
bicycle bicicleta *f.*
big grande
bikini bikini *m.*
bill cuenta *f.;* billete *m. (banknote);* proyecto de ley *m. (legislative)*
bind *(books)* encuadernar
birthday cumpleaños *m. sing.*
bit trozo, rincón *m. (of places);* **a ___** algo, un poco; **not a ___** nada
bite morder (ue)
blame culpa *f.;* **to be to ___ for** tener la culpa de; *v.* echar la culpa

blanket manta *f.*, cobertor *m.*
blessed *(iron.)* dichoso
blessing bendición *f.*
blind ciego; *v.* cegar (ie)
block *(city)* manzana *f.*
blockhead majadero *m.*
blond(e) rubio
blood sangre *f.*
blue azul
board: on ___ a bordo (de)
board junta *f.*, consejo *m.;* cartelera *f.* *(theatrical)*, **___ of directors** consejo de administración
boardinghouse pensión, casa de huéspedes *f.*
boat barco *m.*
bonfire hoguera *f.*
book libro *m.*
bookcase estantería *f.*
bookstore librería *f.*
bootblack limpiabotas *m.*
bored aburrido
boredom aburrimiento *m.*
boring aburrido
born: be ___ nacer
borrow pedir (i) prestado
both los dos, ambos, uno y otro; **___ . . . and** lo mismo . . . que
bother molestar, molestarse en
bottom: at ___ en el fondo
boulder peñasco *m.*
boulevard paseo *m.*
box caja *f.*
boy chico, muchacho *m.*
bracelet pulsera *f.*
brake: put on the ___s frenar
brave valiente
bread pan *m.*
break romper
breakfast desayuno *m.* **have ___** desayunar
breathe inspirar
bribe sobornar
bridge puente *m.*
briefcase cartera *f.*
bright brillante, claro
brilliant brillante
bring traer; **___ along** traerse
broad ancho
bronze bronce *m.*
brother hermano *m.*
brother-in-law cuñado *m.*
brow frente *f.*
brown pardo
browned *(by the sun)* tostado
buffoon bufón *m.*
build construir
building edificio *m.*
bulb *(light)* bombilla *f.*
bull toro *m.*
bullet bala *j.*
bullfight(ing) corrida (de toros) *f.*
bullfighter torero *m.*
bullring plaza de toros *f.*
burn quemar
burning ardiente
bury enterrar (ie)
bus autobús *m.*
business *(affair)* negocio, asunto *m.; (in general)* negocios
businessman comerciante *m.;* hombre de negocios
bustle bullicio *m.*
busy ocupado
but pero, sino, sino que, mas
button botón *m.*
buy comprar

C

Cadiz Cádiz
café café *m.*
caliph califa *m.*
call llamar; **be ___ed** llamarse; **so ___ed** llamado
calm sereno; *v.* calmar
canary canario *m.;* **___ Islands** Islas Canarias *f.*
candy bombones *m. pl.*
cane bastón *m.*
Cantabrian cantábrico
cap gorra *f.*
capital *(city)* capital *f.*
capture toma *f.*
car coche *m.*
card *(playing)* carta *f.*
care: ___ for importar
careful: be ___ tener cuidado
carefully con cuidado; detenidamente
careless descuidado
carpenter carpintero *m.*
carry llevar; **___ upstairs** subir; **carry away (off)** llevarse
cart carreta *f.*
carved esculpido, tallado

case caso *m.*, ___ *(legal)* pleito *m.;* **in ___ (that)** en caso de que, como
cash: pay ___ pagar al contado
cashier cajero *m.*
cast moldear
Castile Castilla *f.*
Castilian castellano
cat gato *m.*
Catalan catalán
Catalonia Cataluña *f.*
catch coger, pillar
cathedral catedral *f.*
Catholic católico
cause causa *f.;* *v.* causar, dar
cave cueva *f.*
celebrated célebre
cement estrechar
cent centavo *m.* *(American)*, céntimo *m.* *(Spain)*
center centro *m.*
central central
century siglo *m.*
ceremony ceremonia *f.*
certain cierto; **a ___ something** un no sé qué
certainly seguro (que), con toda seguridad, sí que
chair silla *f.*
change cambiar (de), mudar (de)
chapel capilla *f.*
character carácter *m.;* ___ *(in fiction)* personaje *m.*
charge: take ___ of encargarse de
charity caridad *f.*
Charles Carlos; **___ V** Carlos Quinto
charm encanto *m.*
charming encantador
chauffeur chófer *m.*
cheap barato
cheat engañar
check cheque *m.* *(bank);* talón *m.* *(baggage);* *v.* facturar *(baggage)*
cheer up animarse
chemistry química *f.*
chestnut vender castañero, -a *m.f.*
chief jefe *m.*
chiefly en su mayoría, principalmente
child niño,-a
choose escoger; elegir (i)
Christian cristiano
church iglesia *f.*
cigar puro *m.*
cigarette pitillo, cigarrillo *m.*; **___ case** pitillera *f.*
circus circo *m.*
citizen ciudadano *m.*
city ciudad *f.*
City Hall ayuntamiento *m.*
civilization civilización *f.*
class clase *f.*
classic(al) clásico
classmate compañero de curso, de universidad *m.*
clean limpiar
clear claro; **it is ___** está visto (claro); entendido
clearness claridad *f.*
clear up aclarar
clever listo
cliff peña *f.*, cerro *m.*
climate clima *m.*
climb subir a
close cercano; cerrar (ie); terminar *(letter)*
cloth tela *f.*
clothes ropa *f.*
cloud nube *f.*
cloudy nublado
club club, círculo, casino *m.*
clump masa *f.*
coast costa *f.*
coat americana, chaqueta *f.;* **fur ___** abrigo de pieles *m.*
coat-of-arms escudo, blasón *m.*
coexistence coexistencia *f.*
coffee café *m.*
cold frío *m.*, catarro, resfriado *m.* *(ailment)*
collar cuello *m.*, collar *m.* *(of animals)*
collect coleccionar, recaudar
collection colección *f.*
college universidad *f.*
collision choque *m.*
colonel coronel *m.*
combination combinación *f.*
come venir; **___ (along) with** acompañar; **___ back** volver (ue); **___ from** nacer de; **___ in** entrar, pasar, ¡adelante!; **___ out** salir; **___ to** volver en sí; **___ to one's eyes** saltársele; **___ upon** dar, tropezar, encontrarse (ue), con; **___ up to** acercarse a; **___ on (now)!** ¡ande! ¡vamos!
comedy comedia *f.*

comfort comodidad *f.*
comfortable cómodo
comical cómico
coming llegada *f.*
commercial comercial
commission encargo *m.*
committee junta, comisión *f.*
commodity subsistencia *f.*
common común
companion compañero *m.*
company compañía *f.*
compartment compartimiento *m.*
compel obligar
complain quejarse de
complete completo
complexion tez *f.*
compliment piropo *m.*
compose componer
composer compositor *m.*
con en contra (de)
conceive concebir (i)
concert concierto *m.*
concierge *(Fr.)* conserje *m.*
conclusion conclusión *f.*
concrete *adj.* particular, concreto; *n.* cemento *m.*
condition estado *m.*, condición *f.*
conduct conducta *f.; v.* conducir
conductor cobrador *(trolley)*, revisor *m.* *(train)*
confine: be ___d to bed guardar cama
confusedly confusamente
confusion confusión *f.*
congenial: be ___ simpatizar
congratulations felicitaciones *f.*, enhorabuena *f.*
connection combinación *f.* *(train)*
conquer vencer
conqueror conquistador *m.*
consent consentir (ie, i) en
consequence: be of ___ importar
consequently por eso, por consiguiente
considerable bastante
constitutional constitucional
consulate consulado *m.*
consult consultar (con)
contain contener
contemporary contemporáneo
content contentar
contented: be ___ contentarse
continent continente *m.*
continual continuo
continue continuar, seguir (i)
contract contrato *m.*
contradict contradecir, llevarle la contraria a uno
contrary contrario; **on the ___** al contrario
contrariwise al revés
contrast contraste *m.*
convenience: at your earliest ___ con la mayor prontitud
convenient cómodo
converge converger
convince convencer
cook cocinero,-a
cool fresco
copper cobre *m.*
copy ejemplar *m.*, *v.* copiar
cordial cordial
cordiality cordialidad *f.*
cork corcho *m.*
corner rincón *m.*, ___ *(street)* esquina *f.*
correct justo, correcto
corridor pasillo *m.*
cosiness intimidad *f.*
cosmopolitan cosmopolita
cost costar (ue)
costume traje *m.*, **bullfighter's ___** traje de luces *m.*
cotton algodón *m.*
cough tos *f.*
councilman concejal *m.*
count contar (ue); **___ (on)** contar (ue) (con)
counter mostrador *m.*
Counter Reformation Contrarreforma *f.*
country *(nation)* país *m.*, *(rural)* campo *m.*
country house casa de campo *f.*
countryman paisano *m.*
couple par *m.*
courage valor *m.*, valentía *f.*
course curso *m.;* **of ___** claro (está), naturalmente, por supuesto, desde luego
court patio *m.*, ___ *(royal)* corte *f.*, **tennis ___** campo de tenis *m.*
courteous cortés
cousin primo,-a
cover cubrir; recorrer *(territory)*
crate embalar
crazy loco
creditor acreedor *m.*
critic crítico *m.*

critical crítico
cross cruzar, atravesar
crossing travesía *f.*
crowded atestado
crown coronar
crude sin refinar
crusader cruzado *m.*
cry *n.* quejido *m.;* *v.* gritar; **___ baby** llorón,-a
culture cultura *f.*
cultured culto
cup taza *f.*
curiosity curiosidad *f.*
custom costumbre *f.*
customs: ___ official aduanero *m.*
cut cortar; **___ it out!** ¡Quita!
cute mono
Cybele Cibeles *f.*
cylinder cilindro *m.*

D

dad papá *m.*
dairy store lechería *f.*
damage daño *m.*
damascene damasquinado *m.*
dance baile *m.;* *v.* bailar
danger peligro *m.*
dare atreverse a
daring atrevido
dark oscuro; *(complexion)* moreno
date fecha *f.;* *v.* datar
daughter hija *f.*
dawn amanecer *m.*
dead muerto
deaf sordo
deal trato *m.;* negocio *m.;* **a great (good) ___ (of)** mucho
dean decano *m.*
dear querido
death muerte *f.*
deathbed lecho de muerte *m.*
debt deuda *f.*
deceive engañar
decide decidir
decision decisión *f.*
decorate condecorar
deed hazaña *f.*
deep profundo
defect defecto *m.*
degree grado *m.*
delicious delicioso
delighted encantado
delivery: free ___ se sirve a domicilio
denominator denominador *m.*
dentist dentista *m.*
deny negar (ie)
depend depender
derby *(hat)* hongo *m.*
descendent descendiente *m.*
desert desierto, páramo *m.*
desk escritorio *m.*, mesa *f.*
desolate desolado, desierto
despot déspota *m.*
dessert postre *m.*
destination destinación *f.*
destroy destruir
detail detalle *m.*, **in ___** detalladamente, largo y tendido
determine determinar
develop resultar
devil diablo *m.*
devote dedicar
dialogue diálogo *m.*
dictate dictar
dictionary diccionario *m.*
die morir(se) (ue, u)
difference diferencia *f.;* **make a ___** importar; **make no difference** dar lo mismo
different distinto, diferente; **be ___** diferenciarse
difficult difícil
difficulty dificultad *f.;* **get out of the ___** salir del paso
dignity dignidad *f.*
dim débil
dine cenar, comer
dining room comedor *m.*
dinner comida *f.*, *(evening)* cena *f.*
direct dirigir
director director *m.*
disagreeable desagradable
disappear desaparecer
disappoint desilusionar
disappointment desilusión *f.*
disapproval desaprobación *f.*
disarrange revolver (ue)
discomfort incomodidad *f.*
discuss discutir
discussion discusión *f.*
dismiss despedir (i)
disposal disposición *f.*
dissuade disuadir

distance distancia; lejanía *f.;* **in the ___** a lo lejos; **only a short ___ from** a dos pasos de
distant lejano
distinctive distintivo
disturb molestar
divided dividido
dividend dividendo *m.*
dizzy aturdido
do hacer; **___ without** pasarse sin; **have to ___ with** tener que ver con
doctor médico *m.; (title)* doctor
document documento *m.*
dog perro,-a
dollar dólar *m.*
domestic doméstico, casero
dominate dominar
Don Quixote Don Quijote
door puerta *f.;* **___ bell** timbre, campanilla
doorway portal *m.*, portada *f.*
doubt dudar
doubtless sin duda
down: ___ the street calle abajo
downstairs abajo; **go ___** bajar
downtown *adj.* céntrico
dozen docena *f.*
drama drama *m.*
draw sacar, tirar
drawer cajón *m.*
dreadfully la mar de
dreamer soñador,-a
dress vestido, traje *m.; v.* vestir(se) (i)
dresser cómoda *f.*
drive conducir; **___ (crazy)** volver (ue)
driver *(automobile)* chófer *m.*
drop gota *f.*
drug store farmacia *f.*
dry seco
dry cleaner's tintorería *f.*
during durante
duty deber *m.*
dye teñir (i)

E

each cada, todo; **___ other** nos, os, se, el uno al otro
early temprano
earn ganar
earthquake terremoto *m.*
easily fácilmente
eat comer
economic económico
edge extremo *m.;* ladera *f.*
editor director *m.*
educated culto
eeriness embrujamiento *m.*
eight ocho
eighteenth dieciocho
eighth octavo
either o, tampoco *(neg.)*
elegance elegancia *f.*
elegant elegante
element elemento *m.*
elevator ascensor *m.*
Elizabeth Isabel
else otro, más; **somebody ___** otra persona; **nothing ___** nada más
embarrass confundir
embezzlement malversación (de fondos) *f.*
embody encarnar
embrace abrazo *m.*
emotion(al appeal) emoción *f.*
emperor emperador *m.*
employee empleado *m.*
empty vacío, desocupado
encounter encuentro *m.*
end final *m.;* **at the ___ of** al cabo de, a fines de *(semana, etc.)*
endless infinito
energetic enérgico
engaged *(busily)* atareado; **___ in** dedicado a, metido en
engine máquina *f.*, motor *m.*
engineer ingeniero *m.*
English(man) inglés
engraved grabado
engraving grabado *m.*
enjoy oneself divertirse (ie, i), pasarlo bien; estar a (su) gusto
enjoyable agradable
Enlightenment Siglo de las Luces
enough bastante, suficiente; **be ___** bastar; **___ of!** ¡basta de!
enter entrar en
enterprise empresa *f.*
enthusiasm entusiasmo *m.;* **full of ___** entusiasmado
enthusiastic entusiasmado
enthusiastically con entusiasmo
entire entero, todo el, total
entirely por completo
envelope sobre *m.*

epic épico
escape escapar(se)
eskimo esquimal *m.*
especially especialmente, sobre todo
essay ensayo *m.*
essentially esencialmente, más que nada
estate finca *f.*
estimate calcular
Europe Europa *f.*
European europeo
even aún, todavía; hasta; **___ if** aunque; **not ___ if** ni que; **___ though** aunque, y eso que; **not ___** ni siquiera
evening noche *f.*
ever alguna vez; *(neg.)* nunca, jamás
every todos los, cada; **___ other** cada dos, un(o) . . . sí, otro no
everybody todo el mundo
everything todo
everywhere en (a, *etc.*) todas partes
evident evidente; **it is ___** es evidente, se ve, se conoce
evidently por lo visto
evocation evocación *f.*
evoke evocar
exactly precisamente
examination: ___ room sala de examen *f.*
example ejemplo *m.*
exaggerate exagerar
excellent excelente
except excepto, menos
exceptional excepcional
excessive excesivo
exchange cambiar
excited agitado, emocionado
exclude quitar
exclusively exclusivamente
excuse disculpa *f.*
exercise ejercicio *m.*
exhaust acabarse
exist existir
exotic exótico
expect esperar
expense costa *f.*
expensive caro
experience experiencia *f.*
experiment experimento *m.*
expert perito *m.*
explain explicar
explore explorar
exporter exportador
exposition exposición *f.*
express *(train)* expreso *m.*
express expresar
expression expresión *f.*
extent: to a lesser ___ en menor grado
eye ojo *m.*

F

face cara *f.*; *v.* **___ (on)** dar a
fact hecho *m.*, **the ___ is** (ello) es que
factory fábrica
fail faltar; **___ to** dejar de
fair *(mediocre)* regular; *(just)* justo
fair *n.* feria *f.*
faith fe *f.*
fall *(season)* otoño *m.*
fall caer; **___ down** caerse
false falso
family familia *f.*; **___ name** appellido *m.*
famished desmayado
famous famoso
fantastic fantástico
far lejos; **as ___ as** hasta; **how ___ is?** ¿cuánto hay de?; **so ___** hasta ahora
fascinate fascinar
fashion moda *f.*
fashionable de moda
fast rápido, ligero; *adv.* rápidamente, de prisa; **be ___** adelantar
fat gordo; **get ___** ponerse gordo, engordar
father padre *m.*
father-in-law suegro *m.*
fatigue cansancio *m.*
favor favor *m.*; **to be in ___ of** estar por; *v.* favorecer
fear miedo *m.*; *v.* temer
feast (of wit) derroche de ingenio *m.*
February febrero
feel sentir (ie, i), estar; **___ like** tener ganas de; **___ well** encontrarse bien; **___ the same way** pasarle a uno lo mismo
feeling impresión *f.*; **with great ___** apasionadamente
fellow individuo, sujeto *m.*
fellowcountryman paisano *m.*

feminist feminista
fertile fecundo
feverish febril
few algunos, unos cuantos, cuatro
fiancée novia, prometida *f.*
field campo *m.*
fifty cincuenta
fight luchar
filigree filigrana *f.*
fill llenar(se)
film película *f.*
finally por fin
finance costear
find encontrar (ue), hallar; encontrarse (hallarse) con; ___ **out** enterarse de, saber, averiguar
fine magnífico, hermoso, bueno
finger dedo *m.*
finish terminar, acabar, concluir *(with inf.,* +de)
fire fuego; incendio *m.; v.* tirar
firearms armas de fuego *f.*
fireman bombero *m.*
fireplace chimenea *f.*
firm compañía, sociedad, casa, razón social *f.*
first primero; ___ **of all** primero, ante todo, por lo pronto; **at** ___ al principio
fish pescado *m.*
fitting digno, conveniente
five cinco
five hundred quinientos
fix arreglar, reparar
flag bandera *f.*
flatter favorecer
flood riada *f.*
floor suelo *m.*
Florida la Florida
flower vender florista *f.*
folk *adj.* popular
follow seguir (i)
following siguiente
fond: be ___ **of** ser aficionado a, gustarle a uno
food *(dish of)* plato *m.*
foolishness tontería *f.*
foot pie *m.;* **little** ___ piececito *m.*
football fútbol *m.*
for para, por
forbid prohibir
force fuerza *f.*
forever para siempre
foreign(er) extranjero
forget olvidar; **I** ___ se me olvida
fork tenedor *m.*
former antiguo; *pron.* aquél
fortress fortaleza *f.*
fortunate afortunado; **be** ___ tener suerte
fortunately afortunadamente
fortune fortuna *f.*
founder fundador *m.*
fountain fuente *f.*
fourth cuarto; cuarta parte
France Francia *f.*
frank franco
Frank Paco, Pancho *(Sp. Am.)*
frankly francamente
frankness franqueza *f.*
free libre; **set** ___ poner en libertad
French francés
frequent frecuente
fresh fresco; ___ **water** agua dulce
freshen up refrescarse
friend amigo,-a; **make** ___**s with** conocer, hacerse amigo(s) de
friendly amistoso
friendship amistad *f.*
from de, desde; ___ **. . . on** a partir de, de . . . en adelante
front: in ___ **of** en frente de
fruit fruta *f.;* ___ **orchard** huerto *m.*
fulfil cumplir (con)
full lleno
fundamental fundamental
funny gracioso; **be, strike one as** ___ tener, hacer gracia
furious furioso
furniture muebles *m.,* **piece of** ___ mueble *m.*
future porvenir *m.*

G

gain ganar
Galician gallego
game partido *m.;* ___ *(hunting)* caza *f.*
garage garaje *m.,* cochera *f.*
garden jardín *m.*
gardener jardinero *m.*
gate puerta *f.*
gathering reunión, tertulia *f.*
gem joya *f.*

general general; **become ___** generalizarse; *n.* general; **___'s** wife generala *f.*
generally generalmente
generous generoso
gentle suave
gentleman señor, caballero *m.*
genuine genuino, auténtico
genuinely genuinamente
George Jorge
German alemán
Germany Alemania *f.*
gesture gesto *m.*
get conseguir, obtener; sacar; recibir; *(become)* ponerse; **___ along with (together)** llevarse; **___ away** escaparse; **___ on** subir a *(train, etc.)*; **___ out** sacar; salir; **___ to** llegar a; **___ there** llegar; **___ together** reunirse; **___ up** levantarse
gift regalo *m.*
gigantic gigantesco
girl muchacha *f.*
give dar, comunicar; **___** *(a look)* echar; **___ up** renunciar a, desistir de, abandonar
glad: be ___ alegrarse de; **be very ___ to** tener mucho gusto en
glass vaso *m.*
glasses *(spectacles)* gafas *f.*
glimpse *v.* entrever
glorious glorioso
glory gloria *f.*
glove guante *m.*
go ir, *(become)* volverse; *(turn out)* resultar; **___ around** dar la vuelta a; **___ down** bajar; **___ in for** meterse a; **___ on** seguir, continuar; **___on!** ¡ande!; **___out** salir; **___ up** subir; **___ up to** dirigirse a; **___ with** acompañar
God Dios
goddess diosa *f.*
gold oro *m.*
golden *(colored)* dorado
golf golf *m.*
good bueno
gorge desfiladero *m.*
gossip historias *f.*, chismes *m.*; *adj.* chismoso
Gothic gótico
government gobierno *m.*
governor gobernador *m.*
grace gracia *f.*
graceful gracioso
gradually poco a poco
grandeur grandeza *f.*
grandfather abuelo *m.*; **great ___** bisabuelo *m.*
grandmother abuela *f.*
granite granito *m.*
grape uva *f.*
grateful agradecido; **be ___** agradecer, estar agradecido
grave grave
gray gris
great grande; **___ many** muchos
greater: become ___ agrandarse
greatly mucho, muchísimo
greatness grandeza *f.*
green verde
greet saludar
greeting saludo *m.*
grief pena *f.*
grilled window reja *f.*
grocery store tienda de ultramarinos (*or* comestibles) *f.*
ground suelo *m.*, tierra *f.*
group grupo *m.*
guarantee garantía *f.*
guard guardia, guardián *m.*
guest invitado,-a
guide guía *m.*
gun escopeta *f.*
gypsy gitano,-a

H

habit costumbre *f.*
hair pelo *m.*
half *adj.* medio; *n.* mitad *f.*; **___ and ___** a medias
hand mano *f.*; **on the other ___** en cambio; **___ to ___** a brazo partido
handkerchief pañuelo *m.*
handle manejar
handsome guapo, hermoso
handwriting letra *f.*
happen pasar, ocurrir, suceder
happiness felicidad *f.*
happy contento, feliz
harbor puerto *m.*
hard: be ___ ser difícil, costar (ue) trabajo

hardship fatiga *f.*
hardware store ferretería *f.*
harmonize armonizar
harmony armonía *f.*
harsh severo, adusto
hasten apresurarse a
hat sombrero *m.;* **top ___** sombrero de copa
haughtiness altivez *f.*
Havana la Habana
have tener; contar (ue) con; **___ to** tener que
headache dolor de cabeza *m.*
headstrong terco
health salud *f.*
healthful sano
healthy looking coloradote
hear oír; oír decir; **___ from** tener noticias de
heart corazón *m.;* **by ___** de memoria
heat calor *m.*
heated acalorado
heatedly calurosamente
heel: take to one's ___s tomar las de Villadiego
Helen Elena
help *n.* ayuda *f.;* *v.* ayudar; **I cannot ___** no puedo menos de; **it can't be ___ed** no hay más remedio
hen gallina *f.*
Henry Enrique
here aquí; **___ is** aquí tiene Ud., he aquí
heroic heroico
heroism heroísmo *m.*
hidden recóndito
hide ocultar
high alto
highway carretera *f.*
hill cuesta *(slope);* colina *f.*
his su, suyo
Hispano-Arabic hispanoarábigo
hiss silbido *m.*
historic(al) histórico
history historia *f.*
hit dar, pegar
hold tener, encerrar (ie); **___ back** detener
holiday fiesta *f.*
holy santo
home casa *f.*, hogar *m.*, patria, tierra *f.;* **at ___** en casa
homebody hombre casero *m.*
honor honor *m.*
hope esperanza *f.;* *v.* esperar; **lose ___** perder las esperanzas
horseback: on ___ a caballo
horse race carrera de caballos *f.*
hospital hospital *m.*
hospitality hospitalidad *f.*
hostess azafata *f.* (air)
hot caliente; **___** *(weather)* caluroso
hotel hotel *m.*
hour hora *f.*
house casa *f.*
housetop azotea *f.*
how? ¿cómo?; ¿qué?; **___ much** ¿cuánto?
however sin embargo; **___ much** *etc.* por más (muy, mucho) que
huddled agrupado
huge enorme
human humano
humor humor *m.*
(one) hundred cien (to)
hunger hambre *f.*
hungry: be ___ tener hambre
hurry darse prisa, apresurarse; **be in a ___** tener (estar de) prisa
hurt hacer daño

I

ice cream helado *m.*
ideal ideal
idiot idiota, bobo *m.*
idleness ocio *m.*
if si; **as ___** como si
ignorance ignorancia *f.*
ill enfermo; **___ness** enfermedad *f.*
illusion ilusión *f.*
imagine imaginar(se), figurarse
immaterial: be ___ no importar, dar lo mismo (igual)
immediately en seguida
immense inmenso
immensely enormemente, muchísimo, la mar (de)
impatience impaciencia *f.*
impatient impaciente
imperial imperial
impertinent impertinente
importance importancia *f.*
importer importador
imposing imponente

impossible imposible
impress impresionar
impression impresión *f.*
impressive impresionante
improve perfeccionarse
incident incidente *m.*
income renta *f.*
inconvenience molestia *f.*
incredible increíble
indefinable (un) no sé qué
Indian indio
indicate indicar
indiscreet indiscreto
individual individual
industrial industrial
industrialization industrialización
industrialize industrializar
inferior inferior
influence influencia *f.*
inform avisar, enterar
informal íntimo, de confianza
ingredient ingrediente *m.*
injured herido
injustice injusticia *f.*
inn fonda *f.*
innate innato
innocent inocente
innumerable innumerable
inopportune inoportuno
inside interior *m.;* **on the ___** por dentro
insist insistir en, empeñarse en
insistent insistente
insolent insolente
insolently insolentemente
inspire inspirar
install instalar
instance: for ___ por ejemplo
insult insultar
intellectual intelectual
intelligent inteligente
intend pensar (ie), tener la intención de
intention intención *f.*
interest interés *m.; v.* interesar; **be ___ed in** interesarse por
interesting interesante
interior interior *m.*
interview entrevista, interviú *f.*
intimate íntimo
intolerant intolerante
introduce presentar
invention invención; cosa *f.*
invitation invitación *f.*
invite invitar
involve envolver (ue)
involved: become ___ enzarzarse en
Irish irlandés
iron hierro *m.*
ironical irónico
island isla *f.*
isolated aislado
Italian italiano
itinerary itinerario *m.*
its su, sus

J

janitor portero *m.*
Jew(ish) judío
job trabajo *m.*, tarea *f.*, colocación *f. (position)*
Joe Pepe
John Juan
join reunirse con
joke chiste *m.*, broma *f.*
journalist periodista *m.*
journey viaje *m.*
judge juzgar
judgment juicio *m.*
juicy jugoso
July julio *m.*
jump saltar, dar un salto
June junio
just precisamente, exactemente, sólo; *(recently)* recién; **have ___** acabar de
justly justamente

K

keep guardar; tener; *(retain)* quedarse con; **___ on** seguir (i); **___ oneself** meterse
kerchief pañuelo *m.*
key llave *f.*
kick dar un puntapié a
kid hablar en broma
kill matar
kilo kilo *m.*
kilometer kilómetro *m.*
kind bueno, bondadoso; grato
kind clase *f.;* género *m. (genre);* **what ___ of?** ¿qué clase de?, ¿qué tal?
kindness amabilidad, bondad *f.*
king rey *m.*

kingdom reino *m.*
kitchen cocina *f.*
knee rodilla *f.*
knight caballero *m.*
knock llamar
know saber, conocer; **let ___** avisar

L

lack falta *f.; v.* carecer de
laden cargado
lady señora *f.;* **young ___** señorita *f.*
lake lago *m.*
lamb cordero *m.*
lame cojo
land tierra *f.; v.* desembarcar
landlady patrona *f.*
landlord casero *m.*
landscape paisaje *m.*
language idioma *m.*, lengua *f.*
large grande
last *(final)* último; *(passed)* pasado; *v.* durar; **at ___** por fin
late tarde; **be ___** *(train)* **venir,** llegar con retraso
later on más tarde, después
latest último
Latin latín *m.*
latter: the ___ éste
laugh reír(se) (i)
laughingstock hazmerreír *m.*
law derecho *m.;* ley *f.*
lawyer abogado *m.*
lay poner
Lazarillo de Tormes *(1554) first Spanish picaresque novel*
lead conducir, llevar
leader jefe *m.*
leak salirse
learn aprender, saber, enterarse de
learning ciencia *f.*
least: not in the ___ ni mucho menos, de ninguna manera
leather cuero *m.*
leave *(behind)* dejar; *(depart from)* irse, marcharse, salir de; *(cease)* pasarse; **take ___ of** despedirse (i) de
lecture conferencia *f.*
left izquierdo
left: be ___, have ___ quedar(le a uno)
leg pierna *f.*
legend leyenda *f.*
leisure despreocupación *f.*
lend prestar
lesson lección *f.*
lest no sea que, no vaya a ser que
let dejar; **___ know** avisar; **___ on** darse por entendido
letter carta *f.*, letra *f.*
liar embustero *m.*
liberal liberal
liberty libertad *f.*
library biblioteca *f.*
lie yacer; *(be)* estar (situado, colocado)
life vida *f.*
light luz *f.; v.* encender (ie)
lighter *(cigarette)* encendedor *m.*
like parecido; **anything ___ that** una cosa así **___ a** parecido a; **___ that** así; **nothing ___ that** nada de eso
like gustar, agradar; **how do you ___?** ¿qué le parece?
likeable simpático
limit limitar
line línea *f.;* renglón *m.*
lion león *m.*
listen escuchar
literary literario
little poco; **a ___** un poco de
live vivir
living vivo
living room sala *f.;* gabinete *m.*
loaded cargado
located situado
location situación *f.*
London Londres *m.*
lonely solitario
long largo; *(time)* mucho tiempo; **too ___** demasiado tiempo; **be (take) ___** tardar (mucho); **how ___?** cuánto (tiempo)
longer más tiempo; **no ___** no . . . más, ya no
look mirada *f.; v.* mirar; *(seem)* parecer, estar; **___ at** mirar; **___ for** buscar; **___ here!** ¡oiga!; **___ like** parecer, tener el aspecto (aire, cara) de; **___ out of** asomarse a; mirar por; **___ up** ver, mirar
lose perder (ie); **___ heart** descorazonarse
lot: a ___ mucho
lots (of) la mar (de)

lottery lotería *f.;* **___ ticket** billete de lotería *m.*
loud: in a very ___ voice en voz muy alta, a gritos; **___er** más alto
loudspeaker altavoz *m.*, altoparlante *m.*
Louis Luis
love querer, amar
low bajo; **in a ___ voice** en voz baja, por lo bajo
lower bajar, *(price)* rebajar
luck suerte *f.*
lunch almuerzo *m.;* **have ___** almorzar (ue)
lung pulmón *m.*

M

machinery maquinaria *f.*
Madrilian madrileño
magazine revista *f.*
magnificent magnífico
mahogany caoba *f.*
maid doncella *f.*
mail correo *m.;* *v.* echar (al correo)
main principal; **___spring** motivo *m.*
maintain sostener
majestic majestuoso
majesty majestad *f.*
major comandante *m.*
Majorca Mallorca *f.*
make hacer
many mucho; **as ___ as** tanto como
manage: ___ to llegar, acertar a
manager director *m.*
mansion palacio *m.*
mantilla mantilla *f.*
map mapa *m.*
mark señal *f.;* huella *f. (trace);* blanco *m. (target);* *v.* señalar
married casado
martial: ___ law estado de guerra *m.*
marvel maravilla *f.*
massive macizo
master amo *m.;* **___ and mistress** los señores
mate compañero *m.*
matter *(affair)* asunto *m.;* **be the ___ with** tener, pasarle a uno; **no ___ how** por muy (mucho, más) . . . que; *v.* importar
may poder, puede que, probablemente; ¡ojalá!
mayor alcalde *m.*
meal comida *f.;* **take one's ___s** comer; **very good ___s** muy bien de comer
mean querer decir, significar
means: by no (any) ___ en modo alguno, ni mucho menos, eso sí que no
meantime: in the ___ entre (mientras) tanto
measure medida *f.;* *v.* medir (i)
meat carne *f.*
mechanic mecánico *m.*
medical de medicina
medieval medieval
Medina del Campo *a town in Old Castile*
Mediterranean Mediterráneo
meet encontrar (ue), encontrarse con; conocer *(become acquainted with)* esperar *(go to meet)*
meeting reunión, tertulia *f.*
melancholy melancólico
melon melón *m.*
memory memoria *f.;* recuerdo *m.*
mention mencionar; **don't ___ it** no hay de qué
mercury azogue *m.*
merit merecer
merry alegre
mess lío *m.*
message recado *m.*
meter metro *m.*
method método *m.*
middle *n.* medio; **___ Ages** Edad Media *f.*
midst: in the ___ of en medio de
mile milla *f.*
military militar
million millón *m.*
millionaire millonario,-a
mind mente; memoria *f.;* **to make up one's ___** decidirse; *v.* tener inconveniente en, importar
mine mina *f.*
ministry ministerio *m.*
Mint Casa de la Moneda *f.*
minute minuto *m.*
misinterpret interpretar mal
misprint errata *f.*
miss perder(se) (ie)
missionary misionero *m.*

mistake equivocación *f.;* *(error)* falta; **___en** equivocado
mix mezclar; **___ in** meterse en; **___ed with** no exento de
modern moderno
modernity modernidad *f.*
modestly modestamente
moment momento *m.*
monastery monasterio *m.*
money dinero *m.*
monkish monástico
monotonous monótono
month mes *m.*
monument monumento *m.*
moon luna *f.;* **___less** sin luna; **___light** luz de la luna; **to be ___light** haber luna
moor paramera *f.*
Moor(ish) moro,-a
more más; **the ___ . . . the ___** mientras (cuanto) más . . . más; **___ ___ and ___** cada vez más; **all the ___ because** tanto más cuanto que
morning mañana *f.*
Moroccan marroquí
mortgage hipotecar
mosque mezquita *f.*
most más; **___ of** la mayoría, la mayor parte, los más de; **at ___** a lo sumo, a todo tirar
mother madre *f.*
motion movimiento *m.*
motorcycle motocicleta *f.*
mountain montaña, sierra *f.*
moustache bigote *m.*
mouth boca *f.*
move *(change)* mudarse; **___ away** alejarse
movie(s) cine *m.;* **___ actress** actriz de cine *f.*
much mucho; **so ___** tanto
mud barro *m.*
multicolored multicolor
murmur murmullo *m.*
museum museo *m.*
music música *f.*
musical musical, músico
must deber (de), tener que, haber de
my mi, mío
myrtle arrayán *m.*
mysterious misterioso
mystery misterio *m.*
mystic místico

N

name nombre *m.;* apellido *m.* *(family name);* **by the ___ of** que se llama
narrow estrecho
nation nación *f.*
national nacional
native *n.* uno del país
natural natural
naturally naturalmente
Navarre Navarra *f.*
near cerca (de)
neat limpio
necessary necesario; **it is ___** es necesario, es preciso, hay que
necklace collar *m.*
need necesidad *f.*, **there is ___ to** hay que; *v.* hacerle falta a uno, necesitar
neglect descuidar
negotiation negociación *f.*
neigh relinchar
neighborhood vecindad *f.*
neither *conj.* ni; **___ . . . nor** ni . . . ni; *pr.* ninguno de los dos
nephew sobrino *m.*
nervous nervioso
never nunca, jamás
nevertheless sin embargo
new nuevo
New Year's Año Nuevo
New York Nueva York *f.*
news noticia *f.;* algo de nuevo
newspaper periódico *m.;* **vile-low ___** periodicucho *m.;* **___ man** periodista *m.*
next próximo, que viene *(time);* inmediato, de al lado *(place);* *adv.* después
nice simpático *(persons)*, bonito *(things)*
niece sobrina *f.*
night noche *f.;* **at ___** de noche, por **la(s)** noche(s); **last ___** anoche
nineteenth diecinueve
no *adj.* ninguno; *adv.* no; nada de; **___ one, ___body** nadie
noise ruido *m.*
noiselessly sin ruido
noisy ruidoso
northern septentrional, del norte
not no

note nota *f.;* apunte *m.*
notebook cuaderno *m.*
nothing nada
notice notar, fijarse en, reparar; sentir (ie, i)
nourishing nutritivo
novel novela *f.*
now ahora, ya; ___ **that** ya que
nudge dar un codazo
number número *m.*
numerous numeroso

O

oak grove encinar *m.*
obey obedecer
object objeto *m.*
observation observación *f.*
obstacle obstáculo *m.*
obvious: be ___ saltar a la vista
occasionally a veces, de vez de cuando
occupation profesión *f.*
occupy ocupar
occur ocurrir, pasar; ocurrírsele a uno; darse
o'clock: one ___, **two** ___ *etc.* la una, las dos, *etc.*
oculist oculista *m.*
offended ofendido
offer oferta *f.*
office oficina *f.;* dirección *f. (hotel)*
officer oficial *m.*
official oficial
often a menudo, con frecuencia
O.K. visto bueno (V.°B.°)
old viejo, *(ancient, former)* antiguo; **be . . . years** ___ tener . . . años
older, oldest mayor
old-fashioned anticuado
olive aceituna *f.;* ___ **oil** aceite *m.;* ___ **orchard** olivar *m.*
on *(about)* sobre
once una vez; **at** ___ en seguida; ___ **and again** una y otra vez
one uno; **the** ___ único
only sólo (que), solamente, no (nada) . . . más que
open abierto; *v.* abrir; ___ **air** aire libre *m.*
opening night estreno *m.*
opera ópera *f.*
opinion opinión *f.;* **public** ___ *(gossip)* el qué dirán
opponent contrario *m.*
opportunity ocasión *f.*
oppose oponerse a
opposite opuesto
orange naranja *f.;* ___ **rose** rosado anaranjado; ___ **tree** naranjo *m.*
orchestra orquesta *f.*
order orden *f.;* **in** ___ **to** para; **be out of** ___ no funcionar; **get out of** ___ descomponer; pedir (i), mandar
ore mineral *m.*
organization organización *f.*
organize organizar
oriental oriental
original original
orphan huérfano *m.*
otherwise de otra manera (forma, *etc.*), si no
ought deber
out fuera, a la calle; *(extinguish)* apagado
outdo oneself desvivirse (por)
outside fuera (de)
outskirts afueras *f.pl.*, arrabales *m.pl.*
over sobre, encima de; *(approx.)* más de; **be** ___ terminar(se), acabar(se), concluir(se)
overcast nublado; **become** ___ nublarse
overcoat abrigo, gabán *m.*
overseer capataz *m.*
overtake pasar
owe deber
own propio; *v.* tener
owner dueño *m.*
ox buey *m.*

P

package paquete *m.*
packer embalador *m.*
page página *f.*
pain dolor *m.*
painful penoso
painter pintor *m.*
painting pintura *f.*, cuadro *m.*
pair par *m.*
palace palacio *m.*
pale pálido
palm: a ___**'s length high** de a palmo
palm tree palmera *f.*
panorama panorama *m.*

paper papel *m.*, *(newsp.)* periódico *m.*
paperknife cortapapel(es) *m.*
parade desfile *m.*
Paraguay el Paraguay
pardon perdonar
parents padres *m.*
par excellence por excelencia
part parte *f.*; *v.* despedirse
partner socio *m.*
party partido *m.*
pass pasar; salir bien en *(examinations)*
passage pasaje *m.*
passenger pasajero *m.*
passing que pasa, *etc.*, pasajero
passport pasaporte *m.*
past pasado *m.*; **half ___ one (two)** la una (las dos) y media
pastry shop pastelería *f.*
pasture land dehesa *f.*
path sendero *m.*, vereda *f.*; **narrow little ___** senderito, veredita
patience paciencia *f.*
patient enfermo *m.*
patio patio *m.*
pay pagar; hacer *(a visit)*; **___ compliments** echar flores
peak pico *m.*, cresta *f.*
peasant labrador, campesino *m.*
peculiar peculiar
peculiarly típicamente
pen pluma *f.*
pencil lápiz *m.*
penny céntimo *m.*
people gente *f.*; *(with numerals)* personas; **other ___'s** ajeno
per cent por ciento
perched asentado
perfect perfecto
perform *(a play)* representar
performance función *f.*; **first ___** estreno *m.*
perfumed perfumado
perhaps tal vez, quizá(s), acaso
permanent permanente
permission permiso *m.*
persevere perseverar
person persona *f.*
personage personaje *m.*
personally en persona
perspective perspectiva *f.*
Peru el Perú
pervade penetrar; animar
peseta peseta *f.*
petition solicitud *f.*
Philadelphia Filadelfia
philosophic filosófico
phonograph tocadiscos *m.*
piano piano *m.*
pick up coger
pickpocket ratero *m.*
picture fotografía *f.*; *(painting)* cuadro *m.*; *(film)* película *f.*; **have one's ___ taken** retratarse
picturesque pintoresco
pier muelle *m.*
pierce pasar
pile montón *m.*
pilgrim peregrino *m.*
pill píldora *f.*
pine forest pinar *m.*
pine tree pino *m.*
pipe pipa *f.*
pistol pistola *f.*
pitcher jarro *m.*
pitiless despiadado
pity lástima, compasión *f.*; **it is a ___** es lástima
place lugar, sitio *m.*; **in ___ of** en vez (lugar) de; **take ___** tener lugar; *v.* colocar, acomodar
plain llanura *f.*
plan plan *m.*; **make ___s for** planear; *v.* tener el plan, planear
plastic plástico
Plata el Plata
plateau meseta *f.*
plateresque plateresco
play obra (de teatro) *f.*; *v.* *(a game)* jugar (ue): **___ tennis** *etc.* jugar al tenis *etc.*; *(music)* tocar
pleasant agradable
please gustar, agradar; hága(me) Ud. el favor de; sírvase Ud.
pleasure gusto *m.*
pocket bolsillo *m.*
pocketbook cartera *f.*
poem poema *m.*; poesía *f.*
poet poeta *m.*
point: ___blank de buenas a primeras; **that's not the ___** no se trata de eso
police policía *f.*
policeman guardia *m.*
polite cumplido
politeness educación *f.*
politics política *f.*
pope papa *m.*

poplar chopo *m.*
popular popular
port puerto *m.*
porter mozo *(station)*; mozo de cuerda *(street)*
portrait retrato *m.*
Portuguese portugués
position colocación *f.*, puesto *m.*
possess poseer
possession: take ___ of apoderarse, adueñarse de
postman cartero *m.*
post office correo(s) *m.*; **central ___** *(in Madrid)* Palacio de Comunicaciones
poster cartel *m.*
postpone aplazar
pottery cerámica *f.*
pour echar
poverty pobreza *f.*
practically punto menos que
practice practicar; **put in ___** poner en práctica
precede preceder a
precipitous(ly) escarpado
precisely precisamente
preconceived (notion) prejuicio *m.*
predicament apuro *m.*
prefer preferir (ie, i)
preferable preferible
preferably preferentemente
preparation preparación *f.*
preparations preparativos *m.*
present *adj.* presente, *(time)* actual; **up to the ___** hasta ahora; *v.* presentar
present *(gift)* regalo *m.*
preserve conservar; **perfectly ___d** intacto
President Presidente *m.*; rector *m.* *(of University)*
prestige prestigio *m.*
pretend pretender, echárseles de
pretext pretexto *m.*
pretty bonito
pretty *adv.* bastante
prevent impedir (i)
previously antes, hace (hacía) una semana *(etc.)*
price precio *m.*
priceless sin par
pride orgullo *m.*
primarily ante todo
primitive primitivo
prince príncipe *m.*
principal principal
principle principio *m.*
print grabado *m.*
prisoner prisionero, preso *m.*
private articular, privado
prize premio *m.*; **first ___** (premio) gordo *m.*
pro en pro (de)
problem problema *m.*
proclaim pregonar
produce producir, dar
product producto *m.*
program programa *m.*
progress progreso *m.*
prohibit prohibir
project proyecto *m.*
promise prometer
promote ascender (ie)
properly bien; como era debido
property posesiones *f.*
propose proponer
proprietor dueño *m.*
protest protesta *f.*
prove to be resultar
proverb refrán *m.*
provided (that) con tal (de) que, como
province provincia *f.*
provincial de provincia
provision provisión *f.*
prudence prudencia *f.*
public *adj.* público; *n.* público *m.*
publish publicar
Puerto Rican puertorriqueño
pull: ___ out sacar, arrancar *(train)*
pulse pulso *m.*
puncture pinchazo *m.*
purchase compra *f.*
pure puro
purple morado
put poner, meter; **___ in practice** poner en práctica; **___ on** ponerse; **___ out** *(extend)* sacar; *(extinguish)* apagar; **___ up with** aguantar, consentir, pasar
Pyrenees los Pirineos

Q

quarrel reñir (i) meterse con
quarter cuarto *m.*; barrio *m.* *(of town)*
queer raro
quell sofocar

question pregunta *f.;* cuestión *f.;* **be a ___ of** tratarse de, ser cuestión de
quickly rápidamente
quiet tranquilo, callado; **be (keep) ___** callarse, estarse quieto; *n.* quietud *f.*
quite muy, todo
Quixote: Don ___ Don Quijote

R

race raza *f.*
radio radio *f.*
rage cólera *f.*
railroad ferrocarril *m.*
rain lluvia *f.;* *v.* llover (ue)
raincoat impermeable *m.*
raise levantar
range sierra *f.*
rapidly rápidamente
rare raro; **___ly** pocas (raras) veces
rash: ___ act temeridad *f.*
rate: at any ___ de todos modos, sea como sea
rather más bien; **would ___** preferir (ie, i)
raw materials primeras materias, materia prima *f.*
razor *(safety)* maquinilla de afeitar *f.*
reach llegar a
read leer; **___ing** lectura *f.*
ready listo, dispuesto
real verdadero; **___ly** de veras
reality realidad *f.*
realism realismo *m.*
realistic realista
realize darse cuenta de
rear *(back)* fondo *m.*
reason razón *f.*, motivo *m.*
recall recordar (ue), acordarse (ue) de
receive recibir
recently recientemente
recognize reconocer
recommend recomendar (ie)
record *(phonograph)* disco *m.*
red rojo
reddish rojizo
redhaired pelirrojo
refer referirse (ie, i)
refuse negarse (ie) a, rehusar
regard: with (in) ___ to (con) respeto a, tocante a
regards recuerdos *m.*
region región *f.*
regret sentimiento *m.;* *v.* sentir (ie, i) lamentar
regularly con regularidad, generalmente
rehearse ensayar
rejoice alegrarse
relative pariente *m.*
relic vestigio *m.*
religious religioso
rely on contar (ue) con
remain quedar(se)
remark observación *f.*
remember recordar (ue), acordarse (ue) de
remembrance recuerdo *m.*
remind of recordar (ue)
reminder recuerdo *m.*, recordativo *m.*
remote lejano
Renaissance Renacimiento *m.*, *adj.* del Renacimiento
renowned renombrado
rent *v.* alquilar
repair reparar
repay pagar
repeat repetir (i)
repel repeler
repertory repertorio *m.*
reply contestación *f.;* *v.* contestar
represent representar
representative representativo
reproach reprochar
request: on ___ a petición
require requerir (ie, i)
resemblance parecido *m.*
resemble parecerse a
reserved reservado
residence: royal ___ real sitio *m.*
resign dimitir
resource recurso *m.*
respect respectar
rest descanso *m.;* *v.* descansar
rest: the ___ el resto de, los demás
restaurant restaurante *m.*
restless inquieto
result resultado, producto *m.*
resume reanudar
retain conservar
return vuelta *f.;* **___ trip** viaje de vuelta; *v.* *(go back)* volver (ue); *(give back)* devolver (ue)
reveal revelar
rewrite volver a escribir

rhythm ritmo *m.*
rice arroz *m.*
richness riqueza *f.*
ride horseback montar a caballo
riding montado
right derecho; **to be ___** tener razón; **___ away** en seguida; **___ now** ahora mismo; **all ___** (está) bien, bueno; de acuerdo; **that's ___!** ¡eso es!
ring *trans.* tocar, llamar; *intrans.* sonar (ue)
ring *(arena)* ruedo *m.*
riot motín *m.*
ripe maduro
rival rivalizar con
river río *m.*
road carretera *f.*, camino *m.*
rob robar
robber ladrón *m.*
rock roca *f.*
rôle papel *m.*, actuación *f.*
Roman romano
Romanesque románico
romantic romántico
romanticism romanticismo *m.*
roof garden terraza, azotea *f.*
room cuarto *m.*, habitación, sala *f.*; *(space)* sitio *m.*
roommate compañero de cuarto *m.*
rough agitado, revuelto *(sea)*; tosco *(not smooth)*
round (of activities) trajín *m.*
row hilera *f.*
royal real
rudely groseramente
rug alfombra *f.*
ruin ruina *f.*; *v.* estropear, echar a perder
ruined arruinado
run correr; **___ning** corriente
rush lanzarse

S

sack saco *m.*
sad triste
sadden entristecer
saddlebags alforjas *f. pl.*
sail salir; embarcar(se)
sailboat barco de vela *m.*
Saint Helena Santa Elena
sake: for its own ___ por sí solo
salary sueldo *m.*
salesman: travelling viajante *m.*
salt sal *f.*
same mismo
sample muestra *f.*
sand arena *f.*
sandwich bocadillo *m.*, sandwich *m.*
sash faja *f.*
satisfied satisfecho; **be ___** contentarse
saving ahorrador
say decir; **I should ___ so (not)!** ¡ya lo creo (que no)!
scandal escándalo *m.*
scar cicatriz *f.*
scarcely apenas (si)
scatter esparcir
scene escena *f.*
scenery decoraciones *f.*
schedule horario *m.*
scholar sabio *m.*
science ciencia *f.*
scientific científico
scientist hombre de ciencia *m.*
scold reñir (i)
scolding: a good, sound ___ un regaño de los buenos
scratch arañazo *m.*
sea mar *m.* *(and f.)*
sea dog lobo de mar *m.*
search busca *f.*
seashore playa *f.*
seasick: get ___ marearse
season *(of year)* estación *f.*; temporada *f.*
seat asiento *m.*, sitio *m.*, localidad *(theatre) f.*, plaza *(train) f.*
seated sentado
secret secreto *m.*
secretary secretario,-a; *(cabinet)* ministro *m.*
section *(of town)* barrio *m.*; sección *f.*
see ver
seek buscar
seem parecer
seigneurial señorial
seize apoderarse de
seldom raras veces
self mismo
sell vender
senator senador *m.*
send enviar, mandar; poner *(letter, etc.)*
sense sentido *m.*

sentence frase *f.*
sentimental sentimental
separate separar
September septiembre, setiembre
serious serio
seriously: take ___ tomar en serio
sermon sermón *m.*
servant criado,-a
serve servir (i); **___ as** servir de
several varios, algunos, unos cuantos
severe severo
Sevillian sevillano
sew coser
shake menear
share *(of stock)* acción *f.; v.* compartir
shave afeitarse
shed derramar, verter
sheer *adv.* puro
shelf estante *m.*
sherry (wine) de Jerez
shift to pasar a
shine brillar
ship nave *f.*
shoe zapato *m.*
shoemaker zapatero *m.*; **___'s wife** zapatera *f.*
shoe store zapatería *f.*
shoot tirar; **___ing** tiros *m. pl.*
shop tienda *f.; v.* ir (estar) de compras
shopping: go ___ ir de compras
short corto; **in ___** en fin
short cut atajo *m.*
shortly en breve; **___ after** poco (tiempo) después
shoulder hombro *m.*
shout grito *m.; v.* gritar
show función (de teatro) *f.*
show mostrar (ue); enseñar; conocérsele a uno; **___ up** aparecer
shrewd astuto
shrine santuario *m.*
sick enfermo, malo
sickness enfermedad *f.*
side lado *m.*
sidewalk acera, terraza *f. (of café)*
sight vista, escena, *f.;* **be in ___** tener a la vista; **___ seeing** ver cosas
sign firmar
signature firma *f.*
silence silencio *m.*
silent callado
silk seda *f.*
silliness tontería *f.*
silly tonto; **___ remark** *(etc.)* tontería *f.*
silver plata *f.*
similar parecido
simple sencillo, simple
simplicity simplicidad *f.*
simply a secas; **___ have to** no tener más remedio que
since *(temporal)* desde, desde que; *(causal)* como, puesto que; ya que
sincere sincero
sincerity sinceridad *f.*
sing cantar
singing *(of voice)* para el canto
single solo; **not a ___** ni uno (solo)
sink *intrans.* hundirse
sip saborear
sir señor
sit (down) sentarse (ie)
sitting servicio *m. (train)*
situation situación *f.*
skip saltarse
sky cielo *m.*
slap dar (de) bofetadas
sleep sueño *m., v.* dormir (ue, u); **get to ___** dormir(se); **feel ___y** entrarle sueño a uno
slender delgado
slight desairar
slightest menor
slippery resbaladizo
slow lento; **be (run) ___** atrasar
slowly despacio, lentamente
small pequeño, menudo
smell oler (hue)
smile sonreír(se)
smoke fumar; **take a ___** echar (fumar) un pitillo; **___less** sin humo
snow nieve *f.*
so tan; *(that way)* así; *(consequently)* así es que; **___?** ¿sí?; **and ___** con que; **___ that** para que, de manera (modo) que; **___** *(then)* con que
soccer fútbol *m.*
social social
socialist socialista
soft dulce
soil tierra *f.*
soldier soldado *m.*

solid sólido
solitary solitario
solution solución *f.*
some unos, algunos; **___(thing)** algo
somebody alguien
something algo
somewhere a, (en, por *etc.*) alguna parte; **___ around** por ahí
son hijo *m.*
son-in-law yerno *m.*
song canción *f.*
soon pronto; **as ___ as** en cuanto, tan pronto como, así que, lo antes (posible)
sorry: be ___ sentir (ie, i)
sort clase *f.;* **of the same ___** por el estilo
soul alma *f.*
soundly *(sleep)* a pierna suelta
south sur *m.*
southern meridional
sovereign: Catholic ___s los Reyes Católicos *(Ferdinand V of Aragon (1452–1516) and Isabel I of Castile (1451–1504) whose marriage brought about the union of Spain)*
space espacio *m.*
Spain España *f.*
Spanish español
speak hablar
special especial *f.*
spectacle espectáculo *m.*
speech discurso *m.*
speed velocidad *f.;* **___y** rápido
spend gastar *(money, etc);* pasar(se) *(time)*
spirit espíritu *m.*
spite: in ___ of a pesar de; con
splendid espléndido
splendor esplendor *m.*
spoil echar a perder; pasarse *(over-cooked, over-ripe, etc.)*
sport deporte *m.;* **national ___** fiesta nacional
square *adj.* cuadrado; *n.* plaza *f.;* **little ___** plazuela, plazoleta
stamp sello *m.*
stand estar, estar de pie; *(endure)* aguantar, resistir; **___ for** pasar por; **___ out** destacarse; **___ up** ponerse de pie
standard: by American ___s según las normas americanas
star estrella *f.*
start *n.* principio, primer momento *m.;* *v.* empezar (ie), comenzar (ie); entablar; echarse a; ponerse a, en movimiento
station estación *f.*
statue estatua *f.*
stay *n.* estancia *f.*, quedarse; parar *(hotel)*
steal robar
steam vapor *m.*
steamer vapor *m.*
steel acero *m.*
steep escarpado, empinado
stenographer mecanógrafa *f.*
steward camarero *m.;* **chief ___** mayordomo *m.*
still *adv.* todavía, aún: *v.* **be ___** seguir (i)
stint oneself quedarse corto
stocking media *f.*
stop *n.* parada *f.;* *v.* detenerse, parar suspender; dejar; dejar de **___ off** detenerse
store tienda *f.*
storm tormenta *f.*
story cuento *m.*, historia *f.;* **short ___** novela corta *f.*, cuento *m.*
strange raro
stream *(tiny)* arroyuelo *m.*
street calle *f.*
street car tranvía *m.*
strength fuerza *f.*
stretch estirar; **___ (away)** extenderse
stride salto *m.*
strike huelga *f.*
strike dar, sonar (ue); **___ one as** parecer; **___ one as amusing** hacerle mucha gracia a uno
strip *(of land)* faja *f.*
stroke gesto *m.*
stroll *n.* vuelta *f.*, paseo *m.;* *v.* pasear(se)
strong fuerte
stubborn terco
student estudiante *m.*
study estudio *m.;* *(room)* despacho; *v.* estudiar
style estilo *m.*
subtle sutil
suburb barrio *m.*, arrabal *m.*
succeed in conseguir (i), lograr

success éxito *m.*
successful: be ___ tener éxito
such (a) tal; cada; **___ as** tal como
suddenly de pronto, de repente
suffer sufrir
sufficient bastante, suficiente; **to be ___** bastar
sugar azúcar *m.*
suggest sugerir (ie, i)
suit *n.* traje *m.;* **bathing ___** traje de baño
suit convenir
suitcase maleta *f.*
summer verano *m.*
summon llamar
sun sol *m.;* **everything under the ___** todo lo humano y lo divino
sunburned tostado
Sunday domingo *m.*
sunny: to be ___ hacer (haber) sol
superficial superficial
supernatural sobrenatural
suppose suponer
suppress *(a newspaper)* suspender
sure seguro
surely *(intens.)* sí que
surprise *n.* sorpresa *f.;* *v.* sorprender
surround rodear
suspect sospechar
suspend suspender
suspicious suspicaz
sweaty sudoroso
sweet dulce
swiftness ligereza *f.*
swim nadar
swollen hinchado
symbol símbolo *m.*
symbolize simbolizar

T

table mesa *f.*
tack *(direction)* rumbo *m.*
Tagus Tajo *m.*
tail rabo *m.*
tailor sastre *m.*
take tomar, llevar; **___ away** llevarse; *(deprive)* quitar; **___ in** abarcar, comprender; **___ long** tardar; **___ off** quitarse; **___ out** sacar
talk hablar
tall alto
tame manso
tapestry tapiz *m.*
target blanco *m.*
taste gusto *m.;* *v. (be)* estar
taxi taxi *m.;* **___ driver** chófer del taxi *m.*
tea té *m.*
teach enseñar
teacher profesor *m.*
team equipo *m.;* **___ play** actuación del equipo *f.*
tear lágrima *f.*
tear rasgar
tease tomar(le) el pelo (a uno)
technique técnica *f.*
telegram telegrama *m.*
telephone teléfono *m.;* *v.* telefonear
tell decir, contar (ue)
temper genio *m.;* **awful ___** geniazo *m.*
temple templo *m.*
tennis tenis *m.*
test prueba *f.*
Texas Tejas
than que, de, del que, *etc.*
thank agradecer, dar las gracias; **___ you very much** muchas gracias; **___s** gracias
that *conj.* que
that *demonstr.* ese, esa, eso; aquel, aquella, aquello
theatre teatro *m.*
their su, sus, *etc.*
theme tema *m.*
then entonces, luego
there allí
these estos, estas
thin delgado
thing cosa *f.;* **to be a good ___ to** convenir
think creer, pensar (ie); **___ of** pensar en, pensar de *(opinion)*, figurarse *(imagine)*
third tercero
thirsty: be ___ tener sed
thirty treinta
this este, esta, esto
thoroughly a fondo; **___ and typically Spanish** castizo
those esos, esas; aquellos, aquellas
though: even ___ aunque, aun cuando, y eso que
thousand mil

thrilling emocionante
through por, por medio de
thus así
ticket billete *m.*, *(theatre)* localidad, entrada *f.*
tide marea *f.*
tie corbata *f.*
tie *v.* atar
tile azulejo *m.*
time tiempo *m.;* *(short while)* rato *m.;* *(in succession)* vez *f.;* *(hour)* hora *f.;* **at one and the same ___** a la vez, al mismo tiempo; **at that ___** entonces; **some ___** una temporada; **what ___?** ¿qué hora?; **have a good ___** divertirse (ie, i), pasarlo bien
timetable guía *f.*
tiny chiquitito
tip punta *f.*, extremo *m.*
tip *(pourboire)* propina *f.*
tire cansar; **be (get, grow) ___ed** cansarse
title título *m.*
to a, hacia; para con
tobacco tabaco *m.*
today hoy
together juntos
Toledan toledano
tomorrow mañana; **___ morning** mañana por la mañana
tone tono *m.*
tonight esta noche
too *(also)* también
too (much, many) demasiado
tooth diente *m.*, muela *f.* *(molar)*
top lo alto; **on ___ of** encima de; **at the ___ of** con toda la fuerza de
topic tema *m.*
torment pena *f.*
tourist turista *m.*, *f.;* *adj.* de turismo
toward(s) hacia; para con
tower torre *f.*
town pueblo *m.*
town hall ayuntamiento *m.*
tradition tradición *f.*
traffic circulación *f.*, tráfico *m.*
tragedy tragedia *f.*
train tren *m.*
trait rasgo *m.*
tranquillity tranquilidad *fl*
transfer trasladar
transform transformar
translate traducir
translation traducción *f.*
travel viaje *m.;* *v.* viajar
traveller viajero *m.*
travelling de viaje
travelling salesman viajante *m.*
traverse cruzar, atravesar
treasure tesoro *m.*
Treasury (department) Hacienda *f.*
tree árbol *m.;* **___less** sin árboles
tremendous tremendo
trick maña *f.;* **dirty ___** mala jugada *f.*
trip viaje *m.*, excursión *f.*
trolley tranvía *m.*
troops tropas *f.*
trouble: the ___ is lo malo es
true verdadero; **be ___** ser verdad
trunk baúl *m.*
try ensayar; **___ to** tratar de, procurar, querer *(in preterit)*
turbulence turbulencia *f.*
turn volver (ue); **___ out** resultar, salir; *(extinguish)* apagar; **___ to** convertirse (ie, i) en; **to be one's ___** tocarle a uno
tuxedo smoking *m.*
twentieth veinte
twenty veinte
twice dos veces
two dos
type tipo *m.*
typhus tifus *m.*
typewrite escribir a máquina
typewriter máquina de escribir *f.*
typical típico

U

umbrella paraguas *m.*
unawares desprevenido
unbelievable increíble; **it seems ___** parece mentira
uncle tío *m.*
uncomfortable incómodo
unconsciously de un modo inconsciente
under bajo, debajo de
understand comprender; entender (ie)
understandable: it is ___ se comprende
understanding comprensión *f.*
unemployed: the ___ los sin trabajo
unforgettable inolvidable

unfriendly hostil
unhurt ileso
unique único
university universidad *f.*; *adj.* universitario
unjust injusto
unless a menos que, como no, a no ser que
unpleasant desagradable
unquestionable indudable, innegable; **be ___** no hay duda de
unrealistic poco realista
unsuccessful sin éxito
until hasta que
untrue falso; **be ___** no ser verdad
unwillingly sin querer
up: ___ to hasta; **___ and down** de arriba para abajo
uphill cuesta arriba
uprising sublevación *f.*
upstairs arriba
Uruguay el Uruguay
use *n.* uso *m.*; **___less** inútil; *v.* usar, emplear, utilizar, servirse de
usual usual, corriente; **as ___** como siempre
usually generalmente

V

Valencian valenciano
valuable valioso
value valor *m.*
varied vario, variado
variety variedad *f.*
various varios,-as
vast vasto, inmenso
veal ternera *f.*
velvet terciopelo *m.*
vender vendedor *m.*
verbally de palabra
verse verso *m.*
very *adj.* mismo; *adv.* muy
vest chaleco *m.*
view vista *f.*, panorama *m.*; **point of ___** punto de vista *m.*
village aldea *f.*
villager aldeano,-a *m.f.*
vineyard viñedo *m.*
violently violentamente, con violencia
Visigothic visigodo
visit visitar
visitor visita *f.*
voice voz *f.*; **___less** sin voz
volume volumen *m.*, tomo *m.*
voyage viaje *m.*

W

wait (for) esperar
waiter camarero *m.*
wake despertar (ie); **___ up** despertarse, amanecer
walk *n.* paseo *m.*; **take (go for) a ___** dar un paseo; *v.* andar, pasear(se); **___ in** entrar
wall muro *m.*; pared *f.* *(house)*; muralla *f.* *(fortification)*
walled amurallado
wallet cartera *f.*
wanderings andanzas *f. pl.*
want querer
war guerra *f.*
warm: be ___ tener calor *(persons)*; **be ___** hacer calor *(weather)*
warn advertir (ie, i)
warrior guerrero *m.*
wash up refrescarse
waste perder (ie) *(time)*
watch reloj *m.*
watchman: night ___ sereno *m.*
water el agua *f.*; **___ing-place** balneario *m.*
way manera *f.*, modo *m.*; **this ___** *(manner)* así; **this ___** *(direction)* por aquí; **by ___ of** por; **on the ___** de camino; **on the ___ back** de vuelta; **by the ___** a propósito; **and, by the ___** por cierto que; **get (have) one's ___** salirse con la suya
weak débil
wealthy rico
wear llevar
weary cansado
weather tiempo *m.*
wedding boda *f.*
week semana *f.*
weekend fin de semana *m.*
weigh pesar
well *adv.* bien; pues; **___ then** pues entonces; *interj.* bueno, bien, pues; **as ___ as** lo mismo que; igual que
west oeste *m.*
western occidental

what *rel.* lo que; **___?** ¿qué?; **___ a!** ¡qué! ¡vaya uno! ¡valiente! ¡menudo!
wheat trigo *m.*
wheel rueda *f.*; **steering ___** volante *m.*
when cuando
where? ¿dónde?
wherever donde (quiera)
which *rel.* que, el que, el cual; lo que, lo cual; ¿cuál?
while *n.* rato *m.*; **a short ___** (al) poco rato
while *conj.* mientras
whirl: my head is in a ___ tengo la cabeza hecha un lío
white blanco
who ¿quién?; que, quien, el que, el cual
whoever quien(quiera), (todo) el que
whole entero, todo; **the ___** todo el, entero
wholesale al por mayor
whose cuyo
why por qué; **so this (that) is ___** con que por esto (eso)
wide ancho
wife mujer, señora, esposa, *f.*
wild loco
win ganar
wind dar cuerda a
winding tortuoso
window ventana *f.*, ventanilla *(vehicle)*
windy: to be ___ hacer (haber) viento
wine vino *m.*
wine cellar bodega *f.*
winter invierno *m.*
wipe enjugar
wish desear, querer; **I ___ that!** ¡ojalá!
with con, de
within dentro (de)
without sin, sin que
woman mujer *f.*; **poor old wrinkled ___** mujeruca *f.*
wonder milagro *m.*; *v.* preguntarse
wonderful maravilloso
wood(s) bosque, monte *m.*
woolen de lana *f.*
word palabra *f.*
work trabajo *m.*, obra *f.* *(art, literature, etc.)*; *(repairs)* obra *f.*; *v.* trabajar; funcionar *(of mechanisms)*; **be hard ___** costar (ue) trabajo
worker obrero *m.*
world mundo *m.*
worn out rendido
worried preocupado
worry preocupación *f.*; *v.* preocuparse (de), apurarse
worse peor; **grow ___** agravarse
worth: be ___ valer; **be ___while** valer la pena
would that! ¡ojalá!
wound herida *f.*
wounded herido
wrinkled arrugado
write escribir
write down *(note)* apuntar
writer escritor *m.*
writing desk escritorio *m.*
writing paper papel de cartas *m.*
written escrito
wrong: be ___ estar equivocado, equivocarse, no tener razón

Y

year año *m.*
yellow amarillo
yes sí
yesterday ayer
yet todavía, aún; sin embargo; **as ___** hasta ahora
young joven; **___er** menor
your su, sus, *etc.*
youth juventud *f.*

Z

zero cero *m.*

Index

References are to sections

acá, allá 74
adjectives
  plural 4, 5
  feminine 11, 176
  agreement 12, 179, 184
  apocope 13, 185
  position 14, 180, 187, 188
  used as nouns 181, 186
  adjective phrases 182
  diminutives 183
  compound 189
  vary in meaning with **ser** and **estar** 20, 270
  vary in meaning according to position 180, 271
adverbs
  formation 16, 191
  adverbial phrases 191
  position 192
  special cases 193, 199
  of intensification 200
apellidos 45
apposition 163
  with **de** 186, 206
article, definite
  forms 1, 155
  contraction 3, 156
  uses 7, 73, 157, 159, 163
  omission 160, 163
  with place names 273
article, indefinite
  forms 9
  uses (and omissions) 9, 158, 160–163
article, neuter 10, 78, 126, 164
augmentatives 170, 275
auxiliaries, modal 127, 135

become 18, 21

clauses, types of 112
collectives 210
comparison
  than 15, 197, 203
  of equality 198, 204
conditional sentences 120, 123
conjunctions
  coördinate 213, 218
  subordinate 214, 219
  correlative 221
correlatives 93, 221

dates 207
days of the week 280
demonstratives
  adjectives 66
  pronouns 67–69
  agreement 75
  special uses 76–78
depreciatives 170, 277
desde, construction with 22, 24, 34
dimensions 210
diminutives 170, 183, 276

estar 17, 20, 149, 246, 270
exclamations 96, 101

fractions 210

gerund 125, 132
gustar, construction of 43

haber impersonal 137, 143
hacer impersonal 22, 24, 137

imperative
  conventional 38
  intimate 38
  of reflexive verbs 58
impersonal construction 136, 140
impersonal pronouns 145
impersonal reflexive 141
impersonal verbs 138, 141, 142
indefinites 205, 208, 209
  alguien, algo, alguno 99
  nada 98, 99, 103
indicative mood, tenses of
  present 22, 29
  preterit 23, 30
  imperfect 24, 30
  future 25, 31
  conditional 26
  perfect tenses 27, 32
  archaic pluperfect 33
infinitive 104
  special constructions 106, 108
  instead of noun clause 114
  after verbs of causation and perception 105
  passive 154
intensification 200
interjections 102, 278
interrogation 8
interrogatives 95, 100

may, might 130
measure 157d, 210, 211
mismo 57
months of the year 280

negation
  simple 8, 97, 103
  strong 98, 103
  ni 103
nouns
  deletion 67, 68, 72, 84, 181, 186
  gender 2, 165, 171, 274
  plural 4, 5, 166
  distributive plural and generic singular 167
  compound 169, 174
  abstract with concrete meaning 172

numerals 207, 210, 279

orthographic changes
  adjectives and nouns 5
  verbs 229

para 107, 109
participles
  present 125, 131, 132
  past 126, 133
  irregular 266
partitive **de** 206
passive voice
  "quasi-passive" 140
  with **ser** 148
  "impersonal" or "reflexive" passive 140, 141, 150, 152
  Spanish equivalents of English passive, summary 151
  special constructions 153
  infinitive 154
personal accusative 6, 99, 118, 168
por 107, 109
possessives
  adjectives 70, 71, 79
  substitutes for 73
  pronouns 72, 79
prefixes 190
prepositions
  simple 211, 215
  compound 212, 216
  distinctions between related 217
  with verbs 269
price 157, 210, 211
progressive or "graphic" tenses 17, 20, 132
pronouns, personal
  forms 35, 47
  of address 36, 44
  subject 39, 46
  object 40, 48, 50, 51, 54
  prepositional 42, 49, 59
  position 41, 60
  redundant construction 42
  reflexive 52
  dative of interest 53, 61
  neuter 55, 56, 64
  reciprocal 63
  with partitive value 65

que 15
  special uses 214, 220

rate 157, 210, 211
reflexive pronouns 52, 53
reflexive verbs 58, 62, 139–141, 144
relative conjunction **que** 94
relative pronouns
  simple and compound 80
  complementary and supplementary 81
  que 15, 82, 89
  quien 83, 90
  el que 84, 91
  el cual 85
  table 86
  cuyo 87, 92
  cuanto 87
  agreement 88
resultant condition, expressions of
  with **estar** 17, 126, 149
  with other verbs 133, 153

ser 17, 19, 148, 259, 270
subjunctive mood
  tenses 110
  theory of 111
  in noun clauses 113, 116
  in pseudo-principal clauses 115, 117
  in adjective clauses 118, 121
  in adverb clauses 119, 120, 122
  future 124
  in softened statements 129
suffixes 175
  see also augmentatives, diminutives, depreciatives
superlative
  absolute *or* general 194, 201
  specific *or* comparative 195, 202
  irregular forms 196, 272

tenses, *see* indicative, subjunctive, imperative
  titles of address 37, 45
than 15, 195, 197, 203

verbs
  regular 222–225
  radical-changing 226–228
  orthographic-changing 229–231
  principal and derived parts 232
  irregular 233–265
  reflexive 62, 139–141, 144
  impersonal 136–138, 141, 142
  substitute 134
  Spanish regimen differing from English 54, 62, 267
  governing direct infinitive 268
  governing prepositions 269
  moods and tenses, *see* indicative, subjunctive, imperative

will and *would* 28
word order 147